LAW SCHOOL

OTHER BOOKS FROM
THE FINE PRINT PRESS

ALSO FOR THE LAW STUDENT

The Insider's Guide to Getting a Big Firm Job: What Every
Law Student Should Know About Interviewing

Later-in-Life Lawyers: Tips for the Non-Traditional
Law Student

Planet Law School II: What You Need to Know (*Before*
You Go)—but Didn't Know to Ask...and No One Else
Will Tell You

The Slacker's Guide to Law School: Success Without Stress

FOR THE SUMMER AND NEW ASSOCIATE

Jagged Rocks of Wisdom: Professional Advice for the New
Attorney

The Young Lawyer's Jungle Book: A Survival Guide

NON–LAW ADVENTURES

Grains of Golden Sand: Adventures in War-Torn Africa

Training Wheels for Student Leaders: A Junior Counseling
Program in Action

LAW SCHOOL

GETTING IN
GETTING GOOD
GETTING THE GOLD

THANE J. MESSINGER

THE FINE PRINT PRESS

HONOLULU

Published by:
The Fine Print Press, Ltd.
Honolulu, Hawaii
Website: www.fineprintpress.com
Email: info@fineprintpress.com

ISBN 10: 1-888960-80-9
ISBN 13: 978-1-888960-80-8
LCCN: 2008902409

Cover Design and Typesetting by Designwoerks, Wichita, Kansas.

The text face is Esprit Book, designed by Jovica Veljoviç and issued by ITC in 1985; supplemented with chapter headings in Castellar, designed by John Peters and issued by Monotype in 1957, section headings in Poppl-Laudatio, designed in 1982 by Friedrich Poppl for the H. Berthold AG Typefoundry of Berlin, and accent uses of American Typewriter, Helvetica Neue, and Law & Order.

PRINTED IN THE UNITED STATES OF AMERICA
15 14 13 12 11 10 09 08   10 9 8 7 6 5 4 3 2 1

ACKNOWLEDGMENTS

This book is hardly mine alone. It has benefitted from review and critique by colleagues including Morten Lund, author of *Jagged Rocks of Wisdom: Professional Advice for the New Attorney,* and Wentworth Miller, founder of the Law Essay Exam Writing System, or LEEWS. Words of thanks do not often convey a proper depth of appreciation, and these words are no exception. Their contributions made this book incomparably better. By catching mistakes and by suggesting better options, the result is ultimately an inestimable contribution to you. To both, a hearty *mahalo.*

My thanks to Jim and Darleen Oertle of Designwoerks, two superb professionals who are a joy to work with.

This book reflects my own experiences in law school and in practice, as well as my observations of others' experiences, and of interactions with and observations of many students in the classroom over the years. Acknowledgement is due to each, and each is reflected here in ways large and small. These reflections speak to a law school experience that many lawyers would echo as less happy and less collegial than it should have been.

The final acknowledgement is thus to you as you embark on your journey, and as you consider and decide from the evidence in front of you the better ways to proceed.

CONTENTS

GETTING GOOD

GETTING THE GOLD

OBITER DICTA

GETTING READY

THINKING LIKE A LAWYER

This is a phrase you will hear many times in law school. What you likely won't hear is just what "thinking like a lawyer" actually means.

Partly this is because *thinking like a lawyer* isn't an "it"; it is instead a way of, well, thinking. That's a bit harder to convey—certainly while your professor drones on about case such-and-so. Yet learning how to think like a lawyer is crucial not only to your success in law school (and in your career)—it is vitally important in the LSAT and in your applications to law school...and thus to your getting into the right law school in the first place.

If thinking like a lawyer is so important—and it is—and if it's something that would be awful handy to have in mind as you begin to actually *think* like a lawyer...then why doesn't anyone define it? Worse, why do some obfuscate and denigrate the very thing that thinking like lawyer represents? One giver of advice actually goes so far as to state: "There is no such thing as thinking like a lawyer." Well, if so, I suspect there will be quite a long line of clients who might be interested in refunds. In other words: poppycock. There very much *is* such a thing, and it *can* be defined. Indeed, if you are to succeed, not only must it be defined, it must be *absorbed*.

Okay, then: Thinking like a lawyer is the art of logical precision, and the ability to express that logic, precisely.

First, this is an art. The best lawyers are *artists*. They draw a picture for a client or a jury, and in that picture they paint the facts and the law in such a way that the outcome is one favorable to their side. In your applications to law school, the "side" is you. It is the artistry with which you craft your statements that might make the difference, to change that Rejection into an Acceptance.

Second, it is about logic. While this might seem to conflict with "art," in fact this is one of the reasons *thinking like a lawyer* is so confusing (at first) and important (once mastered): the artistry is in the ability not just to know logic, but to know how to use it. So, our artist-lawyer doesn't just twist the facts or the law, but instead knows which law is applicable (and favorable), and which facts most strongly support a favorable conclusion under that legal doctrine—all the while standing ready to distinguish the other side's claims under other laws or facts.

To "distinguish the other side's claims" has a special meaning in the law: it's the ability to show how the other side's claims cannot (or should not) be supported. In other words, a lawyer knows not only why their side should win, but also why the other side should not. Crucially, the law is not about mythical theories; it is about two sides in conflict, both of whom want the opposite of what the other wants.

We might think that mere "argument" wins in court, but this is not (usually) the case. What wins is logic. That logic is based (a) in the facts of the case, and (b) in light of the law. Importantly, this very same standard applies in law practice, in law school, in applications to law school, and (as to logic especially) in the LSAT. In your applications, "the law" is the reality from the *law school's* perspective—that is much of what this book is about.

Third is precision. This seems simple, but becomes dastardly complex. It might, in fact, be one reason you find this book annoying. Either way, let's play with this, shall we?

Let's say, for example, that your roommate has become a bit too pesky—shocking, yes?—perhaps by early-morning rowdiness, the taking of one Twinkie too many, and never returning your favorite DVDs. In an attempt to resolve this simmering dispute—which involved at one point the holding hostage, over an open flame, of a certain iPod—the powers that be mandate that you set an agreement in place, and "settle this, once and for all."

Okay. You would like for your roommate to be less intrusive, to leave your Twinkies alone, and to return your DVDs. Assuming explosives or restraining orders are out of the question, how would you craft a statement (which in the law might be called an "agreement" or a "contract") to accomplish that? Not just how, but how *precisely?*

You must cover *every possible intrusion* (and you must define "intrusion" so that everyone knows what it means), *and* you must not cover anything that is either not an intrusion, or would be a protected intrusion. Is coming in at 3:30 a.m. from the hospital different than coming in with an, *um,* "guest"? Is slinking into bed different than mixing a quick margarita and flipping a fast stack of flapjacks?

A lawyer could spend ten pages—no kidding—on defining what constitutes "intrusion," a "protected" intrusion, intrusion by whom, when, where, how, and so on. And this is not made up: it is based on what a real-world person would think "intrusion" is. Thus the infamous hair-splitting on what the meaning of "is" is. The joke? To an attorney, this is not a joke. Sometimes there *is* a difference. And lawyers and the law are all about the "sometimes."

How many Twinkie issues are out there? Must they be labeled? What if they're already opened? What if they're old? Or offered to your *other* roommate? How about if they're in the trash? Near the trash? What if they're replaced? Within how long?

And the DVDs. Goodness: What if, what if, what if.

This is just for one side! We've not even gotten to your roommate's complaints. (Let's just hope they're on paper.)

The last part of *thinking like a lawyer* is putting that logical precision into words. Often, every word carries its own dictionary of meaning. Almost as often, in the law a word does not mean quite the same thing that it means to a non-lawyer.

It's not so easy, yes? But it *is* fun. Every time you think you have it—you'll think of some exception or quirk that doesn't quite fit. Roommate does this; roommate doesn't do that. Smoking might be intrusive (or not), but how about humming? Oh, yes, that too. Okay, what about typing on a keyboard? How loud? For how long? When?

And on it goes.

One example of this type of nitpicky analysis that lawyers do, day in and day out, is in the title of this section: Thinking Like a Lawyer.

Two groups might protest this: English professors, and lawyers. Why? Because the use of the word "like" is not quite right. It should be: "Thinking *As* a Lawyer." Yet this would sound odd to our ears, and because it would seem quite pretentious, the phrase is commonly Thinking *Like* a Lawyer.

The point here? This is exactly the type of nitpicky analysis you will be expected to pick up—on your own—in law school. It is also, notably, exactly the type of nitpicky analysis that is rewarded on the LSAT. It is, in short, the type of nitpickiness that is the essence of "thinking like a lawyer."

Lawyers love nuance. And they love to play with nuance in meaning...often nuance that others would miss. Yet this is done with a purpose—a legal purpose: *Is* there a difference? If there is, what is that difference? Is it intended? Is it potentially harmful? And on and on and on.

This is what thinking like a lawyer is...it's what it *entails*. It is a process of thinking that is expansive (because considering all options is vital), concise (because words create ambiguity), and precise (because every aspect must be nailed down). Why? Because that is the essence of the law. It is also a crucial part of the awesome role of the attorney. And it is *fun!* If you agree, chances are you will do well in law school, and in the law.

If in life you prefer "one, two, three," you might find this all quite frustrating. If instead you're the type to ask "Why three?", "What about 'one-point-five'?", and "I wonder if it should be 'A,' 'B,' 'C' instead?"...you will love the law. And, chances are, the law will love you back.

Why this section? As you read on, you will see this book modeling (or attempting to model) this art of thinking like a lawyer. If you embrace it—if you *like* it—the application process will be a better one (quite likely with a better result), your actual law school experience (and exams) will be better, and your career (read: money) will be as well.

How to Read This Book

This book is designed to be read in the same way that you should study the law: in digestible, relevant bites.

A large part of lawyerly skill is to develop that sense of relevance. Read what is important or interesting to you, and train yourself not to feel guilty to leave the rest. (You should, of course, be interested in what is relevant.) There is simply not sufficient time to read it all. Thus, you should not try.

This is the first of many traps in law school. Beware. Ignoring what is not relevant might seem easy, but it can actually be a major cause of distress to the new law student. A large part of this is the newness of the law school environment and language—and the corresponding lack of familiarity with just what *is* relevant. Worse, the study habits that served you so well in college and before are exactly wrong for law school. The reasons are many, and are discussed at length later.

The key here is to train yourself to build good habits—those that will help you in admission to the right law school, to learn the law well and with a minimum of unnecessary stress or wasted effort, and to begin and succeed in the career that is best suited to and for you.

If, for example, you're just getting started on the LSAT, your time might be better spent reading the section *Getting In* twice, rather than either of the following two sections. Skim the others, sure. But focus where you should. *After* you've read the relevant sections, reread them, completed your necessary LSAT paperwork and begun to study for the LSAT...*then* you might revisit the later sections for in-depth reading.

This really *is* hard. Chances are you'll want to read it all. You've been the best, likely for your entire academic life. This is a worthy goal and accomplishment, and something you should not neglect. But it's yet another trap: the study of law is about *efficient* use of knowledge, not about rote success.

Tell you what: *scan* it instead. Try not to read the later sections as carefully as you read the first. Read whatever is not yet relevant to you quickly—but read what *is* relevant to you slowly. Carefully.

This is a key to success in law school itself, and is also a key to the efficient use of your time.

I've added a preface to each section that mirrors how you should study. This is the Summary at the beginning of each section. As it suggests, this is an encapsulation of the meat of that chapter, either serving as a context for what you then read...or serving as a reasonable substitute for what you then need. This is how one should practice law (to a large extent), and also how one should study law. This is not about "skipping" anything, but about honing in on what is important, at that moment, to you. Focus is key. When sitting in a class on, say, Property Law, one should focus on the topic at hand, and not on, say, Constitutional Law (or an upcoming sale at your favorite mall). Soon enough—and with focus—the connections among the various topics will appear, as if by magic.

In the meantime, you should develop a three-level reading habit. You can apply this right now, starting with this book: (1) you should *skim* materials that you see for the first time to determine its relevance; (2) you should *scan* material to determine its importance; and (3) you should read, *in depth* and *slowly,* material that is relevant and important.

Skimming should be blindingly fast. The prior page, for example, should be skimmed in under ten seconds—and perhaps even under five seconds. It's about how to read a book, right? But the *second* second you spend tells you that it's somehow connected to learning the law. *Hmm.* Your first thought might be "This is silly! I *know* how to read a book!" Your very next thought might give you just enough reason to decide it is worth reading. If not, then skip ahead. No guilt! If you've decided it's not important, then it's not; your time is valuable and you don't—or won't—have hours to waste. You be the judge. Don't let anyone (including me) tell you otherwise.

Scanning should take a bit longer, but not too much longer. If, for example, you've decided it's relevant, you now want to know why—to confirm that relevance and also to give yourself some context for step three. Scanning the first few sections should take just a very short time longer, perhaps fifteen seconds. It's not "backtracking," but is, in a sense, a more in-depth skimming that might take you, say, to the second page.

Why is this useful? You gain more by eliminating irrelevant reading than you "lose" by skimming and scanning. *Lose* is in quotes because you don't actually lose anything: the time you spend puts the in-depth reading into context, which is valuable in itself.

Okay now. You've skimmed and decided relevance, you've scanned and confirmed it. Now you read. Slowly. Yes, you read that correctly. You should read slowly, deliberately, intensely. You do *not* read fast. "Speed reading" is nonsense. [One reviewer—a partner in a national law firm—wrote that this sentence should be "bolded, underlined, and in a 24-point font." So, if that's any indication of its importance, coming as it is from someone most law students would strive mightily to impress, take it as bolded, underlined, and in a 24-point font.] Try a test: try reading something at twice the speed you normally do. Now write a list of ten aspects of what you've just read. Chances are you'll be lucky to list three. This might well be true of most reading—which is the reason one should read slowly. One should especially read the law slowly: one secret of law school is that it's not just about volume—it's about in-depth knowledge. Reading slowly builds that knowledge. Reading quickly masks it; it will confuse rather than enlighten.

Note: this is not to suggest that you read sluggishly. The third step should be done *intensely*. You're *devouring* every word. If not, then why are you reading it? Why did it pass the first two tests?

Note #2: this is exactly how the law works. Every fact pattern will be judged according to a series of tests. Each of those tests will decide whether a case would continue, or not. And each of those tests quite likely leads to another test. This is the essence of the law, and thus of the study of the law.

If you can't "get into" what you're reading, then set it aside until you *are* able to get into it. Do something else for a while. Not everything is great literature, and not everything we read suits our individual style. Sometimes we're just not in the mood. If you're zoning out, then you're hardly doing yourself a favor by wasting time pretending to read. To paraphrase a certain intergalactic Jedi master: Read, or read not. There is no try.

These three steps should become second nature. When you start at a case in one of your casebooks, don't just start reading it. No attorney does that. Or, more correctly, no good attorney does that. Even for someone experienced that's no way to glean the relevant bits—and it's certainly a wasteful expenditure of your time (and clients' money). And that is how you should think of your time; you're *spending* it.

Skim, scan, *then* read. And when you read, really *read*. Don't just go through the motions. There is no try.

The study of law should be about purposeful thought. If you're not in the mood, then do something else. No, not watch TV. Do something else *useful*. Work on your outlines. Categorize your flash cards. Pay bills. Brush your teeth. Clean your room. Clean the toilet. Clean your neighbor's toilet. After a while, reading won't seem so bad.

If, by the way, you're *never* in the mood, you might spend some of that time to think seriously about the career you're about to enter. The law should and can be an engaging profession. But you have to want it to be.

A Disclaimer

It is easy, when writing a book such as this, to take a know-it-all attitude. It is easier still for someone who's been around the courthouse a time or two to slip into a tone that conveys, "Well, when *I* was your age I…blah, blah, blah." The message, implied or direct, is that the newest generation couldn't possibly be as good as the good ole' boys of the last one.

I will attempt to avoid this, for at least a few reasons: First, it's rude. Second, it's unfair. And third, it's almost certainly wrong.

Chances are quite good that the senior partners for whom you will work will have almost no comprehension of the additional burdens you now face. Did they work hard? Sure. Did they not have laptops? Well, yeah. But they also had tuition payments that could be made with relative pocket change, decent savings, and perhaps an odd job or two. No more.

So, I hope the message implicit in this book is one of respect. Part of that respect, paradoxically, is not to pull punches. This is one of the dangers in education today: that in the hope and edict to "be nice," we tell polite lies. Among these lies are continued skirting around issues of genuine importance. If, for example, you open your mouth showing that you've no idea what "precedent" means or how it's applied (or pronounced), your life at that firm is likely to be rocky (and brief)—if indeed you ever get past the interviews. In law school, the stakes are simply too high. And, as you will discover in your law exams, because they are graded on a forced curve—and because they are graded blind—your professors can (*finally!*) tell the truth. In law school, this truth is a grade. And that grade, far more than any grade you have ever gotten before, determines your future.

Thus, please take my admonishments and occasional harsh tone in the spirit intended: to tell the truth, and to tell it in time and in a way that will be meaningful. After all, you read this in the privacy of your own mind. Remonstrate, contest, and curse me all you wish, and I shall not take umbrage. The message, however, remains the same, as does its directness.

Tone. I have thus tried to strike the right balance. Where this advice is a bit rough around the edges, please know that it is intended to help so that you will get into the right law school, learn the law well and without wasted effort, and succeed both professionally and personally. As one example, an editor critiqued a few passages as "conclusory." While true, the deeper concern is that often an advice-seeker does not have the facts—or the facts they do have are incomplete, incorrect, incorrectly perceived, or actively misperceived. The whole point of (useful) advice is not merely "the answer," but in phrasing the question in such a way that the answer makes sense...and can be followed. In this case, it should be a fair statement that almost no applicant to law school has the full facts. They certainly don't have the *right* facts, properly framed. Worse, given the highly intelligent crowd that populates law school, many "know" what they don't really know. We thus have endless puffery that is easily seen (by others who are equally scared) as the way to go.

Patience. There is yet another concern that is quite pointed: whether or not you develop the *patience* to learn the law, and thus to excel. Years ago I complained to a friend in England about some professor or another:

"There's no excuse to be boring!" I lamented.

Her response strikes me to this day. She thought for a moment, and then said, "There's no excuse in being bored."

Go, England.

Law school should not be boring. But it *does* require patience. Your professors almost certainly enjoy the thrill of classroom discussion. Could they simply spell out, in five minutes, what they instead take an hour to goad you into saying? Well, yes they could. But they won't, and they shouldn't. I'll explain why, later.

And while it might be a bit brusque of me to state, it is you who needs to readjust. Allow your professors their excursions, and endeavor to expand your attention span. You'll certainly need to in practice...and for exams. Among other things, you need to turn off your cell phone, stop surfing the net, and *focus*.

In other words, consciously strive not to be so bored.

DISCLAIMER, PART II

As one moves from the cozy world of college into law school, one element that adds to the disorientation is that, while professors and administrators are (generally) quite nice and well-meaning, somehow the world of law school seems so much more harsh. This harshness starts before law school, actually. Years of instant praise lead to a sense of triumph and even invincibility. Yet with each seat in law school coveted by two, three, five, ten, or more "invincible" stars, the disappointments are bound to accumulate.

Once one actually enters law school, the picture changes. In part as a holdover to how law school used to be, and in part as a reality of how the world of law school actually is, there is little coddling. Thus, students not only feel adrift...they feel abandoned. What worked before doesn't seem to work now, and *very* real results are riding on the outcome. Not just the practical—a great job and the ability to repay those enormous student loans—but also the deeply personal. This doesn't hit most law students...until it hits.

In an effort to lessen the effect of that assault, I will attempt to inoculate you at least a bit, here. This will require that I too be a bit harsh. I will tell you, for example, the way the law school world *is*. I will tell not just "the truth," but a larger part of the whole truth. I hope that, despite how annoyed you might be, you understand the reasons for this approach and, more importantly, you have the tools to more honestly evaluate the options open to you. In this, the world as many students know it is actually *dis*respectful: college professors uneasy about correcting a student's poor work give a false sense of security (and success)—and when the blind curve of law school is approached (after months of zero feedback), this can be a ghastly wake-up. Unfortunately, we as a society have built a sense of "respect" that is, in large measure, exactly wrong. Hiding the truth (or sugar-coating it) is *dis*respectful. Clearly one should be tactful. But, as is common with most movements, "being nice" has become "never tell the truth if it hurts." Well, sometimes the truth *does* hurt. Not everyone can get into the law school they would like, and sugar-coating it serves mostly to delay and heighten the disappointment...or to falsely send applicants on their way when they *might* have gotten in with a better approach.

Law school is filled with acid tests: the admissions process, learning the law, and your grades. *Our* tests correspond to those.

Introduction
(Finally!)

So you're going to law school.

This is a statement, not a question. Chances are that by reading this you have thought for some time about going to law school—if indeed you haven't simply assumed that you would attend.

That assumption, in a real way, is almost a requirement for attending law school. Nearly all who go to law school have done well academically throughout their lives, and nearly as many assume that they'll do well in law school too. Yet the realities of actually being in law school are rather different from the popular conceptions of what law school is all about.

WHY THIS BOOK?

Giving advice is a peculiar business. Among other things it sets the advice-giver as the know-it-all (a trait shared among many who become attorneys). Moreover, it's difficult to know whether the advice is actually good or not—until it's taken (or rejected)—by which time it's usually too late to do anything differently. This too is shared with attorneys. Finally, there's the all-important difference that it's not the advice-giver whose life is on the line. That also is a common theme in the law.

Still, it is the very fact that the person giving advice is not the person taking it: it's the distance itself that adds dimension and value. Just think of how many times you see in others what is so *obviously* wrong, which they cannot (or will not) see. Conversely, how many times are we each guilty of failing to see what is so obvious to others?

In an effort to bridge these gaps, I spent a few hours scanning the advice that is currently available to prospective law students. A half-dozen-plus law school guides and a fair cross-section of articles, websites, and reviews. Much of the advice out there (but not all) ranges from okay-to-excellent. Some is misleading-but-harmless. And a small but significant percentage is just plain wrong.

But how can you know which is which? How can you know which (and whom) to trust? After all, you're going to the trouble of reading these sources, and what do you come across but a forest of advice—some of which have trails that seem to crisscross and some that cut across others in no discernable sense or order. Worse, the life of a student is one of constant bombardment, like billboard after billboard on each path, all screeching for attention. As a result of this inundation—classes, the law, spam, distractions, social needs, debt—many tend to lash out at just about anything that's not seen as a quick solution. Most just tune out.

The object of this book is to clear a path. There are many tools, and I will not seek to duplicate the best of what's already out there. Indeed, where I see a good tool, I will point that out to you. More importantly I will hope to point you in the right direction, offering alternatives and, as you are intelligent and curious (having read this far), reasons I might disagree with those alternatives. This is because, when advice is given without reasoning, the advice-taker is left without a basis to assess the wisdom of the advice, and also how important or (in)flexible that specific advice is...or is not. Thus, I will try to provide just such a basis for you. In the end, of course, the actual path you take is up to you. The path recommended in this book is designed to lead you past those thickets, switchback trails, and dead-ends.

The first year of law school is crucially important. It's so important that even a minor setback at the beginning of your first semester can be quite disruptive, and will ripple through the semester and year. Without correction, the effect is deadly. Many, *many* law students don't realize just how lost they are...until right before final exams. By then, it's far, far too late.

So, I shall not discourage you from reading these other sources. Quite the opposite. It can be enlightening and a tool of lawyerlike thinking in its own right to review each of these and decide for yourself which is the better, for you. In this, you are the judge and jury...and defendant. Choose your own path with care.

Law Trek: The Next Generation

A negative dynamic is easily established between generations. It is easy and natural for someone such as yourself to chafe under seemingly endless (and needless) constraints. And it's frustrating to deal with elders who have that familiar know-it-all attitude. If anything, the profession you are about to enter neither understands nor respects its latest generation—you—enough. Here's a secret: much of this attitude isn't a sign of a superiority complex. It's almost—*surprise!*—the opposite. They feel threatened—but not just by you. They feel threatened by themselves. By their own mistakes, missed opportunities, and insecurities.

Most law professors know—or should know—that if they were applying for their jobs today they almost certainly would not be hired. In fact, many would not get even an interview. Seriously. The degree of competition in law school is so much higher now than it was even a few decades ago that it's hard to even compare the two. This, of course, is most impolite to say, and so professors work under the useful fiction that they are the masters. They know, however, that by the enormous pressures you have faced, you are if anything better now than they were, then. (Be careful how you absorb this information. No one likes to be reminded of such things—if indeed they would ever admit it.)

A few additional points: This is not just raw intellectual horsepower at work. After all, there are brilliant individuals in every generation, and individuals who overcome obstacles to accomplish impressive feats. Your professors, like you, had done well. They too were the cream of the crop, and in turn rose to the cream in their law school. They have, moreover, the advantage of familiarity with a body of law that you are not yet acquainted with. They have had years, and sometimes decades, to develop an expertise that is often the best in the nation—by the very design of legal scholarship. These are powerful advantages. So, it's useful to carry a sense of balance. To understand the differences between the two, why each set of characters plays as it does, and to put that into a broader context. Happily, this is exactly the skill that is needed in the practice of law—and that is rewarded in learning how to think like a lawyer (and thus in law exams).

Some books take a negative stance about professors, while others are implicitly (and sometimes explicitly) hagiographic—fawning over law professors without much real critique or advice. Neither extreme should be true for you. Law professors are extremely smart. Most are also genuinely decent individuals. *Very few* fit the Kingsfield model of *Paper Chase* lore. Yet law professors are not your friends, as much as you (and some of them) would like to think so. They should not be your friends. The process of learning the law entails genuine critique as well as the softer side we mostly prefer to focus on. Moreover, it's easy to fall into yet another trap—that a law professor's "liking" of us will make a difference. Not in the grade it won't. It is difficult for law students to accept this, as this is so deeply ingrained in the hand-raised-high/teacher's-pet cycle set over the course of sixteen academic years. Yet it's true: your grade will be determined by a single final exam. Perhaps a single final exam and a mid-term. That's it. In most first-year courses, if there is a mid-term it will count for just a small percentage of the final grade—often ten percent and almost certainly less than half.

It's hard to convey what this means, but this is absolutely essential to your success, and to getting the study of law right. You cannot, cannot, *cannot* be concerned about brown-nosing your professors. Don't do it. Every time you want to raise your hand, ask yourself whether you're doing so to ask a genuine question (in which case, chances are, you should research it yourself, first, and then ask that, one-on-one, as a clarification of a specific point). If you're not, two things will happen. First, it will be obvious to others that you're brown-nosing; second and more importantly, you'll take your eyes off the prize. The prize is learning the law. That's it. The final exam follows *that* prize, not vice versa.

So, rather than asking that question, chances are good that you should instead jot down a quick note to check later...or, if it was just to look good, forget about it and re-focus. You have a job to do, and that job is not to look good. In fact, one way to look at this is that law school provides a unique reprieve. For three years (and especially for your first year) and with the exception of interviews, you don't *have* to look good. Really. It doesn't matter.

Again, this is hard to convey with mere words—certainly in a guide such as this. I have seen students who must have been the dorkiest law students ever to have perambulated down the halls of law school, and because they were in the top five percent of the class, they had whichever interviews they wanted. They were demigods. Sure enough, they cleaned up nicely, stopped perambulating and started just walking...and received multiple offers for their summers and then offers for permanent jobs at stratospheric salaries. (Note: being a dork in law school does not give one license to be so in a firm. Different standards apply.) But without the power of those top grades, such individuals would be wandering the halls just like their metrosexual counterparts.

In this, law firms are amazingly egalitarian. Sure, they look for traits that they would like to see. But, as anyone who interviews knows, the person in the interview room is hardly the same person as when with friends, family, or fellow students. Law school is your chance—perhaps last chance—to enjoy being who you really are.

Says Who?

In addition to my own thoughts and advice, I relied (and imposed) upon a number of colleagues for their critique and suggestions. Among these colleagues are "dream" lawyers: partners in national firms. These are, in short, the types of lawyers that few students will ever get the chance to learn from directly. While that is not, in the words of the law, dispositive as to the wisdom of this advice, it is an important process: I modified and often added sections based on their commentary, resulting in a body of advice that is far superior to what would have been mine alone.

My role here is someone who, as the saying goes, has been there and done that. I've taken the LSAT, worried about money, attended a top law school, worried about money some more, made law review, got an amazing job, passed the bar, and, well, that just about sums it up. Many others have walked this same path, and, to judge by the dozen or so books out there, the advice that's available to someone such as yourself isn't quite as uniform—or helpful—as it could or should be. It certainly wasn't for me.

My own first years in law practice were not what they could have been, mostly because I didn't particularly want to practice. I wanted to teach, but for a number of reasons that path was closed to me. And so, even though I grew to enjoy practice, at the time I took an approach that proved ultimately harmful, to both the firm and to me. I escaped even further from the shores of Hawaii—which might strike you as odd indeed—to spend two years in Micronesia assisting in the development of a new court. I very much enjoyed the professional challenge and personal adventure, and took the time (almost literally on the edge of the Earth) to write a guide for the new attorney, *The Young Lawyer's Jungle Book: A Survival Guide,* as a catharsis of sorts.

A reader in turn wrote a book of his own, *Planet Law School,* which began a decade-long professional conversation with its author, "Atticus Falcon." For the record, Atticus and I have had a prolonged falling out, which I hope serves to strengthen the advice I give here about its contents and my recommendation to read it and to follow its advice. The approach and objections in that book served as the basis for a change in my own thinking about law school, which itself is unusual; most attorneys forget, try to forget, or simply glorify in a false and perverse way their own law school experiences. Sure, they're proud of having survived, and enjoy basking in others' admirations—but in the privacy of their offices, late at night, many look at their three years with a mix of sadness and hurt—if indeed they ever look back at all. Even those who "made it" often did so with academic cuts to their karmic integrity—cuts that start to sting all the more, years later. This should not be, and I have Atticus to thank for my own evolving perspective.

I am decidedly more Establishment than Atticus: I have gone the more traditional route (though hardly as traditional as many), and am constitutionally less inclined to take a partisan position. Yet in conversations over the years, I too share many of the concerns that he writes about—as indeed many jurists and legal educators share. I part with him in some of the particulars, but most are matters of interpretation rather than genuine disagreement.

Why so much about another book? Because I had never intended to write this one. In part this was because *Planet Law School* served, for me, as the Alpha to my book's new-associate Omega. While radical, *Planet Law School* covered the basics—and then some. Yet something happened upon the publication of its second edition…a something that would sow the seeds of our falling out. While I grew more convinced of many of its main points, I felt that it began to veer too far off the path that most readers could appreciate, particularly as they were starting on their path in law school. (This I was sensitive to as I felt *The Young Lawyer's Jungle Book* ran and sometimes exceeded the same risks.) *Planet Law School* seemed to lose at least some of its sense of charm and humor, and its animus towards the law professoriate seemed both misplaced in the context of a guidebook, and ultimately dangerous. Most importantly, it seemed too unyielding in its conception of the proper approach to legal education.

Okay then. Still, why so much about another book?

When I first toyed with the idea of writing yet another book on law school—this was after my first reaction, "You must be kidding…*Me?!*"—I took a jaunt to the local bookstore to have a look at the other guides now on the shelves. In a surprisingly short time at the bookstore I got a sense of what it was that Atticus was so vexed about. In short, a sufficiently worrying percentage of advice out there dealing with issues of any importance in law school…is appallingly bad. Not all of it, to be sure, but enough to cause a far-removed attorney and educator such as I to take a deep breath. No *wonder* law students are in such a mess.

I will not attempt here to repeat all of the advice in these books. To do so would be unfair, and also unwise: it would bury the more important points, the *why* behind the *what*. So, I assume that you will read these other books as well. Many contain much general information—such as first-year sections, FAFSA forms, and so on—all true, but hardly of great importance. The acid test as you distill advice is whether it is reasonable, reasoned, and relevant. So please don't take this as the end of your preparation; it is, instead, a map for the beginning. Nor should you take *any* advice as the final word. The more important question is whether it is the final word *for you*…or whether instead it leads to the next question.

So which books should you pay attention to? (Note: I didn't write *buy*. It's fine—don't tell the publisher—to borrow a book from the library. For free. If they don't have it, ask them to order a copy. Chances are they will, and you'll have a brand new book almost at your doorstep. This will, as a side benefit, help you to think about these points earlier.) You might also search on Amazon for law school books as a rough judge of their quality. Good so far. Yet there is an interesting trend: several books have *bland* written all around them. One title, for example, has mostly-glowing reviews; another has a love-it-or-hate-it collection. The love-it-or-hate-it book (*Planet Law School*) is far better. And no, I'm not saying that because I know its author. It is simply a vastly more detailed look at the mechanics of law school, and in several respects it tells deeper truths while the other book glosses over the same issues and rehashes well-worn frivolities. *Planet Law School* is a radical book; thus, the numerous hate-it comments.

So, be careful before writing off any book. Or piece of evidence, for that matter. Sometimes the unloved is the better.

*   *   *

Much of the advice out there is innocuous enough: how law schools rank, when to take the LSAT, and so on. But that's hardly the stuff that will make or break you. And it hardly imparts the reality of law school or of "making it" or being "broken"—which hits law students all the harder for its suddenness and seeming lack of warning. As I read through book after book I stood there in the stacks and then in an easy chair, and I almost couldn't believe the poor advice in some of them—including one that apparently is the most popular of all.

On vastly more important topics—such as how *exactly* to spend one's time in law school—these books were all over the charts *and* filled with often downright silly suggestions. No, *silly* doesn't quite cover it. For anyone who has graded hundreds upon hundreds of law essays, the result of these tidbits is both insulting to students and professors and dangerous to the legal profession ...and to clients.

That irks me. And it should you too. After all, you're the one who will suffer. Because you're spending your time, and perhaps money, on this book, I'll be direct: advice such as "here's how to brief each case," or "color coding," or "how to impress your professors" is not just wrong, it is *palpably* wrong to anyone who has either taught or practiced law. It's not just that these are dumb—it's that these are a waste of your time when *you do not have time to waste.*

There's another reason this advice is so wrong. That is because it is so seemingly reasonable. When students read about, say, color coding their cases, as many have used highlighters before—or seen others use them—it seems to "fit" within what advice is supposed to be about. It *seems* like good advice. But it is not. It is horrible advice. And perhaps the only way to know this—short of actually wasting dozens or hundreds of hours color-coding cases and then bombing your exams—is to ask a handful of 3Ls. Seriously. Ask. These will be some of the most important conversations you have. There are two problems with even this: if you wait until law school starts, you will already be starting with precious little time to spare—making tricks like color-coding seem the only reasonable alternative—and it's hardly possible to run a scientific survey of and be able to corroborate any 3L's actual exam results, absent law review membership. (This would, however, make for a fascinating study.)

Color-coding is not just a waste of time—as indeed it is—it is a distraction from what you *do* need to be doing: learning black letter law in preparation for learning how to use it. Why does color-coding not teach black letter law? Because that's not what black letter law is. The case is an *example*. It is a fact pattern upon which black letter law is built, and with which one can explore that black letter law. But *by itself* it's not the donut; it's a hole. And through that hole you can waste an entire semester, not realizing how little black letter law you have internalized—and how much you need for exams—until it's too late.

You can learn the law, well, in less time than nearly all of these books' advice will lead you to spend. The answer is so simple that it shouldn't take someone such as I to spell it out—and I hardly have the intent that Atticus has to overturn the system. Broadly, *Planet Law School* stands in opposition to these other books, which he views as part of a vast—yes—conspiracy. As mentioned, in my opinion *Planet Law School* is its own worst enemy. True or not (and it is, in the main, true), its message is overshadowed by its diatribes, *and* it sets up a system of study that few are willing, seriously, to undertake or maintain. The result for individual students is an almost-certain backlash: "it *can't* be true," and "this is just too much *work!*" My suspicion is that many of its readers gasp in shock at the array of sources and lessons laid out. While I don't dispute his reasoning, I believe there is another approach: a middle ground that is both more achievable and, in the end, stronger. In fairness to him, this approach relies on his work as an anchor. And, as I will recommend, so should you.

The approach in this book is thus to impart the importance of a mastery of the law *with as little effort as possible*. Yes, you read that right. This will seem odd indeed, certainly as it is phrased. Yet this is important: learning the law should be about efficiency as well as mastery. In practice, you simply won't have the luxury— though it won't feel like a "luxury" in law school—of spending hour upon hour thinking about a simple point that can be confirmed in minutes. The practice of law, for those who succeed, is *fast-paced,* and *assumes* a command of basic legal principles. Your approach to law school can and must match that, to a better result with less time and better effort. Law school should be an environment in which *all* law students learn both the theory and philosophy of the law *and* at least the basics of what it means to actually practice law. In other words, knowing *why* a rule is important, and having a sense of how that importance will play out in an actual case. And this should take less, not more, time than is currently spent. It *is* possible. This book will show you how.

So, rather than tell you which books are "better," I leave it to you to decide. I encourage you to read *Planet Law School.* Take whatever pieces are useful to you, and re-read sections as needed. Chances are good that as you progress through law school you will come to appreciate its advice with increasing clarity. Indeed, you probably won't appreciate it fully until after you're out of law school. The other books each offer advice of varying quality. Again, most is fair advice, and even books with advice that is to me shockingly bad also have advice that is sound. In the process of reading this book, I hope you'll get a sense of which elements, in my opinion, are worthy and which ones are not. In the end, as with all matters of legal decision-making, it's up to you to weigh and decide. I will lay out a set of opinions that are not mine alone, and that have as their purpose a realistic set of guidelines. I will not seek to duplicate what these other books already do, but will instead serve a different, overarching function.

* * *

There's yet another way to look at this—a way that is most useful in practice as well as life: Ask what the other side's interest is.

What is *my* interest? I will be neither harmed nor helped by your performance—except in the most indirect way of proving or disproving the validity of this advice, and in the karmic pleasure I would gain by your success. I thus encourage you to consider what I write as true (or not true) for the reasons self-contained herein: each piece should stand or fall based on its inherent reasoning and soundness, as applied to you. To dismiss any of the advice (actively or by neglect or cognitive dissonance) is part of a larger issue of Getting Good, and by getting good, Getting the Gold.

Much of what troubles law students isn't a lack of intelligence —this should be clear, as you are by your very presence among the most highly intelligent students on campus—or a lack of effort (usually). Rather, it is a lack of direction and focus. What I will do is to lay out that direction, and to put this all into focus, for you.

I might, just to restate, strike you in some of what I say as a bit brusque, if not downright rude. I'd like to borrow from another colleague, Morten Lund, author of *Jagged Rocks of Wisdom* and partner at a national law firm writing for new associates:

> ...[S]ome rules may strike some readers as unfairly harsh or brutal. If so, I also do not apologize, because that is just too bad. This book is here to be honest, not to be fair. Welcome to the real world. Welcome to law practice.

Jagged Rocks of Wisdom is a book for new attorneys—which I highly recommend, by the way, even though it "competes" with my own—so it's written in a sharper tone than is perhaps appropriate here. I will thus try to temper the advice that should be given to anyone about to embark on law school. Sometimes that advice needs an edge if it's to have an impact. We've all disregarded advice because we didn't believe it, often because we didn't *want* to believe it. Sometimes it takes a literary 2x4 to make a point.

It might sound corny, but in a real sense this book is my pro bono effort. It's my way of giving back, of helping others. You. This will, I hope, help many clients down the road through a better attorney. Also you. You'll be better both as an attorney who has mastered the law, and better as a person, as you won't be scarred in a law school process that is so often unnecessarily harsh. And it's not just professors who make it so, at least not intentionally. Rather, it's the environment and students' fears and maladaptive reactions within that environment.

In a similar vein, please know that all of us—even the authors of books with advice I happen to disagree with—write with the intent and hope to help. Where we sometimes get a bit carried away it is with the intent to make a point. This is also tinged with memories of our own painful lessons, a danger we hope vicariously you might avoid. Sometimes, that point does need to be delivered with that edge lest its meaning be lost. I'll also admit that I can get carried away, writing this as I am on, *ah*, "vacation."

In all of this, please take the advice in the spirit intended: to guide and ease a path for you that was, too often, quite hard and harsh for us. May this thus make your journey better for you than it was for those who've walked the law school path before.

Okay then. Ready for law school?

Getting In

SUMMARY

The law is a peculiar mix of intensely status-oriented elbowing and remarkably egalitarian collegiality. This is true in law practice as well as in law school. In essence, it's a series of clubs with unwritten (and strict) rules about proper behavior within and among each of them.

The rules, condensed:

1. Law schools are hierarchical, and supremely aware of it.

2. This hierarchy is not a linear, up/down scale as commonly seen in national rankings, but rather is three-dimensional, above and across the nation.

    a. National schools soar above all other schools, and are ranked in the stratosphere in rough (but not perfect) relationship to each other. These are the satellites orbiting high above.

    b. Regional schools circle over their respective areas, at mid altitude, and also circle each other. These are the commercial airliners, going about their pragmatic business and hoping to inch just a bit higher above their competitor-brethren.

    c. Local schools hover nearer the ground, are primarily for those intending to practice within that local area or in certain government jobs, and are relatively flat in relationship to each other (as they are, well, at treetop level). Of little concern to employers, they're the ultralights of the law school world.

3. For admission to law school:

    a. Your LSAT is key.

    b. Your LSAT is still key.

    c. Okay, your undergraduate GPA is a key (but a secondary one), as is your alma mater.

    d. See (a), (b), and (c), above.

    e. Other factors such as Nobel prizes, Pulitzers, or grade school honors, are a distant third.

i. The exceptions are:

          1. Two years in the Peace Corps;

          2. An actual Nobel or Pulitzer.

  f. Disregard 3(e) when:

      i. Applying to a top or "reach" law school.

      ii. In that case, everything counts: LSAT first, GPA second, and everything else, through and through.

4. You should divide potential schools into four, not three groups: Dreams, Reaches, Targets, and Safeties.

  a. You should focus your efforts in the middle two.

  b. You should not apply to Safeties.

5. Think honestly about location, personal outlook, and money.

  a. The "lesser" the school, the more important is its location.

  b. Your expectations should be in sync with your qualifications and your approach.

  c. Money cuts in ways many don't consider:

      i. The opportunity cost of law school is high, and easily ignored.

      ii. The actual cost of law school is high. Very high.

      iii. The total cost of law school is very, very high.

      iv. In the short-run, the cost of public schools and lesser-ranked schools can be relative bargains.

      v. In the long-run, how well you do in law school, and at which law school, will determine to a great degree how well you do financially.

6. If you don't get admitted to a Top 50 law school, think seriously, times two, about whether you should go.

7. If you don't get admitted to a Top 100 law school, think seriously, times ten, about whether you should go.

8. Don't rush. If you're not ready, or if your LSAT isn't, your law school will still be there next year. If not, you've just saved yourself far more than your application fee.

About Law School

When applying to law school, the task is daunting, even overwhelming. Worse, advice seems to come from all directions—asked and unasked—and much of it doesn't make a whole lot of sense. It's confusing, or downright contradictory, and much is relayed from those whose ideas about law school are idealistic—or jaded. Also, when hearing advice one usually hasn't yet actually gone to law school. Many have no real connection with the legal profession at all. It's thus difficult if not impossible to know which advice is sound, and which is not. The aim of this section is to put this advice (both mine and what you'll read and hear from others) into context, and to give you the tools to decide which way to turn, when, and how hard.

One key to law school success is to know, going in, what to expect—but this isn't just an academic expectation. Rather, it is deeply emotional and even physical, as the stresses and months-long challenges of the first year of law school build to a level that is difficult to convey to anyone who's not yet gone through it. There are three scenarios that come to mind to give some sense of this reality: (1) a medical residency; (2) military training; and (3) childbirth. Notably, in all of them anxiety, pain, and sleep deprivation compete to out-drain the contender. Law school is, in short, *intense*. It is also an extended intensity. And that plays out in students' minds in varied and equally extreme ways.

This is, in addition, ultimately an individual question: what is right for your neighbor in the LSAT test center might not be right for you. Thus, reading or hearing advice—including advice here—should be taken with a grain of academic salt. So, if you'll bear with me, it's useful to probe a bit deeper into the background questions that will become crucially important to your eventual success.

WHY LAW SCHOOL

A paradox is at work in American society: careers must be chosen and prepared for earlier than ever to satisfy the many entrance requirements—especially at the top—but we often don't know what we want. We especially don't know it earlier and earlier, and few of us have the silver spoons so helpful in the process. Worse, we each look back at our momentous decisions and wonder what on Earth we were thinking. This applies to everyone…remember the decisions you made in freshman year of college? High school? Second grade?

So is law school really for you?

Books, friends, relatives, and passers-by will offer their advice. Much of it is helpful, but it boils down (the good advice, anyway) to some version of *Nosce te ipsum:* Know thyself.

Well, that sounds awful pretty. But what if you don't? After all, not many of us have *always* known, say, a love for insects, book-keeping, or pyrotechnics. Well, the first two anyway. A lucky few might, for example, know in their bones that they're meant for the great outdoors—no matter what, they want to be outside! Law school will probably never figure into this because it tends to be, well, indoors. Your biggest decision might instead be whether you're going into forestry or geology. The sciences or arts tend to be a bit easier, as those who love mechanics or art tend to know it. The skills central to a lawyer tend, however to be confused with a number of traits—not all of them admirable.

The real dilemma? We often don't recognize our own signals. Here are a few ways to interpret those signals. But first, it's often good to decide through the process of elimination: knowing what *isn't* right for you.

Many big-picture types are tempted to go to law school. You know them: the political science majors who spent many a midnight waxing poetic about the latest global calamities, ready always with a sharp critique that usually starts with "Throughout human history…"

A good idea? Nope. Unless you like the big picture and at least some pixel-level detail, the law will be wrong for you. Become a political scientist, a professor, a writer. Are there big-picture types who are lawyers? Sure. Quite a few, in fact. The question, however, is whether they're happy. The answer for many is No. Unless they've become a law professor or have developed an appreciation for detail, the law is simply too detail-oriented and focused on the here-and-now (and on a client's demands) to be the right career for such a person.

A related issue is a tolerance for uncertainty. In what situations do you feel most comfortable? If you gravitate toward the certain and the routine, the law will almost certainly not be right for you. Why? Much of law—the higher, more fun parts, anyway—is in adjusting to *un*certainty. And the law itself is far from the "concrete" set of rules many imagine; American law is almost the opposite, at least in how it is applied. Even the black letter law you will use—which is about as certain as it gets—will be part of a complex picture drawing as much from analytical creativity as from methodical precision. So, be careful if you're a creature of certainty.

One variable that parents will assume relates to being a lawyer—an easy career to recommend to a toddler—is gregariousness. Surely a vocal child is a pre-lawyer, yes? Well, no. Many exceptional lawyers are actually quite introverted. And, depending upon the type of gregariousness, there might be other fields better suited to you than the law. Perhaps most importantly, when non-lawyers think of the law they often think of the courtroom: Litigation. Yet if we actually talk with the best litigators, we find that they're not usually the "car salesman"-gregarious type. Many of the most successful litigators are self-effacing, reserved, even a bit bumbling—like detectives Columbo or Monk. This is not an accident. Even those litigators who are shark-like had better learn to hide it in court; few jurors like being condescended to, and some will punish the client for a lawyer's overreaching. If you'd like to see this in action, visit your nearest courthouse. It's open to the public. Just sit in for an hour and see what you see. Chances are you'll strike up conversations with litigators that will be most enlightening, and nearly all will be happy to chat—at the right time of course.

Okay, then, what do we do with this, since most of us know whether we're the life of the party or not. First, ask what it is that you enjoy. *Is* it being the life of the party? If so, that probably bodes *against* law school. The life of the party is not often the same person who is happy to be the brains of the party. Needless to write, "brains of the party" has not exactly caught on as a catchphrase.

Even this isn't too helpful, as there are many extroverts who are also highly intelligent and who do very well in the law. The question for you is the balance: do you like being the life of the party and really don't like the zillion details of the party and its party-goers? If so, chances are the law might not be the best for you.

What about the argumentative type? This is another parental favorite (and curse). The child who argues a lot surely should be a lawyer, yes? This brings to mind the scene in the film *Little Shop of Horrors* in which Steve Martin, playing Dr. Orin Scrivello, *DDS,* croons that he's found his perfect job: "...You'll be a *de-en-tist!* You have a talent for causing things *pain!"*

Okay, back to the arguer-as-lawyer. Yes or no?

Actually, no.

There is a crucial difference between anger-based arguing and reasoned argumentation. Many who argue *a lot* are in truth quite insecure and maladjusted. The key to enjoying the law is almost the opposite of arguing—even though we often talk in the law of "arguments." The law is, instead, about crafting logic and reasoning to support (or refute) a hypothesis. If the hypothesis is that your client should pay mine, I'd better come up with solid reasoning to support such a claim. Not reasoning that you or I would see as valid (or invalid), but reasoning that a *court* would see. Your client would obviously prefer not to pay, and expects you to fight. This, of course, makes the task rather more significant—and "arguing" with you will be worse than pointless, it will probably annoy both of you enough that you'll fight "on principle" even if I am right and even if you end up losing. If we never go to court, that objective perspective is the only means for us to agree *before* fighting; thus, we anticipate and craft counterarguments and counter-counterarguments. This is not "argument" in the sense that we'd use the term on the playground. It requires a level head and an appreciation for the assertions that are sure to come from the other side. Is there room for bluster? You bet. And when you're in the middle of a negotiation you'll see lots of bad argumentation (as well as the occasional call for extra blood-pressure monitors). The kicker? Sometimes it works. But the senior attorney is not easily fooled—leading us right back to the substance of legal analysis.

This is why it's so crucial, and this is why professors are such sticklers when it comes to their actual exams.

So, if you like to argue and it's based on being angry at the world, please don't go to law school. You won't like it. And your professors and future colleagues won't like you. (I'm reminded of another book's take on this: "If you just want to argue, get married.") Think about business instead, where such "skills" are more appropriate to the task. I'm not being flippant, actually. While you won't be liked there either unless you grow out of your obstreperousness, business does tend to offer greater opportunity for shoot-from-the-hips action. Those angry-types—and there are many—who are in law school find their views more annoying than helpful. Or, worse and more common, they don't see this at all as they're too busy pontificating. But their classmates know it just the same.

That written, it *is* important to be able to argue—including a flash of anger, when and as appropriate. As always, the difference is fact-dependent: whether you control the anger…or vice versa. There is a *huge* difference between angry and reasoned argumentation. In law school, keep your anger to a minimum. And, moreover, eliminate the "I" from your sentences. Law school is not about finding out what you think; it's about you finding out what judges think. Yes, judges trump even professors. Sure, you'll hope to think like your professors—but only because they know how to think like judges.

If, instead, you like to argue because you really do want others to see the situation or world as you do…and you're willing to walk them through your reasoning…then yup, you're a fine candidate for law school. Again, the real test is whether you're willing to concede anything to the other side. If not, you'd better either learn to concede (to win) or consider other careers such as religion or politics.

A lawyer who whispers is the most powerful of all.

So What, Then?

Among the most important factors for a good lawyer is a *desire to perfect*. In a quantitatively-inclined individual this might be seen in an accountant, statistician, engineer, or scientist—someone who wants things *just so*. The stronger that person is in the field, the more likely they can create rather than merely rearrange what is just so. Also, the stronger that person is in the field, the stronger their perfectionist leanings. In a more literary person this is seen in a writer, poet, professor, or lawyer.

A now-common term, Obsessive-Compulsive Disorder, or "OCD," describes an extreme of this personality type. In essence, a desire to arrange the world in its most minute parts is a good indicator to success in the law. OCD-type behavior is prevalent in many attorneys, and the law rewards (most) OCD behavior. So, take the advice of the mother of Dr. Scrivello, DDS, and find the career that will reward *your* natural talents.

Law is a highly detail-oriented profession. Please don't read this as a throwaway phrase; this really *is* true. A lawyer will spend nearly all of the day, every day, focused on *details*. Not changing the world, not curing cancer, not rewriting the Constitution. Details. The study of law should, likewise, be a methodical, detail-oriented process. But it needn't be the dreadful, negative, caustic nightmare many make of it.

IS THERE ANYTHING GOOD TO SAY ABOUT LAW SCHOOL AND ACTUALLY BEING A LAWYER?

Well, yes. For starters, one of the hidden motivations for many law students is to, well, remain a student. This isn't wrong. Being a student, and being relatively free of real-world worries (at least at the moment) can be a wonderful time. It is even better for those who have the right attitude—either because they have the luxury of having the right attitude or because they have a good sense of self and balance. This can be especially important in law school, because the stakes are so much higher.

As to actually being a lawyer, there are many pluses. The obvious ones are money and prestige. These are true for most, and can be an important part of success and of a healthy outlook. (Don't read "money" as being necessarily the same as "mountains of money." Both are possible, but both are not equally likely. And, when you look back, you might realize that a smaller-but-steady stream of income is more than made up in the personal satisfaction in helping clients you want to help.)

There is the personal power that comes with knowledge, and there is the personal satisfaction of being "in the know" as to both people and events. There is the emotional satisfaction of being an attorney. Most people you meet—even if they joke incessantly about lawyers—will at least secretly admire you. A great many will give deference for your opinions—warranted or otherwise. And, as a broad statement, there is simply a *presence* in being a J.D., akin to how a physician feels in medicine, or a senior executive feels in business, or a Senator feels in Washington.

Finally—and, yes, this might have been listed first—the actual, day-to-day practice of law can be an intensely rewarding experience. This is true financially, of course, but it's also true personally. Walking into a conference room with a client who *looks up to* and who *looks to you* for guidance…that's what it's all about. It is a responsibility that is, to use an overused word, simply *awesome*. The lows can be low, but the highs are amazing.

There aren't many other professions that come close: medicine is perhaps the closest that comes to mind. Even business isn't quite right, as the relationship between attorney and client (even for an associate) is simply different than that between an employee and employer. In short, law practice can be almost intoxicating.

So, yes, there's much to be said for being a lawyer. Perhaps one way to find out if these pluses are the right ones for you is to talk with lawyers. If you're not from a family overflowing with them, strike up some conversations, and just ask. It's not hard. Go to bar association meetings and explain that you're curious. Go to the courthouse. Go to work for a firm. Volunteer at a Legal Aid clinic. You will be glad that you did any of these. Don't be a pest (ever), but do put yourself out there. That is, after all, part of the skill of lawyering itself.

All that written, the more power and money are desired, the more time and stress are required. This too isn't wrong…with the right approach and attitude. Importantly, the approach and attitude that will be helpful as a lawyer are very much aligned with what's helpful as a law student, and indeed before you even apply.

AGAIN, WHY LAW SCHOOL?

It's easy when asked this question to come up with a stock answer: to do good, to save the world, to make lots of money, yada yada, yada. Unfortunately, when asked this question we often deceive others by first deceiving ourselves. We either make up what we think is a good answer, or what we think will reflect well on us, or what we think our audience wants to hear. Or we honestly don't know the answer ourselves. And so we simply fall back on pat responses that sound good…to the point that even we start believing them. Rather than getting Afterschool Special on you, I'll admit that this group included me.

NO, REALLY. WHY LAW SCHOOL?

Okay, maybe I should get at least a little Afterschool Special on you. I'll explain why in a bit, but for now, the reality is that lying to yourself will almost certainly be harmful, if not devastating. It's one of those aspects of life that catches up with us, even (and sometimes especially) when we deceive ourselves.

Note: I am not saying that no one should want to go to law school. Not at all. Chances are, if you're reading this, you *are* the right person, and law school *is* right for you. Yet this cannot be simply an assumption, or a pro forma exercise. With so much at stake it is important that you really mean it. Not for me, but for yourself.

The key, first, is whether anyone has ever given you a realistic understanding of what law school leads to; second is whether anyone has ever given you a realistic understanding of what law school is all about; and third is whether you're ready, emotionally and financially, for the journey.

The first—having an understanding of what law school leads to—is important because many law students don't really want to practice law. In a different context this would be surprising, but I suspect that a steady (and high) percentage of every entering law school class has a zillion secrets reasons—except a desire to actually practice law. Many, having been at the top of their class for their entire lives, might want to teach on a beautiful campus, jet to foreign destinations (paid for by clients of course), or just enjoy the fruits of being, well, *an attorney.*

To take these in turn, here's the résumé for a new law professor: top student (usually ranked in absolute numbers, not percentages) from one of the top *five* law schools, often a clerkship with a U.S. appellate court judge and perhaps one of the U.S. Supreme Court justices, and possibly one or two years at a national law firm. That's it. I am not kidding about the exceedingly high academic threshold. Not only are most new law professors drawn from the top five law schools, in reality about half come from just two. You guessed it, Harvard and Yale. (The next nearest school, Columbia, is a distant third. Below that, a handful of law schools provide handfuls of the remaining professors, with the numbers trailing to zero from there.) And at each of these rarified schools, these are the *top* graduates. Following the 80/20 rule (in which eighty percent of the profits/problems/potential comes from twenty percent of the clients/business/candidates), and given the realities of a demographic bulge with few tenure-track professorships available, the odds are in fact far smaller than 80/20: the chances of a law graduate landing a job teaching law are vanishingly small.

I can almost hear the mental reaction: "Well, smartypants, *I'll* be the exception."

Not to be rude, but, no, you won't. Or, more carefully, the chances are very, very slim that you will. It's safe to say that the chances are less than one percent that you will teach law.

How about teaching something else on a beautiful campus? Business law in an undergraduate program, perchance? Here the story is different, but sadly the same: Few universities value the teaching of business law, in part because of the rivalries between business and law schools, and in part because of the lack of inside administrative heft among most business law faculty within the business faculty. The result is that many business law "professors" are in fact adjunct instructors, poorly paid with few or no benefits…and even less respect. In one department I'm familiar with, at a well-regarded business school, business professors joked openly about the business law "department" (which wasn't even its own department but was instead placed under the Finance department).

"Why should we teach business law?" said one business professor with a laugh but quite firmly. It seemed that an unrelated, unpleasant experience with his own attorney wasn't, to him, quite so unrelated. "We can simply hand out lawyers' business cards at graduation. And that is that!" Laughter. None of the three in the conversation stopped for a moment to think of the asininity of what they were saying, and the applicability of that advice to, say, a marketing-research expert. Two taught subjects less important—in terms of both conceptual import and daily need—than business law, which on its own includes multiple topics of sufficient business importance that they might be offered as full courses. Had I had the power, I would have suspended their doctorates for twelve months, that they might take a refresher in critical thinking (or perhaps attend the first year of law school).

As you might imagine, this attitude does not make for a healthy career choice (or for a good business program, for that matter). The business law "faculty" in the Finance department was in reality a single, non-tenured, full-time instructor—meaning he made *much* less than most assistant professors, and not much more than a graduate assistant. He had nearly three times the student load as other professors, he had no benefits, and unlike everyone else his office was in a different building. As an added professional insult, he wasn't offered even the courtesy of renewals of his annual contracts. Instead, each year he was officially fired, and had to re-apply for his job. And he was the *only* full-time business law instructor—in a sizable business school. The others were all part-time adjuncts—practitioners for whom the office, etc., were superfluous. How many students in each class? Fifty-nine. Why that number? That's how many chairs were bolted into the auditorium used. The implied message to adjuncts was clear: they were hardly part of the *real* faculty. The indirect message to students was that business law was hardly equivalent in importance to any of the other, "real" disciplines of business.

So, it's safe to assume that teaching should not be an assumption. If it is, consider seriously what it is you like. If it's being in the classroom, then which subject? If it's, say, history, well then why get a J.D.? Get a Ph.D. in History! (And it *must* be a Ph.D., and it must be a well-regarded one.) Will it be difficult to get a job teaching history? Yes, it will. But you'll be closer to your destination, with less debt, and you might have more fun along the way. If you still love the law, you can take a few classes, or take a joint program; the options are there. The important point is to be honest…with yourself.

Okay, on to "jetting to foreign destinations." Yes, there are some attorneys who fly around the country or world, seemingly in glamorous pursuit of the latest developments in the latest case. The reality? Any travel you do will almost certainly be routine, and will just as certainly be dull—especially if it's done in the first, *oh,* ten years of practice. The exceptions might be in government offices or as a JAG officer in the military, but of course each of those jobs carries its own qualifiers. More on those options, later.

So, what will you be doing? Well, if you are traveling, it will likely be to the local office of a major client to plow through box after box of documents looking for something—often a something you aren't even sure of—in the less-than-glamorous process of discovery (a favorite real-world topic). Sometimes, it's not just box after box: sometimes it's room after room, warehouse after warehouse, or data server after data server. Every scrap of paper, email, etc., is supposed to be reviewed looking for that scrap of evidence that might be crucial at trial (or, more likely, in settlement negotiations).

Is this bad? Well, that depends. First, you're *getting paid* to do this. And, chances are, you're getting paid fairly well. If you compare this with, say, cleaning grease traps, the tedious nature of document reviews is put in a rather healthier light. (For anyone unfamiliar with grease traps, these are the devices at restaurants that collect grease to protect the municipal sewage lines from clogging, as the grease that is trapped is a sludge-like, highly odorous and disgusting blob that is exceedingly difficult and unpleasant to clean. An hour with a grease trap might, in fact, be the perfect cure for a bad attitude—or French Fries.)

It's far more likely, however, that you will travel not at all. Those documents will find their way to you, rather than the other way around. So, in short, if you expect glamour on the job, you will almost certainly be disappointed. And if you even *hint* that you expect glamour on the job—or in law school—you will manage instead to turn off admissions officers and hiring partners, one after the other.

Okay then. So what are these benefits that everyone keeps talking about? I mean, really. Why does it seem that everyone wants to be a lawyer? Well, it's because being a lawyer *does* come with important and subtle fringe benefits. You will benefit from glamour *away* from the job, such as in being able to say, "I practice such-and-so law with Abercrombie & Fitch. Oh, yeah, it's a great firm in town." This will be said with a smile, and it will almost certainly be received with one too. [You might change the name of your firm to the real one, particularly when talking with anyone under 30.]

For many, these are the *real* motives. And…this is fine, so long as you're honest about it. Why? Because the other side of this equation—the ability to *continue* to say that you work for A&F—will be based on succeeding in the non-glamorous aspects of the *actual* job. Part of the challenge is to enjoy, or at least accept, the realities of the latter while not succumbing too much to the egotism of the former.

There's yet one more aspect of this worth mentioning. To take the "document review" as the example, what do you suppose is the pressure applied to that process? There is, first, a time limit—and often lots and *lots* of documents. There is the uncertainty of knowing what you're looking for. And there is the expectation that you'll actually find something. So, all at once you're in a tedious, almost-menial task that is simultaneously stressful—sometimes highly so. This is true in nearly every task of the new attorney: a new world, a new set of expectations, and lots and lots of stress. This is also the world of the new law student.

That is part one of the reality check: knowing that much of a new associate's workday (or law school day) is tedious *and* stressful. With the right attitude, however, much of the tedium is accepted with an appreciation for why it's important nonetheless, and much of the stress is accepted (if not entirely appreciated) for much the same reason. And—here's a paradox—with the right approach it's not as tedious or stressful. If you're looking for a "good time" in the law, or in law school, you will be sorely disappointed. If you're looking instead for serious work, you'll get it, you'll be successful, and you'll find it engaging and even fun. This is exactly the same in your first year of law school. Why?

Because it's a never-ending series of logical puzzles, drawing upon not just intelligence but also creativity and care.

The truth? Many law students find themselves in law school more by default than by any real desire. It's one of those pseudo-decisions we *know* is a mistake, but one that few want to admit. For many it's a decision to avoid making a decision, or to avoid the dreaded "get a job!" imperative repeated *ad nauseam* after college. Law is too important to be a default; it should be a real choice. More to the point, why not take a few years and do something interesting? Whether that's teaching English in Asia, starting a business, joining the merchant marines, hitting the road, you name it…such will help you in many ways, not least in your eventual law school application.

The problem with falling into law school? Unless you fall *up* (into one of the top law schools—and unless you happen to like it)—such a non-decision can be one of the worst you'll ever make. Unlike in years past, it won't be a path you can take and then not worry about. If it all seems like one big joke, it will ultimately be one…on you. So if you do go to law school to avoid life for three more years, your non-decision will be a most dangerous one.

If the real aspects of law don't attract you but you want to hide out in school anyway, consider a Ph.D. program. You'll get to hide a *long* time there, and chances are you'll emerge from hiding at least in the running for a more compatible career. If you have a genuine interest in the law but truly enjoy the philosophical—as opposed to practical—you might consider a joint J.D./Ph.D. program. That way you'll hide a *very* long time, and might indeed qualify for a prized teaching position. In general, however, be wary of joint degree programs. While they can be a good option for some, unless your interest is genuine in *both* fields (business/law, medicine/law, and so on), they are probably not the better option.

Part two relates to a reality before you even get to law school. Indeed, this has become one of the most important elements of advice desperately needed for law students…and is too often mentioned only in passing, or in technical and relatively useless ways. This is the cost of attending law school.

THE MOST IMPORTANT PRE-LSAT TEST YOU'LL EVER TAKE

How much money do you have? No, this is not a question before I try to sell you something you probably don't need for way too much. It is, however, a question one should ask before deciding to *buy* something—in this case, a legal education.

A law degree is required to practice law. In that sense, it's a "union card" for the profession. (For those unfamiliar with unions, the old union card was required to show membership and thus eligibility for jobs that were generally well-paying, protected, and assigned by seniority…all based on membership in the union. No card, no job.) This is intended here not for any political meaning: it simply is. One result of this monopoly power—the right to set law school graduation as a condition of bar membership—is that law schools thus enjoy a relatively price-insensitive market: they can charge almost anything they want, as the value of what they're "selling" is quite high.

Yet there's more. Law schools face two constraints that increase even further the upward pressure on tuition: First is a set of ABA requirements that, individually, are quite sensible. Taken together, however, they add *enormous* cost to the operation of a law school. It is possible, not surprisingly, to take issue with the sensibility of these requirements. A physical law library, for example, is indisputably one of the most expensive components of a law school. It is not, however, as indispensible as it once was. Indeed, it's possible to argue that it is quite dispensable: a computer, internet connection, and research account will match even the largest physical libraries in all but the most esoteric searches. And the computer can be more effective—meaning more inclusive—and far faster. How many students even look at physical books anymore, unless required to do so? (No, this is not a shock to those in legal education. Indeed, the ABA and various judges, professors, and practitioners have been discussing this for some time.) Law schools wishing to retain accreditation must thus spend large sums of money on faculty, facilities, libraries, research, and so on. This, of course, adds to the upward pressure on price. Yet there's more: The nature and impact of law school hierarchy on cost.

A test was done once with chocolate. Blocks of unlabeled chocolate were put in a bin, at a price of $3.99 per pound. The retailer later took the same chocolate and relabeled it at $9.99 per pound. Under ordinary supply/demand logic, sales should have plummeted. Guess what happened? That's right...the expensive chocolate sold *more*. The lesson for a retailer? When there's an absence of meaningful criteria available to a consumer upon which a purchasing decision can be made—*More cocoa! Looks browner!!*—the variable that is relied upon as an indicator of quality is price. Thus, perversely, a higher price can result in more sales (and *much* more profit), as consumers use price as a proxy for quality.

Law schools noticed a similar and highly useful corollary: when the first schools started raising their tuition (ordinarily a tricky task), they found themselves with *more,* not fewer, applicants. Instead of rebelling against higher costs, the message seemed to be "We're not cut-rate! We're just like the expensive guys!"

These two forces add pressure to raise tuition rates to whatever the prevailing rates are—and those are set by the top private schools. There's a historical precedent at public schools as well. In the 1950s, Michigan realized that with its relatively small population it couldn't compete against the best law schools, so it raised its tuition to nearly match the top private schools—and proceeded to invest those funds into building a world-class law school. It worked. For nearly any employer, a candidate from the University of Michigan holds considerable weight: it's "almost-Harvard." This is not meant disparagingly. The University of Michigan's law school is truly world-class. And, philosophically, there's something to be said for not providing, in essence, a state subsidy to beneficiaries who are often from and will almost certainly be among the wealthier of that state's residents.

In contrast, the University of Texas at Austin, the flagship public school in Texas and a strong regional player for much of its history, was the beneficiary of revenues resulting from the state's propitious gift of vast tracks of land nearly a century before. Happily, oil was discovered, and with two-thirds going to the University of Texas System (with the remaining one-third going to the Texas A&M System), UT–Austin was able to buy its way into the realm of world-class institutions through a different largess: luck. Recently, Texas' tuition rates have nearly matched those of the top private law schools as it too realizes the inevitable calculus: for a law school, higher tuition is a no-brainer. With 1,500 law students, that's millions of dollars of additional revenue every year…the equivalent of many tens of millions of dollars in foundation money that can pay for much to boost a school's standing against other law schools. So, the schools would argue, this is actually money well spent on behalf of students— defensively at least, and competitively at best. In sum, the costs of attending any law school have risen faster and higher than just about any other academic endeavor. And the costs of attending even a public law school have risen, often steeply.

For you, this leads to a discussion that might be one of the most important in Getting In. Three years of law school will now cost between $110,000 and $125,000…*not* including books, fees, and living costs. This means that you're looking at total costs of nearly one-quarter of a *million* dollars. And this does not include opportunity costs. If, for example, you're making (or could make) $40,000 per year now—not an unreasonable assumption, yes?— that means that spending three years will cost you an additional $120,000, plus seniority and promotion opportunities, 401(k) matching contributions, medical and other benefits, and a hit to your "net present value," or the cumulative effect of earnings carried forward. In total, *law school will cost you between one-third and one-half of a million dollars.*

If you're not gasping, the answer to the question above must be that your numerous trust funds can take care of such piddling amounts without even needing the trustees' signatures. If so, good for you, and a raised glass of *Cristal Brut 1990.*

For the other 98.9% of us, this is something to ponder. I was serious, by the way, in my comment about older generations not being condescending. I, for example, was a beneficiary of the University of Texas' largesse, as the tuition rates for the law school were counted in the hundreds, believe it or not, and that was in 1989. If memory serves, tuition was already rising but was then less than $1,000 per year. (The law school had higher rates than for other programs. The undergraduate programs cost $4 per cred-it hour, in-state. That is not a misprint. *Four dollars* per credit hour.) Law school tuition rose rapidly during my time there to about $3,000 per year when I left in 1991. With scholarships, I paid between zero and a few hundred dollars per semester. I had no money, true, and had to borrow anyway. But that was a different world...in more than just time. My blind discounting of opportunity costs then and my relative ignorance of just how much was being given to me...these made it easy to simply *go*. That I had a lackadaisical attitude about a law job was rather easy given that there was so much less on the line.

My own story is perhaps a bit out of the ordinary, so I hardly use myself at the personal benchmark. In case you're curious, I came from a family that believed strenuously in egalitarianism, and in hard work. This meant manual labor, often involving animal by-products. There was also a firm disbelief in parents paying for college—a concept so foreign that it still takes me aback. From the time I was 13 we were involved with renovations, culminating in the design and building of a home in Austin in which we all lived over the years. It was thus easy *not* to consider costs: rent was zero, living costs close to that, and Austin a haven (then) for impoverished students such as I. So I ended up, after three degrees, with about $30,000 in debt, nearly all of which had gone to pizza, $1 movies, $300 Chevettes, and the occasional $25 IBM Selectric typewriter bought at an auction, fixed, and used throughout grad school.

As you might imagine, even if your town still has $1 movies, the approach that worked for me would hardly work today. I graduated and went to work for a firm in Honolulu. As it was Hawaii, the cost of living was higher, the salary was lower, and I began making student loan payments that seemed quite high—a few hundred dollars per month. This would be quite modest today. Somehow, loans don't quite seem real when taking them out. They do become real later, however.

As I mentioned, I had not wanted to practice law...and so found myself working at a new court in one of the states of the newly Federated States of Micronesia, about 2,000 miles west-southwest of Honolulu, and from there into business and teaching, two passions of mine. The point? If you're about to enter law school, you had better *seriously* want to practice law. It almost doesn't matter what kind. As I'll get into later, despite the assumption that only the "best" law jobs are the ones to have, that's simply not true. It is possible to live well on a modest salary, including repayment of debt. In any event it won't be possible to simply wish away one-hundred-twenty-thousand-plus dollars in debt—not counting undergraduate debt. On a 10-year loan, that's a payment higher than for a house. Even the post-school pressure for loan consolidation, while easier in the short-run, is often worse in the long-run. As you start your career, this will feel quite oppressive, indeed.

Are there ways to reduce this burden? Yes, there are. More in Getting the Gold. For now, however, the important question is whether or not you have a *real* answer to "Why Law School?"

If it's just to bide your time for three years, *don't do it*.

If, as mentioned, you really want to teach, or to spend your hours and years doing research, then get a Ph.D. Are the markets bad there too? Well, in many cases, yes they are. But it will hardly help you if you have the wrong degree for what you really want to do.

Would you enjoy a more fast-paced business environment? If so, then go to business school. On a purely financial level, the calculus for business school is generally better than for law school. It is certainly energizing.

Do you really want to…[whatever it is that you really want to do]…? Whatever *your* "really want to" is, you should follow *that* dream. Your dream.

In all, this is not to dissuade…unless you are being dishonest with yourself. With the right attitude, law school is wonderful, and many aspects of law practice are enjoyable, even thrilling. But they won't be with the wrong attitude. And that wrong attitude is almost certain to follow if you go into law school for the wrong reasons, or for no real reason at all.

NOW BACK TO OUR REGULARLY SCHEDULED PROGRAMMING: WHY LAW SCHOOL?

There are almost as many reasons for wanting to attend law school as there are applicants. There isn't so much a right or wrong reason—although many (including admissions committees) will judge you on just this basis. Some will say that the "right" reason is to right wrongs, fight for justice, and so on. Others—belonging to a more cynical group—assume that any statement along those lines is just pretend (or, worse, naïve); they tend to believe that the "real" right reasons are practical: a job, a career, a fancy house and car, and lots and lots of money. Many attend because others believe they should. Some attend because others believe they should not. Still others attend because they don't know what they want—but they know it's not flipping burgers. Or, our new reality-check, cleaning grease traps. Were we attorneys to be honest, our reasons for having gone to law school would likely be less honorable than what we had originally professed. In other words, our *real* reasons were quite different from the ones we spoke so loudly and often before entering.

The answer? Don't focus on what *others* believe you should want, or on what you think you *should* want, but rather on what you *really* want. Ask what your real compulsions are.

If it's parents, grow up. Sure, parents are important, and their views are rarely given the weight they deserve. (You'll likely not agree as strongly as when you have children of your own.) Yet it's *your* life. Live it. Be respectful—even if you don't want to be—but don't bend to their will if it's not your will too. One test of adulthood is the ability to say "No"…for the right reason. This, ironically, is one of the tests in the law, and in law school. Also, if in thinking about law school you listen to various advice and end up taking whichever is easier—a bit like asking one parent when the other gives you the wrong answer—that's not making a decision. It's a cop-out. You should consider the options, and do what attorneys and judges must do every day: *decide*.

If it's the fear and hassle of getting a job, grow up. Sure, getting a job is a hassle, and quite frustrating. Yet, as I will get into, there are practical reasons *in* law school that this is important. And if you're fearful and annoyed now, that's not ten percent of how fearsome and annoying it will be once you're in law school. Take advantage of the time when an employer doesn't expect all that much out of you (really!), and endeavor to wow them. If it's a law firm you're wowing, so much the better.

If it's to make a difference, this is a terrific reason. But…

But you'll need to be especially sensitive to the pace at which you will be able to make that difference, and to whom. This is not to give up anything, but to put yourself in a position where you *can* make a difference. More on that later.

If it's to increase options, for glamour, or to enter a mythical genteel profession (complete with bowler hats), be careful. This is yet another reason to work in a law firm, even part-time and even for just a short while. There's not quite any other way to get a taste of what the law is really all about.

If it's money, stop. Law school is the wrong choice. Or, more correctly, if it's *just* money, stop. You will almost certainly be unhappy, and you will almost as certainly *not* obtain your goal: only a small percentage of attorneys make as much as most believe *all* attorneys make.

I once had an English professor who started his first class by asking us what we wanted in life. Rhetorically, he asked "Money?" Most of us were silently responding "You bet!" He waited a moment and said, "If so, you should...*leave.*"

Taken aback, we waited for the explanation. He proceeded to let us in on a secret—one that is well known in the aphorism that "the A's teach, and the B's work for the C's." This saying was from the days before grade inflation, by the way, when the curve was set so that an "A" meant the top 6%—not 10%—and the "C's" were about half of the class. Thus the phrase the "gentleman's C."

He told us that sitting as we were in English class, while of value to him and to us in ways we probably wouldn't appreciate for years...was not on the path to money. He was right, in an important sense. If you want to make money—lots and lots of money—then don't go to school. Even business school is a huge investment that rewards only a relatively small percentage.

Moreover, business school is of a vastly different character than law school, which focuses, essentially, on the allocation of risk. Business, alternatively, focuses on the creation and use of risk. Engineering might focus on the refinement of risks in ever-more sophisticated ways. Every other academic endeavor is fine if appreciated for what it is—and if appreciated for what it is not. One of the things that academics is not is a path to lots and lots of money.

If lots and lots of money is your goal, entrepreneurship is the path. And, by the way, this is not the dream of entrepreneurship that is sold in magazines; it is, instead, years of hard work. One successful entrepreneur once told me that the magic number was 20: it took that many years for a business to "suddenly" flourish. Having run a few businesses, I'd say that's not too far off the mark. In most cases, it is years of work *harder* than in a corporate environment. It is, almost always, years and years of work *in addition* to a "regular" job.

For attorneys at top firms (either national or local), the J.D. does open doors into the corporate world, in both legal and business suites. There are a number of reasons for this—chief among them the analytical skills honed first in law school and then in practice *and* the on-going connections with business clients— yet this too only reinforces the importance of getting into the right school and getting good. So, if you're interested potentially in the corporate world, or are considering an MBA/JD, this can be a path (even without the MBA), but again only if you place well.

This too is not meant to dissuade. Yet if making money is your *real* goal, then don't go to law school. It's fine to want money. It's even okay to want a lot of money. But for law school you need a better reason. Wait until you have one, or find a different path closer to your true self. If you gloss over this in your search for success and happiness and do go to law school for this reason, chances are high that you will achieve neither.

DOUBTS

In a sense, this too is almost a requirement for going to law school. Many have doubts: sometimes secret, sometimes not. Often, the more boisterous the student, the more intense (and secret) are those doubts.

Doubts are fine, as long as those doubts relate to ancillary issues—"Which school?" "Should I buy *Emmanuel's* or *Gilbert's?*" "Will I really do well?"—and not to core issues—"How can I convince so-and-so that I really want to go?"

As the Oracle relates in *The Matrix,* you must know this at your core, "through and through, balls to bones": a sense that law school is for you and you are for law school. It's not for someone else to tell you. If your answer is that you're not sure, then the answer is No, at least for now.

A FEW NUMBERS

You might grow a bit tired of hearing about the numbers, but, as law school has become a sizeable business in its scope and importance to one-hundred-thousand plus students and a comparable number of annual applicants, it might be useful to explore just how the quantitative aspects—these numbers—will affect you.

How Many Want In? The number of applicants varies in any given year, and also fluctuates over periods of years, like a cyclical gauge of how "attractive" being a lawyer is in any decade. A bust in the early 1980s was followed by a massive boom in the mid-to-late 1980s, followed by another bust and then a more gradual rise. Chances are good, as of this writing, that we're set for another bust; perhaps a big one. Why the cycles? Because, to borrow from economics, law firms tend to be on a leading edge (often bleeding edge) of service-industry demand elasticity. Clearly, legal work must be done, and most firms remain stable in terms of their core client base. When recession hits, however, like everyone else firms tighten their belts—only moreso. This is because clients are tightening *their* belts, and because there are fewer clients to go around, and their belts get smaller and skinnier. Firms are hardly going to start firing high-paid partners (although that's an increasingly common practice for those partners not bringing in sufficient business). No, they start with associates, and especially summer and junior ones. One reason is that new associates are relatively value-less. Summer associates especially are a hugely expensive drain, withstood in good years only for their long-term potential and as a practical requirement against competitors. This means, of course, that when recession hits, firms retrench reflexively and robustly. And summer hiring shrinks even more drastically.

This, in turn, means a horrid time for law students unlucky enough to be in law school at that time. Recruiting requirements generally remain roughly the same (firms keep their top 10%/law review "wishes"), but the total number of students hired falls steeply. This, of course, spills down even more steeply, with students below top 10-25% left almost completely in the cold. This, in turn, makes its way into the annual application-crop consciousness, and the next year the number of applicants falls—but not enough to make a real difference to any of the above. Rather, it merely reduces the relative competitiveness of future years' entering classes—which in turn only heightens firms' insistence on their measurements. I know, a lot of *in turns* here. As with any cycle, good timing (mostly by luck) can be wonderful, as a lucky few enter with lighter competition and then more and better jobs, while others enter with severe competition (meaning they probably won't even get into the law school they might have gotten into before) and fight even for interviews. Having lived the latter scenario, I can attest that this is hardly theoretical. So, a few years into a down cycle is often the *best* time to apply, because the cycle works itself out after a few years and students then entering have a better chance of admission *and* a better market awaiting them. This is intensified because firms don't "look back" to prior-year graduates; when they need more bodies, they simply hire more—from the current year's class.

As someone who's missed many cycles in his life, however, I'll not recommend a great faith in cycle-timing. This boils down, in essence, to the same advice: if you honestly, truly, genuinely are ready for law school…that's exactly right. Go.

How Many Get In? The other side of the equation is equally important: the number of seats available. This, as we'll see, has a few important caveats of its own. First and not surprisingly, the number of seats offered is fairly constant. Law schools must plan their budgets, classrooms, faculty, and so on according to some stable, long-term base. That can rise or fall, and over the past decade we've actually seen cutbacks in class sizes. This is a big deal, actually, as it represents a huge loss in aggregate revenue—countered, however, by a steep rise in tuition rates.

What happened during the mid-to-late 1980s was a brisk increase in the number of seats available, as a result of both larger classes and, importantly, more law schools. This was, in part, to meet growing demand, in part to satisfy growing concerns for diversity among student (and faculty) populations, and in (large) part for revenue. As long as enrollments increased, everyone was happy. This pattern was repeated about 15 years later, right up to the time this is being written.

The Real Number. Here's where it gets interesting. The dollar figures for starting salaries rise every year. Sometimes steeply. For the top firms, these starting salaries and bonuses are quite staggering. These jobs go to the top students from the top schools.

What's important to law students from a financial standpoint, however, is not how many total seats are available (as you need only one), or even how relatively easy (or hard) it is to gain admission to this exclusive club. No, what's important is a magic number that's stayed relatively constant. The number?

Fifteen.

That's the percentage of attorneys, give or take, who are—let's see, how shall I put this?—who are *all that*. High-powered, highly paid, top dogs, phrase it as you wish. Over time, almost independent of how the economy, job market, or M&A activity are doing, that's the percentage of attorneys who are in jobs and make the sort of money that most non-lawyers (and quite a few lawyers) associate with being "an attorney": the flashy attorney in the flashy office with the flashy car and flashy house.

Fifteen percent. This has a big impact—or it should—on your thinking. We'll delve into that. (The "should" part, at least.) For now, keep that number in mind if your thinking follows the conventional assumptions of what a lawyer is.

Where this plays out is in the number of seats available. That fifteen percent—again, this is surprisingly constant over time—is drawn almost exclusively from the top fifteen percent (or so) of law schools. That means that the bulk of high-powered jobs go to graduates of the top 30 (out of 200+) law schools, give or take. This does not mean that a graduate of law school #31 has no chance. It does mean that a graduate of even law school #29 had better place quite well. And if at a law school much below that, had better place very well indeed *regardless of the market*. As a practical matter, because (as we'll explore) firms are so status-driven, the real picture is a bit more nuanced, and steep: Top 5 students get just about whatever they want, regardless of how well they place (although the top firms will generally still limit their recruitment to some top percentage, often top-third to top-half of even the Top 5); Top 15 students (those in law schools from #6 to #15, roughly) need to place well (say, top 25% to top 33% in a good year); Top 25 students need to place very well (top 10%); Top 50 students need to place very, very well (top 5%); anyone in a law school ranked below that needs to place very, very, *very* well (measured in absolute numbers, such as #3 in the class) to even be in the running.

Why so much focus on top, top, top? Because, to quote a famous bank robber, that's where the money is. Those stratospheric salaries are there, but only for the top students at the top schools. Sure, a local firm will offer a good salary, and might well consider a "local" grad—but the salary almost certainly won't match what we're talking about, above. And even if you think you won't care, chances are you might, just a little, as your $125,000+ of debt (plus whatever undergraduate debt you carry forward) creeps ever-closer.

Why so much of our number 15? Because, as mentioned, if your real reason for wanting to go to law school is money...stop. Just about every guidebook discusses the reasons student have (both what they say and what they really think) about why they want to go to law school. If your secret reason is money—if you sing *Money Is My Mantra* from the rooftops, or hum it softly so that no one will hear—because of this reality law school is probably the wrong way to get there. This is measured in terms of having a worse cost-benefit profile than other degrees, including especially the MBA (although that has a similar status-reward calculus). It is also statistically unlikely that you will get there. I like raining on no one's parade. But the facts are the facts. There are *lots* of smart people in law school, at any law school. Few of them believe they will end up in the bottom half. Yet, year in and year out, a rather consistent 50% end up there. And that's a mile away from the 15% that firms care about.

Enough of numbers?

Well, not quite. The next number is one to consider before we even start. That is a number that might just set you back a bit, in more ways than one. We've seen it before, but it's worth perhaps adding it here again, for effect:

One-quarter of a million. Dollars.

This is our eyes-wide-open real cost of attending law school—again not including opportunity cost. Add together application fees, LSAT courses, tuition, books, rent, food, late-night pizza, an occasional beer or wine cooler, phone calls home (and to your therapist), bar review...that is how much law school will cost you. A hefty portion of that is likely to wind up as debt. As in money you must repay. And, costs being what they are, this is likely to get dated, fast. Instead of trying to keep up with that, the point here is that, for most of us, we're talking about a *lot* of money out the door.

You will face payments beginning soon after graduation—great job or no—that will rival what you will pay for a home (assuming, that is, you can afford one after paying your student loan debt). Read that again: one-quarter of a *million* dollars. That's two-hundred-fifty thousand smackers or, to borrow from contracts, in ever-present parentheticals that's ($250,000.00). That's *real* money...even if loans repaid sometime towards eternity and the elusive "opportunity cost" don't really *seem* real. They will.

Is it worth it?

Wrong question. Is it worth it *to you?* That is the question to ask yourself while thinking about law school, applying to law school, and before actually going to law school. If you are serious about learning the law, and about your commitment to learning it well (including challenging your assumptions about how you should learn), then chances are this will be a superb investment. Paradoxically, this will be true whether or not you take that high-powered job. This is one of the greatest mistakes we make in life: we know the price but not the value. Repaying $125,000 is not that big a deal...as long as you have the income to do so *and* a plan for how you get there. Plenty of associates at national firms—making far more money than their intrinsic worth at that stage of their practice—struggle to meet their obligations. Conversely, it is possible to do well financially as a public defender, D.A., or civil servant; it does take considerable discipline, but it is possible.

This again is not to dissuade. But, as you can see, it should give one pause. If that pause is followed by a resounding, "I don't care! I really, truly, honestly, genuinely *want to study law!*" Then go! You're just the person who *should* go to law school, and I will be proud to serve with you—whether on the same or opposing side. (Yes, you read that correctly.) You will know, going in, what the score is, and what plan will get you to your individual goal posts.

One more paragraph, because after reading all this you must be feeling a bout of gloom. There's a reason banks are willing to lend money, and a reason law schools remain in high demand: there *are* pots of gold at the end of the rainbow. To find and keep this gold you must work, true, but if you're willing your increased value is far higher than the one-quarter of a million or so that you will spend. If, for example, you were earning $40,000 per year before law school, and can earn $80,000 after, that's an increase of well over one million dollars in your "net present value" (the value of your future earnings, calculated forward). If you do well, this boost will be in the millions. If you do very well, this increase will be in the *many* millions. So, if your intent and goals are pure—and you know both going in and are willing to do the work—it can be a *great* financial deal.

There's yet one more reason not to be gloomy. Despite all the top-15 this and top-15 that, from a purely financial perspective law school *is* worth it. Yes, for just about everyone. Put simply, as a lawyer—any lawyer—you will quite likely make many multiples what you would have made without the J.D. Here's the rub, in two parts: if you're expecting to make the *huge* salaries, *that's* when the top-this and top-that come into play. In a sense, however, that's the jet fuel in your personal career craft: a super-salary takes your law school boost from a mere one or two million to a super-sized mega-millions.

Part two: For everyone, this good deal applies only if you actually practice law. And you will be *happy* only if you *want* to practice law. So, if you do truly and honestly want to practice law, law school is well worth it. Yes, that's why I've been harping on this *if* so much.

ONE MORE NUMBER

This is the yield. A law school's yield is the relative selectivity of that school, measured by the percentage of applications it turns down.

There is a truism that whatever is measured is managed to. In our law school "industry," the extraordinarily powerful incentive to improve standing vis-à-vis other law schools leads to an ever-stronger need to improve every aspect of competitive prowess. Part of this is in a law school's yield.

The implications for applicants is powerful: while not intentionally misleading applicants, there is a not-too-subtle interest of law schools to increase the number of students applying to their school, even if they don't end up going there. Obviously, they'd like to see applicants whose numbers are better than average (*their* average); but it's not a harm if it's from applicants at the other end. In point of fact, it's beneficial. Thus, the standard advice that they "look at all the facts, yada, yada," while also well-intentioned, is simultaneously self-interested. They don't care about you (in the abstract). Your application says it all.

So, in the application process you must undertake your first assignment: an *objective* review of the facts. In this case, the facts are your own. Where, exactly, do you stand relative to the norm for that law school? Don't buy the polite lies written for multiple purposes, leading to a dead end for you.

But what about the one or two students who *get in!?* This brings to mind an explanation I once read about the gaming industry. Casinos have an obvious interest in keeping more money than they pay out, of course. (And they keep a lot.) Why, then, would they not mind the huge payouts? Here's where it gets fun: because of human psychology. Casinos *love* it when they pay out huge sums of money! Why? Not just because not to pay money out would cause the inflows to cease (as indeed would be true eventually), but because payouts cause a surge of *additional* gambling. Why? Because the very essence of gambling is the hope that, on the roll of the dice (pull of the lever, draw of the cards…) magic will happen and a fortune is set at your feet. Huge payouts feed this. In essence, paying money out isn't just a cost of doing business. It's promotion.

Law schools aren't quite so crass, but the same principle applies. Yes, there are a few who do make it in. Chances are the subjective facts are so compelling, and the application so well done, that after hemming and hawing for weeks the committee decides to take the risk. A roll of the proverbial dice. The odds are about the same (or worse). They should not be, for you. This is not about defeatism, but about the ability to objectively evaluate facts (one's scores) in light of the rules (the statistics). And it's about rededicating and rejuvenating your application so that you might well get in. No, that's not it either. It's about rededicating and rejuvenating your application so that you *actually* get in. That, after all, is the goal. In short, each of your applications should be an honest shot instead of merely gambling.

SOUP OR STEW?

Some books state in their advice that "so-called objective criteria" are somehow just part of a larger application stew.

This is an outright lie. The application process is both iterative and comprehensive. It's iterative because, for most, the numbers are it: they're the beginning and end of the application. The numbers (the LSAT and GPA) are those "'so-called' objective criteria." They are no more "just part" of a larger application stew than qualifying for the Olympics is "just part" of competing. It's difficult to overstate this: to a very great degree, the numbers dictate the result. Do *not* fight this. The importance of objective criteria is objectively true.

The comprehensive part comes *after* the numbers meet at least some threshold. (This threshold is not the same as the one advertised; it is higher.) After that, the remaining, subjective parts of your application are not just relevant, they are often dispositive.

Note what this means for you: You *still* need to prepare a flawless, meaningful application for each law school, because you won't know just where in the iterative-comprehensive flow your application ends. Well, that's not quite true: you'll have a pretty good idea. If it's a top school, or a Reach school, your application will almost certainly depend upon your subjective qualities. It's fair to write that, if your stats are anything less than stellar, your subjective qualities will be *the* deciding factor. Indeed, even if your stats *are* stellar, your subjective qualities will *still* be the deciding factor at a top school. (At Yale and Harvard, for example, a surprising percentage of even top-scoring applicants *don't* get accepted.) Notably, the same standard applies to law exams, the bar exam, and day-to-day practice: there is no second chance to prepare for your first shot.

THE APPLICATION PROCESS: AN OVERVIEW

As stated law schools fit within a clear hierarchy, into which a relatively uniform group of individuals go, and from which employment prospects flow. Each entering class is selected in a process that is both straightforward and hugely subjective. In this process most applications are accepted or rejected almost solely based on two criteria: (1) the LSAT and (2) undergraduate grade-point average, or GPA. The other applications are rejected or accepted based on their LSAT, GPA, and everything else.

At the margins, a variety of subjective factors can make the difference for individual applicants. The class as a whole, however, fits within a relatively narrow band of data points for acceptance to each law school. Don't take my word for it: Just look at a book on law schools to confirm this. Pick one at random, and look at its numbers.

While you're at it, pick up *The Best Law Schools' Admissions Secrets: The Essential Guide from Harvard's Former Admissions Dean,* by Joyce Putnam Curll. Its subtitle just about says it all, and happily it's filled with superb advice and a powerful peek behind the scenes. I happened to see this book, by the way, on the afternoon that the manuscript for this book was going to the typesetter. Curll will be most helpful to the most disadvantaged students out there: those unaware of or uncaring about how these levers actually work. It's not a conspiracy, but neither is it unblemished.

Okay, back to the process: as your GPA is set (or nearly so) by the time you apply, the hope and challenge is to do well on the LSAT. In this, the LSAT is very much like the many law exams to follow, and also the bar exam, and also the challenges that will confront every attorney on a nearly daily basis: One doesn't know beforehand what is "enough," and won't know until tested—at which time, of course, it's too late to prepare more. Add to this the reality that everyone *else* is preparing, that everyone else has been at the top of their respective academic heap, and that your standing will be judged *strictly* relative to them. And so, you must overprepare.

Taking the most objective data-point from among the application hurdles, let's start with the LSAT.

THE LSAT: THE RIGHT MINDSET

The range of opinions that can be read (and heard) about the LSAT is indicative of the mystery and misinformation surrounding law school itself. This exam, originally the Law School Aptitude Test and now the Law School Admissions Test, is an intense, half-day, nationally curved exam.

The LSAT is a requirement for admission to ABA-accredited U.S. law schools, as is payment for the LSDAS, or Law School Data Assembly Service. While it's easy to take umbrage at the significant costs, at the same time the LSDAS does an impressive job of packaging the many ancillary parts of your application. Yes, this is primarily for the convenience of admissions offices, but it does provide a standard for you as well. It also provides "access" via referrals to law schools that might be interested in *you,* to a local "law school forum" for general information, and, crucially, to old LSAT tests. Both the LSAT and LSDAS are overseen by yet another acronym, the LSAC, or Law School Admissions Council. Almost as useful as the LSAT test booklets are a number of electronic tools for comparing law schools and for evaluating your fit in each. Do explore the LSAC/LSAT websites, and use these tools in your decisions as to which schools you will apply to.

The LSAT is curved to make relatively fine distinctions—distinctions that law school admissions committees pay close attention to. In other words, it is *the* hurdle for admission to law school. There is grumbling by many authors of law school books about the LSAT—commonly referred to as the "el sat"—and by many who take the LSAT, and by many about to take the LSAT...about the LSAT.

Stop.

This is not the path to take. The LSAT is not to be grumbled against. It is. Don't resent having to take the LSAT. Embrace it. For an attorney it is one of the most important days of your life. Few LSAT-takers will treat it cavalierly, but the danger is in making it worse than it has to be.

First, the underlying problem seems to be one few will admit to: for many, a phobia about not measuring up. While true in any testing situation, this takes on a new life for the LSAT. This is particularly remarkable given the population taking the LSAT—which is exactly the cause. Nearly everyone was one of the ones without the phobia—or, more correctly, with the phobia but without genuine competition; with the LSAT, however, nearly everyone realizes just how serious the competition now is. The possibility of not being at the top anymore seems somehow unfair and even paralyzing.

Second, some have written, and many assume, that the LSAT is a bad test, and a poor indicator of law school performance. Wrong on both counts. The LSAT is a superbly crafted exam, perhaps the most sophisticated exam out there. So much so that its approach has found its way into other admissions exams. It is anything but sloppy, and tests an ability to think around any number of written obstacles. It is reliable—meaning that, statistically, the test itself has been tested to a very great degree. In fact, no actual law exam—or any other exam, for that matter—would pass the same tests of statistical reliability if applied to them. As to predictive value, quite to the contrary: the LSAT has a predictive ability when joined with the undergraduate GPA that would be hard to reproduce in any other way, and impossible in any other practical way.

In short, the LSAT is a wonderful exam. This no doubt strikes you as odd, but it is true. And even if it weren't, that should be your assumption. You're going to have to take it, and study for it, and it *will* be crucially important in your applications to law school, so you might as well have a positive attitude about it.

Reverse the lens. This is an enormously helpful tool. In a single day the LSAT offers a way for you to shine. To even the odds. It's a way to crystallize all that you have been able to do throughout your academic years. Think of it as a challenge that will engage every neuron at your command. Use whatever imagery is best for you: a StarFleet commander summoning weapons to repel the latest attack from the hottest extra-galactic threat, a marathon runner drawing deep upon reserves to make the finish, a musician being enveloped by the music "seen" as the composer would want it...you name it.

I'm serious. Look at the LSAT as a way to make your mark. To show the world just how good you really are.

What if you have a problem taking tests? This is a tricky question, as a great many law school admissions officers would respond, ever so silently, "So?" This might seem harsh or even cruel, but their reasoning does have logic. First, *everyone* is taking the test. Nearly everyone can claim *some* test-taking weakness. Second, if exceptions are made, just as with the law itself a Pandora's Box is opened. Who gets the exception, how is it applied, how much is applied, and how is that person then judged against the norm? See how messy this becomes? Say that we could say with any reasonable certainty that an individual simply had a physiological response to exams very much like stage fright, which for some rises to the level of a disability. Yes, this does exist. And, yes, I have had students with just this condition. Would they be excused? If so, how would they be evaluated in a pool of, say, 100,000 other applicants? And *should* they be given a free pass? Won't they need to be fast on their feet in law school? Once they get out of law school? See where this goes? Nowhere. So, whether or not it is true, law schools simply say, in essence, "Make the best of it." They might take *some* consideration, at the margins, but even this simply will not overcome a dismal LSAT score. Finally, admissions officers will respond that the law *is* a fast-on-your-feet profession, often under intense pressure. The LSAT mirrors that reality. Again, true or not, the LSAT *is*. Don't fight it.

For those with a genuine disability, there are options for accommodation. This opens a world of additional concerns only alluded to above, and, in the minds of at least some who will review your application, the possibility that such disabilities are more imagined than real. There are the practical issues that your application will be viewed and even handled differently, which might or might not be better, but will certainly be tricky. In your case, if you do take this path, you will need to be especially sensitive to this, and to addressing the issue at hand. In many cases, with a legitimate issue and a careful handling of that issue, if anything the response will be favorable, not negative. Even so, be aware of the potential for misunderstanding. Handle this especially carefully.

For everyone else, no whining. Even the hint of this in any way in your application will be the kiss of rejection. The LSAT is crucial, period. It is hard, period. It *should* be a challenge. You want the goodies that the law provides? This is your test. But it shouldn't be a competition—at least not as most conceive of it. Rather, it should be a competition of one: you.

What if you get distracted? Same answer. To borrow from another test, there is no spoon. There is no noise. Where others might hear, say, a noisy radiator, you have a different reaction. What radiator?

This might seem unduly harsh. Too bad. In the law you'll face situations that will make a noisy exam room seem a pleasant distraction. Get over yourself. Do not allow yourself to be distracted. Don't offer yourself excuses. Solve the problem, instead: ear plugs, ear muffs, noise-cancelling headsets, and, since none of those are allowed in the test center, a cone of silence. If this is truly an issue for you, investigate the options, both administrative (with the LSAC) and physical (with the test center officials). For everyone else, don't fight this. Don't make it worse than it has to be.

NOT CONVINCED?

Why is the LSAT so important? To answer this it's necessary to think of the process from the law schools' perspective: there are approximately twice as many applicants as there are positions in law schools. Not quite, but that's a rough approximation for our purposes. For the top half of the law schools, the imbalance begins to bunch far more applicants than there are positions. From a 2:1 average (which might only be a little more than 1:1 for the lowest schools), the ratio of applicants to positions starts to jump, to perhaps 3:1 or 4:1 for Tier 2 schools, on up to 10:1 or even 15:1 for the top schools. That's 10 or 15 applicants for every slot. Still, not too hard, right? After all, there are dozens of top schools, and a hundred in the top half. Well, it *is* when you consider that nearly everyone in those top school application pools is already at the top.

Here's where we switch from averages to absolute numbers. If 100,000 students apply, of that number 1,000 will be in the top *one* percent. That means that Harvard, Yale, *and* Stanford could just about fill *all* of their positions without dipping below the top *one percent* of applicants. See where we are? We haven't even gotten to the other factors—4.0 GPAs, literary award winners, single-mother refugees, and so on.

To a large degree, this is what happens at every level, in steeply cascading tiers. This is why this advice is so LSAT-focused. It's also why this advice applies regardless of where your scores happen to place you. Law schools are keenly interested in any applicant who will improve that school's LSAT/GPA average; they're in need of *serious* persuasion for any applicant who will "drag" their average down. They might protest otherwise. They might proclaim their dedication to a holistic review. Don't believe them. At each level there are many more applicants with scores at or below the median than above it. Thus there's a mixed reality: law schools are constantly striving to improve their attractiveness to attract an applicant pool with higher credentials; yet this soon settles to an equilibrium so that much of this numbers-struggling is happening at the margins.

Without the LSAT, law schools would be faced with a situation far less manageable. Actually, quite *un*manageable. What if we took only, say, the GPAs as the measure? Forget the LSAT! Aside from being less reliable statistically, that would leave law schools with pools far too large. How many students out of 100,000 have GPAs above 3.75? A *lot*. Just about everyone applying for law school has done well academically; a great number have done very well. Just about every one of them feels that they *should* be in Harvard, Yale, or Stanford—and almost every one *could* do a good job at those schools. This is repeated in just about every top-law-school brochure; a polite let-down but a true one nonetheless.

The number of applicants with GPAs above 3.9, 3.75, 3.5, and so on is measured in the thousands, and then tens of thousands. Not just Harvard-Yale-Stanford but nearly every admissions office in the top half would have no reliable means to distinguish among those tens of thousands. What would they do?

How about a lottery? That works for me, but can you *imagine* the difficulties of defining cut-offs, and the very real implications of where those cut-offs were? And how about the potential for abuse? How would we know? (I would have no objection, by the way, to auctioning a limited number of seats. That would at least be honest corruption.) No matter, top law schools would never go for this; thus no law school would, absent an ABA mandate.

Okay, how about let's just take in rank order the Four-Point-Ohs first? That takes us right back to square one, as there would be many fine candidates whose GPAs wouldn't accurately reflect their potential—quite apart from the many qualitative frustrations in comparing GPAs—and this with a measure that, over four years, is not quite as reliable as the single-test LSAT. Can you imagine the howls of protest? We would be arguing about why-oh-why the admissions offices can't look beyond the GPA.

That gets to the fundamental issue: we're asking admissions folks to divine the potential and worthiness of candidates based on whatever criteria, objective and subjective, we can dig up. The instinct when dealing with large numbers *has* to be a reliance on *some* objective criteria, whether that's LSAT, GPA, attendance record, inseam, whatever. The challenge is then to find objective measures that reasonably relate—are reliable and valid—to the qualities of the profession. More specifically for admissions officers, what are the correlations between inputs (GPA, LSAT, etc.) and output (success in law school). In this, the undergraduate GPA has a reasonably high correlation coefficient—somewhere around $+0.29$—while the LSAT has a slightly higher correlation coefficient—somewhere around $+0.35$. Combined, they have a correlation coefficient of between $+0.47$ and $+0.50$.

That's not terribly reliable, you say? Actually, in the world of statistics and of applicants/position seekers, it is amazingly so. To be able to predict one-half of the success of a candidate on two relatively easy criteria (easy for the admissions committees, that is)—is quite powerful. Most hiring decisions, for example, are made after much fuss with reliability closer to zero.

So, again, don't fight the LSAT.

MORE FROM A CONTRARIAN: LSAT & THE CURVE

Yet another reason the LSAT is both valuable (to law schools) and annoying (to test takers) is that its curve is highly attenuated at the tails. Most importantly, at the high end (which is the decisive end, of course, for the top law schools), the difference of each number is increasingly pronounced. As is often true, there's a history here.

The LSAT has gone through a number of generations. In the middle generation, the score topped out at 48. Nearly everyone then pegged their entire self-worth on some number in the 30s or low 40s—and it almost didn't matter where you were, as there was nearly always someone just one number higher. The 98th percentile—a two-standard-deviation cutoff for top schools—was pegged at a 44. This meant that the top two percent was stretched to cover five numbers: 44, 45, 46, 47, and 48. This might not seem like such a big deal, but as one dipped towards and then below 40, the percentages represented grew from fractions of a percent to clumps of percentages. A 40 was just north of the 90th percentile, meaning that 40, 41, 42, and 43 covered about three times the number of students as did the top five numbers. Moreover, the *absolute* numbers of applicants grew from hundreds to thousands to tens of thousands. This scoring system was an attempt to provide law schools some measure of determining just who was at the tippy-top of the LSAT. Even this was not good enough. The number of applicants with top scores began getting too large. So, the Law School Admissions Counsel—the body responsible for the LSAT—reworked the LSAT scoring system to refine these distinctions at the top of the curve even more. Thus, we now see a scoring system from 120 to 180…with a wider range of tippy-top scores in the top dozen (rather than just five) numbers.

Is this fair?

At this risk of seeming to be uncaring: This is the wrong question. Is it fair that some have greater capability in mathematics, literature, music, athletics? Is it fair that some are better-looking, taller, more socially secure? On the other side, is it fair that some are ill, deformed, injured, awkward? These qualities *are*. Philosophers have spent millennia debating these issues, and it's not likely we'll have a ready answer either. (If you're interested, you might read Rawls on this point.) Individually, we didn't earn our ability to earn our score—in the sense that we didn't—and don't—"deserve" our brains. We didn't *work* for them; we simply inherited them. And there will always be someone else just a little bit higher. The challenge, then, is to take maximum advantage of what we do have. That is something we *can* control. And it's something admissions committees look for.

Despite never-ending arguments to the contrary, the LSAT measures, quite reliably, an approximation of capacity for legal thinking. Among other reasons, the law is about abstract reasoning; so is the LSAT. As mentioned, when combined with your GPA—easily enough done—its validity is quite statistically strong. We might agree or disagree, but it's highly unlikely that some alternate measure will emerge—and if it does, chances are rather high that we'll like it even less. How would you feel about, say, a cranial scan? So, perhaps the best thought on the LSAT is, again, simply that it *is*. And, by the way, the LSAT is shorter now than it used to be.

Yet another approach is to appreciate the LSAT for what it gives you: a nearly foolproof "answer." Your LSAT score, more than any other single factor, sets the parameters for your law school selection. You should assume, for example, that the 25/75 percentile statistics for each law school are the ceiling and floor *for you*. You want to get in, obviously, to the law school that you like— for whatever reason—and you shouldn't want to waste effort, money, and emotion. While the answer can sometimes be one that we don't like, the LSAT does tell us that answer. We just need to listen.

The importance of the LSAT is so high that you should focus more on it than you have ever focused on anything in your life. Childbirth and military service are about the only exceptions I can think of—and chances are mothers and former-military applicants will be the most in tune with this advice: Your LSAT is *crucially* important. It will count more than your GPA. You spent four years and many thousands of dollars on your GPA. Shouldn't you put a comparable effort into your LSAT?

WEAPON OR WOUND?

With very few exceptions *everyone's* score is a double-edged sword. This is true at every level. No matter where you rank, there are law schools for which your score is unimpressive—and likely unpersuasive. Chances are this will include law schools you would *really* like to attend. In the end, the question is whether your score will be a mixture of pride-agony, or just the latter.

My thoughts about the LSAT were formed as I was studying for it and as I took it. Just about everything I read then (or since) is some version of "the LSAT is crap." I've long disagreed, and disagreed even before I'd gotten my scores back. (Not that I wasn't nervous nonetheless.) So, while I won't discount the psychological effect on the pride side, that's not the overriding reason for what I write here. You can, if you're curious, confirm the statistical basis of the LSAT's validity and reliability in the materials for the LSAT. And you should consider the rationale from the *schools'* perspective, as this might set your mind in the right place before you study for and take the LSAT.

Treat the LSAT as the most important academic test you will ever take. "Win" or "lose," you will be happy for every extra point you earn based on a good attitude and on a painstaking and dedicated preparation. And you will be even happier if your score gets you to where you want to be...on the first go.

WHICH LSAT?

The LSAT is offered four times per year: in June, October, December, and February.

What follows might be a bit pushy, but here's why: It is not possible to overstate the importance of "think time," both as to the LSAT and also as to the application process. *Think time* equals *downtime*. We've this maddening sense that one must be busy to be productive. In fact, almost the opposite is true. The more one is able to work ahead, the easier the process, the less visible the work— and the better the result. One might be able to crank out a draft of a personal statement—or, with the appropriate beverages, three drafts—in just a few hours. So what? The important point isn't the ability to sit at a computer and type in a few hundred or thousand words. Most of us get quite good at this in college. It's the luxury to have the time to *let it sit*. When you pick your draft up with fresh eyes, you'll see it differently than you did when you first wrote it. You know when something is approaching perfection when you pick it up for the third (or thirteenth) time a week or month later and *don't* have the nagging sense that it should be changed. This is exactly the same test in practice, by the way.

Okay. Assuming you're anticipating starting law school in August of the following year, you back up from there to the almost-year-long process. Most law schools begin their review process in the fall, about ten months ahead. Notably, the better the law school, the more important are earlier decisions. They will swear that they don't exclude late applications, but that misses the point: at the end of the process, the easy Yeses and most of the almost-Yeses are already awarded—leaving precious few slots for an ever-larger pool of Maybes (which admissions officers are forced to cull by progressively weeding out an ever-expanding pool of marginal applications). Do not be in that pool. You want to be in the almost-Yes (because that will mean it's a "Reach" school for you), and you want one of the earlier, "Sure, let's give this one the Go."

Many students use October as their LSAT date. No. This is not the best choice. Why? Because you're busy! You should take the test in June. You should, further, consider June as almost late (with October as the to-be-avoided back-up). Why? Because the whole point of the application process should be smooth, not frantic. I've already mentioned how important think time is for the LSAT and application, but it's important enough to mention again: having a serious go at the LSAT in June gives you several months to switch your attention to the application itself, including the vital personal statement, without a test hanging over your head. If you're trying to take it in December or even October, you will have a million things on your mind—and thus the risk is you'll do none of them well. June is likely the only uninterrupted time you'll have.

There's another reason: if you're still in school, you're still at least partially in the study mindset. The LSAT should be taken at a peak of your (good) study habits. If you're likely to suffer a bout of burnout during the late spring, then take the test in December or February...18-20 months before you plan to start. Choose whichever one will be a month you can focus on for the prior six or twelve weeks or more, with all your heart. Chances are that's February. Again, this is *18 months* before you plan to actually start law school.

Am I mad?! Well, perhaps. But on this, no. Take the LSAT early. "Experience" will have little bearing on your performance; it's about logic, acuity, and perspicacity. These are driven as much by energy and attention as by age and academic credits.

There are debates in some quarters about whether one month is "easier" than another. No doubt there is a mountain of data to support or refute this—but the LSAC would hardly reveal any such data. Two methods are used to validate each test: first, part of each LSAT is used, ungraded, to test each question, and second, each question is validated through "equating," to eliminate or at least reduce test-by-test variations. These statistical steps are one reason the LSAT is such a good exam.

Which month? Rumor has it that February is filled with "make-ups," and thus easier competition, while June is filled with well-prepared nerds. I have nothing statistical to support this, and so if this is the slightest concern, take it in February...18 months prior.

Also, if you are still in school and if your year will be filled with anything like 30 credits, plan to take an additional load either in the summer before or in a different semester. This is so you can take a light load in the semester in which you'll take the LSAT—perhaps just 12 credits—so that you can spend a good part of the entire semester preparing. Obviously, whichever month you're planning to take it, plan your course load accordingly; you need to lighten your load when preparing. It's *that* important.

Did I mention how important the LSAT is?

LSAT PREP COURSES

Yes. Take the course.

Yes, it's expensive. Yes, it's on top of all the other expenses. No, it might not make a huge difference. But, then again, it just might. And, if the above discussion about the LSAT doesn't convince you, the difference of just a few points can make a difference to your chances of admissions if you're on the margin at a Reach school (which, by definition, you will be).

And, as is true in preparation for law school, the bar exam, and any case—you don't know how much you should prepare, so you should prepare a *lot*. Assume that there's no upper limit. This is not just fluff...you need to prepare as if your future livelihood depends upon it. As indeed it does.

Even with an intensive prep course you won't approach the 60-hour-per-week benchmark that I'll introduce in Getting Good. While extreme for the LSAT, that's not a bad mark. Sixty hours per week for six weeks equals 360 hours, or a few hours in preparation for each question on the LSAT. When you're actually taking the LSAT, you'll be thankful during each question for your preparation. The prep course counts, but it's not enough: you must commit yourself, seriously, to this exam. You should assume dedicated study of *at least* six weeks. Twelve weeks is a better mark. And it should be twelve *serious* weeks. Not an hour here and an hour there, but three- and four-hour blocks of time, at least 4-5 days per week. At least. And this does not include attending your actual course.

The purpose of your study is twofold: to familiarize yourself with the LSAT and its peculiarities, and to exercise your mind. As to the LSAT and its peculiarities, that is a large part of what you're paying for, and the brand-name providers have done a creditable job in packaging these tools. As to exercising your mind, as with the other kind of exercise this is not something you can simply turn on. You must, well, just do it.

Which course? While this might change, there are a few brand-name providers. Rather than getting into a static ranking, what's important is that the decision of which prep course should be made with the same seriousness that one buys, say, a house. Yes, it's that important. Okay, it's not likely that anyone will hire an inspector, so let's say just a car. It's at least that important, right? What you want to see are how long the course is (it should not be less than a month), how many hours of classroom and exam instruction (at least a few dozen classroom hours and a dozen exam hours), how many resources (practice exams, online tutoring, etc.), and who's the instructor. In short, this should be of a quality of an all-inclusive professional seminar that costs, yes, about as much as a brand-name LSAT prep course. There are just a handful of courses that offer this extensive a program—which for you should be a requirement. Any less, and you're wasting your money, time, and future.

How expensive? Very. I know that this might strike you as inappropriately flippant on my part, and I am acutely aware of my own history on this...which is one reason I'm taking this stark approach. When I took the LSAT I could not afford a prep course of any kind (and even the brand-name ones were cheaper then). So, I borrowed every LSAT book from just about every branch of the Austin Public Library. I would visit each in turn to get different editions. There weren't all that many then, so I probably only had a half-dozen or so. I did practice exam upon practice exam, and exhausted the (free) supply available at the time. Smart? Not really. Would a prep course have made a difference? I don't know. But it's unlikely it would have hurt, and it might have helped...just enough. As with the law, you won't know how much is enough, and so you must give it your all. The old saying is that the law is a jealous mistress. While that sounds a bit tinny to our post-modern ears, it's true nonetheless.

Take practice tests...*lots* of them. Borrow or buy every LSAT book there is. Consider that equal to the cost of two or three schools you won't need to apply to because your score will be too good. Order every old LSAT practice book the LSAC offers. Seriously. As of this writing the LSAC's website lists 23 test-prep books, plus the Official Guide to ABA-Approved Law Schools. You should plan to spend $150-$200 on these test-prep booklets. If you buy them in batches, as you might want to, you'll need to stay at least a few weeks ahead in your ordering—or use other LSAT books in case you forget.

You'll have access to other publishers' test-prep booklets, either from your library or, new, from a bookstore. To be honest, with so much available from the LSAC, you'll have plenty to keep you busy—but they're there if you need extras or find yourself waiting for a new order. Essentially, you'll never have the excuse of running out of fresh LSATs to chew on.

As to borrowing, here's where you really should have a clean copy. So, if you find a copy marked with X's or circles—correct or not—it's easier and better simply to buy a new copy. If your library does have a clean copy, then please don't write in it. Not even a little, and not even lightly. Splurge on a clean sheet of paper, and grade that. In fact, *even if* you buy it, you shouldn't mark it up; you can sell it later, recouping much of your outlay. And there's no value added in marking up a book. Really. If this is a habit, it's a bad one. Break it. Keep it clean.

Okay, so what do you do with all these LSAT tests?

Take every one, and time yourself. When you time yourself, time yourself short: give yourself *less* time than the official time. Start with, say, two minutes less, and increase that as you practice, until you can finish the LSAC's tests with five minutes to spare. In the actual exam time *will* be short—and will certainly *feel* short—and you must be able to work on an intensely fast-paced, minute-by-minute pacing. Between tests, review the questions of the test you just took. Review them in detail...until you know not just *what* was wrong, but also *why*.

You must take as many tests as you can get your hands on. This should be dozens, if not close to a hundred, practice exams. No kidding. Now you see why I write that even six weeks in preparation is too short. Beyond just comfort and familiarity, something interesting happens: the questions start repeating. Not exactly. Slightly changed, to be sure. But essentially, the same questions. After all, the drafters have only so many analytical options—from a dozen or so different problem frameworks—to choose from. Once you figure out how to solve each logical type, the specific questions will matter less. As you'll find in law school itself, this pattern keeps repeating itself: the process is just as if not more important than the "answer." That's because you're unlikely to get to the right answer without having mastered the process.

As a practical matter, every dozen tests you take increases your score by at least a point or two. The first dozen, perhaps a handful of extra points; by the last dozen, maybe just one. This is nothing to sneeze at—you will cherish every one of those extra points when the time comes to mail in your applications.

CANCELLING

What about cancelling your LSAT score if you don't feel you did well? In a word, no. Unless you absolutely bombed—as in didn't finish the exam and vomited throughout (which likely didn't help the person next to you)—you live with it. This should reinforce just how important this test is, and also the *No Whining* rule. This is not for me, but for your application. There's very, *very* little room for excuses in an application, or even an explanation for that matter, and so it's important to break a bad habit now.

Okay, I wrote that to reinforce how serious this is.

Now for the real advice: if for whatever reason you do bomb— or if you simply don't prepare sufficiently and realize that during the exam—you should *seriously* weigh how badly you want to attend law school. If this is enough to scare yourself straight, there's a legitimate reason to cancel: if you cancel, and if you're serious about law school and re-starting the entire process, and if you actually take that seriously, the presumably higher score you then get will be much better than two significantly different scores. Some law schools will average them; most will, with sufficiently compelling subjective materials, be willing to give the benefit of the doubt, but either way this adds a messy complication in a process that likes neither messiness nor complications.

Whether or not you cancel, you absolutely, positively must take this seriously. If you prepare as you should, you will walk out of the test center with a feeling of satisfaction, not dread.

GPA

This will be a short section, because there's little to write. For most, your GPA is set, or nearly so, by the time you apply.

If it's not completely set, then you must focus on maintaining a strong GPA. This is not just for appearances: in borderline cases especially, the last grades will carry more weight, not least because they're usually for the most difficult courses, and because they are seen to reflect on both quality and character.

What about the type of school, or the degree itself? Well, while the conventional wisdom tends to say, *Nah,* they just look at the score, that's wrong too. And it's wrong where it counts: in borderline cases. If your LSAT/GPA are clearly superior, then you might well gain admission regardless of your college or degree. Conversely, if your LSAT/GPA are clearly inferior relative to the scores for applicants admitted to that law school, then you will likely not be admitted...regardless of your college or degree.

BUT...

It's for the middle group—the ever-crucial middle stack—where this *is* considered. And your application *will* be in the middle stack for your Reach school; that's why it's a Reach. And, even if you've a 178 LSAT and a 3.98 GPA, it *still* won't be a cakewalk for the very top schools.

Too, this is not always a one-way street, or an easily marked path. Clearly, someone with a GPA in engineering is likely to have a slightly better reception when compared with someone with a degree in, say, the ever-popular basket-weaving. Likewise, an applicant with a degree from a top school will probably get the nod over someone from Podunk College. Probably. The better the law school, the more deeply they will look at this, including relative rankings of the college, grade inflation, and just what courses you took and how well you did in each of them. There are other concerns for the law school as well: racial, ethnic, geographic, socio-economic, and other forms of diversity; some indication of overcoming of great odds; when in the season the application is reviewed (the earlier the better); and so on. Most of these will have only the most modest of impacts. Sometimes, however, that's enough.

What happens in this process is that the middle stack gets reviewed by several sets of eyes. The more in the middle it is, the more eyes have it. Moreover, the stronger your application, the more senior are your reviewers. This is taken quite seriously. The task is to weigh both objective and subjective criteria. The more borderline the application, the more importance the subjective and qualitative criteria become. This is why you cannot simply treat all the ancillary material as unimportant—even if they are, in many cases. In *your* case, chances are you want the greatest consideration where it will count the most: when your application is the most borderline, because the school is, for you, a Reach.

What about a graduate degree, or additional coursework, or dual majors, or…? Same answer: it can be significant, when all else is fairly equal. Generally, however, all else is not equal, and other criteria are more important. At best, unless they're truly out-of-the box (a medical degree, dual majors in physics and fine art, and the like), these factors will get only the most modest of pluses.

All of this boils down to two contradictory realities: for most, the *only* factors that count are the LSAT and GPA; and for some, after the LSAT and GPA have put you above the threshold, the extras—everything else—make the decision.

EVERYTHING ELSE

Each application will usually require a main form, a personal essay, letters of recommendation, and any number of housekeeping details. Just about every guide will remind you that your application should be spotless. This is correct. Even one misspelling can be the kiss of death where it counts: with the Reach school. More than one misspelling—or odd or poorly phrased grammar, or rambling, incoherent essays—*will* be the kiss of death.

Law professors, who are among the ones judging you, *care* about writing. And they don't just care about it in the "here's how to write legalese" sense. With most, it's quite the opposite. Nearly every professor tasked with reviewing applications will take the process seriously, and every one of them will assume that they *know* how to write. So, if what you write does not meet their standard, you get dinged, if not rejected outright. And their standard will be high. Just one frown is usually enough. In their minds, this is exactly right. They're looking not only for someone with the requisite knowledge and aptitude, they're looking for someone with the right *attitude*. Someone who *cares*. A typographical error, or sloppy grammar, is proof that you do not care.

If, by the way, you disagree, stop. You're wrong. Typographical errors and sloppy grammar *are* proof that you do not care. In a legal context, they are nearly an "irrebuttable presumption" that you should *not* be in law school. Certainly not in *their* law school. Why? Because law, whatever you think of it going in, will require both technical precision and a high degree of care over how documents are researched, prepared, proofread, revised, and corrected. This *is* important. It's so important that it can make the difference even in a school for which you are nominally above-average: many rejections to Targets and especially Safeties occur because of these types of errors. Law professors (rightly) see their task as deciding who among a large pool has at least enough concern to make sure that what they present is of high quality. If they don't care about a few simple pages, how on Earth can they be trusted with a client's livelihood, or life?

You might think I'm going overboard here. Surely the advent of email, text messaging, and, who knows, cerebral telepathy …renders these conventions old-fashioned and silly. Nope. First, think about who you're talking about. Even the younger of the professors on the admissions committee graduated college before email. And all of them did *extremely* well. This means that they know how to speak and they know how to write English, well. Even if they might be philosophically predisposed to grant certain leeway to new linguistic conventions, they will nonetheless value the ability to "measure up" to formal, proper, correct English. This is both cultural and realistic: they'll do no favors to their school or to themselves if they admit students who don't know how to write, or how to pay attention to detail. And, given how much more of an issue this has become, chances are good they will react quite firmly to any misspelling or poor writing. So, on both philosophical and practical grounds, if there's even the slightest comma out of place…do it again.

So what's a good standard?

The Atlantic Monthly. The Economist. The Financial Times. There are others, but these three are good places to start. Notably, two of the three are British; when it comes to the written language, in all its flavours and colours, that's the mother tongue. If you've not read these recently, you might take a look to see if you agree, then a second and third look with an eye towards emulation. They happen to be excellent periodicals (and the kind that lawyers read), but that's not why you should refer to them. Or that's not the only reason: the level of quality in their writing is your new benchmark. It's the quality of writing for everything you produce in your application, with nary a comma or participle out of place. This, by the way, is the same standard you will be expected to employ once you graduate from law school.

I'm kidding about British spelling, by the way. Although many law professors are indeed Anglophiles—sometimes found saying, to no one in particular, "Right! What's all this then?"—stick with our variety of formal American English. Just think of your strictest English teacher when you think of how seriously you should take this…and take that as the bare minimum.

Okay then. A few words about each part:

The Application Form. For the main form (or, often, forms), if there's even the slightest comma out of place…do it again. (Where have we heard *that* before?) As most forms are now done electronically, and as spell-checkers are available for nearly all software, there's truly no excuse for even a single typographical error. That should be your quality mandate: nary a one. Also, do not feel at liberty to alter a form. If you've some exceptional qualities (or negatives), then add an addendum that must be of equally perfect quality, reasoning, and frame-worthy presentation. And that is that. You might negate a negative with a perfect, well-reasoned addendum…but odds are against it. If your addendum is less-than-perfect, or less than well-reasoned, no way. You've just helped the law school improve its yield—by boosting the percentage of applications it denies.

Also, there's a trend of submitting "cute" applications, in the form of videos, shoes, chocolates, and the like. Don't do this. Don't even *think* about doing this. This is not a graduate program in modern art. It is a professional school. Complete the application, flawlessly, and submit it.

The Perfect Personal Essay. Personal essays might be the only form of cruel and unusual punishment never raised to the Supreme Court. How to find your soul—and then package it just right—for some unknown admissions committee? How to do so when you're busy enough with part-time jobs, classes, crushes, and the occasional all-nighter?

First, your essay cannot be rushed. You should, optimally, think about it for *years*. If you're reading this while contemplating law school once you graduate college (or high school and then college), that's time enough to think about what it is that's important to you, and then how you might—with at least some literary flair—present that to a faceless group of senior law school professors, deans, and admissions officers.

What if you don't have years? Well, this is hardly theoretical as most of us end up throwing something together in months, if not weeks. You must think of something unique. Not off-the-wall. But *unique*. This means unique *to you*. The admissions committee will have read, hundreds if not thousands of times over, about "Why I love the law!" and "Why me 'cause I'm gonna' save the world!" And so on. Does this mean you should not say that you love the law or that you're planning to save the world? Well, unless you have some way to convincingly explain that love, or that passion for utopia…that's correct. You should not attempt a "standard fluff" essay.

You should also not read any book on "best" essays for admission to law school. The moment they hit the shelves, they become exactly the type of essays not to use. Why? Because admissions folks then see hundreds of essays that practically plagiarize. No, no, no.

I was surprised when I spot-checked some of these. The essays I read were such a turn-off that I would have been hard pressed not to toss the entire application into the Reject pile, regardless of the LSAT. This is deeply personal, true, but what they should see is a glimpse of your better self—or your not-so-better self, with some indication of self-awareness, critique, and general ethical value. In other words, are you a decent person? Not perfect. Decent.

What the admissions committee is looking for is some indication of what type of lawyer you will be—the type of *person* you *are*.

While this might seem like a tall order—how can thousands upon thousands of essays be "unique"?—in reality it's a taller order for them than for you. After all, you need to write just one.

So, writing an essay about a childhood experience with, say, a grandparent's involvement in a lawsuit and the impact that that had on you, and the reasons that affected your thinking about what the law should be—*that* might be more effective than a fluffy "I wanna' save the world" (which is easy to read as "I *really* wanna' make a lot of money but I'll pretend to want to save the world").

Now, don't everyone write about your grandparents. It should be something *unique*. To you. Something that, while it might and should strike a chord in anyone who reads it, is intensely personal. No one other than the committee (and whoever you ask) will read it. As with the LSAT, this is something you should take *exceedingly* seriously, and it is something you should want to be proud of. It should be an essay that will knock your socks off when you find it in a box fifty years later.

It's not much of an exaggeration to state that, aside from your LSAT score, your personal essay is the most important part of your application. It almost goes ahead of your GPA. Even with a stellar LSAT score and GPA, a bad essay will kill your application. And if there's anything to save a mediocre LSAT score or GPA, it's your personal essay.

As to asking others to read your essay, it's common to ask parents, family, or friends to read your drafts. This is a mistake. Even if they are exceptional writers, they're the wrong ones to give advice. First, they're too close. That means they're probably too subjective about whatever it is you're writing. Second, they're probably not from the academic or law school worlds, which means that what guides them might (and probably will) be different than what guides the admissions committee. Finally, they're almost certain to be too *gentle*. Yes, that is worse. Unless they tell you *"This is crap!"* as a standard response to any situation (in which case see "they're too subjective," above), chances are they won't tell you what really *does* need to be redone.

So who, then? Most likely, you should ask professors who have known you at least reasonably well, and you should make it clear that you want genuine criticism—and *you should be prepared to take it.* If you even start to talk back when they do critique your work, pinch yourself. Hard. If you can slap yourself without being noticed, do that too. You need *help.* And what you write will almost certainly not be good enough…not yet. This willingness to honestly review and then to revise is the essence of high-quality writing. You should accept with genuine appreciation a real critique, meaning a higher-order "This *is* crap…and here's what you might do to fix it."

The result should be an essay that you read, re-read, and re-re-read many times over, smiling as you wonder who on Earth wrote such a lovely piece. My goodness, how can they *not* let you in?

Letters of Recommendation. These are perhaps the trickiest part of your application, as law schools give mixed signals (often because of how tricky these are), and because few ever explain just how important these can be—or how to actually go about getting the right ones. This leaves the hapless applicant in the position of not knowing whether and how much to focus on them and, if so, who and how *exactly* to go about it.

Some students hesitate to ask professors for a letter, on the assumption that they're too busy, too important, or that they might not write a sufficiently glowing recommendation. (Or, conversely, that they're not important enough.) There are a few answers to this. First, nearly all professors accept that writing letters of recommendation is part of their job description. Some do them well; many do not. Most will willingly write letters, especially for those students who struck them as caring and worthy. Assuming that that's you, your challenge is to make this as seamless and effortless for them as possible. *Stop thinking about yourself.* Or, more correctly, stop thinking about the easy way. First, you should engage in discussions with professors with an eventual need for their professional reference in mind. This is not the only reason you should do this, but it is *a* reason. It is also a reason you should be the type of college student who stands out for quality and integrity—this counts more than anything else in a letter of recommendation. In essence: do you *care?* The recommendation has value to the extent that it confirms something that scores and papers cannot: that you cared about quality and integrity when you thought no one was looking.

As you get more serious (and closer) to actually applying to law school, be ready to discuss your plans to attend law school (and with some real answers as to why and where). You needn't be coy, but you should be polite (always!). A simple request is best. Don't leave them guessing: "Would you be willing to write a letter of recommendation for me, for my law school applications? I plan to apply to…"

This should, ideally, follow a years-long association. Seriously. You should find professors you like and respect, and make sure you deserve the recommendation you hope to get. Assuming they answer in the affirmative, then you need to be ready with part two: "Would it be helpful to you if I were to give you a list of my accomplishments and qualities that might be helpful in preparing your letter?"

We often assume that others know every detail of our (to us) very important lives. Chances are, even if you were a star pupil of the professors you do ask, that they know rather little about you. They know what they've seen, of course, but in reality this is not much: in most classes you're part of a sea of faces. This is true even in seminars, to a large extent and depending upon the professors. Only in one-on-one labs in the sciences is a real bond usually struck. This means that without any help their letters will be perfunctory—and thus of marginal help, if at all. What you should have prepared is more than a mere résumé: it is a window to how you would describe your best self, if you were given that task (as you are).

Note: you are not writing the letter. Rather, you are adding context to the person—you—so that your professor will be pleasantly surprised at some of your many activities and accomplishments, and likely to discuss them, positively, in the context of what is known from your class work.

You thus prepare a detailed summary to add context to what your professor will write. Most important—as with the LSAT and every other aspect of your law school applications—this requires work up front. Don't even go to your professor with the actual request until your summary is prepared *and* refined. That alone separates you from the pack, but that's not why you do it. You do it to make your professor's job easier, which in turn makes the job better.

A warning: letters of recommendation have undergone the same inflation that affects grades. Professors know this. So do admissions committees. Historically, letters of introduction were highly valued, and seriously taken. As much was riding on the recommender's reputation as was riding for the person being recommended. Think of a scene in a *Masterpiece Theatre* special featuring ever-so-proper English gentlemen. That, in point of fact, is where we get the practice.

And now? If a letter is any less than superlative—if, for example, it states that, while the professor didn't *actually* see you walk on water, he heard about it and it certainly comports with the joviality he saw in the classroom and with the, what was it, "B-" you got—that letter might as well have been written on toilet paper. I leave it to your imagination whether the committee will consider it fresh or used. Anything less than "The Applicant?...You'd be Certifiably Insane Not to Accept *This* One!" is taken as a coded, "damned with faint praise" neon sign that you're not so hot after all. On the other hand, some professors are so over-the-top that the committee is left to parse for clues as to how good a student—and person—you really are. And, believe it or not, after a while admissions officers get familiar with individual college professors and their recommendations—especially from "feeder" colleges to that law school.

What if you know someone important...say, the Pope? Well, unless you happen to know the Pope well, chances are that you should stick with recommenders who *do* know you well enough to say so. You can re-live in your mind the time the Pope waived at you, and instead focus on the assistant professor whose courses you enjoyed so much you took all of them, and then were lucky enough to serve as a research assistant to boot. Those recommendations carry more weight. Believe it or not, you can call your Senator and ask for a letter of recommendation. That tells you just how "valuable" certain recommendations have become.

Should you ignore or omit letters of recommendation? No. In most applications you can't, and in any application you won't know just how important they are. As you'll hardly be part of the process, it's not that you "won't know until it's too late," but that you won't know at all.

Consequently, for any number of reasons these letters can be nails in the coffin of your application—and, indeed, most letters of recommendation are read with wary eyes. They can also be what puts your application over the top, however. For your all-important Reach school, this is a crucial part of your application...and an area filled with landmines. The best advice I've seen on this subject is in Curll's book, mentioned above. If there's even the slightest hesitation or difference of opinion: go with her take on it.

Work in a Firm. If you do work in a firm—which is highly re-commended—be careful how you present that. It should not be a primary focus in your application. Sure, you can draw lessons (or perhaps your personal essay) from what you learned, but don't expect kudos. The object of your application is admission to an academic, not vocational, program. Instead, this is a background benefit: you'll have a better sense of what the law (and law school application) are all about, and the admissions committee will look favorably upon an earnest (and low-keyed) display of maturity.

THE THREE STACKS

There are three bins—okay, stacks—into which applications go in each admissions office:

Auto-Admits. This is a small group of applicants whose LSAT/GPA scores are so comfortably above the median for that school, and the personal statement so compelling, and all other elements of the application so without error, that there really isn't a decision to be made. The threshold is set high: very few, and sometimes none, are in this stack. As a general rule, the higher the school, the fewer the auto-admits. This, of course, is because the threshold rises so much higher, the higher one goes. I almost changed this to "Early Admits," by the way, as that might be a bit more fair, but the key in "auto" gets to a central truth that is important: while we want this to be about individuals, this is also fundamentally about the numbers. It has to be.

Perhaps more important are the Almost-Auto-Admits, which are so close that they need only the slightest push to reach the Accept bin. (The stacks are on the tables. The bins are on the secretary's desk...for when a decision is made.)

Maybes. This is the vast middle, upon which so much focus is visited. At the edges, the LSAT/GPA scores *almost* make the decision (Yes at the high end, No at the low), but admissions officers do try to be fair. In fairness to them, they spend more time in this middle stack than most of us would have the patience for.

The more in the middle an applicant is, the more important are the subjective factors—personal statements, overcoming of hurdles, and so on. This is true at both the top schools, where everyone has top scores, and at everyone's Reach schools.

Auto-Rejects. The higher the school, the more there are. Someone is going to contest: "We never reject anyone automatically!" While true, this is a counterfeit truth. The auto-reject standard is comfortably below the median for that law school, and while such applications might get a cursory glance (often from a junior admissions officer or even clerk tasked with picking up on certain extraordinary factors—assuming of course they catch them), for nearly all it's *very* fast track...to the Reject bin.

*   *   *

It's important to see this for what it is: for the law schools, it is a necessary winnowing process. No one likes to give bad news, so everyone tries to be painfully fair. But, when a batch of 2,000 applications weighs on makeshift tables in the admissions office (think of a Dr. Seuss drawing, with the tables nearly drooping to the floor, held up by rickety poles)...and those for just 225 available slots (say, 300 minus 25 auto-admits minus another 50 almost-auto-admits), the ones doing the deciding come quickly to the understanding that they *have* to be critical. Even if they want to give the benefit of the doubt, they cannot. Not to everyone. And certainly not year in and year out. Thus, while they might give a below-median application an extra glance or two, chance are very, very low that it will make its way into the Accept bin. Sure, there's the "waitlist," and also the fudge factor that each law school has (for the assumed percentage who are accepted but who will not attend)—but each of those reinforces the main point: as much as we wish it weren't, this is a numbers game.

Again let's reverse the lens: if you run an admissions department and receive those 2,000 applications, are you going to read every one of them? You'd be negligent if you did. Why? Let's play it out. Let's say you devoted three solid months to an in-depth review of every one of those. What would you find? Nearly all of the applications at the statistical bottom of your pool would be rejected—even (and perhaps especially) after an in-depth review. Nearly all at the top would be accepted, even without the rankings held over schools' heads: they're simply superior candidates, and the LSAT/GPA are coincidental indicators of that quality. Perfect? No, but they don't have to be…and certainly not at the tails. So the process is one of defining ever-more central "tails" in deciding who gets in and who does not. Law schools can thus lop off the bottom 20% or so without any real fear that they're missing a diamond in the rough. Unfair? Wrong question, but for the sake of argument, let's play with that too. An hour spent reviewing a few bottom applications that are almost certain to be denied is an hour that is not available to a handful of almost-great applications. Where should that limited time go? After all, the one element that might save a bottom application is the personal statement…and that can be read in just a few minutes. Also, if it's so important to the applicant, might they have improved their standing? Did they take the LSAT again? An applicant who takes the exam five times to conquer a phobia and discusses it convincingly in a personal statement or addendum might just be one of those almost-great applications worthy of that extra hour.

In this, and except at the least-competitive law schools, the bulk of applications make their way to the Reject bin. Your challenge is to understand this from their perspective…and keep yours in the stack that finds its way into the happy bin. Even for an applicant with a perfect or near-perfect LSAT and GPA, it's hardly safe to consider Yale, Harvard, and Stanford as sure things. This is why, at top schools, not only does everyone have top scores, but everyone seems to have astonishing backgrounds—a Rhodes Scholar here, a math wiz there, a former diplomat shaking hands some-where up front. So, at the tippy-top, they're unimpressed by top scores. At each level lower, there are scores that will impress: yet few applicants have them, for the simple reason that, the more the school would be impressed, the more that school becomes (for the applicant) a Safety. So, for nearly every application, the question is how quickly it heads to the Reject bin...and how possibly it can be diverted to the happier one.

LAW SCHOOL RANKINGS

The law is an intensely status-oriented profession. Much has been written on this, and much is said (and not said) in everyday conversations among lawyers and law students, each of whom is aware of—if not consciously promoting—a pecking order of legal status. Less is said on why this is so. First, let's get a few points out the way.

Are rankings *meaningful?* Yes, they are.

So they describe real differences among law schools? Yes, they do.

Should they be used to decide which law school to attend? Well, in true lawyerly fashion: yes and no.

To treat law school rankings as unimportant—whether out of ignorance or indignation—is foolish. Rankings *do* reflect qualita-tive differences between and among law schools. On the other hand, looking *only* to rankings is equally foolish, and treating law schools with rankings within a half-dozen places of each other as hugely different is simply nonsense. Both extremes set up a bit of a straw man, as few take either approach. Still, it's important to keep the value of rankings firmly in mind, as a decision about attending one law school or another can make a big difference to you and your life. Moreover, as to the last point, it is quite common to use rankings to highlight close difference—*But this school is three points higher!*—rather than treat them as they should be treated. Rankings reflect gross, not fine, distinctions, based on both objec-tive and (hugely) subjective criteria with wide margins of error. So, comparing #12 with #37 or #37 with #92 are fair comparisons worthy of consideration. Comparing #12 with #16 is seductively easy—and qualitatively incorrect. Within a half-dozen, other attributes are more important.

Okay, back to status. Law school is not just some combination of buildings, faculty, students, and graduates. Instead, a twofold reality heightens the sensitivity of lawyers to status. The first is the highly competitive nature of law school. The second is the highly risk-averse nature of law practice. These two factors combine to create a system that is nearly a caste system in its orientation and effect. Is this right?

Wrong question. I happen to believe it is foolish. Many others decry it. But the reality is that it *is*. To hope that we can wish it away—without substantive changes in how our profession operates—is simply that, wishful thinking. For our purposes, wishful thinking is worse than silly. It will set you up for failure, as it's easy to mistake the "wishful" part for something approaching reality. (Even among committed Marxists, Karl himself would never have stood for the silliness that passes for critique today. Among his writings Marx condemned wishful thinking especially, as he insisted upon revolution as the *inevitable* consequence of capitalism.)

There's a paradox in this debate, and that is that law practice has elements of egalitarianism that are almost the opposite of all of the above. In litigation especially, it is the nature of persuasion and of winning, and of a consistent superiority at both, that marks the superior attorney. The paradox comes in that one's pedigree is of little importance in the real world of the courtroom (and even, for a corporate lawyer, boardroom)—but of great importance in getting there. Even more, the airs of a fancy law degree, or of a superiority complex, can work very much against us. Few jurors like being condescended to, and as a result, many top litigators look as if they just arrived to the courthouse via Trailways. Quite a few affect a less-than-holier-than-thou appearance, so as to connect to the individuals who will ultimately, if indirectly, decide their case (and earnings). Even in corporate offices, while senior executives expect a pedigreed counsel (and get it), they generally prefer down-to-earth, let's-get-the-job-done *consigliere,* not snippy bluebloods. If that is your inclination, or if that's what you think is important, knock it off.

This is a difficult section for another reason. There are two ways to approach this: the "egghead" answer and the just-the-facts-ma'am answer. While you might be annoyed if you want just the latter that you have to suffer through the former—unless you just skip it!—these are actually tied together. Law schools are status-conscious because of professors, and because of lawyers. Together—along with a society that knows only brand-name schools—these support a self-reinforcing structure built on status.

So who sets these standards? Law professors are an obvious starting point. But, because their worlds are generally focused in, well, law school, there's another group that heightens this already-strong orientation towards status. That is the world of lawyers and law practice. Firms are populated with individuals who have attended law school, of course. The better the firm, the more likely its inhabitants have attended the top schools. But, in most cases, the experience with law school begins (and ends) there. As a result, the practitioner takes a nearly-monochromatic view of the law school world: there's "my" school...and then there's everyone else's.

The "law schools for everyone else" are clearly worse than *my* school...unless everyone else "knows" that such-and-so school is better. Drats. So, if one attends, say, a well-regarded regional law school, its graduates will relish the ego-boost of admiration from others, especially if practicing in that region. What happens when someone walks in from, say, Stanford? Well, sure, *that's* an okay school too. And so it goes.

How many law schools can most non-lawyers (or even lawyers) mention? Hmm. There's Harvard, of course. And, oh yes, Yale, Stanford. Columbia and NYU, for those on the East Coast. And the Universities of [insert nearest states here]. See where this goes? Chances are most of us can name the top dozen or so schools. We could probably come up with another dozen, and if someone named a few others, we'd get those too. But *two hundred?* No way. Only one group knows even a substantial fraction of that total: those about to apply to law school. Even law school deans focus only on schools near and above them. So, what that means is that the entire population relies on "name brand" and on "me-and-bet-ter" to decide status (above the general status of being a law graduate). This is one reason law schools have begun to spend serious money in branding—to improve name recognition among those who might apply (and, *ahem,* among those who might be asked by *U.S. News and World Report.*) In short, there's a very real emotional pressure to believe one's own school is better than it is—and to help others to believe so too—and so there's constant pressure to connect with those schools higher above. This, in turn, heightens the value of schools—geometrically if not exponentially—the higher they are. Winner take all.

It's an academic version of what happens in locker rooms from junior high on. Perhaps it shouldn't be, but it's hardly likely that we'll change this little aspect of our psychology. More to the point, what this means is that the law practice world—which accounts for the vast majority of lawyers—feeds the weight given to objective measures, which in turn are driven by standards such as how many books are in the library (and you thought measurements would stop), how much money is spent on faculty (of obvious interest to law professors), and professors' own views of their world.

In that, professors deal with the same human emotion: the school *they* went to is best, while the others range from *dreck* to *okay.* And it doesn't matter who you're talking with. If they attended the University of Virginia, their many glories are front and center, and only schools *clearly* better than UVA are in The Club (*i.e.,* the Ivy League.) In this sense, it's like looking through the wrong end of a pair of binoculars: everything around what you're looking at is squished to nothingness.

An important point: the less secure one is, the more important status is. I've seen lawyers almost visibly sizing each other up by their law schools. This happens more often among younger lawyers; this is a no-no among older and better lawyers. Indeed, after working with excellent lawyers from "lesser" schools—and poor lawyers from top ones—few senior attorneys get hung up on pedigree. Among law students, it's often a one-upmanship about their LSAT or undergraduate school or, amazingly, prep school. I remember one attorney in particular who it seemed was thinking for a split second how to respond when hearing that a more-junior associate attended a better school. It was actually *far* better, and both were playing games with the other in terms of one-upman-ship. It was a game both lost, by the way.

Why a focus on this? Why can't we just say "law school is law school" and be done with it?

Well, for one thing, it's not true. For another, there's that human element again. Once one has graduated, there's a natural inclination to live in the reflected glory of that school. This can be for practical reasons (getting a job), or for ego-driven ones. (You went *there!?*)

But still…why? Because our sense of self-worth, particularly for lawyers, is tied up with how we perceive ourselves as smart, and how much we depend upon *others* seeing us as smart. If we can reflect in academic glory, we feel the warm glow of that self-worth. The intensity of law school—and of a bulk of its inhabitants—make this far worse, especially during and just after law school.

There's yet another quirk, in that graduates of the very top schools face a different challenge: it's nearly impossible to even state their alma mater without appearing to brag. Thus, there's an inverse need to avoid this in public altogether. The joke at Yale is that its other name is "In Connecticut." As in "Where did you go to law school?" "In Connecticut." It can be hard to get a Yalie to admit (in public) where he went to law school, and it is certainly considered rude to volunteer it. Maybe that, according to one Yalie, is just their particular brand of snobbery. The joke at Harvard—regarded among Yalies as a good back-up school—is to state the name with a question mark, as if to ask "…*heard of it?*" This too is more of an inside joke than one repeated in public. I've heard more than one Harvard grad saying, with a smile, "…a local school" when asked in or near Boston.

BUT DON'T TOP LAW SCHOOLS TEACH LAW BETTER?

Nope. This used to be a common refrain among (you guessed it) graduates of the top schools. The accusation and assumption was that good law schools taught theory—the ability to "think like a lawyer"—while lesser schools taught mere mechanics of black letter law, like a trade school. This was often said (and written) with a proverbial sneer: a "real" law school taught manly law (*i.e.,* theory), while piddling law schools taught sissy law (*i.e.,* how to go to court).

Although this might have been true at one time, it is no longer. All law schools now teach the same law, the same way. As discussed the bulk of law professors come from the same background: Top 5 law school, top clerkship, a year or two at a top firm, and then on to an assistant professorship. Even the lowest-ranked law schools can get, with today's job market, the same caliber of astonishingly pedigreed new professor. They have all sipped from the same well, and even "local schools" that have an interest to focus on the laws of that state now focus as well on exactly the same doctrines that the "big boys" do. And even if all their professors didn't come from a Top 5 school, they all *want* to have come from one…so they'll be even *more* sensitive to teaching "theory," just like the big boys.

This prejudice carries forward in odd ways. One book states that "top J.D. programs require a lot of work." Um, *all* J.D. programs require a lot of work. It's just that they don't require as much work as everyone seems to believe—and they certainly don't require makework. Top or otherwise. So, if you're going to go to one school over another, don't let it be for this reason. Visit your nearest law school—even one you have no intention of attending—as it's useful to sit in on a few classes. It will be time well spent.

So Law Schools Really Are the Same?

Nope. Law schools are *very* different in two crucial ways: (1) rankings, and (2) students.

Much ink has been spilled on rankings. (And still more will be over the next few sections.) What is missed in the debate is what the rankings actually tell us. If we look at the methodology, we see the impact of a number of factors: the nods of approval of fellow professors, the assumptions of a few senior lawyers and judges, the number of books in the library, and so on. Much of this relates, ultimately, to two factors: money and prestige. These are two factors very much intertwined. More money *does* buy prestige, and prestige "buys" more money. This is another reason law schools now advertise heavily, and produce among the most beautiful "corporate" documents out there. They're trying to sell themselves, and not just to prospective students—with brochures they're also planting the seeds of a reputation in the mind of future lawyers. (I happen to have a better knowledge of—and higher respect for—Case Western Reserve University than I ever would have had without a superlative brochure they mailed me, unsolicited. That brochure, not cheaply done, returned its cost many times over almost exactly 20 years later: in this parenthetical.)

The second factor is the quality of students, as measured by selectivity of the law school, which in turn is measured by the relative LSAT/GPA scores of students admitted. This factor deserves its own mention, as this might be the single biggest difference among law schools—in ways that are indirectly reflected in but in actuality *coincide with* the rankings. Because Yale, Harvard, etc. get to choose the very best, the result is a learning environment populated by the very smartest of the very smart. They might be idealistic and bursting with energy or jaded and seeking success...but, either way, they are very, *very* smart. Now that faculty are nearly uniformly from the very top law schools themselves, the *real* distinguishing characteristic of the rankings is the quality of students, not faculty.

Moreover, the wealthier the school (*i.e.,* the higher it ranks, almost by definition), the more it will be able to offer its students. This is currency paid in tangible benefits as well as intangible ones. At top schools the facilities are usually quite lavish (although you'd be surprised at some of the ancient holdovers at certain top schools, and superb facilities at "lesser" schools), and faculty and elective offerings are often hard to match. But it's not an issue of teaching, or of faculty quality. Rather, it's an issue of resources, and for most law schools the money is there.

Law School Rankings: Attitude and Altitude

Law school rankings are often presented as a linear truth, leading to endless arguments among those with a vested interest in attacking rankings generally...or in relishing *their* school's rank. The academic-snob equivalent of "Is not!" "Is too!" are heard *ad nause-*

am. Soon we forget just what it is that the rankings are measuring, and what, exactly, we should be doing with that measurement. This is especially true for those not yet in law school.

A ranking of law schools is not linear. Rather, it is three-dimensional, extending above and across the United States. Moreover, each law school has a different appearance, as it strives to shine ever brighter and higher in its own way. This too is not quite right, as nearly all attempt to shine like the brightest of them all.

First is the stellar trinity: Harvard, Yale, and Stanford. These are not so much aircraft soaring high above as they are satellites. In fact, they're not ordinary geosynchronous satellites, content to perch miles above Cambridge, New Haven, and Palo Alto, providing all manner of legal feed. Instead they zip across the nation and planet, soaring in elliptic orbits high above each continent and presenting an easy object for raised heads and our collective admiration. They circle closest above their home base, of course, and report in each revolution...but they relish their global reach. They're not exactly stars, but they certainly look that way from below.

The brightest of all is Harvard. A large law school, it is active in seemingly every conceivable area in the law. Indeed, many of its projects become areas of broader legal concentration and concern, such as the Harvard Negotiation Project (under which Alternative Dispute Resolution received an important boost, becoming a major feature of the law and law practice). One of many current efforts is the Berkman Center for Internet and Society...a research center adding to its considerable luster. Yale and Stanford, by contrast, are smaller law schools. Their illumination, while too bright to look at directly, is nonetheless a bit less stunning than Harvard's. Moreover, an interesting phenomenon is seen with the passing of each satellite: Harvard appears as a bright orangish-white, while Yale seems to have more of a bluish tint. Just as visible light can be quite different, depending upon its "temperature," this is the focus, at Yale, on the many academic pursuits in legal education. In short, Yale is more centered on pure academics—leading to the assumption among many academics that *it* is the best law school—while Harvard seems too large and unwieldy to maintain such a focus. A large percentage of Yale's graduates enter judicial clerkships, with the goal of teaching in a law school, or working in public policy or a non-profit. Harvard, by contrast, seems astride the entire profession: each year it produces many hundreds of new associates for the biggest law firms, and nearly as many for judges—and from there to yet more top firms, top agencies, and law schools around the country. With a large population of extraordinarily talented graduates, Harvard populates seemingly every corner of high-powered law. Smallish Stanford tends to take Harvard's generally more pragmatic approach, giving it the same orangy-white shine...but not quite a bright as the one zooming above Cambridge in its daily circumnavigations. As a result, not just the rest of legal education but even the others in the top-tier club look to shine as brightly as does Harvard.

I can hear it now: But Yale is ranked *higher!* Yes, it is. But that is irrelevant. If one looks closely at the methodology of the rankings, they will see that a large part of that reason is twofold: the focus of Yale on the "theory" side, and its lower acceptance rate. The focus of both is of importance mostly to...other law professors. A judge hardly cares that Yale is a bit more "eggheady" than Harvard: both are seen as equally worthy (depending, of course, on whether that judge happened to have attended either of them—not an unlikely occurrence). As to the lower acceptance rate, that's a matter of simple numbers: with an entering class a bit more than one-third that of Harvard, it's hardly surprising that Yale has a lower acceptance rate. In absolute terms, however, Harvard has about twice as many applicants—individuals who would almost kill to get in. And how many stop to think about just how silly this is? After all, both law schools accept the tippy-top layer of the LSAT/GPA crème. Does it really matter that one has applicants a few tenths of a percentile higher or lower? No, the acid test is the one on the street: ask the nearest ten people what's the best university in the country, and you'll likely get a near-unanimous answer. Harvard. It has become part of the *global* consciousness—despite many examples that would disprove it, technically—as the academic equivalent to "the best that there is." Those seven letters, in that order, say it all.

From one Yalie: "They just have better marketing than my people, that's all." Actually, that's not far from the truth. It is a branding campaign underway for centuries, however. For our purposes, this is akin to the ancient question of how many angels can dance on the head of a pin. Whether we like it (or accept it) or not, Harvard-Yale-Stanford form the law school "ideal"—the model upon which legal education rests. And it's the model to which legal employers look.

Below these three are the Top Tier law schools, in their high-altitude positions above the countryside. Many are spotted high above the coasts, with the occasional one above Ann Arbor, Chicago, Austin, and a few other spots in flyover country. These are geosynchronous, holding their positions high above their home bases—some a little higher than others, but all clearly (and proudly) in the stratosphere. Visible for those with the right gear from anywhere, it's possible to see these dotted high above the country. Like Harvard, most have that familiar orangy-white sheen: they're proud to place graduates at the top law firms, and hope to place a healthy percentage with judges—also for eventual placement with top firms and perhaps a professorship here and there, as well as the occasional Senator. Each graduate placed at a top firm or with a top judge adds just a tiny bit of fuel to boost itself a wee bit higher. A few look instead to that smaller satellite zipping above New Haven, and so you see at least one bird a tiny bit more bluish-white, high above Chicago. The rest, however, sit proudly, orangish-white, high above their domains.

As inhabitants below have a habit of looking straight up, an odd phenomenon starts to take hold. Even though all of these are very, very high, each seems to shine just a *little bit* brighter directly below. For this reason, only the top of the top tier are truly "national" law schools, meaning they are visible throughout the country and their graduates are fairly well assured of finding a job, easily, anywhere in the country. The rest of this tier is quasi-national, meaning that among most employers their graduates have almost the same cachet…but not quite, and landing a job isn't quite so easy, especially outside that law school's earthly footprint. So a senior partner in, say, Los Angeles, while appreciative of the pretty cast of the satellite above even Charlottesville, Virginia (and clearly mindful of the storied history of Thomas Jefferson's legacy) seems still a bit more inclined to admire the spell cast by those superstars, and by the ones right above. Gosh they seem bright.

Below these are the Second Tier law schools: some at the lower edge of the stratosphere (still visible throughout wide swaths of the nation), and some at the higher altitudes of the troposphere—just below visual range outside their region. Each burns bright (but not quite as bright as those above)—each with scholars, students, and great energy devoted to all of the many activities that the satellites zipping higher are admired for. Because so many do have that habit of looking straight up, anyone directly below will see the not-quite-so-bright shine of this law school and often be dazzled by it even a tiny bit more than of a higher one farther away.

Further below are the Third Tier law schools: most shining in the sun above various states and regions of the nation—but barely seen beyond that visual range. Some, lower still, are visible mostly in the clusters of cities and towns below them. They too devote great energy to their activities, and as they are piloted by former passengers on those highest satellites, they too seek to emulate that bright sheen seen zooming above the nation. Shiny is good! Higher is better!

Still further below are the Fourth Tier law schools. These hover just above the landscape, often visible in just a handful of cities and towns, where residents acknowledge the sheen...but can't help but admire the brighter glow from the ones higher above.

*   *   *

From this, a three-dimensional picture emerges. This is not technical; it is *visceral*. We look at what we want to look at, and at what is easiest to look at, and at what it prettiest. Hiring partners cannot know 200+ law schools, and even if they could they would chortle at the suggestion. No, they will pay attention only to what they want to: to the stars that matter to them. Those are the ones they can see and admire.

A "lesser" law school, while focusing in the same way on teaching law as Harvard, has a smaller area of visibility. If it happens to be above our hiring partner in Los Angeles, and if it's sufficiently shiny, the firm might well consider its graduates. If not—if it's beyond range, too low for safety's sake, or just a bit too dull—then no dice. And no deal. Sometimes, a firm will consider the token valedictorian, to please the local powers that be. Often, however, the firm has its own pressures to contend with; the shininess of its new hires is one of them. This is not just for vanity. Even the thought of putting a new associate in front of a client sends chills down partners' collective spines. Putting a graduate of Harvard in front of them works (provided the associate's mouth stays closed).

Crucially, the lower the school, the more constrained its graduates are geographically and the weaker is its employment "umbrella" for that crucial first law job. This is *the* value and importance of rankings to you. They perform a highly useful service: they tell you the altitude of the law school, and how brightly it shines (and for whom). From there, the rest is up to you. Not just as a saying, but genuinely. It's up to you to determine the variables that are most important to you, and of course the crucial LSAT/ GPA variables that are the price of admission to any of the rides.

WHICH SCHOOLS, AND HOW MANY?

The subject of deciding which schools to apply to comes up frequently, and is often the source of animated debate—both among those giving advice and within the minds of those taking it. This should not be such a difficult issue, for you. One reason this is a difficult issue (and should not be) is that most applicants look at a list of 200 or so law schools…and gasp. How on Earth can they pick the right ones?

How on Earth, indeed. For most, going to law school is akin to a blind date. One hopes for the best, but by the time you get there, either way it's a bit awkward to back out. Having visited dozens of law schools, I can attest that each has something to offer—and even "hidden" ones have surprisingly pleasant accommodations. Perhaps the overarching lesson is to go where you (seriously) think you want to be…and then strive to want to be where you go. Aside from the Zen angle, you do need to worry (at least a bit), but you also need to be happy. And this doesn't mean for *others* to make you happy. No one—not even a supermodel—can do it for you. It means for you to make *yourself* happy. This is *your* life, after all.

Okay. Again, how to choose? It's better to reverse the process: work backwards from those schools you *don't* want to (or can't) attend. This means defining those qualities that make a school an "I wouldn't attend this school if they paid me" law school...for *you*. Then work sideways, cross-ways, and *then* top-to-bottom, and you'll find the list—a real list, just for you—shaping up. Attrition first, then ancillary qualities, and *then* a wish list.

Well, okay, that sounds nice. But how, exactly, should one go about this?

First is an appreciation of cost. Most law school applications cost fifty, seventy-five, perhaps one hundred dollars. For some, that might be pocket change. If so, a toast to you and to your trust fund's continued returns. If not, then an honest consideration of just how much you should spend is not a bad idea. The LSAT and LSDAS cost money, of course, but are a "fixed cost" in applying to any law school, as are the many LSAT test-prep books you should buy. The real key is deciding whether each school you apply to is worth the money—not to mention time and hassle. If money is tight, you might consider keeping your choices to a minimum. You might even consider a novel approach: one school or two. If you don't get in, then you'll have either the end of the season, or next year. Don't take this approach unless you have at least a decent chance of admission and genuinely want to go only there.

Even if money is not an issue, you shouldn't stray far from that minimum, but you might consider adding a school or two to your list. You probably shouldn't apply to fewer than three. A group of, say, 4-6 law schools is appropriate for most; perhaps more if you're flush or have few geographic limitations and an array of interests. Many more than that, however, and you'll find that you're starting to simply duplicate your odds. That's not what it should be about, but unless you *genuinely* want to apply to each and every one of the 15 schools you've got on a list, think seriously about the costs and benefit. For most, thus, a group of 5-9 law schools is probably "about right"—or even a bit too much. That's a *lot* of money out the door, so keep your cost-benefit antennae attuned. If any of it is paid to a school you're not *truly* serious about, it's a waste.

My purely personal, gut-reaction, ballpark figure? Four to six.

Most important is the question that should be answered firmly in the positive: would you *happily* go there if admitted? If not, don't waste your time or money or paper or ink or stamp.

Okay, now you should begin narrowing the field, for you, to those schools you would not consider. On a quiet night (or perhaps a reasonably quiet spot at your nearest coffee shop), begin to list what it is you seriously would like to have happen in your life. I know, I know. You've been asked this by guidance counselors before, and you come up with what you think they want to hear, or with what you think *you* want to hear. This is not for a counselor, or for me. This is for you, for your *life*. Think about what it is that you like. If it's to escape wherever you are…fine. List that. If it's to follow a love…fine. List that. If it's…whatever…you need to be honest. With yourself.

Then get more specific. If you'd like to live in a city, okay. Which one? If you have a fixation on a certain city, do you know why? Is it because of a movie you saw when you were eight? Have you lived there? Have you visited? For how long? (Again I'm not trying to dissuade you. Rather, if you're going to devote three years and quite possibly the rest of your life to a place, it should darned well be some place you will actually enjoy.) If instead of a city you'd prefer a serene setting, ironically that opens up a different and in many ways highly attractive world in terms of law school applications—not to mention actual job and housing options. Again, it should reflect what it is that you *really* want. To restate this somewhat differently, it should reflect what it is that *you* really want.

This process of narrowing the field should be a dynamic one: try to define a list of qualities that you like, and that you dislike, and keep that in mind as you go down your list. Sunshine, snow. Outdoors, indoors. Culture, serenity. Nightlife, easy life. Again, this is for no one but you. Even if you've a spouse—and clearly that's a *big* part of the final decision—the analysis should be yours (a plural "you," yes, but still with a serious look at the singular "you"). Don't go somewhere that will make you unhappy. Also, don't start looking at law schools…yet. The selection of schools should be guided by what you would like, not vice versa. Yes, we often do the opposite, hoping that the right school will just jump out at us. If you hate cities but have your heart set on NYU, then, well, you'll need to reappraise both and decide which is more important, to you.

This too is not a linear process. Rather, you might define, say, that you want to live near but not in a city, and moreover that you truly enjoy, say, the Mid-Atlantic states. (I chose that for no reason except to play fair with the regions, so please don't assume that the Mid-Atlantic is better than, say, the great Northwest.) You'll then take a look at the question of geography and personal fit—and then perhaps revisit your List of Qualities. From there, you'll have a more manageable list of Mid-Atlantic law schools in your LSAT/GPA realm from which to decide. You might, as part of your research, take a trip to the places you're considering—not just the law school, but the place. I'm serious—and so too should you be. More than merely law school is riding on this; unless you have a serious reason otherwise (or attend a top school), you should assume that where you attend law school is where you will stay.

A sidebar caveat: Many end up with a list that seems to mirror what everyone else wants. New York City is a prime example. But there are many other great alternatives. Again, depending upon what one wants, Chicago and San Francisco are great places to study. No doubt there's screaming out there "What about [your favorite city]?" That's okay. The point is to ask the question, and answer it. There are also great smaller cities, such as Austin, Texas, which I happen to be familiar with as a native Austinite; Eugene, Oregon; Missoula, Montana; Oxford, Mississippi; Madison, Wisconsin; and no doubt quite a number more. How can you tell? Chances are there's an annual influx of students—and a steady accumulation of graduates who don't want to leave. Another is that large universities act as economic and intellectual magnets. These are major reasons that Austin, for example, has been among the fastest-growing U.S. cities for much of the past century.

Third is geography. This is a factor often overlooked—except in a generic sense—by most applicants. In reality, this is a key consideration. If you know that you want to settle on the coast, for example, then don't even consider a school away from water. If you know that you love (or hate) warm weather, cold weather, rainy weather…whichever the case may be…then for goodness sakes cross schools off your list if they don't meet your sincere preference.

This is, in the end, a decidedly personal question…and one you should take, well, personally. Don't just shrug your shoulders and go back to your reference book on law schools, hoping something will jump out at you. You should drive the selection; it shouldn't drive you.

It's quite likely that some reading this will be aghast. How can you recommend that they cross off excellent schools just because they don't meet some personal desire!? Simple. After one has lived life a bit, a realization hits that much of what we think is important turns out to be so unimportant that we shake our heads wondering what it was we were after in the first place. It's quite possible—if not likely—that there will be excellent schools not on your list. That's the whole point. If you want to go to a school (and, as I said, you should look at this "sideways" as well), then that's the time for you to reconsider your criteria. If, for example, you hate cold weather but love Law and Economics and are in the running for Chicago…you've some serious thinking to do. Even that's not a terribly fair example, as Chicago will land you a job just about anywhere. So, even if you do hate the cold you can justify that with an "it's only three years" defense. In most cases (including even Chicago), that is not what will happen: where you go to law school is likely where you will settle.

Don't let the law school tail wag your one-and-only life. It's hardly the better option to live *your* life as a dog.

THE WORLD FROM LAW SCHOOLS' EYES

We don't often look at the world from a vantage outside our own. We are, in short, self-centered. Part of being a good lawyer is learning how to re-center oneself.

From your law school's vantage, *their* "price of admission" is steep. A collection of highly qualified full-time law faculty, a hugely expensive library (both to build and to maintain), and facilities easily equal an annual commitment in the many millions of dollars—and not infrequently tens of millions of dollars. Law schools and their collegiate parents are hardly looking at this as purely academic. Instead, most accept these as the cost of doing a rather lucrative business: hundreds of students paying tuition rates at the highest end in all of higher education, yet without lab and other costs. In essence, the enormous costs of a faculty and physical facilities are the ante to a remarkably profitable business.

At each level in the law school hierarchy, the ante rises. A law school that is in the third or fourth tier can get by with x number of faculty, at y cost, and z facilities. Again, these are substantial costs, measured in the millions, but they're more than paid in tuition—your tuition. As a law school moves up, however, its needs rise ever higher. This is not merely *because* it rises. Rather, it rises because it is spending more money—on faculty, the library, lots of external relations (to build its reputational score), lots of brochures (to improve its yield, or, as mentioned, to decrease the rate of acceptance of applicants such as yourself), and so on. As a school spends more money, it hopes to translate that spending into a higher rank—which in turn will allow it to spend more money. Ultimately, this is about law schools' place in the academic legal sun.

What does this mean for you? The higher-ranked your school, the better that school's facilities, library, and faculty are likely to be. As to the last, this is not just the "star" faculty, but in fact is more likely a result of the hiring of more new faculty. This translates into more curricular choices, and usually a more engaged professoriate.

Is this always true? Should I respond flippantly and write "Here we go again!" No, it is not *always* true. But it *is* generally true. (There is, by the way, a corollary in Civil Procedure: is it *more likely than not* true?) The key for the wise applicant is to study the brochures and other information. While self-serving, the brochures are a window to the general health of a law school. What's key is the type of information discussed: What is happening at the law school? Who's just been "poached"—hired away—from another (usually top) law school? Who are the faculty? How nationally known are they? This can be gleaned in a few fast searches of the full professors, who are expected to have their reputations firmly in place. Take a look at the adjuncts: are they judges and senior practitioners? Federal or state, national or local? What about the alumni? How active are they (*i.e.,* how much money do they give)? How many large donations have been publicized? What renovations are underway? How connected is the school to its legal community? (Clinical programs and externships will be touted.) And so on.

If a law school is connected with a university, you should check the health of that university. It doesn't take more than a few minutes to find the information, and if, say, the university is struggling, that's a bad sign. If it's a state school, how's the state doing? If poorly, chances are money will be "bled off" from the law school even more than normal…which of course hurts the school's long-term odds, especially against private schools. Conversely, if the university just received a huge donation—even if in a different college—that's a good sign, as it will usually "trickle down" to higher overall quality (and reputation) for that law school and parent university.

REPUTATION

Some out there are alarmed, perhaps, at the tossing around of "quality" and "reputation," nearly in the same breath. It shouldn't be, you might mutter, that we focus so much on this. You might well be right. But we do.

If you'll bear with me for a just a little while longer, we'll get to the truth of rankings that might help you in making your decision, particularly if it's a decision that puts you in a quandary as to either rankings or quality. As mentioned (too many times), the law is an acutely status-oriented profession. I can see it now…I will get nasty-grams to the effect that I'm promoting such a system, or at least perpetuating it. (I have gotten exactly such mail already, actually.) My own feelings are mixed, but the more important point is that this *is*. I neither make it so nor threaten it. It simply is, and as a reader I ask that you take the responsibility for accepting that which is. If blame is to be placed, it is on *us*.

Why are my feelings mixed? First, elitism has gotten a bad rap. Indeed, a culturally dangerous bad rap. Elitism is good…if it is based on quality (and, yes, there is such a thing), and if the rules of the game aren't rigged too far askew. Both measures are subject to great debate, and neither is clearly true (or untrue). Moreover, in a very real sense reputation is just about all an attorney has. Even a superstar attorney (or superstar law professor) is a superstar...*to the extent and only to the extent that others believe it to be so*. What this leads to in the rough-and-tumble real world—and in the academic world too—is what economists know as the "winner take all" dynamic. In essence, all or nearly all of the "winnings" go to the top 10% winners, with the scraps left to all the rest. The result is that the top get nearly everything, while those at the bottom scramble for the crumbs. To those who have, more is given; to those who have not, little or none is available. Fair? No, it's not. But what's wrong is not that this phenomenon exists, but that the systems of the legal profession—our profession—encourage it.

Let's look at it from a personal perspective. Say you could get into Harvard. Forget about LSATs, GPAs, letters of recommendation, and so on. You have a golden ticket, found in the nearest chocolate bar, and it says "Go straight to Cambridge. Collect $200,000."

Okay. It's hardly necessary to write that, for nearly everyone, such a windfall would be, well, a windfall. The actual experience at Harvard—the actual quality of the interactions, the quality of the food, the height of the ceilings, etc. may or may not be qualitatively better (they are, for different reasons), but the important point is that that is an entirely different question from the psychic value of those seven letters, starting with "H" and ending in "d."

Harvard has value because of what it is and because of what *we believe it to be*. And, because it has brand recognition—quite literally just about everyone on the planet knows the name—it gains even *more* of a reputational boost, again irrespective of its actual quality. The mere fact of that name is sufficient to convey a constellation of meaning to anyone who can attach that name to their personal (or professional) life. The same goes for Yale, Stanford, Chicago, Columbia, and so on. Yes, many who know the first three of these will argue that, if anything, their smaller, even more selective programs are superior to Harvard's. Again, this is not only beside the point, it actually disproves it. Even if true the key is whether others *believe*.

But note what happens…as soon as we go below that upper-most tier—the top five schools—things start to get a bit fuzzy. Some folks in New York City, for example, might enter the fray with the old contest between NYU and Columbia. Folks in Michigan, California, Pennsylvania, and Virginia might get their debating hats on, each hat featuring the local school prominently. And there's a line of advocates with their own posters ready to protest the value of *their* school.

This alone is proof of the value of reputation. Anyone who knows of any of these schools knows that they are *good* schools. But everyone also knows that they're not at the very tippy-top of our legal hierarchy. We might want them to be—usually because we happen to have gone there and want for ourselves the higher value of that reflected glory. And the schools might actually *be* better. They might have a cadre of professors who are brilliant beyond the brilliance at Harvard, Stanford, *and* Yale. They might have a gleaming new buildings and brand new Federal Reporters. No matter. They're not "generally regarded" as such, and so they aren't. Period.* The asterisk on that period is that, perhaps, they can "buy" their way into fame, as indeed the universities of California, Michigan, and Texas did over the latter half of the 20th century. Still, they bought their way to the middle of the top. It would take quite a feat to jump much higher.

Here's where this takes us: Each law school *knows itself.*

Someone at the University of Michigan, for example, knows that it's a superb law school, that its programs are truly excellent—but that they are likely to remain a poor relative of Harvard/Yale/Stanford. This isn't a horrible place to be. After all, a place like the University of Michigan stands *near* the very top of the heap. That means that its graduates get very, very good jobs (perhaps just a bit less easily than their counterparts in Cambridge, New Haven, and Palo Alto, especially as you move farther from the Midwest), their professors get *very* good perks, and so on.

This can come out in interesting ways. I once was interviewing with the General Counsel of a Fortune 50 (not 500) company, and naturally the matter of *alma mater* came up. He glanced at the University of Texas on my résumé. As I had spent some time in Pennsylvania we briefly discussed his alma mater, Penn, the

University of Pennsylvania. [Penn's motto: *Leges sine moribus vanae.* Laws without morals are useless.] Both law schools are regarded among most attorneys, judges, and professors as roughly equivalent in raw quality, although Penn almost certainly gets the nod as the older and more genteel (and more ivy-covered) of the two. In short, as the *U.S. News* rankings show, Penn is nestled just below the very top, while Texas is somewhere in the middle of the first tier. Why this story? Because, as we were discussing Penn, he said, "...well of course *Texas* is no slouch."

That phrasing carries a rather large suitcase of meaning. While I did not get the job—imagine that!—what it said was that, on one of the mental boxes he had to check, I got a check mark. "Texas is okay." That is very much the type of interaction one gets at the very top, and indeed at every level. What's key is the context. If it were a position in a start-up in, say, Boise, while they might well have known about Texas, it would likely have been fine if it had been any of a hundred—or at least fifty—other law schools. Because I was in the office of one of the largest corporations, it would *not* have been "okay" had it been otherwise. Such-and-so law school would *not* have been "...no slouch."

Additional nuance: certain names have cachet, separate from their quality (even perceived quality). These are often names associated—not to be too blunt—with old money. And old money is associated with old names. So, Cornell or Duke, to take two examples early in the alphabet, probably get better "press" than schools of roughly comparable quality. The name alone might give each a a perch a few spots higher. This too is part of the rankings stew.

There's yet another point, this one related to why so much ink is spilled here on "top this" and "top that." I was once on a panel in which I responded to a question as to how someone who had not graduated from a top school could compete with those who had. I answered that there were many factors in one's success, and while important in initial placement, actual quality then assumed a much more prominent role. Another panelist—a graduate of Yale—told me afterwards, in private, that while he understood why I had taken the gentle, upbeat approach I had, in fact he continued to get job offers right and left: Yale opens doors. I could not argue, as what he said was true. The point of quality is also true, but the reality—like it or not—is that ours *is* nearly a winner-take-all system. Fair or not, many fine candidates would never get the interview, or job, without the name behind them.

Part-Time Law

Most ABA-accredited law schools are full-time, requiring full-time attendance (and prohibiting outside work during the first year of law school). Some law schools offer a part-time program, which usually involves the same coursework, taken in a four-year timeframe instead of three. One guide surprisingly misstates this. In many cases, a part-time student ends up spending longer than four years, particularly if work life interferes, as it often does.

The top law schools are all full-time. There are good part-time programs. The one that comes to mind is at Suffolk, in Boston, but there are more. How to tell? They will highlight their evening program, and it will be a major part of the law school. Almost by definition, they serve a local population, and as good as they can be, they are the exception proving the rule. This is not an indictment of these part-time programs, and certainly not of part-time law students, who bring to their study an often more serious, more concerted, more efficient approach. Part-time students tend to be older, highly focused, and extraordinarily wary of debt. (For good reason, as many have children, mortgages, and the like.) Unfortunately, top firms all but ignore part-time students.

This brings to mind a statement in another guide along the lines that part-time programs have "somewhat" less prestige. Right. You might think of law as a series of cliffs: a great view up high; some interesting archeological finds below; and one helluva' dfference between them.

If you can swing it, I encourage you to attend a full-time program.

Public v. Private

I've a story to tell. [Rolled eyes, yes?] Atticus Falcon, the author of *Planet Law School,* once sent me a note he had received. In the note a prospective law student was trying to convince Atticus of the wisdom of going to a third-tier private law school instead of a first-tier public law school. While I didn't know the private school, it so happened that I did know the public one. So, for fun I wrote a quick response, which Atticus forwarded.

A day later we have a reply: "...but it's a *private* law school!"

This caught me so by surprise that I could hardly approach an answer. Were this posed again—as it is right now—it's hard to know where to start.

I grew up in a rather unorthodox family (for which I am ever grateful) that had an almost-reflexive anti-elitist bias. One way this played out was that it was inconceivable that any of us six children would attend private school—and not just for the anti-snobbish thrill of it. Private schools were simply too expensive. Even that doesn't capture it, as private schools were not even in our consciousness. From that, and also from the years I lived on air, I developed a perhaps too-acute sense of money and value. To me, the assumption that this fellow had that a law school was better simply *because* it was private was baffling.

To address that, it's necessary to think about what a law school is, and what makes it valuable. Regardless of how much ink is spilled on a law school's reputation, in the end it is based on its standing as a legal institution (and often on its standing as a legal institution attached to a university whose standing is just as relevant): Does it perform a valued service to its community, wherever and whichever that may be? A large part of this is the accumulation of legal acumen through a law faculty. This, in turn, is an extraordinarily expensive and lengthy undertaking. Even Tom Monahan, founder of Domino's Pizza and then of the Ave Maria School of Law, with his enormous resources couldn't simply "buy" a reputation. With a clear institutional focus it still had to be built (first in Michigan and then relocated to Florida), and is not yet out of the legal woods in terms of establishing itself as an legal institution to be reckoned with. I don't know much more about Ave Maria than what I've read, but the important point is that a legal education is based, fundamentally, with *some* track record of legal value.

This, in turn, is about precedent: has the law school, through its faculty, produced a body of *persuasive* legal commentary? This is, at base, about substance as well as mere "reputation." *If* a law school can build that legal community, it builds that knowledge, and that value, and eventually the reputation that serves as a symbol of that value. The various Universities of California and the University of Texas at Austin are perhaps the only examples of institutions "buying" reputations, and even there it took the luck of being in ever-wealthier states *and* having decades in which to spend the budgetary surpluses. Only in the "brand name" law schools ("Harvard," "Yale," "Stanford") and perhaps a handful of others ("Cornell," "Duke") does reputation become a value in itself—and that is because they become iconic. When uttering any of those first three alone, everyone *knows* what we mean.

Where does that leave us here? Many private colleges have struggled over the past several decades, and more than a few have closed their doors. This hasn't happened to many law schools, but that's not to write that the same concerns aren't present. There's a critical mass in law schools, just as with any institutional endeavor. I once spoke with a law school dean, and as we were tossing out numbers he corrected himself to say, "Oh no, that wouldn't be nearly enough." What was "that"? It was the "magic number" to sustain a law school's enormous operational costs, which might well require a student body of *at least* several hundred students. And that's just sustenance; reputation requires more.

As to the particular private law school this fellow asked Atticus about, there was a fundamental question: Why is *this* school in the third tier? If a private school has been around any length of time, the question that arises is why it hasn't built a more solid reputation. Perhaps it's geographically isolated. Fine…if it has a solid reputation in that area and the student intends to practice there. That's still two rather important qualifiers…and a *lot* of tuition.

Okay, now over to public schools. Many public schools are the successors to "land grant" colleges formed out of the Morrill Acts of 1862 and 1890, in which the federal government granted lands to the states for the purpose of supporting new colleges for, primarily, the "useful arts" such as agriculture, animal husbandry, engineering, industrial arts, teaching, and so on. While nearly all are now universities with the same array of programs as any other, the enormous wealth dedicated to land-grant colleges was probably one reason the American system of higher education is now so strong: *billions* of dollars' worth of land was transferred to support academic institutional stability and growth. With the post-World War II era and a flood of new talent, these universities grew in both size and stature.

This translates to a school's academic strength. While any school can wax poetic about its mission, unique culture, yada yada, in the end the strength of that school is a direct function of its resources, which in turn are a result of its inherent strengths (powerful alumni, name recognition, state support, etc.) and of how well it is run.

All right. Back to our intrepid prospective law student. He was trying to convince us—two attorneys, as it happens—that a law school that was private was more prestigious *because* it was private. How many ways to say *"Huh?"*

It is true that the very top law schools are private. This should hardly be surprising: two of the three are affiliated with institutions that have had *hundreds* of years as a head start. Will Virginia, Michigan, or California–Berkeley ever break into the top three? Doubtful. That would, first, mean displacing Harvard, Yale, or Stanford. That would only happen if, over some extended period of time, the public school improved significantly (say, with a multi-billion-dollar donation), at least one of the private schools suffered a years-long decline (also unlikely), and no other private law school between them improved at least as well as the public one did.

But why *shouldn't* the public school be at the very top? Why won't it happen? Three reasons: different missions, different resources, and different vested interests in seeing private law schools (and universities) maintain their prestige. Remember, each top private school has tens of thousands of *very* well-placed alumni—who are harmed if the name is harmed and who are benefitted vicariously if the school's name is benefitted. Just go back to our example of someone with a Harvard pedigree. The name says it all. Or at least we think it does.

Public schools, however, have far less deep a pool of vested alumni interest, both because they've been around fewer decades and because many public-school grads go into careers in which prestige is, on the whole, less important. The useful arts, yes? Engineers, accountants, animal husbander-ers, and the like tend to be less at the forefront of, well, power. Students tend to be less well-connected going in…and coming out. Moreover, the public school mission is simply different than that of the private institution.

As just one sign of this difference, which is cultural as well as elitist, the Ivy League prohibits the awarding of athletic scholarships, resulting in their lack of competitiveness in the big leagues. Student athletes qualify for student aid, but their athletic status cannot supersede what they would otherwise be eligible for. Students in the Ivy League are quite active athletically, but they're not competitive as compared to the arguably corrupt athletic system that has developed among the largest universities especially. Notably, the same phenomenon is seen in the military academies. If ever there were schools mindful of athletics, these are it. Nonetheless, the academies—the most public of them all—recuse themselves from the world of big-business collegiate sports.

One might possibly include UCLA and Texas in the above group of three. While all are members of the "Public Ivies" (which includes anywhere from 8 to 30 universities), Virginia, Michigan, and California–Berkeley are at the upper end of this group, while UCLA and Texas are nestled below. Only Virginia would have a reputational claim based on pedigree that approximates Harvard-Yale. Indeed, based on its storied history Virginia straddles the boundaries between public and private in the estimation of many academics (and Southern society), and in its relative independence from public revenues. You might review the book *Public Ivies* by Richard Moll, who coined the term, or the *Greens' Guide* for a list and to cross-reference against your law school selection should any be in your neighborhood.

Conversely, state schools share a strength that few private schools have: the taxpayer. One can argue for or against this, but the reality is that few state schools are at risk, ever. There's simply too much momentum, and too much at stake, even if a state faces budgetary difficulties. At worst, a state school will muddle through, perhaps drifting downward a bit; its relatively inexpensive tuition and local connections will nearly always assure its survival, however. One example is the University of Hawaii, which both benefits and suffers from a close legislative connection and relatively thin population base. While those in Hawaii clearly look to "UH" as the equal of top schools anywhere, and while UH is not at risk, its relative poverty all but relegates it to has-been status in terms of most of its programs and in terms of what it could be. (And it could be much, much more.)

Here's thus another double-edged sword. It would be easy to dismiss all of the above as obsession over objectively trivial differences. Yet these differences, well, make a difference. At least in the minds of many who judge (such as interviewers), and as part of our broader culture, these slight differences—public/private, tippy-top/almost-top—seem exaggerated in our collective consciousness. For most, this really is irrelevant. Yet the same rough comparisons apply at every level. It's important to recognize them and to decide, for yourself, how important they are to you.

Back to our story. As it happens our prospective law student was struggling with a decision of whether to go to the University of Texas School of Law, which is usually ranked #15 or so, with a third-tier private law school (somewhere around #115). Neither Atticus nor I had ever *heard* of this private school. That was not determinative of course—except that it wasn't a good sign—but what was more troubling was the conflation of public/private with higher/lesser quality.

This student, a Texas resident, was willing to give up one of the best legal educational opportunities in the country, at a cost *one-third* what he would have paid at the private school. UT's tuition is far higher now in the path that many state schools took following the lead of Michigan, but even with scholarships at the private school it was not even a close call. And UT–Austin is hardly scholarship poor. There aren't many times that giving advice is a no-brainer, but this was, to stay true to my Texas roots, purdy darned close.

Whew, that was quite an excursion. If you choose a law school, do so for the right reasons. A private law school can be a fine choice, but not *because* it is private. A public law school has drawn on the resources of its larger university and an entire state, usually for generations. It does tend to be a bit more proletariat—which is either better or worse depending upon your background and spirit. The University of Texas at Austin is merely an extreme example of the stability and strength of public law schools—particularly those attached to a flagship campus. While you might not get quite the handholding you might expect at a private school, they are usually good schools (at least), and if in-state, relative bargains.

Now to the advice: For most, the public-private distinction is silly. The only exceptions are private schools at the very top of the heap, or those ranked *significantly* above whichever public school you're considering. By "significantly" is meant that they are, or almost are, in a different tier. Otherwise, paying for the supposed cachet of a private brand is just dumb. Is it really worth *fifty thousand dollars* to you to have a diploma from a private school? *If* you choose a private school over a public one, it should be for the right reasons—just like legal reasoning itself.

A private school should be at least as well-ranked *and* it should satisfy some substantial interest on your part (location, family history, a nifty school crest) *or* it should offer a generous scholarship...to even be in the running. Otherwise, it's simply not worth it. Most public law schools, while more expensive now than in decades past, are still a relative bargain. In some cases, you can establish residency before or during your three years, significantly reducing your costs—and boosting your chances. Indeed, it's not a bad consideration to move to that state if you're serious about practicing there—as you should be. To take UT-Austin as the continued example, moving to the state in time to qualify for residency equals, as of this writing, a $47,000 in-state tuition savings over three years—which in turn is equal to nearly $60,000 of pre-tax income—as well as a slightly better chance of admission. If you're so inclined to make a legitimate move and know that you want to live in that state, this would be worth it at nearly any state school. And a city with a significant university presence is often at the top of quality-of-life rankings.

To reinforce an important point: if you're in-state, chances are you'll be at a slight advantage in acceptance to that state's public law school. It likely won't be more than a modest plus, but a plus is a plus—especially if it's at a Reach school. This means that it's unlikely it will be a decision between an excellent private school and a lesser public one. More often, it's a decision between roughly-equal school, or between a lesser private and slightly better public school.

A personal history, as long as I'm taking up too much of your time. I had to decide among three law schools: UT-Austin, Case-Western Reserve, and the University of Hawaii. An odd collection, to be sure. Why had I applied to Case-Western? One of the silliest reasons of them all: they had sent me a snazzy brochure. I received a scholarship offer (and multiple phone calls) from their dean. While I hated to be impolite, despite the time I'd taken to apply (and for them to review) fortunately I knew they weren't for me, and in any case while a strong law school they couldn't compare to UT–Austin, even with the scholarship money. I got a few similar calls from UH–Mānoa, but no guarantee of a scholarship. They almost kinda' sorta' promised, but nothing in writing, and probably nothing for the first year. So, I was stuck with a school in my hometown, nearly free tuition and living in the house my brothers and I had built...and a lower-ranked school in Hawaii. While I never regretted not going to Hawaii then, I was sad...but I knew after I later moved there that it would have been a disaster. It was enough of a shock to pay rent in Honolulu on an associate's salary; I would have been near *seppuku* had I had to spend money we didn't have while *in* law school.

THE ADMISSIONS DANCE

Before we get to the law schools, we need first to take a look at you...as the admissions officers will.

Law schools provide a helpful series of data points: the LSAT and GPA scores, at the 25th and 75th percentiles, of students admitted to the law school. Often, this is for students actually entering, rather than merely admitted, which can make quite a difference, depending upon the school. These make it fairly easy to see where you stand. The difficulties in terms of evaluation might come if there is a wide disparity between your LSAT and GPA. This can be true in either direction, of course: you might have a good LSAT but weak GPA, or, conversely, a weak LSAT but solid GPA. In most cases, the LSAT becomes the more important of the two, and thus tends to override the GPA—but each applicant-law school pairing should be considered with a dispassionate weighing of these scores. And, when in doubt, chances are the difference will hurt your chances. That too should be a dispassionate assessment, as hard as that often is. As much as we want to reflect in our better selves and put our best scores forward, in a sea of applicants the odd negative is often the application killer. At the very least, you will need to address that aspect of your application directly and seriously, possibly in an addendum.

Law schools will sometimes use an "index," or composite of the LSAT and GPA. Often, it's weighted more heavily to the LSAT; sometimes it's the arithmetic mean. Sometimes it has additional factors, although those are usually internal to the admissions process. For our purposes, it's fine to simply take the simpler result and Index, and compare those with the data points of the law schools you're interested in. Take advantage of the LSAC site for this. Clearly, as you get more involved in the process, you do want to refine your Index to each law school, so that you'll be giving yourself an honest appraisal of your chances of admission.

To a *very* large extent admission to law school is about the numbers. The deans, faculty, and admissions officers *know* how crude this is…but it is what it is. Our railing against it will not change it, and they have no choice. And so, in your analysis you should accept that this is as it is. This can be an important distinction to make once you're *in* law school, as well. The law *is;* the challenge in law school is to figure out the *why*.

Getting Started: Managing Law School Options

Many books about law school separate law schools into three piles when recommending which ones to apply to. Usually this is some variation on Reaches, Targets, and Safeties. For reasons I will explain, I disagree. You should separate the law schools you are potentially interested in into two piles: the ones you would be happy to attend, and the ones you're not so sure about. You will then separate each of those into sub-piles that will be useful in terms of what you should do, and how you should think of each.

At the risk of mixing metaphors, we might call the first big pile the Top-Shelf law schools.

TOP-SHELF LAW

For the Top-Shelf pile, you should separate these into sub-piles: first are the true Dream schools that, were you to get accepted, you would simply not believe your good fortune, and upon hearing of your acceptance might walk around in a happy daze for, well, days. The second category within this pile includes your Reach schools. These are the law schools that are a bit of a stretch, but wouldn't be quite as much of a stretch as the Dreams.

How to tell the two apart? A Dream School will accept *very* few applicants with your LSAT/GPA combination. Vanishingly few. In other words, your LSAT and GPA are both below the 25th/75th percentile ranges for that school. This is more than being outside mere statistical goal posts. The numbers released by the admissions office at that law school might give you, say, a less-than-ten-percent chance of admission. In reality, it's probably a less-than-two-percent chance. That is a Dream School.

How are Reach Schools different? The stats, of course, aren't going to be as severe. The data released by the admissions office should give you an indication that you have perhaps a 20-30 percent chance of admission. In other words, your LSAT/GPA will be somewhere in the lower-half of the 25th/75th percentile range for that school—but they will both be *in* the range. Obviously, this lends better odds than mere Dreaming, even though fewer dreams might be dreamt at this Reach law school.

What if your LSAT is just above and your GPA is just below (or vice versa)? It's a Dream. The greater the disparity between your LSAT and GPA, the greater the uncertainty. This kicks your application into the "let's cogitate some more" stack, which in turn makes the ancillary materials both more important and more irrelevant: chances are there are a dozens of applicants with a similar or better statistical mix and subjective qualities. In the end, just one or two (or none) get the nod.

If your LSAT and GPA shine, you might have a lucky third sub-pile: schools you would be delighted to attend and that are likely to accept you. These, of course, are schools to which you will apply.

Ho-Hum Law

Okay, now to the second batch: these are the law schools you would honestly have mixed feelings about going to. Yes, it's natural to have mixed feeling about any law school below your Dream School. That written, many students fall in love with their law school—or at least develop an appreciation for it—only after attending for a while, regardless of where that school perches.

Again, let's split these into two: First are the Target Schools, with admissions data indicating that you have perhaps a 50/50 chance of admission. This is a good new/bad news statistic, as it tells you your chances are not bad...but neither are they great. In terms of the numbers, your LSAT/GPA scores will be in the upper half of the 25th/75th percentile range for that school. While it might seem that this *should* be a sure thing, given the absolute numbers for most law schools, in fact the odds are often closer to (or less than) 50/50 until the candidate's scores are both at the upper edge of the school's 25th/75th percentile range.

Finally are the Safeties. These are schools that, for you, are nearly assured. An 80% chance of admission or better. The admissions data should reflect a near-certainty that you'll be admitted, as your LSAT/GPA numbers are at or above the high end of the school's admissions range.

But Why Four?

Why separate law schools into *four* groups? Because it's useful to know where to put your resources (and hopes). Yes, other tout three. This is not only not helpful, it will cause you to focus your efforts in the wrong ways.

If the law school you really, truly want to attend is a Dream School, what then? Perhaps there are options other than simply settling for a law school you truly won't want to attend. In this, keep an open mind. Many times, we have dreams based not in reality—or even in perception—but rather in our subjective sense of both. How many times have we done or wanted something, knowing that our *real* motives would be quite silly if anyone actually knew what they were. So, if you want to attend Yale because you like schools with four letters in their name, depending upon your raw scores you might well consider other schools. Duke is rather well regarded, as is Iowa and a fair number of other four-letter law schools. Obviously, that's a silly example...but it's not uncommon to run across reasons that, when we're honest, are almost as silly. This gets back to being honest with yourself, and within this realm is the need to honestly appraise your chances.

If your Dream is a *real* dream: if you would kick yourself for the rest of your life for not attending the school you really, truly want to attend, then let's see if we can make that happen. What follows might seem paradoxical or downright wrong. Stick with me for just a while to see if this will make the difference, for you.

Here is where the application rubber meets the statistical road: *Do not waste your time with Dreams, nor with Safeties. Focus on the Reaches and Targets.*

Yes, this is a bit radical. To take the bottom end first: Nearly every guide says, in effect, apply to some Safeties so that you'll have *someplace* to go. I disagree, with one exception: unless you absolutely, positively intend to practice in the area in which the Safety School is located, *and* unless you *truly* don't care, and unless you truly *won't* care...*don't attend a Safety School.*

There are several reasons for this. First, chances are good that, if you complete your applications painstakingly, you won't be left without at least one Target that grants you admission. Second, most of us *do* care where we go to law school. And even if we think we don't, we change our proverbial tune once student loan repayments loom closer. It's not possible to overstate this: if you're attending a lower-ranked (*i.e.,* Safety) school, the vocational boost from that school drops precipitously with each tier. Finally, law school should not be about "settling"; your every neuron should be engaged. Safeties run at cross-purposes to this, and if that's your approach, unless you've darned good reasons otherwise you might think and re-think your reasons for even going.

What if you apply to Targets and no Safeties and don't get in? This might sound crude, but...so what?

If that happens, then you're left with a question: Why? Why did it not work? Again, if you'd done your application job well and applied to at least a handful of Targets, it really is unlikely that you'll end up empty-handed. But, back to the question, what if that *does* happen? And how dare I write "So what?" The nerve!

I dare because we often think only in the now. Or, more correctly, we don't really think at all. We want to go to law school, we toss our apps in, and see what happens. Toss in a few safeties, just to be safe. No, this is not how it should be. If you're *serious* about the law, about law practice, and about the process of getting into law school, then you must take your thinking to a higher level. There's a reason law school is competitive—both in exams and in admission. This is true even at second and third (and even some fourth) tier schools. *Lots* of applicants want in. Not everyone gets in. The same scenario plays out for every level of law school; the relevant differences are in the actual applicants.

Law schools are looking for more than just scores. This is a half-truth that's bandied about endlessly. It misses what's really going on. Law schools—*all* law schools—are looking for *great* scores. They need those great scores to improve their position vis-à-vis other law schools. Each additional fraction of a point is a little more fuel to boost their orbit just a tiny bit higher. If your score helps, then they're predisposed to admit you. If not, they're not. But again, this happens at every level. Everyone (or nearly everyone) has "dream," "reach," "target," and "safety" schools. Even someone with a perfect LSAT and 4.0 GPA can't treat Yale/Harvard/Stanford as safeties. Chances are, your scores won't be perfect—and that's okay. The challenge is to know where you are, and to figure out just how important this is to you. For each school that you apply to, where does it really rank? And where do you rank relative to it?

Here's where it matters: you need to anticipate how you will feel a few months hence as the admissions letters start coming in. When you apply to each school, you must ask the question: how do I *really* feel about this school? If you get the letter back with "Congratulations!" on the first line and your response is some version of "Whatever..."—if your *real* response is disappointment rather than elation—then why did you send that in in the first place? What a waste! And, not least, a waste of *their* time too.

If you get back nothing but a perfunctory let-down, "After an extensive review..." you need to predict, now, how you will really feel, then. If you're upset in the mere anticipation of such a fate...*good!* That's a good sign. Now is the time to redouble your efforts to make sure you're doing the right things, now. Whether that's re-reviewing targets, locations, your application...all of those will avoid the empty-handed fate. If you absolutely, positively *have* to go to law school, the fight is *now,* not then. Add Targets and Reaches, not Safeties.

If you're the least bit iffy, don't apply. If that makes you nervous, good. Go back to the question of why you're iffy. Then go back to the question of which law schools. This is a list that should be dynamic, not cast in stone. If it's not quite right, now's the time to change it.

For the next question, you need to sit in a dark room. Alone. With not an electronic device within twenty feet.

Ask yourself, in your most private thoughts, *what happens if you don't go?* At all.

It's my suspicion (and the basis for this advice) that many students go to law school by default. If this is true for you, going to a Safety will be the worst fate, times two. Are you *really* interested in law school? Are you subconsciously sabotaging your own efforts? If law school *is* for you, you need to make that happen, whether that's adding one or two or five target schools or retaking the LSAT until you're satisfied that it will make the difference, *this* makes a difference. Don't just go through the motions. Don't settle.

And don't wimp out. If it's important enough to you, then dammit it's important enough to improve your chances and try again, next year. If you bombed on your LSAT, and if you reasonably feel that that didn't capture your genuine ability, then why *not* try again?

In business there is the common phenomenon of jumping on a bandwagon...whether it's a deal, interest rates, the latest fad, you name it. The truth is that many of these deals should be met with a single word: "Pass."

It might seem a dreadful thing to wait a year. It is not. If anything, it's likely that you'll look back and that additional year will seem like the best investment you've ever made—in yourself. If you're working, then you'll have the chance to save more money. If you're not working, then perhaps you can find a job (even a part-time job) in a law firm or law office, which will further boost your chances with a Target. At the very least, that year will be the acid test of whether law school is really for you—and you'll certainly have some fodder for your new, better personal statement. If law school is for you, then the year will be nothing. If it is not, then that year will be everything. And it will save you one-quarter of a million dollars...and a lifetime of regret.

In short, don't attend a Safety. Don't even apply. Focus instead on your Targets. This focus should be genuine, all-inclusive, and intense. Rather than tossing a few extra applications to the winds, *target* your applications, instead.

* * *

Nearly every guide also recommends that you apply to Dream Schools. I disagree. While dreams are wonderful things, there are serious disadvantages in the law school context. First, it is almost certainly a waste of money. By definition, the chances are extraordinarily low that you'll get admitted to a dream school. In reality, the bulk of applications rejected from candidates for whom that law school was a dream school had no chance. It's not a "ten-percent roll of the dice"; it's closer to zero percent. Unless you have extraordinary positives that aren't reflected in your LSAT and GPA, don't waste your time or money.

Keep in mind the rule as to LSAT and GPA in the application process: they are nearly the whole game. The reason they're nearly the whole game is that you matter to law schools as much as they matter to you. Dream law schools want *fantastic* scores, not just good ones. If your scores are not just below their 25th-percentile numbers but are *substantially* below them, now we might as well complicate things further with new sub-categories: Dreams and Fantasies. This is not just academic; it is deadly serious. If your scores are below their average, your admission *hurts*. The farther below, the more it deflates their standing. So, even if you *do* have extraordinary positives that aren't reflected in your LSAT and GPA, it's *still* almost certainly a waste of your time and money. Also, be honest about the relative importance of all three—the LSAT, GPA, and your subjective criteria—if the first two are borderline but the last is truly magnificent, is it a Reach or a Dream? And, if it's a Dream, can you make it a Reach instead? How? *Reset your LSAT*.

I know you're getting tired of reading this, but if it's not already clear the advice is that you stop fighting your LSAT. If it's not what you want it to be, then take it again. And again. Whatever it takes.

Do you want it or not? Don't think of this as a one-time lottery. If it's truly important to you, and if you feel, honestly, that your score doesn't reflect your ability, then *take it again*. Take the time to prepare—just think, you'll get to take one hundred LSAT prep tests again—and *give your all* to the next LSAT. Now you see the second reason why taking the LSAT early is better: if need be you can re-focus and still have a fighting chance.

Now you know why I also made such a fuss about preparing for the LSAT the first time around. Even if you do end up not hating it, it's hardly an exam you want to take twice if you don't have to. And you won't have to by taking it seriously the first time around. This is *exactly* the same advice that applies to law exams, the bar exam, and every day of your working life: do it right the first time.

Perhaps that dream will become a mere reach. With the extra time, you can focus as well on all of the ancillary aspects of your application: personal statement, recommendations, perhaps even GPA if you're in your last year of college. Maybe audit a law class at your local law school, and write an article or two. Get a job in a law office and get a better handle on what it is that the admissions committee might—just might—be attuned to. Go talk with the admissions officers, after the season is over. You can, in essence, take at least some of the *luck* out of the equation. (As the saying goes from Seneca, a Roman philosopher, "luck" is what happens when preparation meets opportunity. You control the preparation, and it might be that the opportunity is waiting for you, not vice versa.)

So, then what?

Then nothing. As hard as this might seem, again this should not be seen as a one-time process. If law school is important to you, and if you've taken this process seriously, chances are you will be accepted to at least one of your Targets. If not—which is unlikely, if it's a true Target—then revisit your application. Was your personal statement real? Was it genuine? Was it spotless? Were the recommendations and other details sufficiently glowing?

I know that this section will strike you as odd—if not downright batty—but for the reasons above you should focus on neither Dreams nor Safeties. Don't waste your money. Don't waste your and their time. Don't waste your hope. Focus on Reaches and Targets.

If you ignore this—and it's hard to counsel anyone to ignore a dream—then try this: place a one-hundred dollar bill (we'll use that as the fee for your dream application) in front of you as you study for the LSAT and as you draft your personal statement. This is not about the dreams, or glories, or salaries...but about the thought of flushing that bill down the toilet if you don't take the process seriously. At the very least, your personal statement should be one that brings readers to tears. It should cause, in certain admissions offices, law professors and deans to exclaim, "To Hell with the LSAT! Here's a student I want to see in *my* class."

If it's a true dream, follow it. Apply. But do your darnedest to change it from a mere dream and *make* it a reality. Your reality. This is done—exclamations aside—with your LSAT and with a superb application, not a one-hundred-dollar lottery.

If you get accepted, you have my sincere congratulations and a promise to somehow embarrass myself given all that I've written above. If not, perhaps you might still consider your options, not discounting the one that takes the additional year.

OTHER CONSIDERATIONS

In addition to a law school's rank there are a few additional variables to consider—and these tend to be more subjective. And thus, in a sense, they're more important. After all, if your LSAT/GPA locks you into a fairly narrow band of a few dozen law schools in your LSAT/GPA range, it certainly seems important to focus on the subjective factors that will make this the right decision...for you.

If you plan to stay where you are (often a financially wise choice), then your options are likely to be quite limited—and thus easier. It's likely, for example, that you'll have just a handful of law schools to choose from within commuting distance—and often just one or two. It's unlikely, as well, that they'll be in the same tier. Clearly, if geography is a limiting factor, the school's rank becomes secondary. Almost. If, for example, you happen to live in New Haven, Connecticut, then of course it would be helpful if your LSAT and GPA are within Yale's range to avoid the commute to the University of Connecticut's law school in Hartford—a good hour's time even without rush-hour traffic—or Quinnipiac University's law school in Hamden—a closer twenty minutes or so. Importantly, all three schools happen to represent their own law school worlds: Yale at the tippy-top; UConn somewhere respectably in the middle; and Quinnipiac a bit further down the law school atmosphere.

Note: This is not at all a comment on Quinnipiac, which I have not visited and do not know. It is likely a fine law school. As is often the case when exploring the options, however, one's knowledge of a law school is either zero or perhaps a bit better if you happen to be considering law schools in your area. After all, unless you live near a law school, or happened to have relatives or colleagues who are alumni of that law school or affiliated university, it's doubtful the knowledge extends much beyond a single page in a law school reference book.

Law School as a Person. Each law school *does* have a personality. Sometimes this is as much imagined as real, but as is often true, the popular imagination can become a self-fulfilling prophecy.

Yale, for example, has assumed that more purely academic cloak (in the sense of focusing on producing future law professors) than Harvard. This offers an interesting contrast, because Harvard is a much larger law school and one that produces more future law professors—in absolute numbers—than does Yale. The difference is that Yale produces almost three times more professors, adjusted for its size, than does Harvard. Thus, while Harvard and Yale are equally "top" schools, in the minds of most law professors and many senior practitioners, Yale is a bit more "academic" than Harvard.

The University of Chicago, which is renowned in both law school and university worlds as the epicenter of the Law and Economics movement, tends towards that impulse in its course offerings and applicants. Will an employer care? Probably not. Chicago and its graduates are going to find a warm reception just about anywhere. But, if you're someone who despises capitalism and all that it conveys (which, as a beneficiary, you should not), then you might think twice before applying and then attending law school at the University of Chicago.

Why a focus on just the top law schools? Because that's what everyone focuses on, because that's what everyone will continue to focus on, and because "lesser" schools tend to strive toward the Harvard model: success in practical as well as academic terms. Thus, most law schools (with a few notable exceptions) attempt to be the "it" school to their respective group of law firm recruiters and local firms and judges.

To reinforce the impact of this in the popular legal consciousness, the only exceptions that come to mind are the "environmental" law schools of Vermont and Oregon. If you're absolutely, positively planning to focus in environmental law, if you just love issues involving the environment, and if you've decided to sell your love beads and "Have You Hugged a Whale Today?" button stash to pay for law school, these might be a good fit. Conversely, if you're someone who despises environmentalism and all that it conveys (which, as a co-inhabitant, you should not), then you might consider twice before applying and then attending a law school that has embraced this area of legal expertise. Not least, this expertise exists because their law professors—possibly *your* law professors—have this expertise, and passion. If that's not you, beware.

If you're highly conservative, you might consider whether you'd be happier in a bastion of conservative thought, or in a highly liberal environment. If you're highly liberal, the reverse question applies.

I am not arguing, by the way, that we shouldn't seek to challenge our preconceptions, and in this perhaps we should each seek out experiences that challenge our beliefs. The danger is that cognitive dissonance rears itself, putting up a resistance to such a new environment...and for most, the result is profoundly disruptive. Also, law school is not college; the assumption is that you have already found yourself. Again, the real question is where you see yourself, and where you see the connections between yourself and others.

Are there other law schools with comparable personalities? Yes. But most law schools, while they might have law professors and even groups of law professors rising to a local specialization, still maintain that pragmatic approach vis-à-vis employment for graduates.

How to tell? The course catalogue is the place to start. First, is there a weighting of courses? In any academic setting, professors teach courses they are required to (such as first-year courses), and are usually allowed to offer a course or seminar they like. Law schools will thus usually offer a sampling of courses based on the expertise of its faculty. The more faculty, the more that will be available. There is a likelihood, however, that all but the smallest and largest law schools will have focused in their faculty recruitment on a *limited* number of areas. As a result, you will often see a corresponding offering of courses and seminars in those areas.

It's useful to keep in mind, as well, that not all courses, seminars, and professors are equal. So if, for example, you absolutely want to specialize in environmental law—not just as a lark but, say, to round out your master's degree in geology—you might delve a little more deeply. Who is teaching these courses, and how well-regarded are they in their field? In academia, nearly everyone will have a keen sense of "who's who" in the field. How to tell? Check to see how many times a faculty who teaches in an area has been cited in other works, especially articles and cases. For a top "department," the expectation is that faculty will be *the* reference for other professors and for courts. And, yes, this too becomes a self-fulfilling prophecy.

In practice this is of only marginal importance—except that a firm specializing in environmental issues will almost certainly recruit at the law schools with an established faculty known in the field. (Careful, however: most firms seek associates for defense, not public-interest, work.) Nearly always, this corresponds to the overall quality of the law school. This is because top law schools can more easily poach those professors who've *already* established their reputations, thus enabling top schools to "buy" a better institutional reputation, even if in just a narrow area. So, if this is a concern for you, at the top of your list should be research on which law schools are "players" and which are just "bit players" in the field of genuine interest to you.

Part II is that, for nearly everyone, it really doesn't matter. Unless you have strong personal leanings, you'll find plenty of like-minded souls in any law school. The larger the school, the more options both as to fields and friends. And if you don't have a clear area of interest (which is common and entirely okay), or if it's in a general area such as business law, then few law firms will take a second look. In honesty they could not care less. They will focus on the quality of the school and of the job-seeker. They will train you, later.

Where this *can* come into play is in the general sense of camaraderie (or, on the other end, aggressive competition) within each law school. Some schools do have a reputation as being more collegial...while others seem especially competitive, even cutthroat. This boils down to two variables: first is the market that that law school occupies, and second is the cultural backdrop for that school and especially its students. To take two examples, Hawaii and Vermont benefit from well-defined markets and unique cultural environs that are, shall we say, a bit more laid back. Students in both schools tend to be local, and thus tend to know where they're headed. Likewise, law firms and local offices tend to accept their graduates without much fuss. As a result, competition is primarily within each class, and reasonably sedate. Why? Because chances are there are more jobs relative to graduates, especially in the middle and bottom of the class, and thus less intense competition. Moreover, there are strong, local cultural forces that moderate competitive pressures. Conversely, law schools more exposed to the markets and especially those that are below nominal peers (thus fighting for their own altitude) and with students intending to migrate elsewhere...tend to be more cutthroat, especially in a bad year. This is in large part because the competition is felt not only within a class, but also is perceived as being against graduates from other, usually higher-ranked law schools as well. The more exposed a law school's graduates are, the more likely they are to be hyper-competitive.

Even so, much of this collegial-versus-cutthroat atmosphere relates to your approach and attitude in law school: the more cutthroat you feel you have to be—especially after exams—the more likely those around you will respond in kind. If you have already worked in a firm, and continue in your first summer and again with part-time work thereafter, you'll have little need to worry. Thus, you'll reduce—just a bit—the über-competitive forces that swirl in many law school circles.

Urban/Rural. This might not seem such a big deal, but it can be if there's a mismatch. If you plan to move and if you like cities, then think seriously before applying to a rural law school. Why waste your time? Visit the school if you are even considering it. Traipse the halls and surrounding community. Sit in the cafes and ask yourself whether you'd go stir crazy (or whether your preferences might just be a bit made-up, rather than real).

Conversely, if you think you're not cut out for the urban life and instead assume that pastoral views are for you, focus your efforts there. This assumes, too, that your career interests are in line with your preferences. So, for example, if you like rural settings but hope to work in a big firm, you might take a look at both. If by "big firm" you really mean "lots of money," chances are that that money will be available only in cities—the bigger and more noisy the city, the more money. Chances are if you are looking for a pastoral life, you'd probably also be more comfortable in a smaller practice—perhaps a small firm in your hometown or a branch of a medium-sized firm nearby. All are viable options (depending upon how well you do, and where), but all should be considered as part of your process of elimination of law schools to which you will apply.

My own take on this is perhaps unusual. I was once in New York City—a city that held attraction to me more for its architectural, cultural, and engineering qualities than for the presumptive qualities of many of its residents—while traveling with a friend and his fiancée who lived on Staten Island. While in Manhattan we happened upon a side street just below Greenwich Village. My friend, who had lived there, inhaled deeply, commenting how he missed it. I looked down the street (more of an alley, really)—past row upon row of garbage—and wondered just what the Hell he was reminiscing over. I later traveled there many times, and could see how life in Manhattan could be quite engaging...but only with the right mindset (or a lot of money). In short, New York City is not the place for me; I would choose many other cities over it. This is, for me, almost in reaction to the presumed superiority of New York City and the East Coast generally. Once one travels abroad it's harder to hold such a centric view, and after one slaves away in an office for the fifth midnight that week, the metropolitan attractions grow cold.

But enough about me. This is about you. What do *you* like? That is the question to ask. If you think you like (or don't like) a city you're considering, for goodness' sake take a few weeks and visit there. If you have school-subsidized rent in San Francisco, Chicago, or The Big Apple, that's a wonderful opportunity. If cities are not for you, there are many, many more options open to you—but that decision will impact your eventual path.

A corollary to this is the issue of safety. This includes the community surrounding the school. As one example, I once traveled to New Haven, Connecticut, the home of Yale University. I was stunned at how awful the area surrounding Yale was. Although Yale has worked to minimize the near-cliff of social decay that seemed to have enveloped the edges of its campus, I was floored. I had pictured a bucolic campus, and while the campus itself is magnificent, walking just a block away puts one in a near drop-off of seedy storefronts, run-down streets, and so on. Crime, I learned, had been quite an issue. Imagine that.

Were I applying to law school today, I would think seriously about *not*. Yale or no Yale, it was damned depressing. And—this might strike you as quite sexist—were I a woman I would think very, very seriously about not attending there. In either case, I would visit again to see whether it is still as bad as I remember it.

Perhaps I should check with a source. Hang on. [Keyboard clattering, replaced by sounds of the coffee-maker. Fingers tapping. Indistinct coughing. Toenail clippers? Some time later...]

Okay, got it. Here's what he reports:

New Haven really *is* a horrid little town. My wife and I (foreigners from the Midwest) pulled into the Motel 6 outside of New Haven and turned on the news, only to see a gleeful news anchor declare with pride that New Haven now had the *fourth* highest violent crime rate in the nation. This was, apparently, a big improvement over years past. (We spent the night soul-searching on why we hadn't gone to Stanford instead.) We lived just a few blocks off campus (in Bill Clinton's old house, actually), yet tried not to go outside after dark, and carried Mace everywhere we went. We were encouraged not to use the Grove Street exit from the law school, because it wasn't safe, particularly after dark.

There were two crackhouses on my block, four blocks from the law school. It has gotten quite a bit better since I left—noticeably so. Current students are horrified at my tales. I go back for interviews/reunions every so often, and always walk about. New Haven is just as awful as ever, but Yale has pushed the boundary back several blocks. No more crackhouses on my old block now, or for several blocks behind, and there are students living on streets I would never have dared to visit.

And, on balance:

I would add my opinion, in line with your "golden ticket" theory earlier, that if you get in to Yale, Harvard, or Stanford, you stop the analysis right there and go. No matter what. Failure to do so will result in a lifetime of self-flagellation. No matter how many crackhouses in New Haven. Just go. Sell a kidney to pay for it if you have to, but go.

So there you have it. I can hardly wait for the subpoena from the good folks at the New Haven Visitors Bureau.

Other cities offer nearly the opposite. My hometown of Austin is one of the best places in the United States to live—and I don't say that (just) as a former resident, as indeed I did not appreciate

Austin as much as I should have. Austin is simply a superb city as a combination of the best features of a small city and a uniquely intellectual, musical, governmental, and technological population (and, to confirm this, bumper stickers that declare "Keep Austin Weird").

If UT-Austin is a possibility for you, the city of Austin should be a strong draw. Likewise, there are a number of cities offering a comparable lifestyle. In no particular order: Missoula, Montana (the University of Montana); Oxford, Mississippi ("Ole Miss," or the University of Mississippi); Madison, Wisconsin (University of Wisconsin–Madison); Ann Arbor, Michigan (University of Michigan); Athens, Georgia (University of Georgia); Eugene, Oregon (University of Oregon); Boulder, Colorado (University of Colorado–Boulder); South Royalton, Vermont (Vermont Law School); and, no doubt, a few others. There are many great cities and towns, some with law schools in or nearby. You might check out *Places Rated Almanac,* by David Savageau, for a detailed look at any number of geographic preference factors.

I left out one of the obvious ones, Honolulu, because its law school is small and focused on students who have at least some connection to the islands (and thus is relatively harder for "outsiders" seeking admission just to live there), and because Honolulu itself is quite expensive and, as with San Francisco and New York City, is difficult on a student's budget. Even with a careful student's lifestyle, I would recommend any of the above cities before Honolulu.

If, by the way, you do have a serious intent to live and practice in Hawaii, then UH–Mānoa is your ticket. It's really the *only* ticket. The "comparable" schools (*i.e.,* those that are given "equal" weight among employers in Hawaii), are the likes of Harvard/Yale and the well-known West Coast schools. Even schools like, say, Penn—while "okay"—won't be the natural *in* that UH is, or Harvard/Yale/Stanford/UC–Berkeley/Hastings are. If you are from Penn hoping to work in Honolulu, chances are it will take some independent work to even get the interviews. It might sound funny, but that's exactly how a small-town scene works, and this is true especially if you don't have a connection in the islands. "Small town" includes cities too. As the saying goes, all politics is local.

Especially if you're single and intend to move, take advantage of the opportunity to move somewhere *fun*. Wherever you do move, it will almost certainly affect the rest of your life.

You might, by the way, think me crazy for including such cities while excluding others, such as those in California or Florida. This is perhaps the broader point: there are wonderful cities and towns out there—wherever "there" is for you. Personal preference shades our personal views. If an area of the country is where *you* would like to be…then go! Law school can be a catalyst for your personal as well as professional life. Don't do it haphazardly, however.

One more story, if I might: Many moons ago my father faced a choice as he left the Air Force. Would he attend graduate school in Seattle or Austin? While either would have been a good choice, we were lucky that, well, by luck he chose Austin. When I write "luck," I mean that, dejected, he happened to run into a dean on the steps of the UT Tower. Perhaps helped in his conversation by mention of the seven mouths depending upon him—a wife and six children—he found a home there. A chance meeting made a *huge* difference for a Newark-born child of the Great Depression.

It can make a huge difference for you…but it shouldn't be chance. If you have your heart set on a place, confirm that your head is there as well…and go for it!

If you've not got your heart set on a place, think, seriously, about what it is you like. Then research places that fit your dream. That, more than mere ranking, might make your law school a true dream.

If you don't know what it is you like, you really should search deeper. This *is* important, and will make a difference.

I hope the above lists have raised questions in your mind, particularly if you've never visited most or any of those cities. Each is not for everyone, but each has been well-regarded by others. Thus, while you shouldn't go to one of these law schools just because of where it's located (or because of what I say), neither is that irrelevant. It *is* relevant to where you're going to live for three years at least. You might as well enjoy where you are. Moreover, one lesson I have learned as I've travelled around the country and world—it's easy to stay too focused on work (or school), and lose sight of what is equally important: actually living. As in all things, a key is *balance*.

Top 50 or Bust

In the summary I included a statement that might have shocked you. It was: "If you don't get admitted to a Top 50 law school, think seriously, times two, about whether you should go."

Am I actually saying that if you don't get into a law school ranked somewhere in the top 50—or even in the top 100—you probably shouldn't go?

Well, yes I am.

This might seem like very odd (or horribly elitist) advice, as the top 50 effectively cuts off nearly three-quarters of all law schools. Even more, counting unaccredited ones. As it's rather dramatic advice, the burden of proof is on me to show why.

If it were merely a question of gaining the credential to begin a practice of law in, say, a small town with just a few tiny firms and solo practitioners, then, yes, any accredited law school will do. Small-town practice can be wonderful, but you need to learn how, first. Paradoxically, small-town practice draws on *more* skills than does big-firm practice—because clients' needs tend to be all over the charts. Being a good generalist is harder than being a good specialist. And even in a small town one's alma mater does matter—to get your foot in the right door. My suspicion, however, is that you're probably not interested in such a life or practice.

If you are contemplating a solo practice immediately after law school, I will go past "I strongly advise against that" all the way to "don't you dare." Do *not* plan to practice solo out of law school; you won't be ready, and you will do a severe disservice to your first clients. In the words of one partner: "Rookie solo practitioners are walking malpractice machines."

So, if your preference is to live in a city and practice in a good firm, or a good agency, or in some way with reasonably good income—or if, upon reflection, you would like that option—then the *Top 50 or Bust* rule is in full force. This is because the odds of your achieving any of this (good firm, good agency, etc.) fall steeply the further below the Top 50 you go. In fact, they fall even before you get to that Top 50 marker.

I can just see the hate mail. Yes, there are many good law schools not ranked in the Top 50; yes, it's quite possible to learn the law well at a sub-Top 50 school; and yes, it's possible to get a good job with a good firm (agency, etc.) as a graduate of a "lesser" school. This is a pre-LSAT test: I did not write what I will be accused of. I wrote that the *odds* of your achieving any of this fall—and fall steeply—the further below the Top 50 you go. That is a correct statement, verifiable by any career services counselor in any law school. I also did not write not to go. I wrote that if you don't get admitted to a Top 50 law school, you need to *really* think about whether you should go.

But that is not why I write this. The risks (and costs) are difficult to overstate. If, for whatever reason, you do not end up staying in the locale of that sub-Top 50 school, or if you do not end up in the Top 10% of that school's class, or if the market turns south...you will be in a world of hurt. Three years' income gone; three years' tuition gone; and *massive* student-loan repayments and a career yet to appear. This is not where you want to be. Sometimes in life we must play the odds.

A second reason: *why* can you not get into a Top 50 law school? I'm not being flippant: If you look at the criteria of the schools in the lower part of the Top 50 (much less, the top 100), you'll see that the LSAT/GPA scores are not outrageously high. Clearly, if you're already past college, your GPA is set—which takes us again to the LSAT. Was that a fair test? Not metaphorically, but *for you*. Did you do as well as you could have done? If you are serious about the law, and about doing it right, and if your LSAT doesn't reflect your true qualities, then why put yourself in an environment that—fair or unfair—will not give you the practical boost that your intrinsic strengths deserve? We can rail against the system as it is, but for the seventy-third time it *is* as it is. Polite lies will not make it less so. Taking the extra year or two or three will be time well spent if it puts you in a better position in getting the type of job you are capable of and want. Again, I'm not being flippant. You should not be "law school crazy," insisting that you have to go *now!*

Why? What's the rush? If you're serious, then you should be serious not only about the process, but about your *objective* fit within that process. Admissions officers will certainly look at this; that's pretty much all they have to go on. This is, in fact, one of their deepest concerns in *their* world: how to choose those students who "get it." At the margins, these subjective signs of maturity can be just the ticket. If you do take the extra year or two or three, chances are you will get the benefit of the doubt as to your new, higher LSAT score, and the extra year's reflection in your personal statement. That Dream might just become a Reach, or perhaps even a Target, which just might become a letter of acceptance. They will appreciate that you take the longer view, as their school (one should hope) will be there next year too.

What if your stats are unlikely ever to be within Top 50 reach? As with any advice, its usefulness depends upon circumstances. Your circumstances. If your college years were marked, say, by multiple distractions and personal crises, and such cannot be readily explained in your application materials, or if you've taken the LSAT two or three times to disappointing results, what then? That boils down to the same question: do you really, truly want to be a lawyer? If so, then go! Don't let me stand in your way. That's exactly the drive that's needed. Part of the "really, truly wanting," however, is an acceptance that you might have to (and should) work harder than others to Get Good. Chances are, getting good will give you the boost that you need to meet your financial as well as emotional needs.

What about the needs of underserved populations? Doesn't this advice hurt them? There are a number of responses to this, not least that you shouldn't limit yourself—or sell yourself short—if that's you and your goal, and you really, truly want to be a lawyer and help those who need it. Were I the Emperor, I would broaden the issue to far more than simple socio-economic factors: there is a *huge* underserved population: everyone in the bottom 85%. Even middle-class individuals are at a severe disadvantage in our legal system, which, by its nature and structure, is designed for only the wealthiest clients (both people and corporations). There is much that could and should be done, but it hardly does, *ah,* justice to non-wealthy clients to assume that they should be helped only by those who are not from top law schools. Perhaps most importantly, one way to get good in serving a public interest is to get good in serving private ones. There is very much a Catch-22 here, and it's important not to succumb to the inverse snobbery that only certain students from certain schools care about (or should care about) public-interest work. This is something we should *all* care about, and *do* something about. What's in this section is different: it's about your place in this debate. If you wish to do public interest work and attend a lesser-regarded law school, the burden will be even higher to get not just good, but to get *better* than those you will be up against. If that's a burden you accept, then you have my genuine respect. You should, however, still work in a traditional law office for at least your first few years (so that you will get good in practice as well as theory), and you should still attend a Top 50 law school, if you can. If you then decide that a serious dedication to *pro bono* work is sufficient, you can do good as well as well. If you decide that you'd like to dedicate all of your time to public interest work, you will then have the skills to make a difference, and you will. In any event, the same tests apply, and the same reasoning favors a Top 50 law school.

If your LSAT is not what it could be, then, to borrow from a certain Starfleet Captain, "make it so." No excuses, no back-talk, no whining. Just make it so. This, in a sense, is one of the most important tests of all. If it's not right for you, or not right for you now, don't go. The planets aren't always aligned when we want them to be. And, by the way, you shouldn't go because you think that if you don't go now you never will. That is a sure sign of why *not* to go. A genuine interest should be, well, genuine. You shouldn't play games with yourself, nor should you rush just for the sake of getting somewhere fast. You need to get to the right place, in the right way, for where you will want to be.

If law school is truly for you, the extra year will be a plus. If not, then it won't matter.

How Does All This Stuff About Top Schools Help Me?

Despite the focus in much of the above about Top This and Top That, in actuality this advice is *more* important in the middle.

After all, if you can get into a top law school (Top 5, Top 25, whatever), it won't matter nearly so much: you'll likely have a good shot at one of those jobs everyone covets. If you go to a school in the fourth tier, chances are you will focus in local jobs, because those will be the only ones open to you. And, despite my admonition to think thrice, it's entirely possible to have a good career from a fourth-tier school. It almost certainly will not be a top job in the conventional sense, however, which is why—with the cost of law school so high—this is truly a decision to ponder. Just as in the law school application process, it's for everyone in the vast middle where this assumes special importance.

All law schools operate in the ways described above, and those "'so-called' objective criteria" *will* be constraints that apply to (and against) you. Choose what's best for you, knowing as you enter what the rules are. The real rules—the ones that you will actually face—and not those we would like to believe should be true.

IF YOU'RE STILL IN COLLEGE

Are there any courses that might help you on the LSAT and once you're in law school?

Yes, there are.

Law schools no longer require a pre-law curriculum for admission, and most brochures have some version of "any undergraduate degree is welcome." True enough, but not enough. There *are* disciplines that are helpful in law school: those that hone skills in critical thinking and a close reading of text. Ironically, English majors seem just as lost as everyone else. Without getting into theories why, the disciplines at the greatest advantage are those in mathematics, the physical and biological sciences, Talmudic studies, and the like. Philosophy ought to be a shoo-in, but is often more concerned with navel-gazing (navel gamesmanship, really), rather than truly critical thought. Even so, do find a good instructor and take at least a course in logic, if possible.

I've added a note in the *Obiter Dicta* section, at the end, with a list you might consider. Happily, if you're still early in college (or in high school), you can plan all or nearly all of these as part of your lower-division and electives, so that you can have the benefit of a real "pre" law education—without spending an extra dime or semester hour.

TO PREP OR NOT TO PREP

One debate of sorts that rages—well, simmers—among advice-givers is whether a student should prepare before starting law school, and, if so, how. One camp, which might be labeled the *Don't Worry, Be Happy* school of jurisprudence, argues that it's pointless to study and that it's more important to be fresh and ready for the adventures to come. The other camp—filled with Type-A overachievers (which includes much of law school popula-tions)—proclaims the opposite: "Goodness, you have to prepare! You'll be lost!! Why aren't you done yet!!! Where's my Prozac!!!!"

The first camp is not the camp to be in. If you decide not to prepare you will be way, way behind *and* lost. It might be useful, however, to discuss why this is true, so that the importance of preparation will make sense, and so that you'll know what and how to prepare, in a way that is manageable and beneficial. You *should* enjoy your summer before law school (as you should enjoy all summers). But you absolutely should not blow off preparing for what's to come.

Advice-givers of this camp assert, often strenuously, that any pre-study is pointless. "You won't know what to study!" "You'll study the wrong things!" "Everything you need to know you'll learn when you get there!"

Wrong on all counts. First, you *will* know what to study. How? Because that is the way of the law. Any good attorney can tell you at least the main points of every first-year subject. Look at the table of contents of any commercial outline, hornbook, or casebook, and you will see...exactly the same major concepts, for every course. The law, to *be* the law, must be predictable. It must be structured. This is (or should be) the essence of the study of law too.

So, as to points one and two ("You won't know what to study!" "You'll study the wrong things!"), you will know exactly what to study, and you will not study the wrong things. If, for example, we look at Contracts, you will find that every single contract under-goes the same basic tests: formation, legality, breach, damages—

leading to the insight that, gee, wouldn't it be useful to begin thinking about these topics, at least in the most overarching of ways.

To those who say, "…But your profs might focus on different areas of the law!" First, no they won't. Law professors are not only uniformly trained at the top law schools, they are expected to cover the major areas of each discipline. Second, these major areas are "well-settled," a term of art in the law meaning that everyone knows what's what, and everyone also knows what is to be covered. They are the legal "canon," or near-sacred text of what is accepted as basic among the profession. Third, might a professor deviate on one point or another? Sure. The answer? It doesn't matter. Even if they do deviate, it's not likely to be more than a minor difference of emphasis. Actually, even this doesn't go far enough: *especially* if they deviate, "pre-study" becomes more, not less, valuable. The more you know about the general framework of that area of the law, the more you will recognize the differences—and deviations. It is the difference between a novice and intermediate player. Not yet expert, but a world of difference between the two.

So, in short, you should begin preparation in a careful way: you should begin laying out the major headings for your master outlines. You will have six: Contracts, Property, Torts, Civil Procedure, Criminal Law, and Constitutional Law. Even if there is a difference in your first-year courses, which is unlikely, it would be *highly* unlikely that any of these will go to waste. Even if your law school pushes one to the second year, let's say, you've "wasted" perhaps a few dozen hours' time. We're not talking about a huge amount of work. It's less time than you'll spend on the LSAT, by far.

An example of a first-level heading for, say, Contracts is *Formation*. Once you have the first-level headings, you should begin the process of delving into the second-level headings, which begin to flesh out the subject. So, under Formation you might have *Offer, Acceptance, Consideration,* and *Legality*. The third-level headings under Offer will run through a number of tests, such as (1) *Commitment* (2) *communicated* to an (3) *Identified Offeree* with (4) *definite terms*. Each of those terms will be fourth-level headings, so, for example, a *commitment* is an *objective test* in which the question is *whether a reasonable person hearing words under similar circumstances would believe the sender intended a contract*.

Notice what is happening. In just a few minutes you're laying the groundwork for an understanding of black letter Contract Law. As you move forward in the course, you will add detail to explain each of those phrases and terms. Moreover, when you define the term *objective test,* for example, you will be defining a term that applies across legal disciplines. You will, to put it bluntly, be learning a foundational definition for *dozens* of exams.

Yeah. Preparation is important. And what you are learning in class will make far more sense because it will fit within a framework you have already built, and have re-chewed a few times. Before your very first class, you already know, for example, there's a basic question in Contract Law of how a contract is formed. So, if your professor delves immediately into a discussion of, say, *Texaco v. Pennzoil,* you won't be lost wondering what on Earth an oral contract has to do with a billion-dollar dispute. Instead, you'll be saying (silently!) to yourself, "Of course! How could they have been so *dumb?*"

Indeed. A multi-billion-dollar dispute (and a multi-billion-dollar bankruptcy) because a roomful of bigwigs forgot a *first-year* law school lesson in what makes a contract. *That* is the level of comprehension you should aim for, and your outlines—which you should start *before* law school—are a key to getting there.

Also, isn't this more *fun?* Isn't it better to know what the professor is talking about, and to be able to appreciate it…rather than slinking from class to class in a fog? If you neglect your outlines for even a few days, a fog it will be.

Note from a Top 5 reviewer: "And a fog it was. Boy do I wish I had done this."

Note #2: there is not a single right way to build your outline. You might, for example, have *Consideration* as a first-level heading, or another second-level heading *Termination Before Acceptance?,* or some such. That doesn't matter. It's on a computer. You can switch it around if you don't like it. And your professor will appreciate the sophisticated structural question you'll ask if you do need to ask.

How to get started? Follow the primers and commercial outlines. Note #3: Your job is not to simply copy it. Commercial texts will have *lots* of detail that won't make sense (such as cases and tertiary rules). Skip that, for now. You need, instead, to build the *framework,* into which you will later add the wiring, walls, outlets, paint, and so on. This isn't so much "getting a head start" as it is getting ready to start off right. Once law school starts, you'll have very little time to backtrack. And, by definition, backtracking is a poor use of time.

To mix metaphors, this brings to mind an old joke:

> Two explorers are on safari when they notice a tiger so famished it starts snaking its way toward them. As they stare in horror, one explorer starts to tie his shoelaces.
>
> "What are you doing?" whispers the first, "We can't outrun the tiger!"
>
> "I don't need to outrun the tiger," comes the reply, "I only need to outrun you."

Carnivorous humor aside, this applies with all too much force in law school. While we might want for law school to educate every student to a 90+ average, in reality this is not the way law school is. With the forced curve, graded blind, it is a competition. You will have a better chance against the tiger if your shoelaces are already tied.

I recommend, again, that you read *Planet Law School.* In fact, I feel so strongly about it that this is one of two sources I will recommend you use multiple times. For your preliminary work, focus on chapter 16 (especially pp. 432-42; 452-56; and 458-68). Follow the advice there and read, or ignore, whichever parts of the book don't apply (yet). This advice—to go to another book for advice—might be viewed as a bit odd (and, no, I'm not the author of *Planet Law School*), but that misses the point. This is part of a broader lesson of efficiency: take advantage of the best of what is already out there. The materials recommended in *Planet Law School* are the materials you should have—and read; it would be pointless to simply restate them and the points he makes, less well, here. (Not to mention unethical.) The broader point is that *Planet Law School* is correct: preparation *is* important. It need not and should not be extreme, but it should be substantial, and concerted.

One other source you might look at, and this one I did have a hand in, are the *Great Law Books* pages at www.fineprintpress.com. These include a number of references that you might find interesting or useful to prepare for the LSAT, application process, or law school itself. In most cases, I suggest you borrow these books from the library—there's no point to waste money better spent on future pizzas, yes?

A ONE-MINUTE TEST

If you're still debating whether or not you should prepare, consider how you will feel as you walk into your first week's classes...with professors opening the semester by talking about cases as if you already knew the law, cold. You'll suffer a sinking feeling, made worse because there's no break: the cases keep coming and coming. Times six. And discussions that *seem* to be about what you read somehow don't quite fit.

To reinforce this feeling, how about a metaphoric challenge? Go to the nearest large pool. Grab some diving weights—six should do—and strap them to your feet. (Not your waist, as it would be too easy to remove them.) For an extra measure, tape 'em on real tight. Now, jump into the deep end. If you can, get a good run going so that you're a good way from the edge. Not that it would matter, really, but after all we are talking about that sink-or-swim feeling. Now, reflect on the sensation you'll feel—at the bottom of the pool—over the succeeding sixty seconds. That should be more than enough time. Without knowing a general contour—an outline—of the rule under discussion in each class, *that* is your first year of law school. In every class you'll feel that you're in way, way over your head. You're smart, but, but...

But that is not what your first year should be *for you*.

A legal disclaimer, in two parts: First, the above is an attempt at humor. (And gravity at the same time, come to think of it.) Do *not* try this at home...or, indeed, near any body of water. Second, if you forget and try this anyway, please do make sure there's an emergency rescue team nearby.

It's not possible to restate this strongly enough: for your classes, you must go into class knowing what the cases are about. Simply knowing a case is not good enough. In many cases, it's misleading and even confusing, because it might be an illustration of an exception to a rule. You must know *why the case is there*. That means that you must know the rule that is at issue in the case. With that understanding—which, with your outline, is not too hard—understanding the case itself becomes easy.

Okay then. Ready for law school?

GETTING GOOD

Summary

The term "getting good" can have several meanings, from doing well on exams (clearly important to your success), to being a decent human being to your fellow classmates (more important than one would ever know *in* law school), to actually learning the law *well*.

Which you focus on is, of course, up to you. In my mind these are not contradictory. Indeed, they are very much complementary and even necessary to each other: one doesn't do well on exams unless one actually learns the law well; one finds it harder than expected to remain decent when one's future is fading into nothingness because of poor grades; and one will find it more difficult to learn the law well and to act well in interviews and elsewhere if treating others poorly.

The rules, condensed:

1. In law school success, grades are the only thing that count.

2. Classroom participation does not count.

3. For career success (and also for personal growth), etiquette, deportment, and integrity count—in subtle yet powerful ways —more than can ever be known at the time.

4. Classroom participation still does not count.

5. Classroom notes are not a good way to study law (or anything else, for that matter).

   a. Notes should be one-half page or less per class. No more.

   b. This is not high school; impressing others with pointless make-work does not count.

6. Outlines are a key to success. They count big.

7. Outlines must be done by you, and only by you. These will be crucial on law exams, and important for the bar exam.

   a. There should be two: a master outline and a summary outline.

i. The master outline for each course should be between 30 and 50 pages. No less, no more.

     ii. The summary outline should be 1-2 pages. No more.

8. In law school, outlines are your life, Part I.

9. Study groups can be invaluable, but must have members with the same goals, the same dedication, and the same approach and habits.

    a. Study groups are not for the "study" (or, worse, division) of outlines

    b. Study groups are for the purposeful discussion of hypotheticals and for the working of exams.

    c. Do not try to form a study group immediately. Instead, wait until you have a sense of the dedication and approach of prospective members.

10. In law school, hypos and exams are your life, Parts II and III.

11. Multi-tasking is bad. Do one thing at a time, and do it well.

12. No, classroom participation still does not count.

Getting Good, while a goal in itself, should be about more than just the right approach to and in law school. It should be about the right approach to the law. Your three years should be engaging, fruitful, and even enjoyable. If they are, so too will be your career.

    Law school should not be about exhibitionism. What were Rules 2, 4, and 12, above? Classroom participation does *not* count. That means that nothing you say in class will help you—but it can hurt. And Rule 3 *does* count. Try not to get trapped in the petty one-upmanship, mindless drama, or nasty tricks prevalent among some law school crowds.

> Take extensive notes, ask questions, study hard. Really, it's that simple. You will be reading so much once you get to law school—don't burn yourself out before classes start.

The "advice" above was written by a law student to other law students. If you follow this advice—which *seems* to be common sense, and is certainly common—you will almost certainly fail.

The advice itself fails on all counts. For reasons why, and for the right ways to study in law school, I invite you to read on.

LAW SCHOOL PRELUDE

Law school should be an engaging, immensely satisfying adventure. For many, it is not. It is, instead, an adventure that begins with great promise…and ends with heartache.

This is no exaggeration. Nor is it written just to scare. Talk with any group of 2L or 3L law students, and chances are that nine out of ten will—after you've chatted a while—tell a tale of gut-wrenching woe (if not for them than for at least a few of their compatriots). I know of one fellow student in particular, a decent and *very* smart guy, whose spirit was crushed in law school. He was a shell of a person even years after. More than just hopes and dreams are dashed—the realization that those tens of thousands of dollars in student loans loom large, and there might not be the high-powered job to sweep the debt away. Even that doesn't quite capture it: this is a deeply personal wound for many, including my friend above.

First we'll consider how law school is for many, if not most, law students. Then we'll consider how law school could and should be, for you. These sections tell no great secret, by the way. Law school administrators and ABA officials have studied the darker elements of this reality. It *is* a reality, and one that senior leaders have lamented for decades, yet despite everyone's wish that it would go away, it won't. There are too many reasons that law students fall into these traps, like so many trapdoors on a stage hidden from view until you're on top of them. Many don't recognize them even then, as they're disguised to look like solid foundations from habits that worked before. The first step is to recognize them as the traps that they are. Let's then take a peek, to pull the curtain back on what goes wrong.

SETTING THE STAGE: OR, HOW TO DO LAW SCHOOL WRONG

Here's the scene: a group of eager new law students file into the front doors of a law school sometime late in August. Filled with nervous energy, they're nearly bouncing off the walls with excitement. The halls bustle with this energy. Anything seems possible. Yet much of this energy is channeled negatively. To cover intense feelings of inadequacy and nervousness, nearly all seem to blurt their life résumé when meeting each other: "Hi!...I'm Chip!...Yale undergrad and Exeter!...*Heard of it?*" "Hey!...I'm Suzy...just got back from my second summer in [pick some Third World spot]...guess it helped me get in here...did I mention I went to Princeton?" It's amazing more students don't pass out; they're so busy racing through their life accomplishments they don't seem to have time to breathe. And so it goes. For anyone within earshot (which is nearly everyone, as voices rise to eardrum-piercing levels), each self-flattering declaration causes, simultaneously, even *more* self-conscious nervousness, pangs of inadequacy, and, more than occasionally, dry heaves. Like electrons, students bounce nervously from one to another, eager to electrify others with their impressive credentials. Like spastic, autistic caricatures of themselves, many morph into almost-unrecognizable, egocentric boors. "Me, me, *me!*" Someone then mentions that the assignments for the first day's classes are posted, and more than a few students gasp. Huh? You mean we really *were* supposed to have prepared? Quickly they make their way to the poster (or web page), jot down (or download) the assignments. They grab their casebooks, and start reading. Ohmygod. This isn't like any reading they've ever seen. They attend a presentation on how to brief a case, and of course are eager to get started. They already have a *dozen* to do! Okay, they buy the extra highlighters and start to brief cases. Dutifully. Painstakingly. *Man* it seems to take forever. Each case seems to take *hours*—and it's sometimes hard to focus halfway through on what was just read. Their minds start to wander ninety seconds into the first "hereinafter." A holding? *Huh?* Procedural history? *Gah!* In the first week it seems that they're spending every *second* of free time reading and briefing cases—and they're supposed to go to class too! In class they take notes. Lots and lots of notes. *Surely* this will help to make sense of the Greek (well, Latin) they're reading in the cases and hearing from the profs and other students. Oddly, the notes don't seem to help. At the end of the week, they look at their piles of notes and it's hard to tell what they're even about, much less to help understand the cases. If they forget to put the class name on the note, they can't even tell what the subject is! If they get out of order, they've *no idea* which way they go. So they put them in a stack that grows ever more disheveled, and on and on it goes, week in and week out, as they bumble through their first week, second week, and then first month. Someone mentions *another* task—outlines!—and now they're starting to panic. How can they possibly do *more?!* The cases are taking *all* of their time, and they're struggling just to keep up. Class is getting to be a joke. It's fine to pretend to know what's going on, but they're worried about getting called on and goodness that is a sure killer, right? Then they're called on. Ohmygod. I'm dead, they're thinking. If only I understood that case! The facts! The holding! What are they *getting* at?! The prof must think I'm a real moron, you fear silently. *Everyone* feels this way—even the cocksure gunners (who hide their fears by having their hands nearly constantly raised). Surely they know how lost we are and will help. Now it's a *real* panic. It's the middle of the semester, they've been attending classes like clockwork, the professors are certainly nice, but it's just not making *sense*. Gosh it's hard. Hmm, outlines have been forgotten…there's no *time!*…but with exams just around the corner, they know they have to start doing *something*. They've also read they're supposed to practice with exams, and gee-it-would-be-good to have a study group. No *way!* This is a madhouse. It's hard enough to keep up with the readings, much less deal with others and their peculiarities. Especially not *those* assholes! Didn't you *see* how so-and-so looked at some other so-and-so? Exams! They've always done well. Surely these won't be *that* bad. The semester is drawing to a close, and panic hangs in the air. Students are wide-eyed with fear. In just about every class something is said that brings utter dread: what are they *talking* about?! Some are like the undead...they've never come close to *failing* before. But will they pull this off? The law *still* isn't making sense. It seems mysterious, even bizarre. All these phrases they're supposed to know. What do they *mean?* Well, cramming worked before, and it doesn't seem like there's much choice now anyway. Exams are right around the corner! So, just like in a scene in *The Paper Chase,* cramming it is! *"I'll show them!"* says nearly everyone to themselves, silently. More silently, they're praying just to make "B's." Maybe one "A," just to keep some dignity. Students huddle together and separately (this might seem an oxymoron, but that's what will happen...like an academic fetal cry for comfort, students will almost hug themselves). Some will seem as if they'll burst into tears at any moment. Others have distant looks, as if they see something important far, far away. Anywhere but here, they seem to say. Just let this be *over.* Taut faces and even shorter tempers give their fears away. Panic is contagious. Even those who were doing a good job and who *do* know the law succumb to a foreboding dread. Like cattle to the slaughter, they file into the exam rooms. Even with polite chatter, they can sense their impending doom, and the certain knowledge that they're just not ready. If only a meteor hit, destroying the exam rooms and giving them even just 24 hours more! Perhaps ancillary fires will engulf the neighboring buildings, buying a *week!* Sadly, no meteor hits, and three and a half hours later they leave the exams *knowing* they could have done better. If only, if only... Their thoughts trail off, and they pray that they're not one of the ones in the bottom half, as by now they've seen and heard what happens to students in *that* dreaded statistical pool. Now starts the bargaining. Just give me this, Oh Lord, and I promise I will be good. Even committed atheists begin negotiating with deities great and small for their future lives. Like a bad science fiction movie, they stagger the hallways, putting on a show but knowing all the same that their dreams for a high-paying job are dead—along with how they feel. Many start acting out, and many of those go to the dark side—secretly planning to cheat, lie, or otherwise do whatever it takes to reverse the fate that's been so unjustly handed them. Or they profess never to have cared at all. But *they* know better. Before, they'd been *the best.* Everyone had said so. Now they were a whole heap of nothing. Not just fighting for a good job—fighting for *any* job. With anyone! Pleeese? It's so *humiliating*. The winter holiday is hardly worth enjoying as the stress of the semester never quite leaves—how can it with exam scores still hanging in the balance? Somehow, they eat the turkey and smile weakly through the family accolades. The new semester starts, and one by one grades start to come in. The reactions are painful, and predictable. A few positive surprises, but mostly very, *very* long faces. With the curve's uncaring median, nearly everyone is seeing grades *far* below what they would ever have expected—or have ever gotten. For those hoping for an "A," it's a long, long way down. From undergraduate classes where nearly everyone gets an "A" or a "B," in law school even a "B" seems shockingly rare. It's as if hundreds of students are hearing the worst news they've ever heard—and for many, that's exactly right. Classes are already a few weeks underway, and in a sort of post-traumatic shock, the whole process starts up again. Cases. Briefs. Notes. Panic. Frenetic worry. More notes. Panic. Cramming. More panic. Another, final set of exams. This time, however, the exams count. Spring fills with even more intense dread, if that's possible, and for most, very little that's remotely positive or productive. In less than a year, hundreds of the most intelligent, most decent individuals who've excelled in college have been reduced to a quivering mass of despondency—a surprising percentage of whom have suicidal thoughts. (But who won't confide in a counselor for fear of an impact on bar examiners' committees for fitness to practice law, which can investigate even intensely personal counseling.) Even the lucky few who actually did well—if you asked them privately—would find it hard to explain just *how* they did it. So the next year somehow starts with the undead wandering the halls, putting on their brave faces, and watching as an eager new crop of law students bounces off the walls with excited, expectant faces to class.

* * *

The above, admittedly way-too-long paragraph might seem unbelievable. It *is* unbelievable. It certainly was to me, and to everyone I knew. Yet this is what happens, year in and year out, at every law school.

You've been at the very top of the academic heap. You've been praised for sixteen years for your intelligence, qualities, promise. Why should the next three years be any different? Although you read variations of this story in nearly every book about law school—each telling you that it *is* different—you still don't *believe*.

That's understandable. This is a reality that doesn't quite hit…until it hits. And, for at least half of every law school class, the "hit" will be very much like a mental version of what we see after a train derailment. Tens of thousands of tons of metal, twisted at places beyond recognition, all because the wheels smehow jumped the track.

If it helps in the important process of understanding—*really* understanding—just how true this reality is, I'll recount my own experience. I attended the University of Texas Law School, which is generally regarded, give or take, as being in the middle of the Top 25. Within Texas it's pretty much a Texas-sized Number One, and so "UT" strives mightily to compare itself not with any Texas school but rather with the dozen or so schools above it (naturally) in the rankings. In short, UT is the best law school for a thousand miles: you can pretty much drive to the coasts or Chicago before finding its equal. Why so much (more) ink about rank? Because of the experience I had graduating in 1991. The bottom had fallen out of the job market, and we students stood aghast as firm after firm cancelled their on-campus interviews, often just days before they were scheduled. To say that panic set in would be to report a mild version of events.

The national firms—which considered UT as very much a secondary school in their recruitment—required the standard Top 10%/law review standing, which of course few had. As mentioned, in 1989, when I entered, law school applications were at a peak, with intense competition pushing qualifications ever-higher at every school. The bust led to a steep drop-off, which took years to recover. There were a few firms, mostly regional or local, that would consider Top 25%, or perhaps even Top 33%. As the firms interviewing shrank, so too did job prospects. And this at one of the top law schools in the country! I write this not for self-flattery, but to reinforce that, in a bad market, even those in Tier 1 schools suffer. And, in a winner-take-all system, everyone lower down feels the crunch earlier and harder, in a steeply cascading tumble. As I had lined up a position in Honolulu, I was embarrassed even to repeat that among fellow students—half of whom had no job at all. To repeat, this was at a Tier 1 law school; the job market makes a *big* difference in the level of anxiety and near-psychosis among law students.

The atmosphere in those days was heart-wrenchingly depressing. The scenario above is a reflection not only of what exists now, but of what has existed for many decades, and is true at every law school. The only difference is where the drop-off starts. In a good market, Tier 1 students must *still* rank in the top 10-25%, usually, for a *top* job; the exception might be for students at a Top Five law school. But even there, the top jobs still go to the top students. Students at "lesser" schools must rank ever-higher for the same chance. In a poor market, the odds grow progressively (and steeply) worse. So, even if attending a Tier 1 or Tier 2 school, the job market has much to do with the level of success (and failure). At every law school, for a majority of students the scene described above plays out, exactly as above. Year in and year out.

It should not. Break the pattern for *your* play.

If you follow the above screenplay (and fall into even one of the above trapdoors), chances are high that you will fail. This does not mean that you will literally "fail" (usually), but you will be lucky to earn "B's," and will probably see more than you want of "C's" and even "D's." And, believe it or not, you'll have *no idea* why you earned each grade...but you will know, deep down, that you didn't really deserve a better one. I suspect that, if you're like me, a "C" is worse than failure. Even an "F" can be explained away a little less awkwardly—you were deathly ill, you were prescribed the wrong medication *and* being wheeled into the emergency room, the exam was held in the wrong city. Just try to explain away a "C."

This is a *crushing* experience for a dismaying number of highly talented, intelligent, caring individuals. An "A" might be an expectation, but law schools *strictly* limit number of "A" grades. That means that just about nine out of ten of those highly talented, intelligent, caring individuals—you and your future colleagues—

are about to experience one of the worse experiences in their lives: failure.

Break this pattern. If you sense *any* of the above happening, stop.

Stop! Something is wrong. This is not the way law school should be. It is especially not the way law school should be *for you.*

FIRST YEAR: EMOTIONS

Let's take a look at the various emotions described above—and, as this is a book about how to do well, not how to wallow in the risks—let's then take a look at how it should be.

Nervousness. This is a good emotion. Nervousness is a reaction that carries physiological and well as psychological meaning. Among other changes, a person who is nervous undergoes heightened awareness and sensitivity: it's as if life is turned all the way up. That is very much what you *should* feel as you learn the law. Most learning requires some active participation; it's not like watching television. Law requires more, because it is both substantive (rules, exceptions, and exceptions to exceptions) *and* procedural (the ways those rules fit together). So, consciously maintain the right level of nervousness. You should darned well *be* nervous. Grades *are* important—whether or not you say you care. Don't let yourself get carried way, however. When (not if) you start to go overboard, find some way to "decompress."

Try for this not to be alcohol or drugs, by the way; while they might help in the short-term, they almost certainly won't in the long-term. Better alternatives (by far) are: exercise, sports (not spectator, but actual playing of), a bit more exercise, hobbies, and still more exercise. One additional reason exercise is important—aside from the physical, emotional, and sexual benefits—is that it mirrors the process of learning the law. When one exercises, there is only one truth: whether or not it is *done*. Playing with the weights, or faking a crunch, or just going through the motions—the only one hurt is you. The result will follow—or not—based upon the effort put into it. And the number of mirrors is irrelevant; your body knows. Likewise, in the study of law, your mind knows. Be sure that it does.

Balancing your level of nervousness ties in with overall stress, which is important to control. After all, the practice of law will be filled with similar (and more impactful) episodes; better to conquer this now.

Did I mention exercise?

Stress. In much the same way, stress acts physically as well as emotionally. The key is to balance and maintain the "right" level of stress. What's right? Well, whatever's right *for you*. Some individuals respond poorly to stress, and under stress. If that's you, you will have to be especially careful, as the law does carry more than its share of stress-inducing experiences. If this is you, you should consider the stress levels in potential employers, as it is high in most law offices. As much as possible, try to build your tolerance for stress, and de-stress in ways that help in your overall health. How about exercise?

An important sub-point: stress not only has immediate effects (as if we haven't all suffered the feelings of impending doom in highly stressful situations). It has long-term effects as well. Too much stress, over too long a time frame, will eventually be seen in serious health (and mental health) side-effects. Pay attention to what your body is telling you, and moderate your stress. If you're a "Type-A" person, be *especially* sensitive to this; burning yourself out won't help, but it will burn.

Frenetic, Harried. This is the "spastic" effect that seems to infect law school and its inhabitants. It should not infect you. Inoculate yourself with a conscious effort to *slow down*. Yes, you read that correctly. Learning the law is not boosted with mere "action." Instead, get your life into order, get your health into order (exercise!), and concentrate on focused effort. You should not be harried, nor should your actions be frenetic. Think instead of Bond, James Bond: cool, collected, confident.

Multitasking, for example, is a sign of *poor* time management. Moreover, it does not work. Though you might think you're doing more, in reality you're getting less done, and what is done is done less well. Do one thing at a time, and do it well. The study of law should be focused, purposeful, concise. Not spastic.

The Most Dangerous Emotion of All

Some go into law school with a chip on their shoulder. A few have chips nearly large enough to require surgical removal. It's natural to assume that law school is a place for smart people to argue. It's also natural for really smart people to assume that they're there to "set the record straight" for everyone else.

A few points of caution are in order. First, if you have a chip on your shoulder, knock it off. It won't help you, and it almost certainly will hurt. Moreover, no one will care what you think after about, oh, your second rant. After your seventh, others will avoid you, and you will then carry that stigma with you for the rest of your career. I have seen attorneys roll their eyes when the name of another attorney with whom they happened to have the same first-year section is uttered. Needless to say, that's hardly a helpful start.

The second caution: Most professors love to rant. That's what they *really* like about the law. Not the boring, black letter law stuff, but the cutting-edge, fun, edgy stuff. Sometimes, they have a political axe to grind, and the law provides a wonderful tool for that. Sometimes it's just boredom, or the excitement of a new area.

The third caution: None of that matters, except in how you learn (1) black letter law and (2) how to use it.

I know that I'm getting monotonous, and I know that I have a disability as described above: I have deleted section after section (believe it or not) because it was too much of a distraction. These were painful deletions to make, because that's what makes the law interesting to me. I *love* these distractions. Chances are your professors do too.

Here's how to use this to your advantage. First, understand that your role as a law student is most closely analogous to that of the straight man. In comedy, the straight man is the person who sets up the joke for the comedian. The straight man gets none of the attention—and often gets laughter directed at him. But that's their role. Without the straight man there is no joke. Your professors have stories to tell, and usually want to tell them either philosophically or humorously. Let them. Do not interrupt, do not preempt, and do not distract. Whatever it was you were going to ask, don't.

Second, use the professor's version as a means to confirm your understanding of the basics. That's right...black letter law. Even if your professor has a wild interpretation, or starts with out-of-the-box cases, *they will make sense in light of black letter law*. Once you have a grasp of the general rule, fitting exceptions into that framework is easy. The important point is to make sure you know which is the general rule, and which are the exceptions. Do *not* rely on class for this. Rely on your secondary sources, instead.

Finally—and this might be the most difficult—is the issue of patience. Most students today are used to a world that is faster-paced than professors are comfortable with (or even aware of). Your professors grew up before computers, before the internet, before text messaging. While a few might have caught on, many have not. And, following one of our human traits, when pressed they don't embrace; they retreat farther away. So, try not to press your preference, assuming that that should be the preference for all. Many professors like the pace that they like, and so they'll pontificate, meander, and (if you're lucky) regale you with war stories. The question for you is practical as well as limited by patience: is the class worth your time? Not in the sense of "learning" the law, but in the sense of being able to engage in the discussion with the black letter rules you have already learned. If so, bear with your professor. If not, skip class and work on your outline, instead. No regrets, but no great fury, either.

One final note: don't be so impatient. You might find that the old fogeys actually have a thing or two to impart—both in the classroom and on the job. And, once you do get their rhythm, you'll find it far more pleasing (and productive) than the hyper-paced one of today. It's perhaps useful to realize that professors and practitioners have spun their wheels too.

A Chasm

Most professors—by temperament and job—take education quite seriously. Even those who were radicals from a long-gone era hold the basic elements of the classroom experience as sacrosanct. There is thus, seemingly, a different conception of what the classroom is all about. It's my suspicion that the divide that worsens the law school experience for many students is nearly a class (*er*, clash) of cultures: a growing gap between students and faculty in their very definition of what learning is—and ought to be.

Talk to any student and you see a person who is almost certainly overburdened. This burden is not (usually) practical, but is instead attentional: a constant drain on one's concentration. As a result of numerous factors in a highly changed and charged environment—the Information Age, instantaneous communication, and a barrage of competing messages—students today have adopted a different view, and a different set of demands. There is in addition to a shortening of attention spans an aggressive impatience. This afflicts nearly everyone...including me, such as when I get a phone call with the cryptic message "Give me a call!" My mental response is usually "Um, *no*. A, it's rude; B, it's annoying; and C, with email I hardly know how to use a phone anymore." I simply no longer have the ten minutes a call takes, and have fallen out of practice (and patience).

It's my suspicion, further, that many students view schoolwork with contempt. Initially this is because it is boring—all too often true—and eventually because it's irrelevant. There's simply not enough time. So, rather than pushing non-essential activities (video games, instant messaging) off one's plate in favor of, well, getting the work done, instead the imperatives are reversed: *classwork* becomes the distraction.

This is a broad statement, true, and certainly does not apply to all. If my own experiences in the classroom (as both student and instructor) are any indication, I suspect this is an unacknowledged sea-change. I too felt that classwork was unacceptably dull. But I didn't have one-tenth the distractions that students have nowadays (or at least the electronic distractions), and I would have relished them just as much as most do now.

I came of age as the social experiments of the 1970s were taking hold. In an effort to equalize the educational experience, the laboratory school in which I was a student was changed to an "open" classroom in which JDs (juvenile delinquents, in this case) were admitted...and managed to destroy not just the academic environment but also the fabric of the class. This was, moreover, not about socioeconomic standing, as the lab school had had a balance of "townies" along with children of faculty. Happily, we were barely aware of this distinction, then. The open-classroom experience was horrible, and I remember especially a deep sense of betrayal as teachers focused their energies on the worst among us. They had little choice, but even in retrospect it was hardly the right approach.

What happened? After more than a century in operation—and after just two years' experiment and much in-fighting—the lab school closed its doors. An educational light of great brightness was extinguished. Something similar has happened in American education. Rather than taking the best aspects of early and hugely important social constructs (compulsory and free attendance chief among them), we instead rejected much that was known to work in furthering an "enlightened" theory. As a result, educators began to focus on ensuring "success" for all students. While admirable in principle, this has two problems. The second problem—the one of importance to us—is that it cannot raise all students to an "A" level. Instead, the focus is at a different level: a "B" (inflated) or "C" (in truth). It was a race to the middle. What that meant was that the best—you—were abandoned to help the bottom reach some floor of achievement. Moreover, a traditional tracking, which became anathema in the new theory, was also neglected, resulting in the bizarre thought that to be worthy *everyone* needed to attend college. What all this meant in reality was that neither the best nor the worst—nor, in fact, the great middle—were truly helped.

Education for gifted students—never strong to begin with in a system necessarily designed for the masses and in a culture never far from anti-intellectual roots—was gutted, both pedagogically and ideologically. The curriculum *had* to be dumbed down. What this means for us is that most students in law school have spent their academic lives bored out of their minds. They've been shadow-boxing with material far beneath their potential...and boringly written, to boot. And they've received false praise nearly the whole time. The result? Most—understandably—simply tune out. It *is* boring, and mindless (literally), and if you can ace your classes without really trying, why *should* you? More to the point, how can we *not* be cynical about the classroom in such a peculiar world? And how can we not look at *class* as the distraction? In the law school world, the comparison is to case briefing: it is an attempt to get all the "children" in a row. The result is that almost no one actually stays in that row (or understands what the row was all about in the first place). A counter to the above history is seen in magnet schools for a few lucky public-school students, usually in larger cities. Many, however, have been in operation just a short while, and nearly all face uncertain if not treacherous political futures. They are thus the exceptions proving the rule.

We then add the impact of technology. Not just the many benefits that that provides, but also, apparently, a change in how we relate (and are capable of relating) to the written word. This is hardly my thinking alone, and as with other points is not meant to be disparaging. One author argues that technology is not just making things easier, it is actually changing our brains, making us less able to maintain a focus for extended periods. While we flitter from site to site, absorbing vastly higher quantities of data (often in more targeted and useful ways), at the same time we might be losing the ability to understand the broader and deeper implications of what it is we're reading—because, as with a lack of exercise, we simply *don't*.

We certainly are losing the patience of sitting still for longer. Have you seen any old movies? One aspect that is immediately noticeable is how *plodding* they are. Lasting three hours, their scenes linger and seem to stretch far too long—according to our sensibilities now. Directors today would snip an hour from an old movie without even thinking about it. It's much too soon to tell whether this is all bad (as it's likely not *all* bad), but it's almost certainly not all good either.

To borrow from a discussion in a recent Association of American Law Schools meeting:

> Today's law students, members of the "millennial generation," tend to be confident, pampered, accustomed to immediate feed-back, and not afraid to demand changes.

If that description includes you, be very, *very* careful when entering the world of law school. While some professors will be sympathetic, every descriptive term above is a potential landmine. Even if you do prepare, no law student should be confident—that is practically begging the fates for a comeuppance, and I knew many confident souls who all but melted away after grades came out. Pampered? Not in law school. Immediate feedback? How about a month or so after the end of your first year? And as for changes, while the changes in law school *have* been noticeable, they are more a result of pressures on the institutional side—and they've hardly been swift.

What does this mean for us in law school? More importantly, what might this mean for how to do law school right? This might well be yet another double-edged sword. As I repeat, ah, repeatedly, one should be both intense and efficient in law school. So, when I write that one shouldn't read cases for five hours, I'm quite aware that few students still actually do this; most stop long before then. But the result won't matter. What *will* matter is that many students today aren't replacing the bad old ways with anything better. So, there's cynicism built upon cynicism. It's important to separate the qualities that any good student has with habits that are maladaptive in law school. The reality is that most undergraduate students can all but ignore every serious aspect of their education...and still survive. Perhaps not straight A's, but survive. Worse, several generations of countercultural influences have led to a situation in which at least some students are substantively underprepared as well as temperamentally ill-disposed to law school.

The answer? Use these many tools, of course. But be mindful as well of your own impatience. Your professors will almost certainly not change their habits, nor their expectations on exams. That's what it's all about in law school. All of the above reinforces the need to stay *ahead*...by one day. This is done by a methodical approach that is precise—both in terms of not jumping about, and in terms of staying on target. You must prepare prior to every class, and not stray sideways or forwards (and certainly not behind). Preparation is refining *that day's* section of your outline, which incorporates a *brief* study of the cases. This isn't hard (or, more correctly, it's not horrifically hard)...but it does take discipline.

HOW TO READ THE LAW

Several law school books speak of "reading loads," making the task of reading sound very much like drudgery: x hours per day, y days per week, plus z extra on weekends. Well, if that's the approach, it will be.

Your approach should be different: reading the law can and should be *engaging*. Note, this isn't necessarily "fun," but it should be interesting, and it should *connect* with you. With the right context and the right approach, reading the law will not be drudgery, and will not be exhausting. With the right context and the right approach, reading the law *will* be enlightening, and even satisfying. It will be the difference between a chore—which, almost by definition, causes clocks to slow to near-interminable speed—and a hobby that you actually enjoy. You can and should look forward to time when you get to study. How wonderful would that be: three years of your life devoted to something you actually enjoy—that you find intellectually and even viscerally stimulating. Like a job, but better.

Setting the scene as you get started—so that the study of law answers questions of interest to you *and* starts to expand what it is you find interesting—is akin to making your "job" of learning law more like a hobby. This is (or should be) the holy grail of one's life: finding something you like, getting good at it, and finding a way to make a living doing it. In the law, this can be a very good living. But this is not a static challenge: a hobby is simply something we like doing. Usually it's something we do after we finish doing what we *have* to do...and *don't* much like doing. Much of liking something is a matter of whether we *want* to like it. Thus, if you're treating law study like a chore, it will be. If, instead, you're approaching it more as a series of quests—answers to interesting questions *that you get to pose*—then it will be interesting, if not downright fun.

Paradoxically, this will take less time than the boring, plodding, all-too-common approach takes. Yes, it will still take time, and study, and energy—but the results are almost certain to be better if you *like* what you're doing. That's part of the task of this book.

It's important to put your hours of study into context. Many students treat study as an extension of some grueling, macho gantlet. Again, if you take this approach, it will be. But you won't get credit for it. Instead you'll be stuck with the worst of both worlds: studying like mad, and *getting* mad. And you'll get less and less out of it—including, quite possibly, grades lower than you have ever seen in your life.

While we're on grades, it's important to keep these in context as well. It's easy for law students to become fixated on this, leading to an upside-down frenzy that ends up being ultimately disastrous: for many students, the crash of a "C" (or of several "C's") hits *very* hard. And it's equally hard to convey to a group of new students, such as you will be a part of, before the reality of the forced law school grade curve. But I and many others have seen our friends suffer this fate. Don't let this happen to you.

In a corollary, many students assume that time in-seat (or eyes in-casebooks) equals knowledge. Or equals, in the context of feel-good education, something-that-should-be-rewarded-just-because. In law school, there is no extra credit just-because. Don't mistake the symptom for the disease. To do well in law school is to *learn the law,* well, and to learn how to *apply* that law. Mastering these two elements—the substance of the law plus the "procedure" of how to apply it—will boost your exam results. But that result only follows a regimen of actually learning the law and actually learning how to apply it. More on both points, later. In fact, you'll probably get sick of my repetition. In the meantime, it's important to separate yourself from what worked before. Law school is not college. And law school adds an important additional burden: the requirement that you be able to *prove it.* Not just knowing something well enough to say so on an exam, but knowing it well enough to know how to *use* it.

The challenge is twofold: to learn the law, well, and to learn how to apply what you have learned. In a sense, the essence of law school—stated and implied—is what "education" is supposed to be: not to learn a specific subject, but rather *to learn how to learn.* What we think of now as "education"—sit in class, take notes, regurgitate, graduate, get job—is not education at all. Or, at least, that's not what it's supposed to be. But, reality is reality, and most of us are concerned about real-world needs of career and debt, rather than fulfilling the assumptions of academic curmudgeons.

I will add a third challenge: to accomplish the above two tasks with less effort. Maximum results with a minimum of exertion—not laziness, but an ever-finer skill that *seems* effortless—such as when you might see a professor or senior partner discuss a legal issue. It will seem almost as if they're able to toss out answers with only micro-seconds of thought. The trick it that it's not effortless, but it's seen that way by those who thrash about, hopelessly squandering precious time with wasteful and useless study habits.

As you get started, it might not be as smooth for you as it will be later. That's okay. The challenge is to force yourself not to fall for what has worked before—because it won't work in law school. Period. Etch this in your mind: *what worked before will not work now*. Be focused, instead, on what it means to learn the law, what it means to learn the law well, what it means to apply the law…and how this can all be done with an intense efficiency that absolutely rejects a wasting of your time. That is your goal.

EFFICIENCY VERSUS LAZINESS

The classroom today is filled with many distractions. How many of us are actually cross-checking references during a lecture—rather than emailing a friend or scanning the latest blog on the club scene? How many of us actually *learn* when we sit there thinking about the latest blog on the club scene?

If you want to do well, you must force yourself not to be distracted. Most of us would prefer to do what we *want* to do, not what we *have* to. This is human nature. There is a difference, however, between being efficient—using one's time well—and being lazy. Okay, that sounds like something one might expect to hear at some chirpy seminar. The real problem isn't the statement—*"Efficient, Not Lazy. Check."*—it's the reality. Efficiency is hard; laziness is not only easy, it's seductively easy.

Efficiency is hard? Well, it's not hard in the doing. It's hard in the *not* doing. It's hard to stay focused. It's *hard* to challenge one's habits and unquestioned beliefs—especially about what has worked before.

Laziness is easy? Well, yeah. That's the point. But it's more than just not doing anything. Actually, that kind of laziness—

deciding, say, to see a movie instead of working—can be a good thing. In moderation. No, what's worse is a laziness of mind. This is a laziness that refuses to be challenged. Part of the challenge of this book is that I will attempt to persuade you that nearly every technique that has served you so well before will not work in law school. If you stick with what is "tried and true," you will in the end be fried and blue.

Actually, I will argue more than this. I will go further to say that the "techniques" that are used by *all* students in college (and before) are generally ineffective. They have been effective *for you* only because your competition has been so relatively light. Not to be too blunt, but it was never a fair fight; you were always going to win. In short, there was a ready supply of folks lower than you in the classroom curve—very helpful in lifting *your* academic boat. Not anymore. Welcome to law school, where *everyone* is the academic star...and always has been. So, being unwilling to question long-held assumptions about how you have studied in the past is being a worse kind of lazy.

You're either insulted at this point or you're silently saying, "*Yeah, yeah...*" The problem is that, even with every book out there repeating some version of the story that law school is somehow different, it's very, very hard to break the cycle. In a sense, laziness is the reverse of the efficiency question. It is lazy to simply do what we *want* to do. And what we want to do is nearly always the easy way. Part of the easy way is not to challenge ourselves—whether that's in actually working hard, or in working *differently*. Most of us have worked hard; few have worked differently. The object of this book is to show you how you can learn the law, well, in less time. In other words: the maximum amount of learning with the least amount of wasted effort.

It's easy to mistake that, however, for the promise of, say, great grades with no work. Even if I had a magic wand, for this assignment it wouldn't work. It is natural to want accolades, admiration, great grades, a great job, a great car, you name it. But that will not happen if you are not efficient. It certainly will not happen if you are lazy.

While understandable, in the law school context laziness takes a few forms: (1) burnout; (2) genuine laziness; (3) both.

If you are inefficient, you will burn out. And you will at some point decide to give up. You might not give up entirely...and in fact you probably will hang in there, which will almost be worse. But all those dreams of the great grades, great job, etc. will be replaced by a desire simply to make it to graduation. A devastating psychology takes over at that point. After all, you were one of the academic stars. Everyone said so. Everyone at home still thinks so. But you know better—and you confront humiliation (real and perceived) every day in law school. And so you hide. From them, and from yourself. And you begin to hate law school, your classmates, and anything remotely connected to either. This, of course, is hardly a healthy approach. To exams, the profession, or life.

Genuine laziness is a bit harder—and easier—to deal with. It's easier because, if you *are* lazy, there's little that can be done about it. Unless *you* want to change. Chances are—unless dad's a sitting justice or mom's a senior partner—chances are you will not do well. Not doing super-well might in fact be your goal, in which case you will likely meet it.

We all have lazy tendencies. I certainly do. But there's a difference between knowing one's tendencies and acting upon them. Or, in this case, not acting at all.

The answer is in eliminating make-work. Case briefs, for example, are makework. They do little to help you learn the law in the way you need to learn it, and they take a *lot* of time. The cost-benefit is simply too high. Arguably it's near infinity, despite the "conventional wisdom" that that's how the law should be learned.

The answer, equally, is in accepting—honestly—that even without all the make-work there is still a *lot* of work to do. Outlines are part of that work. So are hypotheticals, and team work, and practice exam upon practice exam.

Briefing cases is foolish. Thus, not wasting time briefing cases is efficient. Reading casebooks cover-to-cover is foolish, as is reading hornbooks. Thus, not wasting hours reading casebooks or hornbooks is good. It's efficient. Saving just one hour by not doing one of those things frees that hour up for something that *will* help.

Preparing an outline, on the other hand, is *essential*. Thus, "dividing" outlines among a study group, while seductive in seemingly saving time (and, according to conventional wisdom, the very reason for a study group), is not smart. It is merely lazy. Even if it does save time, the cost to you is far higher. It is almost impossible to do well on a first-year law exam without having done your own outline. *You must do your own outline for each course.* In fact, as I'll show, you'll need to do two.

Efficiency, or a desire to do the minimum amount of work to achieve a result, is not laziness. Please keep this distinction in mind as you decide what to spend your time on. Don't be lazy. If you are, you will almost certainly fail. Don't be inefficient. If you are, you will almost certainly fail—or at least you will do much less well than you could. To restate, the objective is, or should be, *the maximum amount of learning with the least amount of wasted effort.* That is the path to riches, and to personal satisfaction.

That is our path.

SETTING THE STAGE: THE RIGHT ATTITUDE

You will find that everyone in the office—whichever office you happen to be in, whether at the Registrar, with a professor, or in a law office—*everyone* has abilities, desires, motives. They might, in fact, have abilities, desires, and motives stronger and better than yours. Even if not, chances are good that they want to—or are willing to—contribute to your cause. Let them. That someone might be twenty-six or sixty-two. The challenge for any effective attorney is, first, to understand that, and second, to maneuver through. Or, perhaps more correctly, to maneuver *with*.

Some will rebel against this, saying, in essence, "No way! It should be about *substance!*"

Well, perhaps it should. But it's not. That's simply not life, and many, many have rebelled against this, for thousands of years. Nearly all fail...if they don't "get it" in time.

Or, some might rebel, saying, in essence, "No way! I betcha' I can sneak *my* way past!"

Well, yes, you might. But it's not likely. Most of those you will ever deal with in life—professors, bosses, judges, clerks—are willing to give *you* the benefit of the doubt. Let them. Be courteous, enthused, positive, decent. What you should want is to make it in their interest to say "Golly, I sure wish we had more folks like [fill in your name] around here!"

Make it *easy* for them. Most want to help. Really. Even the harshest of bosses—in their own minds—simply want competence. (See the first statement, above, about "No way!") When they find it—however they define it—they'll almost certainly reward it. Why? *Because it is in their own interest to do so.*

Help others to make it in *their* interest to help you.

How?

At this stage, one way you do this—if not *the* way—is to excel. That excellence centers on law school: learning the law in such a way that you approach mastery.

This is not empty rhetoric. Many years ago, I heard a fellow law student discussing a section of the UCC. She commented something to the effect that "Section 2-xxx *can't* mean that, because there are only two sub-sections." This blew me away. I wouldn't have known Section 2-xxx well enough to have restated how many subsections were there even had the dean threatened me with expulsion on the spot.

But there's more. It's not about memorizing Section 2-xxx of the Uniform Commercial Code, or about any section of any statute. Rather, it's about falling in love with the law. I'm serious. This is something that happened to me *after* law school, believe it or not. I moved from Austin to Honolulu a few days after my last exam. In a rainstorm, actually, slogging six enormous suitcases through several hundred feet of mud as we couldn't afford a mover. I started work at the law firm the next week, and the bar review course the week after. It was, as they say, an interesting time.

The bar review course—which happened to be by BAR/BRI— was held in the evenings, four hours a night. Subject after subject, in a rapid-fire, condensed format that encapsulated all that we had learned—and much that we had not—over dozens of hours for each of eighteen subjects. I loved it. It brought all of law school together for me, and legal concepts that seemed obtuse suddenly seemed like common sense. I remembered shaking my head, wondering why I hadn't gotten it that well before. It seemed that I had lucked out with my best grades—how had I fooled them?

Call me weird, but I actually enjoyed the bar exam too. It was suddenly a chance to play with the law, and each essay seemed, well, interesting. The Hawaii bar exam was then three days, plus a day for the MBE, or Multistate Bar Examination. So, for four days I was getting paid to play. Told you I was weird.

One episode captures this. At the end of the fourth day, a partner and senior associate picked up another of the firm's new associates who was also taking the bar exam. I suppose they couldn't very well leave me there, so they brought me along. As I'd not shaved in two or three days, I can only imagine their debate after an exchanged glance: "Do we *have* to invite him?"

During lunch the senior associate posed a question that he had been researching all morning. It involved a question of commercial paper (*i.e.,* a promise to pay, such as with a personal check). Despite my dreadful sight—which brings to mind a phrase common in the military: *There's never a time you're not being observed*— I answered: "So when is your client going to cut another check?"

The partner immediately got it, and chuckled. The senior associate did not, and proceeded to go into the case. The answer was that, under commercial paper doctrines, all that he had investigated that morning was irrelevant; in commercial paper a promise to pay is a promise to pay. As I reeled off the tests we had studied for two months, I was nervous that I wouldn't get all the prongs right, then relieved when I did, then happy. My first real test! Fifteen seconds and I had *nailed* the answer to research he had spent all morning on. It felt *good*. Even so, my imprudent—and impudent—conversational approach was inappropriate. Not surprisingly, I never got along well with that senior associate, who became a partner not long thereafter. Beware. It is *not* just about substance. Moreover, there might well have been other ways to serve the client's interest; so my "answer" might not have been the right answer after all.

The woman I mentioned above, by the way—the one who commented in law school about UCC Section so-and-so—was an art history major. Quiet, and exceptionally nice. She earned the highest grades in our section, and was at the top of our Texas-sized class of 540 souls. That's where you should be. Not just the top rank (although that's nice too), but in a *mastery* of the basic elements of the law. Before it's tested. Law school should be fun without being frivolous. It should be engaging without being about mental one-upmanship. It should be challenging, without being cutthroat. It should be you.

You should be able to say (or at least whisper), "I *am* the law!"

A VIEW FROM THE FRONT

Professors are people too. This might seem a bit silly to write, but it's a point that most law students tend to ignore…to their peril.

Most law professors are nothing like the monsters we see and read about. Most are decent, earnest individuals who truly wish to do a good job in imparting the law. A notable minority views students as pests…a necessary evil for their "real" job: thinking about the law. Nearly all are exceedingly intelligent, and, despite having (usually) little or no practical experience, really do know the law. So it should go without saying that the gulf between their ability and knowledge and students' pre-ability and lack of knowledge in the law is cause for anxiety, at least. It is also, for professors, cause for frustration. Many are at a loss as to just why students are so flummoxed. The minority of professors who don't care, well, don't care.

Law professors are not blank slates, waiting to cheerfully pour knowledge into roomfuls of dutiful students. They see their role quite differently. A healthy percentage are left-of-center—much has been written on this, of course—and a notable percentage are extremely so. A relatively smaller percentage, even in supposedly Establishment-minded law schools, are right-of-center; a smaller percentage still are reactionary. This is important because the essence for many of these law professors is a critique of the structures of the law—the very structures you are expected to learn (and *must* learn, to do well). Ideology aside, law professors see their role as more than mere teaching. They recoil at the very notion of "education" as it has come to be in undergraduate studies. They are, in their minds, facilitating your growth into a mind capable of dissecting fact patterns and arriving at coherent, cohesive legal analysis. This requires something far more—and far different—than you have ever known before.

There is something else. Being nice, and extremely smart, and desiring of affection as much as respect, law professors hope to engage in a mythical battle of wits among equals. They expect to win, of course, but what they hope for—really!—is a contest in which the other side (you) is able to respond intelligently, and to *contribute* to the discussion. Sure, a few are less kind, and enjoy seeing you squirm. These are by now very much the exception, thankfully.

Where this comes into play is that many students come to law school expecting to voice their opinions, or expecting to be spoon-fed. Neither will be the case, and while common both are highly frustrating to your professors. Worse still are the students who expect to fake their way through. How will your professors respond? Chances are it won't be in the classroom. Because of the ubiquity and power of end-of-course surveys and a general need to be liked, few law professors will make a scene in class. Where their real thoughts will play out is a place far more dangerous to you: on exams.

What happens—regardless of what actually occurs in the class-room—is that only a small percentage learns the law sufficiently well (including an ability to use it) to write an "A" exam. What then happens is that, as soon as a law professor reads such an exam, what they see is a *lawyer* jumping off the page, not a student bumbling through facts and bits of the law.

The reality is that—on an absolute scale of legal knowledge and analysis—only 10% of exams *deserve* an "A"; from your profes-sor's perspective, most of the rest deserve a "D" or an "F." On an absolute scale, they are simply legal dreck; a law firm partner would concur by tossing them unceremoniously in the trash. Well, that's not quite right: they would ceremoniously hold their fingers high—as well as their nose—while looking you straight in the eyes and releasing the pages to the trash bin. That would likely be the end of the meeting—and almost as likely, your career. I'm not being all that facetious, by the way.

Your professors are equally slaves to the forced curve, however, and so a range of "B's" and "C's" are given. The point of this book is to show why this is the case, and why and how it should not be, for you.

There's yet another issue for professors. Law school is not about *changing* the law. Professors *love* to think about this—there's probably not a professor alive who doesn't think the world would be a better place if only legislators would listen. And so, they love to discuss these thoughts in class. It's fun! But it's crucial to understand that, at best, classroom discussions are "armchair legislating" and "armchair judging." Crucially, what is tested on the exam will bear almost no resemblance to any of these lofty discussions in class. At most, they will be the thin layer of tasty icing on the cake that decides who gets #1 and who gets #2. Still fun, and still important...but only *after* the basics are *mastered*. That is what is missing for most law students.

There's yet one more danger, in three varieties.

First is the "mechanical" student—the one who seems endlessly concerned about utterly boring and inconsequential aspects of cases and the law generally. These are the students who used to ask "How many questions will be on the test?" and "Will *this* be tested?" Most professors respond politely, but behind their smiles inside they're annoyed...and after a while, they start to seethe. "Dammit, can't these students *care* about *the law?!*"

(To answer the question, yes, it will be on the test.)

Second are the bored students—those whose heads are nearly falling onto their desks for lack of sleep, perhaps with a string of drool descending ever so steadily onto their laptops (...leading neighbors to fear the impending sparks). Others seem in a trance from playing too much solitaire. Still others are seemingly deep in dialogue with instant-message buddies, busily typing away with no apparent connection to the classroom discussion. Yet more are searching for the latest charm bracelets, or, well, just about anything but what they're in class nominally to do. Your professor's thoughts? Same as above. And yes, professors *do* notice. They're not stupid...or blind.

Finally are the disrespectful ones. These can be students who are simply argumentative without being thoughtful, or perhaps who are quasi-autistically unaware of how inappropriate their interpersonal relations are (in a room full of future colleagues, no less). Others can have a personal axe to grind, and quite frankly don't care what the professor (or others) have to say. These can be the worst of all. It's not just a disrespect of the person (although that's hardly good training for a career in *any* law office) as much as it is a disrespect of *the law*.

Don't expect your professors not to care.

I'll recount two episodes that come to mind: In business law classes I like to start with the (in)famous McDonald's hot coffee case as a way to connect with something students have likely heard of and as a way to explore the importance of precedent, tort law, tort reform, procedure, punitive damages, media practice, and the broader impacts on how businesses respond to (and should respond to) risk. The progression is nearly always the same: a number of students have heard of the case, and nearly everyone "remembers" how utterly ridiculous it was. (The plaintiff was awarded $2.86 million dollars after having spilled coffee on herself.) The very mention of the case is an invitation to ridicule—having spawned numerous late-night jokes—and so those who've not heard of it join in the exasperated disbelief at our legal system run amok.

From the front of the room, this is enjoyable. This is because we know—we're directing—what comes next. What we want to see is not to make anyone look foolish, or embarrassed, or angry. Quite the opposite. We want to see light bulbs go off—new and enlightened ways to think not only of that case but also of *all* cases. In the end we content ourselves to think that if just a few students "get it," it's worth it.

What happens in class is that we then go through the case, fact by fact. That takes perhaps twenty minutes. What seemed a ridiculous case becomes, in fact, an example of a horrendously callous decision that caused grievous harm far out of proportion to the assumed risk. The jury—filled with people just like those in the classroom—was furious at McDonalds' *gross* negligence and thus insisted on punishing it in the only way a corporation understands. In the end, most students are not just in agreement with the verdict (which was automatically reduced by the plaintiff's comparative negligence and further reduced by the judge as a general limitation of the punitive damages)—most want more.

Why? *Because the facts matter.*

This is the essence of law school—because it is the essence of the law. And this is what law professors hope *you* grow to enjoy.

On occasion class does not go according to plan—usually for a disrespect of the facts—and two classes in particular come to mind. In the first occurrence, weeks after having gone through the exercise and seeming to have solidly made the connection in students' minds, a student who had been active in the original discussion and who seemed to "get it" made a comment showing that he had completely discounted the entire discussion. I would have had no problem had he given the slightest credence to the facts, or had he distinguished the case we were then discussing, or given *some* indication of thought; but, in essence, he did the opposite. In an instant I was flooded with the realization that cognitive dissonance is our destiny. ("Cognitive dissonance" is the psychological state when a person realizes that something believed to be true is, in fact, *not* true. In short, we often choose to reject information that does not fit within our preconceived notions of "truth," rather than suffer a change in our beliefs.)

It was a humbling and depressing moment, because it told me that even the significant classroom time spent going through facts of the case, point by point and seemingly to good effect, was rendered futile. In essence, learning—for this student at least—was dead.

In the second class, some years later, a student flat-out did not care about the facts. At least he had the decency to disagree up front. But his disagreement was not rational. He simply disagreed. And that was that. This is the type of "argument" that is guaranteed to fail a law student ("fail" as in an "F"); what is important is not the answer, but the reason. This student didn't care about the reason, only the answer. *His* answer

In approaching the "dispute" as a genuine hypothetical—as is the model for classroom discussions in law school—I adopted whatever facts he presented as (in his mind) clear proof of how absurd the case and law were. No matter how many times he was pushed onto the limb until it broke, he simply refused to accept even the slightest possibility that McDonald's had in fact done wrong.

Chances are good that if you read about the McDonald's hot coffee case, including an in-depth review of the facts—which takes just a few minutes, by the way—and if you have the slightest change of reaction at the end of reading those facts, you will do quite well in law school.

In essence, he disagreed with the very concept of legal liability as it applies to a broad spectrum of business law. He also failed to appreciate that individual cases do not stand alone: they are built on legal principles and rules that must be consistently applied across fact patterns, even when occasional outcomes appear undesirable. If they're consistently undesirable, we then modify the rule, or create an exception to that rule. Moreover, a fair reading of the facts in *this* case should have led him to question his prejudices.

The most arch-conservative of justices would have a hard time with such an extreme position—and would at least do the courtesy of hearing the case. More than that, such a person accomplished in the law would recoil at a refusal to care. So will your professors. While it seems that law school is about "the law," in truth law school is about the law *in light of fact patterns*. These hypotheticals are more than mere tools. They are the essence of legal thinking. Change one fact, and the analysis (and answer) might well change. From the front of the classroom, this is both the central importance of law school...and the fun part.

Why is this important to you—aside from the obvious interest in doing well? Because, after a few rounds of such classroom interactions, your professors are likely to get jaded. The same thing happens among senior partners in practice, by the way. They reach a new equilibrium, in which they come to understand that a certain percentage of law students "get it," and the rest do not. The danger is that it's quite easy to equate the 10% who get it in exam terms—an ability to think through an essay's fact pattern and write a cogent legal analysis—with 10% who are worthy of getting it.

In reality, the percentages are inverted. 10% of students really *don't* get it...not because they cannot but because they will not. Of the other 90%, the vast majority are simply lost: the disconnect between how law school is and how law students understandably (but wrongly) react all but condemns them to the bottom half.

You should enjoy classroom discussions for the value they add—an exploration of fact patterns very much relevant to law exams—and for the connection they provide between the theory and practice of law. And you should seek the same equilibrium your best professors enjoy: these *are* fun. But as will be shown, this equilibrium is possible only after you have mastered the basics— *before* class—which will not happen if you follow the crowd.

Professors are neither out to get you, nor are they your best friends. They *are* there to help you learn to apply the law that you must learn before class. Give them the respect they deserve, and do your part. The respect comes in appreciating what they offer, what they can relay, and how they wish to relay it (*i.e.,* via a classroom hypothetical, in which, yes, the facts matter); "your part" comes in learning enough before class to be able to appreciate why.

BEING COMMITTED

Several books on law school speak of the importance of being committed to law school. One book out there takes almost the opposite tack, saying in essence that if you're too committed you'll *be* committed (...presumably to an institution even more structured than law school).

On the "commit" side, one book speaks of "[n]ights, weekends, and holidays...sacrificed to the cause."

Nonsense.

It is not only possible to learn the law without killing yourself, you can learn the law *better* with a more-focused, more business-like approach. This translates into less time—although it will still take a considered, serious effort. The law is not a sprint—and no one can successfully devote nights, weekends, and holidays for nine *months*. That's not smart; it's foolish. Even that's being too kind. It's downright *stupid*. The difference? The author of that advice should darned well have known better. It's fine to take a little literary license, but not when readers are relying on one's word.

If you take this approach you will burn out long before you get to the finals, and you'll realize (too late) that much of the time you spent was wasted. An *attorney* who needs to learn the law cannot spend weeks—much less, months—learning a new area. Yes, they already know the general doctrines of law into which the specific legal area will fall, but the analogy holds: you need not and cannot spend so much time "learning" the law. Your efforts should be— no, *must* be—highly focused and highly productive.

Greater learning with less effort. This too takes commitment, but of a different kind. *Planet Law School* lays out a detailed plan for study. This is much closer to the mark, although the risk is that many students who see that will either gasp in horror (and walk away) or spin their wheels. Its author warns against this, of course, but it's simply too seductive. You've always been successful cramming, so why stop now? So, you'll do some things, let others slide, and wind up—along with your classmates—in the same miserable, leaky boat.

If this happens, you will almost certainly fail. I don't mean literally, and I don't mean to be rude. But it is the truth. "Failure" is relative, and chances are that you, along with most of your colleagues, consider a "B" as a failure. Well, with the forced curve, you might find yourself with more than one "C" or even "D" or "F" if you take either of the above approaches. To be on campus after grades are out is to see a sizeable group of walking wounded—academic stars who, for the first time in their lives, are no longer even above-average, much less stars. Along with their crushed egos, they face the almost-worse realization that they might not get the great law job they were counting on—or even *any* law job.

It's hard to convey just how strict the forced curve is in law school—and how much of an impact this will have on you. As much as I hate to keep drawing on the University of Texas as the example, that's as good a law school as any.

In educational theory, assessment involves some scale of comparison: either Student A against Student B, or correct answers against incorrect ones. As we think in a base of 10, the most easily identifiable assessment scale is xx out of 100. Odd systems are thus more useful when converted to a base of ten. For example, the LSAT scale of 120-180 converted to percentiles—from *per centum,* or "out of one hundred"—so that admissions officers know so-and-so is in the ninety-eighth percentile, or just below the top one percent and above the bottom ninety-eight percent.

The University of Texas Law School, circa the late 1980s, managed to insult every one of its students with a scale of 55-91. This is not a joke. Aside from being, *prima facie,* an affront, it set students at a disadvantage relative to other students (despite protestations that firms would keep in mind the relative scales), and served to keep most students morose.

The median was a fraction above a 73. Not just that, but the curve was strict. The vaunted "top 10%"? That was an 82.5. Think about that: a grade law students would just about kill for would, in any other academic universe, be a "B-." Most students had grades in the 70s—the *low* 70s. It's not too hard to imagine how hard this was for nearly all students to get their minds (and hearts) around.

The scale was changed in 1990-1991 to an "A–F" scale. As a final insult, the new transcript incorrectly reports the earlier scale as "0–100," not "55–91," leading anyone to reasonably assume that an 82.5 on the front of the transcript is in fact equal to a "B-."

No matter. Regardless of the scale and in any law school, the forced curve *is* the reality. It's a reality that hits the *majority* of students hard. Very hard.

There are a number of ways to avoid this fate. And, no, they don't all revolve around being in the "top ten percent" (a phrase that will become almost monotonous in law school). While that certainly is a solution, by mathematical truism it is hardly guaranteed. So, part of your approach should be to (1) decide where you want to be, knowing what that entails; (2) maintain a focus in getting there (and an equally important focus not to get distracted); and (3) plan for alternatives. As to number three, this is not defeatism, but rather a means to land on your feet no matter what, and to accept that you might eventually decide that you want something different after all.

This happens in both directions, by the way. Some of the "best" students decide they don't really want to take that high-powered, high-paying job—while nearly everyone else would just about kill for that same job. Unfortunately, in both directions law students feel trapped, constrained to do something they don't want to do. So, part of our task is to put you in exactly the position *you* want to be in—whether or not that's what you want right now. This is much harder and trickier (as it's done by most now), but, paradoxically, is easier (as it should be done). Discipline is key, but not in the sense that most use it. Rather, it's the discipline to stay current and not to succumb to bad habits.

THE BUSINESS OF STUDYING LAW

So, you must commit yourself to the study of law. Check.

Well, that certainly doesn't *sound* very helpful. Kinda' like "Brush your teeth," "Don't forget to wear clean underwear," and oh by the way, "Be sure to do well in law school."

To say that you must commit yourself is not to say that you should simply work hard. That, in fact, is the beginning of where many law students go wrong. Nor is it to say that you should search for the secret to success. That is the not-so-secret desire of just about everyone. And, when exams come along, exam-takers realize that they either have it or they do not. And, when exams come along, if they don't have it, it's too late to get it.

Your commitment, thus, must be to *get it*. But this too is too broad. You must get it in terms of black letter law, and you must get it in terms of applying that law to fact patterns—*hypotheticals*—because your professor can and will constantly change the facts to get you to think about the legal consequence of that change. Thus, these ever-changing facts are "hypothetical"—and crucial to your analysis of the law.

Yet another part of the commitment is an equally important commitment not to waste time on anything that doesn't (1) help you to learn black better law; (2) help you learn how to apply it; or (3) help you to be a good person. Number three is not a joke: you should not only strive to be better than you were (or could devolve to), you should consciously seek balance. This is in cooperation, laughter, fun, play, and sometimes doing nothing at all. These are not just okay, they're a necessary part of studying well. All of these should be directed to maintaining a sense of balance, and to being a good person.

Your commitment should be *manageable*. This means that you should consciously and steadfastly force an *efficiency* to your study. Some of this efficiency will come from this book. Much will come from forcing yourself not to spend too much time on any task. You must, in short, take a business-like approach.

What is a "business-like" approach? Well, anyone with at least a few years' experience in business knows that the 40-hour work-week is now a pleasant fiction for most exempt employees. "Exempt" refers to an exemption from the rules for most employees under the FLSA, or Fair Labor Standards Act. In essence, an exempt employee is on the management side of the labor-management divide. This includes professionals and, of course, lawyers. Exempt employees are now expected to work 50-60 hours per week or more, often perpetually on-call and with no real time off when it comes to thinking about work. Indeed, that might be the real definition of being exempt: when you can't *not* take your work home with you.

In many law firms, new associates are expected to spend 70-80 hours per week just to meet expectations. For reasons I'll explain, this can be a dangerous assumption as you're getting started. And not only is it not necessary in law school, unlike what everyone else seems to assume, striving for an hourly martyrdom will actually hurt you. Your health will suffer (both physical and mental), and you simply won't learn the law as well. So, what's a good assumption for us?

Sixty hours per week.

This is your new job. And it's definitely exempt. This includes time spent in class; that's part of your new job. Like a job, it doesn't include time spent getting to, near, or in-between class. Okay, you can include time commuting, as you can use that time to listen to law CDs, running through hypos in your mind—watch out for that car there changing lanes!—or simply to think about the law. In essence, you agree to devote a full-time, *real* job learning the law. To restate, this is not a nights-weekends-holidays "sacrifice"; it's a deliberate, serious commitment *to learn the law*.

If classes take, say, 15 hours per week, that means that your study time is 45 hours per week. Is that reasonable? I hope so. Again, that 60-hour workweek will be on the light side compared to your first job in a firm. And, believe it or not, that's the traditional 3:1 study-to-class rule for undergraduate studies.

Looked at a different way, if you keep a healthy sleep pattern (as you should), a 60-hour week will leave you with 52 hours for entertainment, laundry, socializing, or doing nothing at all. Thus, a bit more than half of your waking hours are spent on and in the law. Fair?

This leads to the second reason that it's better to shoot for 60 hours per week, rather than, say 80 hours: You need to get efficient. In a firm requiring new associates to bill, say, 2,500 hours per year (which will take you 70 or even 80 hours per week, week in and week out, to achieve), there are those who get there efficiently, and those who do not. The ones who do not fall into two categories: those who technically make the number but who burn themselves out doing so, and those who simply fall away. Either way, the threshold in larger firms is only possible in the long run with an efficient approach; chances are high that the ones who don't become efficient in law school will not make it in a law firm. Indeed, this is another reason firms seek top-10%/law review students: they assume, correctly, that grades are a reflection of efficiency as well as quality.

As with anything, there's a "mission creep" aspect to billable hours: the expectations seem to climb ever-higher. And often it's an informal rather than formal expectation. Also, the distance from real to billable hours is not one-for-one: it takes more of the former to equal one of the latter. But there *is* a difference. Some get there faster, and better. Even for those who *want* to make it, a "billable machine" approach simply doesn't work. 80 hours per week is equal to 14 hours per day, Monday through Friday, plus 10 hours on the weekend. Adjusting for Friday nights, that's Monday through Thursday from 9:00 a.m. to 11:00 p.m., every night. Friday from 9:00 a.m. to 9:00 p.m., every week. Saturday 10:00 a.m. to 10:00 p.m., every weekend.

That's *crazy*.

This is serious. And it's also regularly misconstrued. Even senior partners—whose income is at least partly based on the total volume of billable hours for clients under their purview—are looking for those who can do their work efficiently. They're looking for more than the mere "workhorse" associate. They want a smart one, too. They know better than anyone that such an extreme worklife is simply not sustainable. Indeed, this is one of the greatest dangers of the law school myths: everyone in law school seems to "know" what they don't really know. Yes, firms expect a lot. But, despite mountains written and said about billable hours (more, more, more!), law firms are about *quality* first of all. Such quality does not come from walking zombies.

You must thus get *efficient*.

So, part of your approach in the study of law is to do more with less. The "do more" part is the learning of the law—not just a superficial "Yeah, the rule is *x*" but a deeper "The majority rule is *x*, but there's been a trend toward *y*, and with the *Restatement* reasoning, the majority rule is likely to become *y* with a little *z* twist." Whether it actually becomes *y* with a little *z* twist is irrelevant; you know *x*, you know *y*, and you predict *z*—and you know *why* it's *x*, *y*, and *z*.

The knowing is the first step in thinking like a lawyer. You must know black letter law *in your bones*. And, as with our gestation, you have nine months.

The "...with less" part is *time*. You should devote a substantial time—60 hours per week—but you should not allow it to consume you. Not 70 hours to get a "jump start." Not 75 to really show 'em. Sixty hours. No less, no more.

This is true even if you do love the law: once you know the law, *then* you can be consumed by it (which still won't be too good for you, as a person). In this, you agree to be committed, but to a moderated, achievable, *sustainable* level.

Moreover—and here's where the commitment really comes in—you must be committed *when you study*. Five hours spent "reading" cases is five hours wasted. And they won't be five pleasurable hours. Chances are, after even thirty minutes you'll have no idea what you just read. You almost certainly will not be able to restate it. Etch this into your mind: never spend *hours* reading cases. Never, never, *never*. That is a colossal waste of time. And it is a colossal waste of time that precedes a colossal failure. If you waste your time in this utterly foolish way, you *will* fail.

Try instead a different reality:

Five *minutes* spent confirming a rule, another five minutes finding the part of the case at hand on point (*i.e.*, the part that focuses on that rule), five minutes getting a sense of the relevant facts, and yet another five minutes updating your outline. That time will produce results: twenty minutes and you've accomplished far more than the five hours ever could.

How to confirm the rule? *Don't start with the case!* Don't even *look* at the case, at first. The rule is why that case is there.

What does the rule look like? That's the black letter law that says what the law is. It will be a definitive statement. For example: "The finder of lost property, a 'bailee,' holds it in trust for the benefit of the true owner, and has rights superior to everyone but the true owner." Actually that's two rules, but you get the point.

Look for the rule in the section that the case is in. Look for it in your commercial outline. Look for it in a primer. Look for it in the *Restatements*. Look for it in your professor's syllabus. Look for it in your secondary sources—not the case. These secondary sources are *crucial* to getting started, and to getting efficient. They're "secondary" in name, not in importance.

The result? You'll gain an understanding of the specific point of law *exemplified* by the case as well as you understand what you get when you multiply 2 and 2. You will simply *know* it—and you'll find yourself focusing on ever-finer points of the law. The case itself *doesn't matter*. What matters is that the case has precedential value, based on the law *in light of its facts*. That is your task: find the precedential value. Facts are "merely" tools that highlight those rules. In other words, you're *looking* for rules, *using* facts.

Okay. I'll nag you more about this later. For now, realize that if you agree with nothing else in this book, take it as gospel truth that studying simply for the sake of looking like a law student is a near-guarantee of failure. Don't do that. Study efficiently, instead.

Agreed?

To PREPARE OR NOT TO PREPARE, PART II

There is, as they say, a "split of authority" among, well, authorities on this question. Nearly every law school guidebook has some take on this issue, and much the advice is some variation on the *Don't Worry, Be Happy* tune. In other words, "There's no need to 'pre-study,' for goodness sakes! Just relax and enjoy yourself before law school. You'll learn everything you need to once law schools starts."

This advice is so wrong it's hard to approach this sufficiently carefully so that you get a sense of just how wrong this really is. Here goes: First, there's more than a tinge of laziness to this advice. Even if couched in "rest up so you're ready for the real battle" language, it's hard to see this as other than, "Goodness, you're going to be burning out soon, so save your strength!"

If you burn out, it will be because you are studying poorly. Usually, this is because you realize once you start law school just how far behind you already are. And if you burn out, it won't make a bit of difference whether or not you were rested when you started. Burnout is burnout. The focused, intense approach I discuss is by design and necessity sustainable. It *is* hard, but it is *less* hard than what most students do now. And it is the way to avoid burnout. The path of *bad-bad-bad* study (which nearly everyone assumes is the "right" path) is a near-guarantee for burnout, emotional and spiritual as well as physical and pedagogical. What's worse, bad study—and bad advice—seem to "fit" our preconceptions better: study hard, take notes, and so on. That *sounds* right, but...no, no, no.

Reading and color-coding case after case after case—and understanding none of it—and taking bucket-loads of notes in class and then cramming just before finals? Not only won't it work, but *of course* you'll burn out. And, if you do, it will serve your right. Or, knowing that there is an alternative—if you *insist* on studying badly, it will serve you right. Sorry to be so brusque, but if you want to get into the minds of veteran professors and hiring partners, that is how *they* will see it: If you don't "get it"—in time for exams—then that's just too bad. You don't count. Literally. If you don't get it, as measured by grades, you are invisible to these two groups. They're looking to reward those who *do* get it, in time.

That is reason number two that you must prepare.

Here's how the summer-preparation issue was written in another book for law students, *Later-in-Life Lawyers: Tips for the Non-Traditional Law Student* (which, notably, was a rebuttal to the conventional "wisdom"):

> There are perhaps three points: First, if your preference is not to prepare, let it be for more noble reasons than laziness. Law school requires enormous dedication; if you're not willing to dedicate time now, ask yourself, seriously, whether you're *really* going to "make up for it" later. Second, understand that many students *are* preparing. As they will be your competition in the all-important first year of law school—where absorption of the material is most difficult—do you really want to risk a *do-nothing-but-relax-and-be-merry* approach? Too, even if advance preparation is not entirely helpful, what if it is partially so? What if, as is likely, it just takes a few times before a legal doctrine makes sense? What if that one extra time before finals would have been the just the right number, for you?

The last point is the third reason. I lucked out in my law school grades because I really *didn't* get it until the bar exam. Mostly, this was because I didn't really want to get it. Even so, it does take a few passes before it makes sense. Your goal should be to have a strategic pass under your belt as you get started. Note: this is *strategic* pass— a 40,000-foot view requiring just a few dozen hours for each subject—not the minutiae that everyone gets hung up on. This overview will help by being a first pass, and it will help by making the second pass "fit" better. The law you then learn *during* law school will make more sense.

Going into law school "cold" is a nearly certain path to sub-par performance. Is it possible to do well (and thus get the gold) without any preparation? Sure. As a matter of statistics and experience, this happens. But that's not the way to bet. The odds are already 9-to-1 against you. And there's something greater at stake: actually knowing the law. It's one thing to memorize a bunch of stuff...it's quite another to internalize six sets of hundreds of rules and many hundreds more sub-rules, exceptions, and exceptions-to-exceptions. That *is* the law. Moreover, to think like a lawyer (and thus do well on exams and in practice), you must know these *in your bones,* and you must know how to apply them to a new set of facts, cold. The rules themselves are just the starting point; even if memorized in time, going in cold is still too late for most.

Law professors have a command of the law not just because they're very, very smart (as indeed they are), but also because they've been spending their time on that subject for years, and sometimes decades. In a sense, it's like the pro who is tossing a ball around with a novice. Because they are pros, it *seems* effortless. And when compared to the novice, it seems miraculous. In reality, it is neither; practice makes perfect.

A large part of this is the fact that law professors are not learning the law for the first time. You are. Moreover, your professor has the luxury of focusing on one or two areas of the law, while you're expected to learn six, simultaneously. While obvious, this is more than a mere disadvantage. This is not intended, by the way, to be disparaging of law professors. Rather, it is intended to point a way that should be obvious to you: having studied the *basics* of the Big Six, you will be miles ahead—and you will be on your way to *understanding the law.* You still won't be to the level of the professor (nor should you expect to be), but you'll be able to hold an intelligent conversation that you simply will not be able to do the first time around. That is the key: knowing enough to be able to put it all into perspective.

You need not know every rule. You need not parse every source. This is a misconception that law students stubbornly cling to. No, no, no. You must know the *framework,* and you must know the *basic* rules, exceptions to those rules, and the highlighted exceptions-to-exceptions. And, more importantly than those, you must be able to apply them—which takes us back to the framework.

One frustration in the first year of law practice, by the way, is that most junior associates never seem to get the same type of assignment twice. They're often bandied about from partner to partner, adding stress to an already-stressful job. Paradoxically, this only adds to the importance of having that knowledge of the law *in your bones,* which will prove most helpful in having some sense of what on Earth the project is all about.

So, you should, in a concerted-but-not-overwhelming effort, undertake your first pass before law school; your second pass in law school; and your third pass for the bar exam. The first two passes will be crucial to Getting Good: your exams. Three passes will—as you look back—be just right for your success in your first position: Getting the Gold.

As to the many—too many—resources being pitched to you, I will not recite (or plagiarize) all that is already out there, as to do so would be wasteful of my time, and yours. This includes a number of sources, references, services, and, to be blunt, scams and quasi-scams. It seems, in fact, that one problem law students face is that there's simply *too much.* It's like life within a can of spam. And so, we tend to shut down. Just like your professors do with your fast-paced life. We don't believe *any* of it, with a most depressing result that we fall further into the only study habits we have—our old, *bad* study habits.

To Heller With Law School

In his 1961 novel, Joseph Heller coined a term that would come to symbolize a bureaucratic paradox—or rules that conflict in their very meaning. The term, Catch-22, applied to the novel's anti-hero, John Yossarian (played in the film by Alan Arkin). Yossarian, a World War II bombardier, wishes to be excused from combat. To be excused he must submit a medical diagnosis from his squadron's flight surgeon that he is unfit to fly because he is insane. According to regulations, however, any sane person would naturally not wish to fly combat missions. By requesting to have one's sanity evaluated, Yossarian demonstrates that he is in fact sane and therefore *is* fit to fly, because one has to be sane to recognize one's own insanity.

Law school is one gigantic Catch-22. Professors are wonderful, but not at "teaching" the law. This is not an insult, as they will be the first to proclaim that their job is higher than mere "teaching." Rather, professors are wonderful at leading discussions of hypotheticals...which require that you *already know the law.*

The Catch-22 in law school is that class does not mean "learn the law"; class means "learn how to use it." If you believe nothing else in this book, believe that this is the basis for why law school is different—painfully different—and so disorienting. It shouldn't be for anyone. It won't be, for you.

And now for the good news: In any particular class, we're talking about one or two rules and two or three or a handful of sub-rules. That's it. In some classes, you'll spend a few days or even weeks on a single rule. In this sense, learning the law is *easy*. You're not learning [fade in dramatic soundtrack] *The Law;* you're learning a specific, finite, defined *rule*. One at a time. Just stay one rule ahead, and keep up. If you know those few rules and sub-rules, class is fun—even exhilarating. If you *don't* know those rules—again, we're talking about a handful, at most—class time is not just a waste, it is a counterproductive waste. It's likely to be confusing more than enlightening.

In Asia there is an expression that students are like Coke bottles, waiting to be filled with knowledge. To the extent that that's true in American education, it is *not* true in law school. As bizarre as it might sound, in law school you will not be taught the law. The assumption is that you bring to class what you have *already* taught yourself; a knowledge of black letter law is *presumed*.

You are, instead, a gladiator. Your weapons are a knowledge of black letter law, and knowing how to wield that knowledge: black letter law, plus learning how to think like a lawyer.

As currently practiced, you should view class as, generally, a diversion. This is not because it's not inherently valuable, but because few students are up to the challenge. Among many other factors, there is simply too much going on, there are too many distractions, and most students' study habits are all but useless. What you *can* do is to use the discussions *from the professor's side* to check your knowledge. What is said by the professor *should make sense*. You should smile inwardly because you'll know where the discussion is going. In short, you should be able to predict which legal limb the student is being pushed onto, and when it will break. *That* is the essence of the classroom hypothetical. And it's exactly what you should be doing in preparing for exams. In class you become a silent professor, sitting in per chance on a happy discussion of some legal point. When that starts to happen, you'll zoom beyond "getting good"…you will *be* good.

THE CYNIC SAYS

"Cut the crap. Just give me the answer!" seems the battle cry from row upon classroom row. "Why can't you just *tell us the law?!*"

The collective answer from law professors? No.

There are a few reasons for this response. First, professors *love* theory. Or, more correctly, professors love theory…if you're lucky.

In the law, *theory* is related to but quite different from "black letter law," a term that means a specific rule of law that is commonly accepted and can be stated fairly simply. Let's run through two examples, for two courses, to see if this makes sense. And to see if you're having fun.

The first example of black letter law might be, say, the rule in Criminal Law that if a defendant *voluntarily abandons* an attempt before completing a crime, he will be able to use the defense of "renunciation" to avoid criminal liability.

Dastardly Dan waits outside his enemy's house and intends to shoot Evil Editor. Five minutes before Evil Editor appears, Dastardly Dan remembers something his second-grade teacher told him ("Play nicely with others, Danny."), and realizes that he should not kill Evil Editor, despite the truly wicked comments written on one of Dan's manuscripts. So Dan returns home. Just before sipping his mint julep on his front porch (and after placing the gun safely in its case), Dan is arrested and charged with attempted murder. Result? Courts would acquit Dan because he voluntarily abandoned his plans—even though his actions might otherwise have risen to and met the tests for attempted homicide.

As you dig deeper into the black letter law of renunciation, you find more black letter law: the terms above have specific meaning. The renunciation must be *voluntary*. Dan cannot avail himself of this defense if he went home because of (1) a threat of imminent apprehension; or (2) a general fear of apprehension. Further, it must be a true *abandonment*. Dan cannot have decided to postpone his plan, or (given how eloquent is his victim) have been dissuaded from the shooting by Evil Editor

The *theory* is that a crime is based on a *voluntary act* (the "actus reus") in *connection with* ("concurrence") a *culpable intent* (the "mens rea"), and also *causation* between that and the victim's harm. This is based on the public policy interest in punishing criminal acts ("retribution") *and* in reducing the likelihood of future criminal acts ("utilitarianism"). In our example, if Dastardly Dan in fact voluntarily abandons his crime, he has, arguably, removed the need to punish him for the act (because it did not yet occur), *and* society should encourage criminals to abandon their crimes. Thus, while you can play with the facts to make Dan qualify (or not qualify) for the defense—How will you know? Black letter law!—you can also discuss the reasons behind why we have a rule called "renunciation" and why and how it fits within the broader rules of criminal liability.

Maybe it's wrong! Maybe we *shouldn't* excuse this. If so, you'll need to reason through why it's wrong, step by step, and also reason around the counter-arguments: what happens as a society if the rule is otherwise. *That* is "legal reasoning"—and how one connects the theory behind the black letter law, which together are the basis for legal reasoning.

Note too that on your exam you can neatly sidestep the irrelevancies (the mint julep and front porch) and focus on the important facts (everything else) related to the relevant points of black letter law (the voluntary abandonment of the crime).

Is this fun?

[If, by the way, it doesn't make sense, don't worry about it. Really. This would take a few hours in law school to get familiar with, and a few hours more to play with. Try this: re-read it, *slowly,* and see if it makes better sense the second time around. Does it? Isn't it just plain *interesting* to read about Dastardly this and Evil that? That's much of why law school *is* fun.]

For our second example, as long as I mentioned *causation* let's go with that. Let's look at another fun subject: Torts (*e.g.,* what happens when Person A harms Person B). For a negligence action to proceed there must be a "proximate cause" between the act and the injury; in other words, proximate cause is a *legal* limit on the "reasonable foreseeability" of harm. In other words, would we have been surprised that the harm happened?

The *theory* of proximate cause is that *not* limiting causation results in nearly limitless liability: it's too easy to find causation with the simple "but for" test. To apply this to the real world: if you think we have a litigation explosion now, just watch what would happen if we didn't have this rule. Thus, the public policy rationale is one that "conserves judicial resources" by limiting tort liability, generally. As a result, courts began to limit the legal reach of "causation" beyond that of "cause in fact" to a reasonableness test—a phrase you will hear repeatedly in law school, by the way.

Thus, in Torts you will almost certainly study the *Palsgraf* case, which set the standard for proximate cause. While the black letter law is fairly straightforward, so too is the theory behind it: if you let it be. It's possible, too, to argue exactly the opposite—just as the dissent did in *Palsgraf*. And this is what you need to get a sense of *after* you have absorbed the black letter law on that point. Why? Because then you can handle any fact pattern thrown at you (such as on a final exam). Knowing merely "the rule" isn't sufficient. Necessary, yes. Sufficient, no.

Again, this is a *lot* to throw at you in a few paragraphs. Don't be upset if it doesn't make complete sense—or even *any* sense. The above rule in Torts, for example, causes grief for many law students...in large part because they go into class without an understanding of the underlying legal rule.

One reason I didn't edit this out, by the way, is to make the following point: Law school is disorienting in large part because there is so much thrown at you (six subjects at a time!), and nearly all of it draws on interconnected themes that aren't immediately apparent. This is why it's so important to outline each subject, and to take it one step at a time. Reduce the mass of "stuff" to a manageable series of rules. With those, you can *play* with cases, facts, and hypos. It becomes not just fun, it's easy. Really. Try this: re-read (or just scan) this section after your first week in law school. You'll laugh, because it will then seem so easy. And it will be even easier if class was merely a review for you, given that you already know the law from your outline.

Professors love the very aspects that are so frustrating to many law students, and they are bored stiff by discussions (or—gasp!—recitation) of black letter law. Both pedagogically and by temperament—they were and are the stars of law school—they dismiss "mere" black letter law and gravitate to the esoteric, the wonkish, the edgy, the fun. Who wouldn't?

Second, professors have a point: While it is true that law exams draw upon a precise understanding of black letter law, the catch is that these rules won't make sense without an understanding of the broader context, a respect for the meaning behind the holdings. *This* is what professors love. So should you. This is, happily, also the part that adds meaning to the law. After all, anyone can come up with a few rules here and there; it takes a bit more to understand *why*. This is thus the reaction among professors: a steadfast insistence upon theory over black letter law.

Third, students and professors (still) come from different worlds. It's useful to remember that most professors came of age in a different age: nearly all studied before computers, before the internet, before text messaging. To them, these tools are distracting and even rude. In short, many professors are wary of the impact of technology. In their view, it serves to limit, not expand, one's abilities. Rather than using technology to scale greater heights, the fear is that it serves mostly to shorten attention spans. As I'll illustrate later, even if true this can be your ally as well as enemy in law school. One of the points in this book is that what happens in the classroom doesn't count [!]—so you needn't worry too much. But, more deeply, they have a point here too. They learned the law just as well (if not better) with far fewer gadgets, tools…distractions. Use these tools; don't let them tool you.

Finally, from the professors' collective perspective, the rush to impatience takes another form: mental laziness. This, to be blunt, is what they hear when they hear "Just give me the answer!" This is why the *No* is so firm. They want you to walk the path, without shortcuts, because they want to know that you *understand*. Not just "the rule," but the *why* behind the rule. The trick here is that they're right: you *do* need to walk that path. The counter-trick is that there *are* shortcuts—but not the ones most take. *Those* "short-cuts" are in fact dead ends. They lead nowhere. (Actually, they lead directly to bad grades.) The shortcuts you *should* take will take you to a true understanding of both the rule (black letter law) *and* the why (an ability to talk through variations—the "hypothetical," or "hypo").

So, try not to be impatient. *Use* your professors' love of theory to confirm your own understanding of both the rule *and* the why.

A CHIP ON THE OTHER SHOULDER

An opposing problem is the student who loves theory...and who wants to be sure that others are in on the secrets of the universe.

If this is you, stop.

Law school is not a political science seminar where every voice gets its day. There are simply too many voices, and even if that were the goal (which it is not), it would hardly be workable. It is to the professor to guide the discussion, to bring out and highlight those nifty secrets, to add the joke here and there. This does not mean that you withdraw in a huff; in fact, you need to be quite attentive. But your attention needs to be silent, and acute. Think of it as a stealthy approach to law school: go in under the radar and show 'em, in the end, who's really boss. That's what will happen anyway...make it happen for you.

Your job is not to be the center of attention. If that's your goal, reconsider your interest in law school, or focus on grades and extracurricular activities as your place to shine.

In the classroom, no, no, no.

LAW SCHOOL AND LAW PRACTICE: TWO WORLDS

It might be surprising—or not—but there is a world of difference between law school and law practice. Much of this stems from the move spearheaded by Langdell at Harvard to "professionalize" the law school faculty—which in the world of academia means almost the opposite of what it means in practice. To Langdell, it meant the development of a law faculty that focused on research and teaching. What that meant was that, over time, the number of law faculty who had, say, twenty-five years of experience as practitioners before embarking on a semi-retired career in teaching dwindled from a majority to just about zero. I include this here not as a commentary—as there's plenty of that elsewhere—but as an important note to much that *is* of importance to the law student.

Many law students, for example, are "academic." They enjoy the intellectual challenge of school, and engage with gusto in conversations (and arguments) about, well, just about everything. That is certainly a lot of fun, and is shared by many…but it is not the world of law practice. Or, to be fair, that's not *just* what it's about, and for a new associate, that's definitely not what it's about. Other students are less concerned about academic niceties—they'd rather have the great job, thank you very much.

Both worlds intersect—and collide—in important ways. First, much of what you read is based on an academic view of law schools. If, for example, you look at the methodology of the *U.S. News and World Report* rankings, you will see that an important factor in rankings is the view of professors. In essence: professors and deans evaluating the reputation of their own law school as well as others. While they certainly have a broader awareness of the qualities of a larger number of schools, they hardly think about all 200-odd accredited law schools. What this means is that prejudices among faculty (literally, judgments made prior to or without sufficient facts) tend to be self-perpetuating. The factor that includes a reputational evaluation of law schools by practitioners is even more limited, because practitioners have less practical ability to keep up with the array of law school goings-on—and even less interest in doing so.

For this book, I will attempt to keep these views separate (as they are nearly always separate among occupants of both worlds), and I will identify the source where it's appropriate. So, if your interest is academic, you might give less weight (with some caution) to what practitioners think; and vice versa.

YOUR JOB

To get good, your responsibilities in law school are narrow, and firm. The "narrow" part is the good news, because your job is quite achievable when taken step-by-step; the "firm" part is the bad news, because you cannot follow anything other than a methodical, consistent approach. Cramming will not work. Why? Because even if you could memorize six summary outlines (much less six master outlines), you would still not be able to effectively apply each to six fact patterns: your law exams.

Note-taking, hand-raising, brown-nosing...none of that will work either. Why? Because grades are based solely on exams, and grading is curved and done blind (*i.e.,* your professor *must* assign a certain percentage of each letter grade, with only a small fraction of "A" grades, and doesn't even know whose exam is being graded).

What worked before—memorize and regurgitate—will get you a "C" in law school. Perhaps a "B" if you're lucky. Why? It's the difference between a chemist who memorizes the periodic table...and one who actually *uses* it. Or between watching a novice who stumbles through the motions...and enjoying a ballet. Black letter law is just the beginning. "Knowing" the law is just the beginning. To be worth the "A" on a law exam—much less, six of them—you must be able to take this far beyond mere memorization.

Your responsibilities? You have two: First, you must learn the law. Then you must learn how to use it.

"Learning the law" means learning "black letter law."

"Black letter law" means the consensus view of what the law is. This can include a consensus of a majority of jurisdictions and a consensus view of a minority of jurisdictions, even if this view is disliked *within* those jurisdictions. Black letter law is spelled out not in cases or in your casebook but in "secondary sources": primers, commercial outlines, and the various *Restatements* of law. Crucially, you must learn black letter law *on your own,* and *before* class.

Disregard what anyone says or has ever told you about "primary" versus "secondary" sources. In the law, a primary source is what a court (or legislature) says. A case is a prime example. Is that valuable? Of course. Is that the way to learn the law? Nope. No attorney learns a new area of the law that way. Neither should you. Instead you go to secondary sources: compilations summarizing what the law is. This is not to cheat, nor is it to uncover some "secret"—it's simply a way to put those rules into your mind in a recognizable context so that the cases and discussions make sense.

You absolutely, positively cannot expect to be *told* what the law is; you must ferret it out *on your own*. The sections on outlining and mini-briefing will show you how. Happily, this is not all that hard, if done right. You must, moreover, learn those few specific rules before class; you cannot let this slide. *This* is hard.

HARVARD:
OR, IS THAT AN ELEPHANT IN THE CLASSROOM?

This heading might strike many of you as odd indeed. (If not excessively annoying, as I've mentioned Harvard, what, 312 times?) Nearly everyone who's got an opinion on status and education has a love-hate relationship with Harvard...including those who go there. This is because Harvard, like it or not, agree or not, is the benchmark for all other schools. That might rile the good folks in New Haven, or Palo Alto, or Chicago, or Ann Arbor. No matter. Harvard sets the standard to such a degree that to even say the name brings with it connotations that are nearly impossible to match, or overcome.

Why include this section, and why "...an Elephant..."?

Harvard Law School is undertaking a revision of its first-year curriculum. What Harvard set in place more than a century ago (the 1870s, to be more precise), Harvard can replace. It's quite likely, moreover, that whatever the result of Harvard Law School's new curriculum, it will soon find its way into *all* law school curricula. This might seem a bit Big Brother-ish, unfair, or downright creepy.

Wrong. This is how the law works. Someone proposes an idea. This could be a judge or legislature (although one might write legislature first, that's not how most law schools teach it), or a group of judges, attorneys, and professors, as in the American Law Institute's highly influential *Restatements,* or a social movement accepted by any of the above.

In this case, a group of individuals—senior faculty at Harvard Law School, along with a number of others—propose, debate, and wrestle with an issue (the curriculum), and after a years-long process implement their ideas. Because they *are* the benchmark— and they know it—they cannot and do not take such measures lightly. As indeed anyone who's worked in higher education will know; design and approval of curricular changes are glacial. For Harvard, it's glacial with a wee-bit-more-deliberate twist.

So what happens? What is almost certain to happen is that whatever changes they enact, others will look to. Is it fair that they'll look to it just because it's Harvard Law? Wrong question. *Because* it's Harvard Law it will probably be more innovative— because Harvard is too powerful to be threatened by innovating— but that's not why it's the wrong question. It's the wrong question because this is simply how human nature works. Ergo, this is how the law works. Those who are influential...influence. Don't get mad at this reality. Ask instead...based on what? If that influence is based solely on daddy's money, or uncle's connections, or the end of a gun...*that's* problematic. And not just because it's unfair. Rather, it's because such a corrupt system is nearly inalterably set to fail, and to harm many, many in the process. If, instead, the influence is based on logic, thought, peer review, and some form of considered debate—chances are the result might actually not be so bad.

A story I just have to share about Harvard: The first time I was there I was invited to an event. No, I wasn't anyone important; I was in fact decidedly sub-important. I made my way from the law school at the northwest corner of the majestic campus to the southeast, where there is a mansion: the Faculty Club. A stately building, it spans floors, rooms, and patios that seemed to expand farther than even a mansion should. We—being sub-important— were shown to the basement for this event, where we proceeded to meet and greet as any nerds do, often congregating around the food and drink. The food included seemingly endless trays of scallop and shrimp hors d'oeuvres and delicacies that most would never enjoy on any regular basis. The drink included foreign and microbrew beers that would make ordering a regular beer seem a genuine faux pas. (This, by the way, is just like interview season.) A friend and I just about laughed as we looked at each other, shaking our heads as we marveled at this world.

I told you that story to tell you this one: At the law school cafeteria one does not simply order, say, a sandwich. Rather, one selects the type of bread from among a half-dozen varieties, one or more meats and one or more cheeses from yet another half-dozen types each, mustards, mayonnaises, and relishes from a dozen or so bins; sandwiches are made very much to order. It seems that they would cure the meat there with daily rubs, if they could. It almost goes without saying that the food there is far, far better than in most cafeterias, and it didn't take much of an excuse to go there…often. Moreover, the prices are surprisingly reasonable, as they are subsidized.

In thinking about this there is an impression that anyone from Harvard has about, well, just about anywhere else: they might as well have been dropped off at a cattle ranch. After such refined treatment in Cambridge, a post at another school pales by comparison, and so there's an ever-subtle impetus to either treat the new host school with a restrained contempt, or to remake the host into the home school. Either way, the process is subtle and powerful, and very much directed to co-optation rather than conquest. I must admit the pull on me was—and is—quite strong. This is thus perhaps the most American—and, by derivation, British—of caste systems.

In a sense, there is yet another driver: the assumption of most who have been in both worlds that Harvard really *is* the gold standard, and every school ought to at least aspire to be like them. I would argue that they should aspire to be better, as in more innovative, yet I have seen first-hand how schools lock themselves into place, for admittedly practical reasons. So, when the latest academic novelty emerges from Cambridge, it is absorbed eagerly into the fabric of academic life nationwide, even and perhaps especially with those who attended other schools.

What this means for us is that Harvard will likely once again reset the law school table: the patterns in law school we "know" to be true might not be so true anymore. With luck, these changes will be for the better. Perhaps they won't. (My first impression in reading them is that they will.) The point here is that, whatever the changes, your role should be exactly the same: to go into law school with an open mind, and with a mind ready to first absorb, and then to wrestle with, but not to *mindlessly* challenge just for the sake of challenging.

Most importantly, the essential challenge will be the same: to learn black letter law, and to learn how to use it.

FIRST YEAR: THE BIGGIES

Most students entering law school read about the "Big Six" courses they're about to study. These are courses with words that everyone knows (except perhaps Torts, although it's hard to miss a discussion of tort reform nowadays). Still, a dangerous pattern develops: Students begin immediately—well, sooner than immediately, as they're supposed to prep before the first classes begin—to study cases in each of these areas. The problem is that the cases make no sense. And the more you read, the less sense they make.

I can almost hear you thinking now, "Right. *I'll* know what they mean!"

No disrespect, but, no you won't.

The cases make no sense because they're in no context. If you start reading about, say, a chase involving foxes, you're going to wonder what on Earth—literally—that has to do with Property Law. (And that's well before you get to The Rule Against Perpetuities, a simple idea that perplexes just about everyone, and has caught even experienced attorneys in its grasp.)

As mentioned in the introduction, the author of *Planet Law School* is beside himself with vitriol at the state of legal education. In this sense, I am too. Law school begins with the misconception that if we begin with the minutiae we build to the big picture. Not sure about you, but that's not the way I learn.

So, part of the message that should be conveyed to the new law student is how to put each component of study (cases, codes, statutes, Restatements, commercial outlines, and so on) into a context that will have meaning and that will make absorption stronger and easier, rather than obtuse and frustratingly difficult. In reality, what happens is that many law students give up and tune out, in utter frustration, rather than nodding in agreement and understanding of the purpose and complex *beauty* of how these rules, concepts, and philosophies all fit together.

Yet further, the Big Six are not taught as different views of the same legal prism. But they *are*. One cannot deal, in practice, with a tort case that doesn't also involve some property or contract right (and often both). Contract issues necessarily involve a property right, and also perhaps a tort claim. Nearly everything implicates procedure—civil or criminal—in one way or another. Just ask a senior partner. As long as I brought up the actual practice of law, once upon a time an elderly client got off on the wrong floor of a large firm. The gentleman ran into a litigation partner, who after pointing him to the right floor but before seeing him off realized that what he was about to do in his will was a prescription for disaster. So, gently, the partner suggested an alternative to reduce the risk of a property dispute and contest of the will. All because he got off on the wrong floor. Procedure and positioning *matter*—sometimes more than the claim itself.

Professors will respond that they can't possibly teach these courses in such an integrated fashion, as to do so would be too complicated, and would confuse rather than enlighten. Nonsense. Anyone smart enough to take and "pass" the LSAT is sophisticated enough to understand the interwoven threads of the law. The key is to highlight each thread, and to put that thread into its broader legal framework. Let's give it a shot.

PROPERTY AND CONTRACTS

Property and contract law are two sides of the same commercial and societal coin. To explain that, let's take a "frolic" (to borrow a term from Tort Law) into the reasons why.

Hernando de Soto, a Peruvian economist, once asked a question: why do some societies succeed and others do not? He wrote his answer in a book, *The Mystery of Capital: Why Capitalism Triumphs in the West and Fails Everywhere Else*. This title might strike quite a few as more than a bit loaded, but any such criticism misses the vastly more important point: When de Soto (or other economists) speak of "capital," "growth," and so on, what they *should* be saying are things like "infant mortality," "sufficient food supplies," "clean drinking water," "education of girls," "mutilation," "incidence of abuse," and so on. This really *does* matter.

We often talk about how important the "rule of law" is. But we don't often stop to think about what that *means*. Among other important aspects, the law has a dual role: it is, of course, a set of interrelated rules, but it is also a transparent framework through which every other aspect of life passes. So, for example, when we mention the word "economics," the essence of that discipline carries importance not just within economics, but also *through the law* to the many ways in which law must consider the impact of its rules. We thus have not only a movement called Law and Economics, but also a more subtle imposition of economics in ways large and small, in cases far and wide. This cuts, as well, in many directions. We might think economics would lead a court, for example, to hesitate before extending liability to an employer for, say, the actions of an employee, based on the negative impact of that rule on all employers. But those same thoughts—the impact of money on behavior—will lead a court to just the opposite conclusion: *not* to extend liability is to cause greater future harm. We thus have countless judges—not the wildest group—continually reinforcing a legal doctrine based at least in part on principals that another discipline propounds. The impact of money on behavior. In this, the law absorbs as well as it reflects.

We might connect the dots here, briefly, to see just how true this is. And, yes, it does tie into how we learn, think about, and practice law—and how we should learn property and contract law.

With echoes of Adam Smith, de Soto examined the differences between successful and unsuccessful societies. While others have more recently studied the same question, arriving at a number of possible explanations (the impact of climate on disease, the presence or absence of navigable waterways, etc.), de Soto arrived at an (again) noteworthy conclusion: a successful society is almost wholly dependent upon the working presence of the rule of law. Specifically, upon two legal doctrines: Property Law (the ability to own something) and Contract Law (the ability to trade that something for something else).

That's it.

What de Soto argued, essentially, was that all of civilization rests upon these two doctrines being sufficiently in place for citizens to take advantage of their talents and to trade with others for *their* talents. Economists have gone 'round and 'round seeking explanations, but none appears to have done it more concisely and persuasively than has de Soto. *This* is why Property Law and Contract Law are important.

Economists at world bodies use the diplomatic phrase of "developing" versus "developed" economies, despite the clear—to economists—reasons behind why certain economies simply don't keep up or, worse, fall further and further behind. This has given rise to the newer literature surrounding "failed states," which implicates the rule of law as the missing component to economic development.

It's easy to be in law school and read these as mere academic terms...until one actually *lives* in a failed state (which is difficult, as there's often that risk of getting shot), or in a developing economy (where accomplishing the most simple task, like having a telephone or internet connection installed, will make this discussion quite relevant). It's a shame that the only people allowed to talk about the rule of law aren't those who've survived life in a system without it; nothing else will lend quite the same appreciation.

My sister, who once served in the Peace Corps and later wrote a book about her experiences *(Grains of Golden Sand: Adventures in War-Torn Africa),* was visiting from Zaire. We took a trip to Mexico and, avoiding the tourist area in favor of local ones, we ran across a hardware "store"—more of an alley, really—and she exclaimed: *"Wow!* You can actually walk in there and *buy* something. You can just walk in and buy it! Look...a *hammer!"*

This is the difference the rule of law makes.

Communitarians of a communist bent might resist the necessary implications of personal ownership of property, and yet eight decades of empirical evidence shows that they are wrong, both as a matter of practice (and Marx insisted upon pragmatism) and more deeply (and controversially) as a matter of philosophy. Likewise, those who resist the importance of a functioning economic system miss much more: The ability to criticize is dependent, at base, on the functioning of the very systems derided. It's akin to wailing about what meanies mom and dad are. With Property and Contract laws in place and reasonably well-enforced, all else is possible. Without them, nothing is.

It might sound a bit melodramatic, but the choice isn't really about how successful a society is. Rather, the choice is whether the society *is* a society. Where the rule of law exists, there can be disputes about whether blueberry subsidies should be four percent or four and one-half percent, and whether they should apply to wholesalers or growers. These are *good* disputes.

Where the rule of law does not exist, the disputes are usually whether it's safe to take the main route through town to scrounge badly needed supplies...hoping that no marauding teenagers with assault rifles happen to be along the path. This is not hyperbole. It really *is* this stark. One girl—taking water home to her family in one of the many failed states in the world as of this writing—was accosted by a group of armed "soldiers." She was so badly mauled that a U.N. helicopter was called in to take her to a hospital. Ask her what the rule of law means.

This is why you should be proud to study law...and willing to learn it. *Really* learn it.

*   *   *

I remember in one early Property Law class—taught by a professor whose field of expertise had little to do with property law, as I later learned—the case of *Pierson v. Post,* which law students study as the basis for property rights. In this 1805 case, Lodowick Post was hunting with his dogs on community land and had pursued a fox when Pierson, aware that the fox was being hunted, killed it within Post's sight and carried it off. Not very gentlemanly, true, yet the court ruled that mere pursuit was insufficient; instead, possession (or actual dominion) was required for the creation of a property right in a wild animal.

We might think this a funny case to study in Property Law, but in fact it is a crucial building block. The law does not depend upon the value of a case, or even on what is being disputed, but rather on its reasoning: Neither Pierson nor Post would likely have believed that billion-dollar oil cases would ride on their unhappy connection in a hunt.

Property Law necessarily casts political and social shadows. Soon after studying that case (which made little impact on me until years later), we studied the cases involving, essentially, justifications for pushing the American Indians off their land by denying them legal recognition of their right to live where they had lived for countless generations. When we were studying this I remembered thinking, "This is like two fleas arguing over who owns the dog." Again these cases made little sense, and we seemed to move on to the next cases without any real closure as to the meaning of each. And, even when we *thought* we understood it, our poor study habits meant that we were constantly confused by the progression of cases and seemingly bizarre facts and more-bizarre language and unfathomable exceptions-to-exceptions. While I did well, I fell victim to these bad habits just as had my classmates, Scott Turow in *One L,* and hundreds of thousands of other law students.

These early cases were important to the development of American law and to the nation—and, centuries later, were used to reestablish ownership among quasi-sovereign tribes. Years later, the Mashantucket Pequots and Mohegans in Connecticut among other tribes won the right to develop gambling establishments. Perhaps not the best of industries, true, but darnit, they were finally *using* the law rather than being abused by it—and the law was, finally, living up to its supposedly neutral purpose...and promise.

The important point here is that legal doctrines, concepts, rules, and procedures do not occur in a vacuum; they are very much a part of our social fabric, and reflect that on-going tussle. Moreover, judges—who tend to be both judicially and politically conservative (not the same, by the way)—think quite seriously about the impact of their decisions. Overworked as they are, they know that a simple case might well be used against someone else in a court of law—and if their reasoning is poor, the shame will be on them.

We thus have a never-ending struggle between philosophies (big government v. small government, radical v. reactionary, and so on), laws (written and rewritten in a never-ending struggle reflecting those social changes), regulations (likewise in reaction to the changes above), and on and on in social and sometimes epochal cycles. Thus, we can read a case from the early 1930s and fairly well predict the change in outcome as compared to the 1940s (after the "switch in time that saved nine" on the U.S. Supreme Court, which paved the way for much of the New Deal), and then into the 1970s (with broadened interpretation of consumer protection, for example), and on to the present. Entire areas of law, such as a good chunk of employment law, simply did not *exist* even two decades ago. What clients and managers deal with now—nearly continuously—are the ever-expanding impacts of those broader societal expectations. And, of course, lawyers are right there in the middle (...and on both sides).

Each of these reflects the times—and serves as an unintended mirror to the reasoning of the past. In law school we can and should look at these various topics as an inevitable tradeoff: we can have either bright-line legal rules (black letter law), with the resulting unfairness to one side or another, or we can have a messier, vastly larger and more complicated legal system. We have, for now, opted for the latter.

*   *   *

Okay then, back to Property and Contracts. It might seem that I've given too high-level a view of Property. My goodness...Property Law as one of two saviors of civilization!? Where's the practical advice? What do I do on day three? Maybe *this* is crap!

Perhaps. But before concluding this let me counter with two rebuttals. First, it *will* make sense, as the day-to-day advice is very much relevant and very much important. Second...

Patience, weedhopper. I hope this reference isn't too flippant. It refers to the 1970s series *Kung Fu,* starring David Carradine as Caine, a Shaolin apprentice. In the pilot to the series, Caine meets his Master, whom Caine pities as blind. The Master shows, however, that he can hear the grasshopper at Caine's feet—even though Caine himself cannot. From then on, Caine is referred to as "grasshopper." As there are more weeds in my story than grass, "weedhopper" it is.

Later sections will spell out not only ways to learn the law, but ways to *master* the law with *less* effort than nearly all law students spend today. It is possible to be both effective and efficient, and that is our challenge. Okay, enough frolics!

Property law is the distillation of rules for the *practical* use of things. A rather important qualifier in there: this is a field of law enmeshed in what is *practical.* While courts spun pirouettes explaining the logic behind accepting or not accepting a certain basis for property rights, in essence it is about power. Not just the power of those who have property over those who have not (which gives rise to "critical legal studies"), but also the power to *do* something. For example, the American system recognizes the possibility of patents, copyrights, and trademarks. These are state-sanctioned monopolies, granting the owner the right not only to use and benefit from the patent, copyright, or trademark, but to prevent others from doing so. This is no small thing. This is a *legally protected monopoly*—a direct contradiction of the philosophy and law of free trade and competition. This *does* make a difference, and we're still arguing the extent to which such power is appropriate. Your professor might just have a "side" in this debate (mine certainly did), but the law that is tested has little to do with these philosophical disputes.

Property can be real, as in the land under a farm; it can be personal, as in the tractor over the land; and it can be intangible, as in the patent covering the design of that tractor's rear tires. All three are valuable. Intangible property, for example, was the un-sung stepchild of property law...until companies discovered gold in their R&D vaults. One high-tech company has made more money in its intellectual property than it has, in decades, for its "real" products.

Crucially, property can be sliced in many ways: by owner, by tenancy, by license, by time...the courts will recognize just about any slicing or dicing. These are the famous "bundle of rights" that professors will use to simplify the concepts, and this is, to get melodramatic again, one of the underpinnings of American economic success. This is why you have a car instead of a cart. This is why you have a home instead of a hut. Seriously. In too many parts of the world, a "landlord" is exactly that. In some parts, this includes the virtual (and sometimes real) ownership of tenants. Property law is a *big deal*. The ability to slice ownership by, say, *time* gives us the ability to create nifty legal tools such as mortgages: the right to possess a home before paying for it. In essence, the ability to bring future productivity forward in time. If you think this a stretch to connect "home" with "productivity," think about how productive you would be without one. Who says there is no such thing as a time machine?

How many ways to state that property law is a big deal?

It's worth restating an important point: the underpinnings of property law, while capable of philosophical defense and critique, are not for our purposes philosophical. They are oriented towards the *practical*. Do not rant. Do not rave. That is not your job. Your job is to learn what property law *is*.

What property law is is a set of crucially useful, *pragmatic* rules. As with the LSAT, do not resist. Do not resent. Moreover, a corollary of learning what property law is is learning *why* property law is. I hope this has helped to set that right, or at least to get you pointed in the right direction. There are many criticisms, as mentioned, and it's fine to delve into them. Your professor might want you to do so. But *avoid this trap:* even if your professor, for raw political reasons disagrees with the basis for property law, guess what will be tested on the exam? Like it or not, black letter law is what is tested, along with your ability to use it. That is the definition of what property law *is*.

Keep in mind the bigger picture: even the most biting of critiques are set in opposition to a system that is designed by thousands, over hundreds if not thousands of years, for a very real societal need. It's easy to cast stones. It's rather harder to *use* those stones to build something of value. That is property law.

*   *   *

It might seem that I've given short shrift to Contracts, but in fact Contracts as a subject is easier to put into a framework: Every contract raises the same procedural set of questions. And thus, like other subjects, every Contracts exam will assume the same set of questions and will focus on pretty much the same basic doctrines and potential flash points.

When faced with a contract, we must first ask: *Is it* a contract? That takes us to the question of formation, which in turn takes us through the tests of offer, acceptance, and consideration, and then to the relatively minor tests of legality, capacity, and so on.

Only after we determine that we have a contract—and we almost always do, as they're alarmingly easy (in the real world) to create, and as the opposite conclusion would make for a shorter and less exciting exam question—do we focus on remedies: what happens next, who owes how much, what happens if it's a peculiar contract, and so on?

The "sexy" part of Contract Law comes in ancillary doctrines such as unconscionability—which should be viewed in the context of what they *don't* show. To take this example, very, very few contracts will ever be held as unconscionable, for the reasons alluded to by our juristic ancestors: to begin voiding contracts based on unconscionability renders nearly every contract potentially invalid. Such as state is not just wrong, it is dangerous. In just the same melodramatic way as I waxed eloquent (I hope) about property law, contracts are a bedrock of our economy and civilization. Really. Take away the right to enter into or enforce a contract, and no deal is safe. If no deal is safe, it's not that such-and-so group will have to put up with, say, being nice to their counterparts. We wish. If no deal is safe, that means, in most deals, no deal is *done*. That means that people starve (as food doesn't get transported because the parts needed for vulcanizing the tires never get bought), people go homeless (as banks would hardly give away money if courts didn't back them up in getting it back), and no one works (as there's little reason to work if there are no deals to be done). Gee, you're probably waiting for that sentence where I write that this is a big deal. Yup, this is a big deal.

Once upon a time I spoke with a fellow who happened to be the general manager for a local branch of a Chinese business. This was early in China's reengagement with the Western world. This company had planned to leave the area, but for appearances (and without consultation) had renewed a ten-year lease for their large commercial space.

He was incredulous when I told him that, yes, he was bound to pay not just the rent...but the rent for the *entire* 10-year term, minus offsets.

"But why should we be held to this?!" he half-sputtered, half-pleaded.

Why indeed. This is the *essence* of contract law. Someone will almost always be upset if a deal is badly done, as it was here, as there's nearly always a change in value or circumstance that makes it in one side's interest to escape. Courts don't care about the side that wants out—or even the other side, to a large degree. They care about both sides of *future* contracts. This is the whole purpose for Contract Law: if one could escape because they felt like it, contracts would be meaningless. If contracts are meaningless, everything stops: Lessors can't build those buildings because no lender would lend because no contract for future earnings would be safe.

Contract disputes involve at least one side that is displeased—and often both. The courts' response?

"Too bad."

If pressed, they'll elaborate just a bit: "You shouldn't have signed it. That's why they're called *contracts.*"

This is important because very often clients (and law students) treat contract law like just so much mush, ready to be tossed aside with the merest of wishes or flimsy counterarguments. It is the opposite: it is among the most binary of legal doctrines.

Have you heard of the Prisoners' Dilemma? In game theory this is the scenario in which two suspected accomplices are given the option of staying silent or ratting each other out. Neither can communicate with the other. If both remain silent, they will each receive two years in prison. If both confess, each implicating the other, they will each receive three years in prison. And if only one confesses, implicating the other, the one who confesses will not be jailed and the one who did not confess will receive five years in prison.

Contract law presents a grand Contractors' Dilemma. In a contract, either party can at any time cheat the other by breaching the contract. Clearly it's better when both parties willingly agree to complete their part of the deal, presumably because it is profitable to do so, yet that is not always the case. Were courts to allow parties to breach contracts without fear, the calculus would shift—harming not just the non-breaching party but future parties and all of society as well. Even if it benefited the breaching party, and even if it didn't harm the non-breaching party too much, it would *still* harm everyone else...by altering *their* behavior. It is the knowledge of consequences that tends to correct bad behavior, whether that's a default, substituting counterfeit or inferior goods (just imagine an aircraft parts supplier who could save *lots* of money by providing recycled parts), or the like.

Even more than theological and moral rationales (where breaking one's word invites banishment...or worse), this is the philosophical underpinning for contract law: a jurisprudential reverence of and loyalty to the *pragmatic* reasons for and necessity of contracts. A paradox, yes? Property and contract law are meaningful because of what they *do,* and because of the void they prevent. As you enter the cathedral of legal learning, you should stand, sit, or kneel in awe at how important this simple legal construct is. I'm being just a little bit tongue-in-cheek here, of course. We no longer think in these terms, and chances are that, in any other circumstance, we'd all burst out laughing. All true...but this is *still* a big deal. I bring it up here not to incite mindless "Oh isn't this great!"—and, by inference, "Aren't *we* great!"—but rather to frame this so that the law will make better sense, and so that the *assumptions* of judges past will make sense. Very often, those assumptions are hidden in the open. If the assumption is known—such as the assumption that contracts are the *sine qua non* (loosely, "without which there is nothing") of our economy and society—then the reasoning and decisions of all those cases make a whole lot more sense.

I'll go further and argue that, in most cases, the law is *right*. In most cases, "postmodern" critics are foolish, misinformed, or downright intellectually dishonest (or just plain ignorant and lazy). The rules that we have inherited are created across jurisdictions and time with sound reasoning, and with a healthy appreciation for the more-evil alternatives. That, often, is what is missing in law school: an understanding of *why* the law is as it is—not because of its intrinsic beauty alone but because of how much worse it would be if the rule were otherwise. *That* lends a deeper appreciation and, perhaps, less resistance. And that leads to better comprehension and fluency...and better grades.

Okay, back to contracts.

The essence of contract law in the Anglo-American legal system is that courts will not look to the relative quality of the deal. In other words, they do not care whether the parties struck a good bargain. In essence, they say to the parties: "Shoo! Go out and do your business! Do a good deal, do a bad deal. That's up to you. We're giving you an astonishing ability to make a contract over just about anything, with just about any terms you like. We *like* commerce. We support contracts. We thus support the enforceability of contracts. You do the deal, but don't come crying to us if you decide you don't like it later."

That raises a real concern, then, when a deal is obviously and egregiously imbalanced. Rent-to-own contracts are notorious for this, as they usually have terms that are outrageous, such as, say, paying $1,500 for a refrigerator worth $450. This in turn brings images of the "company town," where virtual slavery took shape in the form of credits extended that had almost no chance of being repaid, as the terms of the deal added usurious interest and fees far in excess of the underlying value of the property—and taking "undue" advantage of the weaker party's weaker position.

But what to do? As soon as we open the door to saying, "Yes, poor consumer, you really shouldn't have signed this contract agreeing to pay $1,500 for a $450 refrigerator, so we're going to reform the contract, letting you off the hook"...what does that mean?

In the law, "what does that mean" really means "what does that mean for every *other* 'poor consumer'" who will then, as a matter of law, be able to apply the same test. This isn't merely idle academic chatter. What of the person who agrees to pay $900? How about $625? $495?

Now we're in a real mess. What constitutes a deal that "shocks the conscience" of the court? What, *exactly,* constitutes a deal so bad that it is "unconscionable"? See how this evolves? The reason that courts seem so harsh is because they *are.* They have to be. If a judge simply ruled on what seemed "fair" at the moment, the result is chaos—the opposite of what "law" is supposed to mean. A nation of laws, not of men. That's an old saying that actually means something when we stop to think about it.

There are many, many angles to just this one doctrine within Contract Law—a narrow exception to the broader doctrine of contracts that assumes legality—which is one reason the study of law should be both enjoyable and enlightening. The important point is to understand the context of each of the doctrines, rules, exceptions, and exceptions-to-exceptions—all within the broader context of that subject. Once you know what a contract is, and when it's at risk, it all falls into a surprisingly sensible set of rules.

To be more explicit, as this might be the only chance to put this into such a context: the essence of Contract Law in the United States is a *strong predisposition to uphold private contract rights.* Once the parties have met the tests (offer, acceptance, consideration, etc.) and assuming none of the secondary tests for legality are tripped (infancy, incapacity, etc.), the contract rights attach...think of a massive electric breaker—the kind you might see in a movie featuring Frankenstein—being pushed into gargantuan brackets with a bright zap of electricity. Once that happens, the entire body of Contract Law is brought to bear should anything happen involving that contract. If relations sour and one or both parties begin to back out—which as mentioned is likely if the deal, economy, or value of the property in question sours—the next question is: Who must pay, and how much? This often turns on who defaults. *This* is tricky, as both sides are usually (re)acting against the actions of the other—or they *think* they are. If one side doesn't perform, or doesn't perform well (or as well as the other side expects), what then happens if the other side doesn't pay? Who is in breach? More to the point, who is in breach *first?* This is critical, both in law exams and in real life.

Happily, in law exams, you need merely point out the dilemma and then draw conclusions of what happens if one side is declared the first defaulter, and alternatively what happens if the other side is so declared. You point, you score.

The "damages," or amount to be paid, is almost always an amount that would put the non-defaulting party in the position it would have been in had the contract been fully performed. Whew! But it makes perfect sense when you get past the language: the essence of U.S. contract law is to *enforce contract rights*. That means thinking *as if* the contract had been fully performed.

This might seem more than a tad convoluted, but if you put yourself in the position of a Jedi master just before he battles the bad guy—*"Use the Force, Luke. See the Contract!"*—it makes perfect sense: What is the purpose of contract law? (To enforce private contract rights.) How do we know? (Offer, acceptance...) What if? (Duress, unconscionability, etc.) What about when things go wrong? (Default, damages.) What then? (Remedies.)

The courts seek to "set the world right." In the case of a contract, this means to set the world right between the parties had they both performed as promised. That's it.

If it's an unusual contract, such as for a personal performance (always fun to discuss in class) or for real estate, or for a few other quirky exceptions, the courts might step in to award "specific performance," or a command to one side to do something (such as to transfer ownership of real property), as compared to a command to pay an amount (which is a command to transfer ownership of money, a form of personal property). You'll get the chance to discuss the Statute of Frauds—a most excellent-sounding doctrine, don't you agree?—and memorize the situations (sometimes archaic) to which they apply. But all of this is a variation on the theme: to *enforce contract rights*. Everything fits within that grand strategy.

Does this overview strike you as enjoyable? Interesting? Important? If so, chances are you will do just fine in law school.

If not, if you're utterly bored, distracted, disgusted, or just plain uninterested...wondering when on Earth this meandering "advice" will end...consider whether or not the study of law is for you. This should be at least an *engaging* process. At best, it can add deeper meaning to your view of the world, and it can even provide the means for you to change and help at least parts of it, and enjoy a healthy living in the process. But, first, it must be for you.

TORTS

Tort law is, in many ways, the fun branch. There are many tales to be told that involve someone doing something to someone else. Someone is forever getting hurt, and the fact patterns get deliciously bizarre. And, as with our fascination with accidents, when someone gets hurt, it's just plain interesting. A morbid curiosity on our part, yes, but there's plenty of room for such tales in tort law.

That, perhaps, is not why the study of torts should be appealing. Rather, when an issue arises between two parties, it is almost always because of what one party does—or does not do— to the other party. Even this gets a bit obtuse, so let's try that again.

When an issue arises between Plaintiff and Defendant, it is almost always because of what Defendant [the person blamed] does—or does not do—to Plaintiff [the person blaming the other].

Plaintiff is upset. Perhaps Defendant hit Plaintiff. Perhaps Defendant embarrassed Plaintiff. Perhaps Defendant failed to help Plaintiff. Perhaps…

When we look at the case, we then discover that Defendant has his own story. Perhaps Plaintiff had hit Defendant first. Perhaps Defendant *thought* that Plaintiff was about to hit him. Perhaps…

Then we're back to Plaintiff, who might argue that he *did* hit Defendant first, but only *in response to* what he saw as a threat against his family. Or perhaps…

See? Told you it's fun.

Social interactions are filled with possibilities for outcomes both positive and negative. Despite all the fuss above, 90-plus percent of all contracts are performed without a hitch—because it is in the self-interest of both parties to do so. The 10-minus percent that are not become issues, and some percentage of those (not many, actually) end up in court.

Torts, on the one hand, are the extreme version of what happens when something goes wrong between individuals and, on the other hand, a milder, private version of criminal law (which is a wrong between the *state* and individual).

As with Contracts, Torts involves a procedural approach that is followed in each case. Was there a duty the Defendant owed to the Plaintiff? Was there a breach of that duty? Was the harm caused by the Defendant? Was that harm reasonably foreseeable? What was the harm?

In each of these areas you'll go through case after case—*lots* of cases in Torts—with the hope that you'll develop a sense of what each of these main areas is about. Again, I think that that's the wrong way to go about studying law. First it's important to know *why* it's important, and then it's important to study *what* is important. The *why* is conceptual; the *what* is usually one line. A handful of lines at the most. *That's* how you can master the law, in less time. Understand why it fits together, and learn, in no more than a few sentences (hint: in no more than five minutes), what it is that is fitting together. This is black letter law. The *why* is…how you begin to actually think like a lawyer.

As a student, it's important to know, precisely, how a case fits within a broader context of the legal doctrine. If you *do* know, the case will fit, *ah*, like a glove, and you'll be rewarded with plenty of "Ah ha!" moments. It all really does make sense. If not, the cases will quickly become a confusing morass of words, each with meaning more empty than the last. Choose not the latter path. Don't fight it. Again, judges have thought about these rules for centuries. Ours *is* to reason why…but 999 times out of a thousand, your answer should be exactly the same.

Tort law is based on the premise that duties are owed from one individual to the next. Actually (and as a matter of law), every individual owes *many* duties to many other individuals, and is in turn owed duties from many others. A woman can be a mother (thus owing duties to protect members of her family); an employee—thus owing duties to her employer); and, say, a physician (thus owing special duties to patients under her care). It doesn't take long, obviously, to see duties nearly everywhere—one reason Torts is so fun on law exams.

"Duty" carries a meaning more specific in the law than as used in lay terms. To simplify greatly, in the law a *duty* is something that provides *a right to sue* when it is not met. So, in essence, it's defined in the negative. The woman above fails to save a drowning boy. Result? In most cases, no liability. Why? There's no "duty to rescue" another person. This is coming under assault in many jurisdictions not only for the emotional impact in these hypotheticals, but also in reaction to heart-wrenching cases, such as one involving a child abducted and killed in a Las Vegas casino. Again, the law does not exist in a vacuum, but ultimately reflects the mores and fears of the society and its time.

What if the boy was her son? Then yes, there *is* liability as there *is* a duty to rescue when a "special relationship" exists, as would be true also if, say, the boy were a patient or if she were serving in a medical or lifesaving capacity. Unless...a rescue would have put the rescuer in danger (usually).

This then becomes the logical pattern for tort law, and indeed for all of the law:

> The general rule is x...

When you read that, you should read "The general rule is x..." and then you should wait.

This is important.

Wait.

What are you waiting for?

You are waiting for a comma, and then a word. The word is:

> , unless...

Huh?

That "unless" is the *exception* to the rule.

Wait, wait, wait for the *unless*. The *unless* is the true meaning of the law. Anyone can memorize a general rule, or lots of general rules. Whoopee. The key is to know when an *unless* applies, and how it applies, and then how to actually apply it. Black letter law (rule, exception, and exception-to-exception), and how to think like a lawyer (*i.e.,* "...how to actually apply it").

That is the law. Both the study and the practice of.

How will you know whether an *unless* applies? A *fact* will tell you so. In the above case, we learn that the general rule is "no duty to rescue." (Note: you might get a fraction of a point on an exam for mentioning the social utility—or disutility—of that rule. You've fifteen seconds. Mention it and *move on*.)

Okay. Agree or disagree, that's the rule.

...unless it's not. Perhaps the jurisdiction has passed a new rule. Perhaps a number of jurisdictions don't like the old rule, and start passing the new rule. Chances are, if it's truly against a new public consciousness, this "minority rule" will over time become a "majority rule"—and all of a sudden we have a...*new general rule!* The old majority rule then becomes the minority rule, and *it* becomes the *unless.*

Unless is key.

It's also (and especially) key with regard to the facts. We learn that the boy is her son, a fact that removes the case from the general rule and places it instead within the exception to that general rule:

> There is no duty to rescue, **unless** a special relation-ship exists between the rescuer and victim. A "special relationship" includes an immediate family member.

> The woman had no duty to rescue, unless there was a special relationship between her and the boy. There was a special relationship, therefore she had a duty, therefore she is liable for failing to rescue the boy.

But there can be exceptions to the exceptions. If, for example, she would be put at special risk to try to save the boy—say, a rescue attempt that would be impossible due to weather or her own condition, then that case would then fall within an exception to the exception.

> There is no duty to rescue, **unless** a special relationship exists between the rescuer and victim, **unless** a rescue attempt would place the rescuer at undue risk...

> There was a special relationship **but** she would have
> been at undue risk of harm, therefore she did not have
> a duty, therefore she is not liable for failing to rescue
> the boy.

Also, these two *unlesses* can operate independently (so the above construction is itself a simplification). This means that, in a tort case (or on a tort exam), you might (and will) have multiple *unlesses* operating all at once. The key is to separate each of them out, and address them, separately. This is crucial. And it's also crucial that this be at a *brisk* pace—as if your mind is itself a human supercomputer. Thus my nagging about the importance of studying *intensely*.

This is a fact pattern that reinforces the interconnections of legal doctrines. Such a fact pattern could almost as easily be on a criminal law exam.

This is fascinating, yes?

Fun, even?

I picked this topic because I happened to think of it. There are many, many others, and indeed the process above should be repeated hundreds upon hundreds of times. It should be *fun*. Not the actual hypothetical—it's easy to get emotional about a boy in need of rescue, but that's a trap *in this limited sense of learning the law*. These are *hypotheticals*. We can change the facts, and we should do so to define just what facts apply, in what ways.

More importantly—and this might strike you as a bit odd—we might not even be *right*. That's okay. The important point when working through hypotheticals is that we nail down the legal variables. It might be, for example, that a special relationship would trump a risk to oneself. I doubt it, but it's possible. Result? Exactly the opposite as what's indicated above.

How can *this* be right? Because the important point in the law—and thus law school—is to understand how one defines the question. The important point in law *practice* is to confirm the actual rule, with actual statutes and actual case law, and square those with the facts. For an attorney to simply state "the answer is *x*" without doing *some* research is malpractice, or close to it. In law school, it's the essence of learning: you lay out the rules, exceptions, and exceptions to exceptions, and rather than "answering" the question you instead *reason* through the hypothetical. That shows that you (1) know the rule (*i.e.,* black letter law, including the exceptions and exceptions-to-exceptions, which are really fairly basic, as above); and (2) know how to think like a lawyer. And it shows that you will know how to find the real answer when a real case comes before you.

I repeat this too often, I know, but your professor will know *within seconds* whether you have it. *Getting* it requires (1) learning black letter law, and (2) learning how to use it. Part One is acquired through creation of your own master and summary outlines. That's it. No notes, no case briefs, no color-coding, no nonsense. Two outlines, done by *you*. Not just memorized but *internalized*. Part Two is acquired through working hypotheticals. If schizophrenic, you can do this alone. Otherwise, you'll need a team. More on that later.

With cases in law school, the facts are given. The same process is involved as with hypos. In *real* cases we can and should feel for the individuals. That is a hardening that affects all too many lawyers, and that you should resist. But the *process* is the same. Like or dislike a case—or a client—the legal analysis should be, well, analytical, not fluff. You don't arrive at an answer because you "feel" that Party Z should win. You don't even necessarily have to arrive at an answer. You *do* need to arrive at a question, properly framed, and fit the facts of Party Z within that analysis.

What if she rescues the boy but he is injured as a result? Answer: it depends upon whether she acted with "reasonable care"—which might then turn on whether a non-physician or physician standard is used (and, if so, whether it will be as a general practitioner or as a specialist). It also depends upon the jurisdiction, as many have limited or eliminated liability for rescuers, to encourage rescue.

See where this takes us? To a truly *engaging* discussion of a fact pattern to determine which facts are relevant, which rules apply, and what other facts might alter the outcome of the case. This is one reason law professors enjoy teaching torts, as nearly everyone feels comfortable with the general fact patterns—and nearly everyone can be tripped up by simply accepting an answer without understanding the exception and exception-to-the-exception nature of Tort Law especially.

Note too that this is just how an attorney will likely first hear a case: a client enters the office and begins to vent a stream of relevant *and* irrelevant facts. The attorney must sift through the blob of a story to determine which are relevant, which are not (at least not immediately), and where that leads the case, even and perhaps especially if it's against the client:

"Was the boy related to you?"

[Answer.]

"Oh, yes, he is your *son*. Very interesting. Was there a reason you decided not to jump in the water?"

[Another answer.]

"Ah, yes, I see. Let me see if I have this correctly. The river was filled with ice, the battery in your wheelchair was running low, you had lost your cane, you were apparently suffering from a reaction to your insulin, you thought he was your *other* son who is a champion swimmer, and, let me see if I have this right, once you realized who he was you remembered that you never much cared for this one anyway."

[Pause.]

"*Hmm,* well yes this does raise a few possibilities in our defense…"

CRIMINAL LAW AND PROCEDURE

Law schools usually teach Criminal Law as part of the first year curriculum (usually as a one-semester "stand-alone" and sometimes in the fall of the second year), while usually offering Criminal Procedure as an elective. This too is a shame, as a survey course of both, putting both in the context of each other, would be more effective. It would also be quite possible to pair Criminal Law with Torts (the former dealing, as mentioned, with offenses against the state and the latter with private offenses), or Criminal Procedure with Civil Procedure (both concerning, differently but with similar mechanisms, issues of how the law actually operates), or Criminal Law with Torts and Criminal Procedure with Evidence. See how interconnected the law is? This too is a fun aspect of the law, once you get the hang of it.

To keep it reasonably simple:

Criminal Law is the legal end of the societal stick: What happens when a person violates the norms of that society?

Criminal Procedure, in the United States, is tied closely with constitutional considerations of due process.

It's easy to bring one's personal feelings about crime, punishment, and general social commentary into a discussion of Criminal Law and Procedure—and that's not unreasonable. It is, however, a trap. It's a near-guarantee of a bad grade, if that's all you do. Give the law a chance to explain itself. Suspend your beliefs for just a while. Don't worry; you can re-invite them back if you wish.

As I write this I keep thinking of the scene in *The Matrix* where Morpheus is attempting to convince Neo that he can achieve incredible feats if only he will free his mind of preconceptions that limit him to artificially low potential. This is because Neo is trapped, mentally, in a false reality.

This *is* the reality, for most, in law school. And it is a reality because most assume, consciously or otherwise, that their own opinions (although most don't like to think of them that way) count. They don't. At least not yet. This is not intended as an insult, but rather as a matter of fundamental truth: the law cannot be beholden to a single perspective—or it's no longer the law. It especially is not beholden to a single perspective of a non-judge.

Free your mind.

For example, one doctrine that invariably causes difficulty for students (and the general public) involves insanity as a defense to a criminal charge. First, it's important to know that this defense almost never flies. There are very, *very* few successful cases of an insanity plea. Second, this doesn't (usually) mean that the defendant walks; instead, the person is confined under a different set of rules. Third, this doctrine (doctrines, really) developed in tandem with our understanding of mental illness. We can agree or disagree, but the tests for insanity mirror our conceptions of what it means to be criminally liable. This in turn takes us to the first weeks of your criminal law course, where we talk about these concepts. Unfortunately, when we first hear them we don't realize how fundamental they are, and that nearly everything that follows that semester will hang on them. And, because we're pissed off—if only the law were the way we saw it!—we deride every sentence, never getting beyond our own limited sense. *Free your mind.*

It might well be that the better social response is "Sorry, we don't care. You commit a heinous act, we ain't letting you use this defense." But before you reach this conclusion, let in the reasoning of dozens of judges, for just a hearing. Remember, these judges are hardly the wild-and-crazy, funkalicious, do-anything-but-be-serious types to simply throw some decision at the bench and then retire for a fast game of the latest version of *Grand Theft Auto.*

In class you should play your own Devil's Advocate: why is the professor wrong...and why are you? Once you can answer both sides, equally well, then you'll realize this is all child's play. It's almost like law (elementary) school. You will know the law, which you will know how to use to question either side. *That* is what it means to Get Good.

Criminal Law involves the power of the State, and as a result, in our system and with our history, we react hesitantly to that power. As a result of that hesitation, we constrain the State and attempt to empower the individual, even though we *know* that this will result in injustice. Why? Because much as we like to hope otherwise, we cannot know what happened. We cannot climb into the mind of the defendant to see what happened, or what they thought. We rely, instead, on twelve jurors to decide which side's witnesses are the more believable. Hardly a reassuringly accurate system. The choice, essentially, is between overconvicting in the hope to get all the bad guys, or underconvicting in the hope that we don't get the good guy who *seems* like the bad guy, caught up in the wrong place at the wrong time. How many of us have ever been there? We also want the State to stay pure. Not to cut corners. Remember, with the power of the state, an ability to cut corners means that we don't know *whose* corners will be cut—but we do know that there will be blood. And so we punish the State (officially its agents, but unofficially all of us) when it does cut corners, or gets sloppy, or simply fails to prove its case.

This is not a happy reality, and it does no good to say that we can somehow avoid the horns of this dilemma. No, we can't. This is the choice, and our society has chosen what we see as the lesser of two evils. Once that decision is accepted, or at least understood, then Criminal Law and Procedure fall into logical place.

Free your mind.

It's not, by the way, that you should suspend your beliefs permanently. Rather, you should hold them aloft for a different viewing, and then reexamine whether they still fit a new understanding. What *should* happen is that, even if you hold the same views— as you likely will—you should have a more refined understanding of the other side's views.

Moreover, what should happen is a moderation in your views. It's hard to remain an extremist if you give a fair hearing—a truly *fair* hearing—to the other side. (An interesting phenomenon happens to a sizeable minority, particularly those with strong beliefs: they can flip to the opposite extreme. I knew a radical leftist in first year who became a reactionary conservative in his second year. This seems to be a danger the more extreme one's views are.)

Keep in mind that Criminal Law and Procedure involve the State *as a party,* and that will keep most of the discussions that follow in context. Victims are not parties; they're witnesses. The court is not the "State" for purposes of its relationship with the prosecutor and defense attorney. This is the essence of the court's sublime role as a co-equal branch: It sits apart from the State's executory arm. And the Defense serves as a "necessary evil" in a purposeful tension with the State. In essence, even where the State pays for it, the Defense's role is to keep the State honest.

"Prove it," says the Defense to the State.

And *free your mind,* say them all to you.

CONSTITUTIONAL LAW

Our society has over the past few decades been in a "down cycle" in its view of history, including a history of what makes our law and society unique. What began as a critique of conventional wisdom devolved into an assumption that whatever existed before must have been bad, or wrong, or just-about evil. This includes, for now, both the Constitution and its Framers. It's entirely appropriate to examine, critique, and even castigate the Constitution, its framers, or indeed any of the law—but one ought to do so with a fair reading.

The U.S. Constitution is simply the most important document—outside the Old or New Testaments, Qur'an, or other religious text—ever written. It is the culmination of a multi-thousand-year conversation, and it has proved influential ever since. It drew from a "Grand Conversation" of thinkers stretching from Greek and Roman philosophers through to the Enlightenment and then-contemporary European agitators. Along with the Declaration of Independence, its framers—who could probably not get elected to the lowest local offices today—were well-read, aristocratic, and ready to put their lives on the line, quite literally.

The U.S. Constitution is the most important document in history not because we say so (and certainly not because I say so), but because *others* say so: it has been used as a model, if not *the* model, directly or indirectly, for every other constitution in every other nation on the planet. *That* is precedent.

Moreover, it is important because it *survives*. It strikes an astonishingly resilient balance between principled structure and flexible interpretation. Other cultures are quick—with some justification—in critique of American adolescence. Ours is, however, the oldest major continuous government on the planet. For good or bad, that is an accomplishment that ought not be taken lightly.

U.S. Constitutional Law is, of necessity, a product of the American experience. The concerns of its framers were unique to the American circumstance, and thus we have doctrines that are quite different from comparable doctrines in other nations. Whether theirs or ours is superior is a qualitative judgment, and one that depends upon both who is doing the judging and what, exactly, is being judged. Happily, we need not focus on that in law school. Or, more precisely, we need not (and must not) focus on such philosophical musings in a law exam. Spend no more than *seconds* on "public policy" in an actual exam. It *is* useful to put the doctrines we do need to know into context, and it certainly is helpful for the extra point here and half-point there—but it's not the main event. Black letter law plus hypotheticals *are*.

Thus, as with the other areas, it's important not to go into class with an emotional, quasi-intellectual chip on your shoulder. This, for the twenty-second time, gets to one of the deepest issues faced by many law students: the thought that their thought counts. This might come as a shock—and a rude shock at that—but embrace this: the law doesn't care what you think. That bears repeating: *the law does not care what you think.*

The law does not care what I think, or what anyone I have practiced with thinks, or what anyone I have ever known thinks, or what anyone *they* have known thinks. In groups we can change the direction of the law, in small ways (usually), but that is a different animal. Even those few lawyers who change the law do so at the margins, and in the context of a much larger picture that *does not change.* In a sense, it's like an ant building a new home in a vast landscape: yes, the ant can change the landscape, but only in the most infinitesimal ways. To the ant, those changes might be profoundly important; it is, after all, its home. But compared with the other beasts roaming above, it's hardly worth noticing, much less valuing. In this, we are the ants.

The same could be said of most disciplines—mathematics, astronomy, biochemistry—yet because law is closer to the social arts than to the sciences, it's easy to misconstrue our own role. It's easy to believe that our opinions count more than they do. Or, indeed, for us to think that our opinions are more than mere opinion.

The law *does* care that you familiarize yourself with its meaning and contours. Some of you, perhaps, *will* serve to change the law. As legislators, or legislative aids, or star professors, or top attorneys, you might have the occasion to argue for some change in one of the many rules within our legal framework. If so, my genuine respect for the future you. I mean that. For the vast majority of attorneys, however, our role is rather more limited: to serve clients, including governments, defendants, and students.

For all law students, the task is even simpler: Learn the law.

Part of this is to challenge your understanding of how the law operates, but that is not the same as challenging the law. It's fine to act as an "armchair Justice"—but understand that that role is for education and amusement, not for anyone listening.

This will come as a hard pill to swallow. I know. I was and am that person who wants to change the law. Yet that is at cross-purposes to the essence of what law school is about. First, it's about gaining a proficiency and then mastery of at least the basic principles of law. These principles are susceptible to political or emotional judgments—but they are not susceptible to being changed, at least not in law school. Free your mind. Rather than rant in class against the tort rule that there is no duty to rescue, or against the criminal law that the bad guys get away with murder, or...whatever rule gets your knickers in a bunch...know instead, in your bones, that *your job is to understand what judges have said the law is.*

What will happen, if you take this seriously, is that you'll very likely find that judges have *already made the same arguments that you thought were original.* They're not dumb. We might disagree with *x* case or *y* dicta, but they've been fighting these jurisprudential battles quite literally since before your *grandparents* were born. And, for considered reasons, judges have ruled consistently one way or the other. Sometimes you might agree, and sometimes not. You might be right, you might not. Whatever the case, understand that your role is, first, to understand. Atticus Falcon perhaps said it best in *Planet Law School:*

> Sometimes the pace [of change] is glacial, sometimes almost hectic. Yet, if and when you do practice law, it will be rare for you to have anything whatsoever to do with those changes. This is not meant as an insult to you. It's just the way the Law is, for 99.9% of those who are in it. It's safe to say that will include you. It certainly includes me.
>
> In fact, the *weakest* argument you can make to a court is to merely say "The law ought to be changed." That's tantamount to merely making the child's plaint, *"It's not fair!"* This is a favorite argument of law school students—and if that's all you can come up with, it's nearly *guaranteed* to get you *low* marks, whether from a professor, a supervising attorney, or a judge.

Then, a bit later:

> It isn't much of an exaggeration to say the courts don't care what *you* think; courts only care what other *courts* think, especially higher courts.

Bingo. I'm more than a little embarrassed to write that *I* didn't get this—truly get it—until I read the above statement, *years* after having been in practice. If you honestly, truly want to change the law, then plan to go into a staff position in a legislature (or run for local office), or into the courts. Neither is an easy option, and neither will grant immediate access to change the world (probably), but both offer a good life, a more intellectual life, and plenty of "big picture" issues that are simply absent outside of being a law professor.

In the meantime, free your mind. Approach Constitutional Law (among other subjects) as a mosaic to study and appreciate—but save the pontificating for worthy jousting friends who, like you, need to blow off steam. Just keep it all in stride, as the bigger purpose is not to critique the law, but to learn it. Again, this is not intended as an insult; give judges a bit more credit, and you'll be amazed at the power of reading what it is that they've already written.

Okay, then. That's a fair amount of seeming hagiography. What, again, is constitutional law?

As the saying goes, it is what the justices decide it to be. There are times when constitutional law is, arguably, wrong. There are even times when constitutional law is almost palpably wrong—or at least arbitrary. To take just one example, everyone "knows" that polygamy is wrong, yes? The Federal government all but forced Utah's Mormon community to renounce polygamy (in practice, polygyny) in order to join the Union. This happened, conveniently, when the then-head of the Church of Jesus Christ of Latter-Day Saints had a vision of God telling him that Mormons should renounce polygamy in order to join the Union. The timing, a bit suspicious, led to the splintering of the church into a dozen groups. These groups, continuing the practice of polygamy, are quite active today. In fact, they are among the most successful (if hidden) of religious groups in the country. Clearly there are related issues of involuntary, underage "marriages," but while related those are, logically, separate issues.

In 1878, the U.S. Supreme Court held that polygamy was, well, not normal: polygamy was "contrary to the spirit of Christianity." Aside from the uncomfortable truth that the justices were historically and theologically wrong, such reasoning was, well, thin at best. One of the reasons the law is enormously engaging is that it's possible to put forth argument after argument—and still lose. It's also possible to lose and lose and lose—and still have the better argument. It's happened many times. As to the Court's being wrong, for example, polygamy has been practiced throughout history, in most societies, and is on any reading sanctioned in Judaism and Islam and is an integral part of the Christian biblical tradition. Think Abraham and his three wives; King David and his 18 wives; and his son King Solomon—whose *Song* is read at weddings as a hymn to monogamy—who somehow handled 700 wives. Anthropologists estimate that three-quarters of societies have, at one point, allowed for polygamy. What the justices *really* meant was that it was not normal for polite society at the time. Men were expected to have mistresses, not multiple wives. The law is wonderful because the truth can be told—even if it's ignored. The assumption and hope is that, at some point, deeper truths will in time overcome the petty ones.

There are many, many examples of this—examples "proving" whatever one is predisposed to want to prove. There are even cases where the justices didn't just ignore precedent, logic, and facts, but where they actually, blatantly *overruled* the clear meaning of statutory language. Often, the legislature is complicit, as it very much prefers to let the Court take the heat for positions that would be political suicide. Some of these decisions are hugely important—affecting each of us—right now. I leave it to you to find them, and also to question your own predispositions. When looking at the law, it should be a matter of suspending your beliefs for long enough to question whether your reasoning is valid, or not. If not, it's important to know why.

Having written all that, these cases are just the icing on the jurisprudential cake: I happened to use this example because I thought a word like "polygamy" might be a tad bit more interesting than, say, "interstate commerce." Chances are you'll find these cases more, *ah,* stimulating—just as your professors will. So enjoy. Really. Don't feel that you have to get stuck in the rut of any subject. Yes, there are rules to learn…but you can test those rules with the wildest of cases…or hypotheticals.

There is a dynamic aspect to the law that is important to consider: courts are asked to interpret the law given facts that are often unconsidered when the law is drafted and might involve, for example, a technology that didn't exist when the law came into effect, or social mores that simply change, such as with Civil Rights, or involve facts or issues at the outer edge of what the law requires. The courts are supposed to look first to the statutory language or precedent, in that order, then to "rules of construction" as to how, exactly, to interpret the law to apply to a given set of facts. If Congress and the President disagree with the U.S. Supreme Court's ultimate decision, or with any lower court's decision, they may pass into law a rule that overturns what the court(s) just decided. So far so good. This does not apply, however, where the Court (when capitalized, this refers to the U.S. Supreme Court) decides that a law is unconstitutional.

Constitutional law, as it's currently interpreted, gives the U.S. Supreme Court the ultimate authority to decide just what is or is not constitutional. Notably, this authority is found nowhere in the Constitution, but is instead inferred. And, crucially, for political and practical reasons both the President and Congress have, for the most part, acquiesced. It's unlikely this will change, but one additional curiosity is the thought of what the picture might look like if the President or Congress—for their own political reasons, to be sure—ever told the Court "No." They would have a strong argument, as they are given co-equal obligation to uphold the Constitution…but it's unlikely ever to happen. It would, however, make for an interesting constitutional crisis.

Note: No, I am not arguing that this is what the President and Congress *should* do, although they no doubt would like to now and again. Rather, it's important to think through *why* each has demurred in forcing an issue. They might disagree politically or disagree jurisprudentially—and chances are good that they would be right. At base there are real and powerful reasons—pragmatic, real-world, non-legal reasons—they do demur. And the Court, of course, benefits (as, arguably, do we all).

This is one of the joys of thinking about the law—and it's one of the joys that should transfer in law school from faculty to you. After all, this type of "armchair quarterbacking" is an essence of legal reasoning, and is *the* essence of one of your major tasks: the hypothetical. And it's the fun part. Thus my constant harangues about working hypotheticals: this is the essence (and joy) of learning (and using) the law.

What if, what if, *what if!*

If Constitutional Law is the granddaddy of "big picture" law, the next sits at the opposite corner.

CIVIL PROCEDURE

We thus arrive at perhaps the most feared subjects in First Year: Civil Procedure, or "Civ. Pro."

This might be the most painful first-year course for most because it hits no readily known landmarks. Everyone knows words like "contract," "property," "burglary," and so on. But "12(b)(6)," "permissive joinder," "impleader," "interpleader," "interventions," and on and on? Ack! And by its nature, civil procedure is, well, procedural. It's not about any of the grand elements of the law. It's about keeping a litigation train on its judicial tracks and trying to keep the squeaking, squealing, and slipping to a minimum.

In fact, that's as good a way to think of it as any. A train leaves a station, starting on its journey. That is the filing of the case. In the real world, this follows many steps, such as the initial meeting with the client, demand letters, negotiation, threats, and so on. It should also follow a serious investigation, quite apart from what happens with the other side. That might be likened to the passengers getting their suits spiffed up and getting ready to board the train. In this case, there are just two passengers: the Plaintiff and the Defendant. There is a conductor (the judge), a few stewards (attorneys for either side), and the occasional expert mechanic or two.

The train starts on its journey, and its accelerator is locked. It continues, lumbering down its path. The litigation will continue until something happens. Maybe the case is a bad one. So the conductor orders the train to take an early sidetrack, perhaps to stop completely (if dismissed "with prejudice"). This doesn't happen often, however, as the conductors have been told to get their passengers to their destinations—and as passengers who get tossed out can get rather unruly, and complain to the railway. Very messy. Maybe the issues are confusing and poorly (and numerously) stated, so the conductor orders a slow run through pre-trial hearings, to clean the train of unnecessary weight. Maybe the conductor has other passengers to worry about, so he orders the car to a side track—say, mediation—in the hope that those quarrelsome passengers will go away. Or maybe there are more passengers who want to go to the destination. Perhaps they should climb aboard, joining along for the ride.

This is one determined conductor. Nothing will stop this train until it finishes its run. If it continues down the path to trial, we begin to see steam and other signs of speed and excitement. Maybe the award is disputed, so the train continues on to a destination with better appeal.

The task in law school is to understand the fundamentally linear nature of civil procedure. Everything that is discussed is something that will happen, or could happen, on or to that train. Why do we care? Because the destination of that train is something we care about: dispute resolution. We care about this because it's important to our society, and to our economy: We don't like disputes. They're messy. They're costly. They're distracting. We do like resolution. It's cleansing (usually). It's cheaper. It's re-focusing. Ultimately, it's highly productive.

The courts in the U.S. have long been pro-business. This is not written in the political sense, but rather in the pragmatic one. We often forget just how impactful the Industrial Revolution was, but as we moved from an agrarian to an industrial society, the courts were there, cheerleading the enormous developments that affected all aspects of society. This was true because the elite of society believed, for the most part, in its mission, which included such social thoughts as Manifest Destiny and Social Darwinism. We can (and do) certainly criticize these now, but they explain a lot. The truth is that our wealth is possible only because of the commercial inclinations and midwifery of U.S. courts throughout American history.

As a result, courts are predisposed to act in ways that further the financial health of future parties, generally. This is not idle chatter. If considering the impact of a rule, courts will consider what happens if a different rule is adopted…with the result that courts will nearly always adopt a rule that is self-regulating. This means that the courts (1) want businesses (especially) to correct mistakes that led to litigation in the past; and (2) courts have neither the manpower nor inclination to "watch over" litigants. This means that civil procedure works, to a very large degree, with surprisingly little input from judges.

So, our conductor might stop by every once in a while, such as for a pre-trial conference or two, but otherwise occupies himself with other passengers. Other than that, passengers and attendants are expected—to an amazing degree—to take care of their own needs. While we study the "official" interactions involving the conductor and stewards, it's important to keep the litigant-focus in mind. Much of what we study in Civ Pro thus relates to these other interactions, such as the questions we ask of each other (interrogatories) and other forms of discovery, and how the litigants can reach the destination (resolving the dispute) based on what each brings to the train.

With all this in mind, and with your outline underway, Civ Pro will not be the nightmare it is for most. It will, instead, be a pleasant ride through the legal countryside.

LEGAL RESEARCH AND WRITING

This is a more difficult topic to broach here—not because it should be, but because of how it is broached in law school.

You are likely to face some version of a hypothetical to which you are to write a brief or memorandum and in which you are to consult a relatively known (and small) set of cases and rules. You will often be broken into smaller groups for "intensive" writing, again with the idea that this will bridge the theoretical world of law school with the pragmatic world of law practice.

This was a result of the infamous MacCrate Report, commissioned by the ABA and resulting in a report critical of law schools' retreat from the messier world of contracts, briefs and—horrors— timesheets. There is much that might be written about both the ABA's report and also its reactions. For our purposes, law schools have undergone a decade-long process of responding to this critique—part of which is the now-universal Legal Research and Writing course.

The difficulty comes in that learning about how the law is actually practiced is quite a bit different (and more difficult) than it is presented, and does not neatly fit into the law school world. Among these realities is that your writing class will likely be led by an instructor, who may or may not be a professor and who may or may not have practiced law for any appreciable length of time, and assisted, usually, by upperclass "TAs" (or their law school equivalents). Often, these TAs have backgrounds in English or other evidence of writing ability—but this too is quite different from *legal* writing.

The real difficulty comes in that one does not master legal writing—in the sense of knowing, for example, what a court would really need to see, or how a provision should really be modified— for *years*. It's safe to say that an attorney doesn't get really good at the practice of law for eight to ten years. About the amount of time it takes to make partner, give or take. And even that is just the beginning of true proficiency. It's fairly safe to assume that you will not be taught by such a person. This is not intended as an insult to legal research and writing instructors, who are among the most dedicated you'll meet. Still, most have not practiced for more than a few years, and some not at all.

To be honest, I'm a little conflicted about the advice to give in this area. Research and writing programs have improved, and they address an issue of crucial importance to your success in the law. My own feeling, however, is that they are mostly a waste in first year; they should be central during the second and third years in expanded clinical programs. But, as I wrote before, no one will care what I think.

That's not, however, the greater concern. What is of concern is that many programs are—how shall I put this?—crap. This might be unfair, and again, it's not a reflection on the instructors. Rather, it's a result of how law schools are addressing, in fits and starts, the critiques of the MacCrate Report. On the ground, this means that you might have a (required) course that is, essentially, a lot of work with little benefit. Moreover, and here's the irony, most law firms don't really care. This is because they will teach you what they think you need to know, in the manner of that firm. Clearly, they will not be pleased with a bad grade—but they'll hardly shower accolades over a good grade as they will with "real" courses.

What to do? First, guard against spending an excessive amount of time in any such project. How much is "excessive"? Well, using your 60-hour-per-week benchmark, you should not devote substantially more to it than a per-credit pro rata share would indicate. So if it's a one- or two-credit course (not uncommon), it should not get as much time as one of your three- or four-credit courses. Here again, I'm being a little unfair, because these projects *are* time-consuming. Perhaps the best advice is to keep this in mind, and don't allow it to drain too much time from your other work, and especially not as you approach finals. Focus on its immediate value: a writing sample for potential employers.

That written, this *is* important. So, instead of spending lots of time, you might instead attempt the same trick that you will be doing with your classes: becoming highly efficient. You need to get to the point where you can almost draft language that is "airtight" *without substantial editing.* This is *much* harder written than done. Most attorneys, again, don't get good at this for years. Some don't get good, ever. The key is to think, intensively, about what it is that you're trying to convey. Who is it about, who is to be included, who is not to be included, what is being attempted, and so on. From there, you want to draft that *in the fewest, simplest words possible.*

Brevity is prized in (good) legal writing. If it's not at your program, I encourage you to do the absolute minimum, give wild and effusive lip-service to it, and endeavor to learn *good* legal writing in your summer and part-time work. Among the resources, you might consult those written by Bryan Garner. He's written quite a few, and is superb.

But What if I Don't Want To?

Concision and precision are gold. Both are harder than they seem. Try, try, try not to write simply for the sake of writing.

There, I've written too much already.

What You'll Need

The resources available to law students have blossomed since I was in law school. So much so that few can keep up—much less, provide an objective view of the relative qualities of each.

There are two categories of writing in the law practice world: primary sources and secondary sources. Primary sources are the actual text of statutes, regulation, and cases: what legislators, administrators, and the courts say the law is. Secondary sources are…everything else.

The paradox in both practice and law school worlds is that, while primary sources *are* the law, they are not the best way to *learn* the law. When an attorney is asked, say, to draft a memo for a client in an area of the law that that attorney is unfamiliar with, the attorney will almost certainly *not* go first to the cases. Sure, if the local journal has an article about an important new case, the attorney might go read it…but chances are high that the attorney will rely on that article, instead. That is a secondary source.

You should learn the law in almost the same way. Why only *almost?* Because the attorney will already have a broad understanding of the law, and needs to fill in specific questions. The attorney also has a concrete fact pattern in mind—the one given by the client's situation. So, your task in law school is to mirror the general approach of relying first on secondary sources, not primary ones.

So what are these secondary sources?

Primers. These are the "introductions to…" that serve as general, well, introductions to the topic. They usually are short, written for an intelligent but lay audience, and intended to deliver just the rough contours of an area. Given the profusion of new sources, many primers are becoming increasingly detailed, almost rivaling hornbooks. You do not need a hornbook. You need a *brief* introduction. The Nutshell series are an example—although not the only ones—and as with many primers suffer from uneven quality. I suggest that you refer to *Planet Law School* for the better ones, and also that you compare specific sections in whichever competing books you're considering.

Hornbooks. These are mini-treatises on a topic, usually written by one or two demigods in the law school world. An example is Prosser & Keeton on Torts. Although West (a major publisher in the law) has developed a line of mini-hornbooks for students, be wary of these. Why? They are far too detailed for your needs. Some explanation might be helpful, as it strikes many students as odd to be "too good." In fact, one way students fail is to get bogged down in the process of learning "the law" in too *much* detail. They start to drown in detail, never gaining the broader insight necessary to the higher-order need to "think like a lawyer." In short, hornbooks are okay after you have developed an understanding of an area of the law. If used, it should be to confirm a specific, narrow question. That's it. It is not to "learn" the law.

Treatises. In law practice, the needs are highly case-specific. There are thus a range of series—treatises—most so large they have their own shelves. These are multi-volume compilations (leather-bound or loose-leaf in massive binders). Usually, these started from demigods and are now mostly updated by editors or corporate-publishing staff. With the advent of electronic sources, these too are undergoing change, if not obsolescence. If hornbooks are too much, treatises are way, *way* too much. In fact, hornbooks are often condensed treatises. Avoid them both until you're drafting your law review article.

Casebooks. These are the "textbooks" in law school…but there's not usually a whole lot of "text" in these books—in the sense of interpretive commentary. What there is is usually a collection of cases, edited in the (vain) hope that that will help students to uncover the reasoning of the court as to that point of law. The problems are twofold: first, they presuppose that you will glean the meaning from the facts; and second, they are written by judges who already know the law. Thus, little explanation—or context—is in these cases.

And now to the more "canned" study aids:

"Canned briefs." These go by a number of names and series, and are, in essence, *Cliff Notes* for cases. They break down, usually on a single page or two, cases students are expected to read. Highly seductive, the danger (and professorial condemnation) is that like cocaine they will not "boost" your reading but will instead substitute for it.

Commercial Outlines. There is a sense that professors have condemned these for eternity. The reality is that, when they first appeared, they were indeed condemned—for the reasons I'll get into below. But few professors condemn them today, as they've become part of the law school landscape. These are, in short, a hierarchical view of rules, sub-rules, and exceptions. They are *essential* to your study of the law, as they are a way to structure the law and to "zoom in" on a specific area and easily "zoom out" to the broader meaning. This is a crucial skill, and outlines are fundamentally important to that skill.

Examples & Explanations. This is a series started by Aspen and deserving its own section here, because it is so useful as you and your learning team get into the discussion of hypotheticals. The author of *Planet Law School* is probably the single-most important catalyst for the success of this series, because his was the first voice recommending them. I leave it to him to point the way to specific books you will find of use. Importantly, Aspen has expanded its series considerably since *Planet Law School* was written, and thus you might consider those additional titles as well—once you've used the primary ones recommended there.

Restatements of [Each Subject]. This too was a resource largely exposed by the author of *Planet Law School*. The "Restatements" are among the most important references in the law, not just because they contain the combined wisdom of legal thinking from the brightest stars in the legal universe but *because* of that, their value is hugely persuasive. In field after field, teams of these legal stars cogitated and conspired to set forth not just what the law was but also what it should be. Because they were the stars, and because their work was so well reasoned, the *Restatements* were transformed from mere "restatements" to proto-legislation. Courts would find comfort in a line of reasoning pointed out in the *Restatements*, and thus find "cover" for changing the law. In this way, the *Restatements* are as much a predictive as descriptive tool—and especially so for the student editions, which you absolutely should use. For you and your learning team, they serve another purpose. The *Restatements* are written in a wonderful style in which, like Aspen's *Examples & Explanations* series, they set forth the rule and then provide a series of mini-hypos to illustrate those rules. If law is a mistress, this is one you'd forever regret you didn't marry.

Flashcards. These are a derivation of the old 3x5 index cards we'd use to memorize whatever was needed on an exam. If that's the way they're used, they're worse than useless. As with other secondary sources, however, they have grown up, and they are useful with your learning team as a way to break the routine and confirm your understanding of various areas in each subject. The ones I've seen from Aspen, the *Law in a Flash* series, are nicely done. Use with caution.

Dictionaries. *Black's* is the gold standard. For your purposes, however, you really won't need one—and you certainly won't need one in class. You should be able to find a definition in seconds online, and you'll save back and shoulder strain in not carrying around additional deadweight. As with other sources, it seems that we don't feel complete without a law dictionary, so if so, there's a pocket edition of *Black's,* but even it isn't cheap. If you're inclined to buy used, don't buy one before the 7th edition. You might also be able to find a sexy leather-bound edition in a used bookstore. *Très chic.*

Other. Law school bookstores are filled with any number of supplementary products, such as outlines on a single (sometimes bi- and tri-folded) sheet; exam series; audio and computer versions of all of the above; and no doubt more to come.

The exam series seems to be the latest addition to the shelves. I'm not sold, however, as to their being quite ready for prime time. The ones that I've seen are decent, but won't begin to replace what is needed in terms of working hypos. That is the key: if you get one and use it as a *supplement,* that's a plus. If you use it as a substitute for the work you need to do, then it's more of a detriment than aid.

My suggestion? Share these "extra" purchases within your team. There's no point in everyone having six sets of flash cards, exam series, and so on—but one copy in each subject is useful. Use the exams especially as yet another source of hypos to work through at the end of the semester—when your familiarity with black letter law and with working hypos allows you to take advantage of them—and take them under *timed* conditions. Don't cheat. Even a little. Use these to test yourself before the tests that count.

As to all of these aids, avoid either extreme: don't discount them as a needless expense, but don't go "whole hog" until you have genuinely used them in a course and find them to be effective and efficient uses of your time. How will you know? They'll be effective if they help you to learn black letter law or to think through the hypos. They will be efficient if, upon reflection, you couldn't have done it faster or better without them.

*   *   *

All right then. So which of all of the above should you use?

You should rely on primers and commercial outlines to start your own outlines. To repeat, you are *not* simply transposing from the commercial to your own outline—and certainly not simply using the commercial outline instead of doing your own. Either is a near-guarantee of failure. You *must* create your *own* outline. And you must do it *in pace* with your class.

In class, you should follow the 2-4 line briefing that I include later from Wentworth Miller. You might or might not use canned briefs; they're not bad, or wrong, but neither will they get you much mileage. Again, classroom participation *does not count*. What does count is what's in your brain, and whether and how you can use it.

What of the radical advice from some quarters that you not buy casebooks at all? After all, if they're not the real source, why bother? Well, I'm of two minds on this. First, it's a hard pill to swallow for anyone who's lived life in the classroom. While it isn't wrong, per se, and it would be entirely possible to, say, read the case via your laptop before and during class, I doubt that many students would feel comfortable without a big, heavy book sitting in front of them. I certainly wouldn't. In this sense, it's a (rather expensive) (and heavy) security blanket. That's fine and well, but keep in mind its use: a casebook is useful *after* you have learned the narrow set of rules for that portion of the course. This you must do with these other resources. Do *not* think of your casebook in the same way that you thought of your undergraduate textbooks. They are not the same *at all*.

In your learning team, you should share the expense of these secondary sources—because you don't need to have any of them on your own. This is a third, huge benefit of a learning team. You should, for example, each agree to purchase the *Restatement* for one course. Thus, everyone has something to go on for at least one subject—and can't blame others for "not having what they need to get started." You do the same for primers, commercial outlines, *Examples & Explanations,* and so on. You agree to "round robin" these sources, no less than once per week. In this way, you can all share in the benefit of an expense one-fifth or so less than if you bought them all yourself. Moreover, your learning team can use these changeover times as a good time to confirm that all members are on track, and are actually keeping up with the work.

NOT GOOD ENOUGH. I WANT SPECIFICS!

I want to know which *exact title* of each kind should I use! Which series is best? Which author? Which edition?

These are trick questions, with a trick answer.

The answer? It doesn't really matter. One train of thought is that, in comparison to the enormous costs of law school, even the exorbitant costs of *all* of the above resources is fairly modest. In the long view, even $1,000 per semester—on the high side, obvious-ly—is only about five percent of your tuition. Of course, these books come *on top of* your tuition and other costs, so it certainly doesn't *feel* modest. Were anyone to have said this to me, way back when, my response would have been unprintable.

So, let's move to the new-versus-used debate. Some guides state (unwisely) that you absolutely, positively must have shiny, brand-new, clean books...lest any inferior mind have soiled what you are about to glean, presumably. This is utter nonsense. I scoured the used bookstores in Austin for whatever I could find, and as I lived there had the advantage of first dibs on the best used books at the two law bookstores.

Even that doesn't go far enough. Here's the trick: *For your purposes in your first year of law school, it doesn't matter.* Even a mediocre secondary source is fine. This is perhaps one of the hardest aspects of law school to get your mind around—not least because everyone is saying how hard law school is, and everyone assumes that because it's hard there must be *something* to all these books. But law school isn't "hard"; it's disorienting. The law that you need to learn is "merely" the first three or four levels in your outline's hierarchy. You don't *need* to know *all* of the law. You don't need to know the fine points of the law. You *cannot* know all of the law, or the finest points. You *do* need to know the basics. All of them. And you need to know how to use them.

For that, just about any guide is sufficient. Yes, even a book written ten or even twenty years ago, faded and crumpled with use. Unless you're looking at an area that has undergone a judicial upset—in which case you darned well should know that from reading the papers and from staying awake in class—the rules that you read in a hornbook written *fifty* years ago should be almost identical to the same text you read in the same series written now. Okay, perhaps the uses of "he" have been changed, but aside from that, the law is the law. That is the essence of precedent, and the reason this is such a tempest in a law school teapot.

If you enjoy the sensuous feel of a brand-new book, and if you can afford it, by all means. But it's not required to do well. Personally, I bought whatever was available at pennies on the dollar. I was proudest of finding *Emanuel's* and other guides for fifty cents or so at bargain bins and flea markets. On balance, perhaps I shouldn't have spent so much time being quite so cheap, notwithstanding the few hundred dollars I lived on each month. The more important point is not to distract yourself on this

I have spoken with two executives at Aspen, by the way, and I like their products. They are expensive—seemingly more expensive even adjusting for inflation—but the books are also more developed and more numerous than when I was in law school. Again, this should not be the driver. There are ways to save, there are many resources, and a key is not to go overboard either way. Do not resist, buying into the (false) guidance or pretense that "the assigned texts are all you need"—nonsense—but neither should you buy every book in every subject, assuming that you'll somehow absorb all that knowledge as if by paper-to-mind osmosis.

To be worth anything you must *use* these books. Better to buy a single source and use it until its edges are dingy, than to have a shelf of untouched books. That is what happens to many, many law students. Don't let it happen to you.

OPERATING ASSUMPTIONS

This might seem a silly section, but it might be one of the most important in the book. The reason why will be apparent as each is discussed. Here they are:

1. Law exams and only law exams count

2. Classroom participation does not count

3. Your first year of law school is everything

Law Exams and Only Law Exams Count. I suspect that as you read this, yet another understandable mental response is heard: "Yeah, yeah. Got it."

No, I don't think so. One more time: "Law exams and *only* law exams count."

"Yes, yes. I *got* it!" Now you're annoyed.

Nope. I still don't think we're there. Now you're *really* getting peeved, yes?

"Look, mister. I know how to read and write English, and I know the meaning of the words you just wrote. I really don't want to read it again."

"Too bad," comes the response. Now this is starting to annoy even the typesetter. "I really don't think you get it."

"I've *told* you I get it." Exasperation now. "Why don't you believe me?"

"Because," annoying-writer continues, "law students will read this statement (or one like it) a dozen times…but they won't *believe* it. They won't believe it sufficiently *to change the way they've acted and interacted in classrooms for sixteen years.*"

Waiting for a moment, annoying-writer continues:

As a result, in their frustration and panic they will revert like academic lemmings to the tools and methods that served them well before—why *shouldn't* they use what worked before?

But these are near-guarantees of failure. Yet only those who've already gone through law school will recognize them. Why? Because for everyone else these ways have always worked before!

There's a reason that law school is so "hard." Students *make* it that way. Or, at least, they make it worse than it has to be. Things like taking copious notes, participating aggressively in class, detailed case briefs, sabotaging fellow students and playing "psy-ops" to gain the upper psychological "edge"…these are the *wrong* things to be doing in law school.

If you follow this path, you will almost certainly fail. Yet because they're so deeply ingrained, it is nearly impossible to push them aside and accept something new, something radical. Something scary.

Still a little peeved, you still want to know the secret, and you're just a little intrigued. So you decide to humor annoying-author.

Law Exams and Only Law Exams Count. This is repeated (again) for effect, and to refocus the discussion. Law students go through first-year with the delusion that profs can't *really* not consider their fine qualities. After all, they study hard, they attend and participate in class—all the good qualities of students anywhere. They try to make the professor (and themselves) look good. These should be rewarded, right?

Even when the professors themselves explain to students that the course grade will be determined solely on one exam, or perhaps two exams with a 10/90 weighting, or perhaps even an exam plus one or two bonus points for "good participation," it *still* doesn't sink in.

Free your mind.

Everything you thought prior to law school, you should un-think. All of the ways you succeeded in high school and under-graduate studies...most of them will be useless, or downright counterproductive. Law school mid-terms, to the extent that they count at all, are often worse that meaningless: they create a false sense of security in those who do well, and they're taken too seriously by everyone else. If they count for only ten percent, then they count for only ten percent. And they often count for only ten percent.

Why do mid-terms count for only ten percent? Because professors know that they can't really test what you're expected to learn: black letter law *and* the ability to use it. Professors know that it takes longer than just a semester to master both. It's also a way to ease you into taking law exams; it's the professors' way of "encouraging" you to break your bad habits.

Nearly every trait that students everywhere have taken for granted their entire lives *do not work in law school*. If you believe nothing else this book, believe this: College study habits are *bad* study habits. Yes, there's a lot in this book that you should believe "if nothing else."

Well, then, what does work?

Before we get to that, more (annoying) aversion therapy:

Classroom Participation Does Not Count. This too is restated for effect, and to re-re-focus. This should be superfluous, as it clearly fits within the first assumption: if law exams are the only thing that count, then as a matter of logic anything else, including classroom participation, does not count.

This is included because...we can read "law exams are the only thing that count" a hundred times and we still won't believe it. Worse, we won't *act* like we believe it. If classroom participation doesn't count—as indeed it does not—that carries significant meaning for how one should go about the study of law, and especially how we should go about the study of law in the classroom.

After all, isn't *not* acting on information worse than not having that information in the first place?

Why does this cut so much against the grain?

Because it *does*. For our entire academic lives, we have been rewarded for classroom participation, from "teacher's pet" to "brown-noser" to "extra credit for [you name it]."

No, no, no. Law school does not work that way.

In life, what is rewarded is encouraged. Teachers from grade school on reward classroom behavior—for good reason—so it is encouraged. This behavior becomes ingrained, so that as we move from elementary to secondary to higher education, we simply can't help ourselves. We *have* to show how smart, good, and worthy we are. In class. While this has its uses earlier, and while the law school classroom certainly *looks* like a classroom, this approach is useless in law school, and it is counterproductive in ways that do count. Namely, focusing on classroom participation will be a drain on efforts you *should* be focused on.

One book writes of the "nerve-wracking" aspects of preparing for class. What?! Yes, the way most students "prepare" for class (by attempting to read case after case after case) would make anyone's nerves, well, wracked. Egads. That's an awful way to spend law school. And it won't work. What's the rule again? Classroom participation does not count. You should thus not live in fear of whether and how well you stand up to questioning. The paradox is that if you instead focus on your outlines and 2-4 line briefing, you will do far better in class, with less effort and far less worry. Repeat this to yourself: *classroom participation does not count*. If you find yourself slipping into that old, brown-nosing habit of wanting to impress, repeat this again. That mousy student at the end of the row is likely to zoom past you when it counts: on exams.

Should you be courteous? Of course. Should you be rude? *Never!* Really. Don't *ever* think you can pick a fight with a professor or administrator or even a fellow student and assume that it won't count. It will. You might not know how, or when, or how severely...but it will. Count on it.

Okay, once again here's the rule: *Do not focus on classroom participation*. Period. You might make the occasional comment, where the topic presents itself and you have a truly important contribution to make. This will happen rarely. *Rare* means, well, rare. Not more than once or twice a month, perhaps. Maybe less. Maybe not at all. Rare.

If you're talking more than once per class—or just once per class—you're talking too much. Do not waste your time and mental energy in this way.

This does *not* mean that you are a lump of nothingness in class. Quite the opposite. You should be *actively* engaged in the dialogue: think ahead of, around, and in-between the conversation, almost as a mental joust. This is the art of *active listening,* one of our most powerful skills—and one of our most neglected. Active listening involves—as it indicates—a real awareness of and interaction with the conversation. It is *intense,* not passive. You're not sitting; you're practically ready to jump out of your seat.

Rather than being a spoken interaction, however, it is mental. So, when the professor is talking about, say, the *Erie Doctrine,* you are asking yourself whether a student's comment about *Swift v Tyson* jibes with your understanding *Erie*. It certainly didn't sound right. *Hmm*. You jot that down. That was most confusing, as you thought the rule was fairly simple: when sitting in diversity jurisdiction the federal courts must follow rules laid down by state supreme courts. Class ends and you find a place for thirty minutes of post-class outlining, which you do, yes, right after class. You have only a few quick notes to review and address, and the *Swift* case is bothering you. You don't bring your commercial outline, so you type in "Swift Erie Doctrine" in Google and in 0.24 seconds you have 32,200 answers. You have time for just one or two, however, and in an additional forty-five seconds you have the explanation: *Swift* was *overturned* by *Erie!* Well, *of course!* You should have known that that student didn't know what he was talking about. Too bad the prof didn't make that clear in class, but it's pretty easy now. The rest of that discussion was confusing though. I'll reread that section of the outline when I get home. Another few minutes to type in two more notes from class, including one on *forum shopping* that makes perfect sense now because Erie was decided to prevent litigants from "shopping" for a more favorable court, and the *diversity jurisdiction* point mentioned in class, which of course makes sense because the other option, exclusive jurisdiction via a federal question, wouldn't involve state law to begin with. Now that makes sense. Got it.

That is how you "participate" in class.

Later that evening, you spend fifteen minutes reading *Examples & Explanations* on *Erie,* and from that you get—in fifteen minutes!—a summary of the theory behind the decisions in *Swift* and in *Erie.* You re-read this for another 15-minutes, just because it's so darned interesting, and then you refresh with your team in your Q&A section as you chew through these a half-dozen times, and you're using the secondary sources as your primary means of learning the law. The case itself is just the skeleton. In a matter of mere hours, cumulatively, you're on your way to mastering an elemental doctrine in Civil Procedure that most now spend dozens of hours on...and many never truly get.

Crucially, "participation" is not what you do *in* class. It's what you do *before* class. You must remain steadfastly up-to-date. You cannot let any outline slide, because your outline *is* your study. Might you fall behind by a day? Sure. Life happens. But a week? Never! That's what weekends are for. Not "catching up," but reviewing and fine-tuning, and preparing for the next week's rules. Focus on your *outline*—not case briefs, notes, questions to ask, or other makework. If you need to impress, impress with your courtesy...and grades.

The Socratic Method is Dead. Long Live the Socratic Method. Anyone who's seen the (now rather dated) film *The Paper Chase* will remember Professor Kingsfield, the imperious professor of Contracts who chastises and embarrasses his students in, supposedly, an intellectual version of tough love.

His weapon? The Socratic Method.

Kingsfield famously claimed to take a young man (yes, in those days law students were nearly all men) whose skull was "full of mush" and, if he survived, would leave "thinking like a lawyer." This burned its way into the American legal psyche so that "thinking like a lawyer" became a catchphrase—and Kingsfield became an icon for many a law student (and a model for many a law professor).

"You teach *yourselves* the law," thunders Kingsfield, "I train your *minds.*" This sets the stage for what law schools are all about: the topsy-turvy world in which college graduates find themselves and into which law students lose their academic bearings. It is so, well, *weird* to be told to teach *yourself* the law—and yet that is very much the key.

Kingsfield was a bully, and supposedly a bully with the best interests of his students at heart. This was because his method—the Socratic Method—was seen as central to training the soon-to-be lawyers to build legal awareness and to build legal thinking on their toes. It was, in essence, the professorial equivalent of playing the role of judge. Any number of critiques are possible over the Socratic Method. For our purposes, the most important critique is that few law professors still employ anything remotely resembling the Kingsfield model. For one thing, most law professors are cut from an entirely different mold, and are quite sensitive to what their students think of them. This is either for the practical reason that student evaluations are part of the evaluation process, formal or otherwise, or simply because—despite the counsel of Machiavelli—most law professors would rather be liked than feared. The Socratic Method, well done, is also a *lot* of work. The fictional Kingsfield labored morning and night to hone his knowledge of contract law and perfect his side of the classroom exchange. Worse and more importantly, few law students are up to the challenge; they are, instead, more often hopelessly lost. This is hardly the stuff of informed debate that is the nominal basis of Socratic dialogue.

So, the Socratic Method, in any form remotely resembling that in *The Paper Chase,* simply does not exist. You are likely to face one or two professors who like to call on students, perhaps raising their voices to mimic the intimidating tones (they think) of a courtroom, but chances are good that most of your professors will engage in a pseudo-lecture/dialogue hybrid. Their thinking, to be honest, is that they know their students are lost, and it gets tiresome to "interrogate" someone who is clueless about the case or point of law—and so they quickly dodge the dialogue and simply start lecturing. We thus see endless dancing and kid-glove questioning, often with no real legal conclusion.

This, in a sense, is worse than the Socratic Method of old, because at least with the Socratic Method the importance of *learning the law* was clear. When we slip back into a quasi-lecture model, the old habits reappear: miss preparation for a class, wait for the lecture, write lots of notes, miss preparing again, wait for the next lecture, write more notes, stop preparing altogether, borrow notes when you skip class, write even more notes when you're there, repeat, cram, fail.

Even if you could learn all of the law from your professors' lectures (which will not and cannot happen to the level that you need for exams), you would *still* fail. Black letter law is an absolute requirement...but it's not enough. Listening passively to someone's lecturing is the opposite of what you need to do to get good.

So how do you handle the times you will be called upon? As hard as this might seem, don't worry about it. If you've prepared your up-to-date outline as you will have, you'll be at least passable in a classroom discussion...and you'll probably do quite well, as compared to others. If you've not read the case—an alarm bell not as to the case, but as to how steadfastly you've prepared—then you might have to pass. Not a good sign. Not fatal, but not good. Happily, if you have prepared your outline and scanned the case, you'll do just fine. If not, here comes the hard advice: accept that you'll be embarrassed, and don't worry about it...it *won't* affect your grade. Really. As long as you're not obnoxious about it, no one other than you—not even the professor—will remember. Really, really. Dust off your wounded pride, and move on.

Do your best. But keep your eyes on the prize.

Your First Year of Law School Is Everything. There is no accurate corollary to the importance of your first year in law school. Perhaps the closest is the SAT, or the LSAT. In either of those, your performance on a single day determines, to a large degree, where you can realistically apply and get accepted to.

In your undergraduate program, even if you bomb an exam, or two, or three, it's unlikely that that would make a categorical difference. Sure, if *all* of your grades are poor, then not many employers (or admissions committees) will come a' callin'. But if you have a 3.5-odd GPA and get a D in some course—particularly if it's not related to your major, chances are it will take a short explanation that you were sick that semester, etc., and that will be that.

In law school, your first year grades—six exams—will determine almost completely your future in the law. By that is meant your chances of landing a summer clerkship, your chances after law school for your first full-time job, and, to a very large degree, your chances at whichever firm and stratum you get into after law school.

Summer clerkships are hugely important, and for most are in between the second and third years. At top schools, for students who do well in mid-terms, there's a chance of landing a clerkship between the first and second years. Both summers are important, as both offer money and the chance for a full-time position (or leverage for a different full-time position). The money is quite nice, of course, but in reality even that doesn't quite capture it, as your grades in first-year will also determine your ability to get a good part-time job during second and third years. If you're not on law review especially, this can be quite important. (Law reviewers are too busy, and generally more than make up for the extra work during the semester by their fantastic salaries during the summers.)

Even if you decide not to go the big-firm route, grades will determine your attractiveness to the best government and corporate positions (both attractive in their own ways), and in just about everything else.

I am not disparaging of anyone who doesn't do well in first-year. In fact, my heart went out to those among the walking dead—friends and others—and to those who face that same problem today. The moral of the story is that it is not helpful to discount this, and it is important to understand just how important this is. One cannot "make up" for a poor showing in first year exams with a great showing later. It's difficult (and unlikely), and for most employers it won't help. The ranks of employers seeking third-year students for a full-time job (or clerkship) are just about zero. In law school, first-year grades are *extraordinarily* important.

YOUR "SECRET" WEAPONS

There are three: (1) outlines; (2) teams; and (3) LEEWS.

Part One is not merely the focus on outlines—as indeed that is the focus—but on rejecting bad study habits, including the mindless taking of excess notes.

Part Two includes two main purposes of a team, as well as important subsidiary benefits.

Part Three is both a preface and capstone to the proper approach to the peculiar world of the law exam.

OUTLINES

I've gone through outlines in a number of ways, above, and left the meat of this crucial task in the section on "to prepare or not to prepare" before law school, in large part because this *is* so crucial.

To Recap: You should have *two* outlines for each of your courses. The first outline is your "master" outline—needed for you to master that subject. Your second outline is the summary outline, which is your master outline, condensed to 1-2 pages. You don't "memorize" these as much as you *internalize* them. It's akin to your ABCs. You would hardly consider that you "memorized" where "T" goes...you just *know*. You have long since internalized "T"—and you must now do the same for the rules in your outlines. Yes, there are more than 26. You can do it. And, with the right attitude, it's fun. In this, it's akin to how our chemist *knows* the periodic table: not (just) because it's required, but because it's *used*. After the first thirty-eight times one checks the atomic weight of Hydrogen (*um*, 1.008 right?), it gets to be second nature. You don't have to think about it; you just *know* it. That is your goal...not for atomic weights, but for the law.

You should start your master outlines before law school—one for each of your first-year subjects. In this, you are "merely" setting out the structure for the course, and beginning the process of delving into each major sub-topic with second-level topics. Do not get bogged down. Don't spend more than an hour or two at a sitting—and don't get sucked into the tar pit of the minutiae. You're looking at the big picture: what is that course about, and what are the major topics for the course? The total time you spend should not be more than a dozen hours or so for each subject—at most. This is a marathon, not a sprint.

Your outline changes. Encourage its growth. Relish in changing its sections and contours as you learn more. This is hard. It seems that once something is in "black and white" it seems somehow sacrilegious to change it. Or, it seems like just too much work.

No, no, no. You *must* change your outline. It should reflect your growing familiarity and comfort with the subject. As you go through the semester, it should be increasingly more *refined*.

What Not To Do. A related concern is expressed in the negative. This is because the proper use of outlines requires that you *not* do what most students do: take too many notes.

No More Notes

This should be one of the easiest fixes, but I suspect it might be one of the hardest. It seems that note-taking is so deeply ingrained that even when students are commanded to put down their pens (or shut their laptops), they fidget in the assumption that they *must* be missing something. Or they glare in the audacity of a professor to curtail their electronic activities, note-taking or otherwise. (By the way, I just read where law professors are agitating to do just that: to ban laptops from class. I'll leave it to the *Obiter Dicta* section at the end to disclose my thoughts on that.)

In the meantime, here's a pedagogical heresy: note-taking is bad. It's not just bad in law school—as indeed it *is* bad in law school—but it's bad before law school too. Note-taking is a substitute for active thought. It is a crutch for poor attention and poorer habits. And it is almost always fruitless, as the cramming that implicitly follows could as easily happen with crib notes. These would have the benefit of saving both ink and carpel tunnel syndrome—as well as offering high-quality notes. As will be discussed, in law school this not only will not work, it cannot work.

So why take notes at all?

BACK TO THE FUTURE: OUTLINES

Well, to answer that, we need to back up. Before you enter your law school classroom, you should already have sketched out the relevant legal sections in your master outline. In other words, you have already taken "notes"—but they're far better than mere notes; they're your *structured* exploration of the essence of that area of the law. How to do that?! You have the syllabus. You have a commercial outline. You have a casebook. You have the internet. You have more than enough (quite literally, more than you need) to craft a workable section in your initial outline. I use the word "literally" on purpose: you cannot and should not duplicate everything. You're attempting to *distill* the essence of the law into something that makes sense *to you*. You're not focused on the leaves: you're focused at first on the forest and on only the tallest and most notable of the trees. In essence, as you start you're concerned about the broadest import and impact of black letter law in that area of the law. This black letter law is not all of the law. You need to know only about two pages worth, per subject. No kidding. That's a *year's* study boiled down to twelve pages.

Okay, you're ready for your first class. Let's pick, say, Torts. For example, under Torts, chances are that negligence will be a major focus—if not the major focus—for the course. As you begin your outline, however, you fill in the major area. They will look something like this:

Torts

1. Intentional Torts
2. Defenses to Intentional Torts
3. Harm to Economic and Dignitary Interests
4. Negligence
5. Strict Liability
6. Products Liability
7. Vicarious Liability
8. Joint Tortfeasors

9. Immunities

It's not unlikely that your professor will "recommend" a different ordering, or hierarchy. That's no problem! What was the rule about changing outlines? You take the course as you find it. And so your outline reflects that.

The outline above was the skeleton: the first-level. To add the next level—let's say, the musculature—let's take these to the second level. They'll look something like:

Torts

1. Intentional Torts
    a. Battery
    b. Assault
    c. False Imprisonment
    d. Intentional Infliction of Emotional Distress
    e. Property Torts

2. Defenses to Intentional Torts
    a. Consent
    b. Self-Defense, Defense of Others, Defense of Property
    c. Necessity

3. Harm to Economic and Dignitary Interests
    a. Defamation
    b. Defenses

4. Negligence
    a. Duty
    b. Breach
    c. Causation
    d. Damages
    e. Defenses

5. Strict Liability

6. Products Liability

7. Vicarious Liability

8. Joint Tortfeasors

9. Immunities

Okay, your master outline is started. Here's how you'll proceed:

1. The main subject area. While you'll complete each of the other major sections, let's say that your professor intends to start with negligence—not uncommon. (More likely is Intentional Torts—which will give you a chance to practice, yes?) We'll skip ahead to Negligence, then Duty, then standard of Care. In outline form, it would look something like this:

Torts

*   *   *

[These three asterisks stand for omitted text, which happens to be filled in above. The point is that you focus on that day's class and only on that day's class.]

    d. Negligence
       i. Duty
          1. Foreseeability test

             a. Cardozo's majority rule: foreseeable "zone of danger"

             b. Andrews' minority rule: everyone is forseeable

          2. Standard of Care

             a. [I have 9 sub-sections and about as many sub-sub-sections. Each would be filled in as you approach that class.]

2. Using your commercial outline, you fill in the major headings, and a brief description. Note: you do not simply copy the commercial outline into your own. That would be silly. Instead, you choose the fewest number of words that seems to make sense to you, in explaining just what that legal doctrine is.

3. It is okay if the doctrine doesn't make sense. That's what the class is for—sort of. If it doesn't make sense after the class, you'll need to discuss this with your team, and make sure everyone is clear on its meaning.

4. Elapsed time: 30 minutes.

5. You cross-reference, very quickly, your master outline with the other references you have. A casebook, the internet. Elapsed time: 40 minutes.

6. You scan the cases in your casebook. Note: you do not read them. You absolutely do not "brief" them. That is an obscene waste of time.

   a. You are looking specifically for one thing: Why is that case there? That's it.

   b. The answer? It is in the casebook because that case highlights a single point of law.

   c. That's it.

   d. A single point of law does not deserve more than ten minutes of your time. Seriously. As you revisit it, you might well refer to that point and case again—especially in topics such as Constitutional Law and Civil Procedure—but by then you're not merely learning that point of law. Rather, you're building a complex structure that incorporates that point, and consequently that is time spent refining—rather than learning—what is important.

   e. So, you scan the case so that you have some sense of how it fits. Don't even worry too much about the facts. If you get called on in class, you can give the correct answer—annoying the professor who won't have the chance to lead you down the path in the hopes of getting that right answer. But it won't hurt you. Really. Just scan the case. Do not read it. Do not brief it. Do not waste your time.

   f. Elapsed time: 50 minutes.

7. Review your outline before class. Perhaps scan the cases again.

8. Elapsed time: 60 minutes.

That's one hour in preparation for a class. Note, you're not wasting time trying to learn what doesn't yet make sense. You're trying to *make sense of what you need to learn* for *that day's class.*

Note 2: your commercial outline probably has a half-dozen pages on *Palsgraf,* the case you will study as to the forseeability test. While it's fun to read through this, be careful. It's too much, too soon. After you have a sense of the main rule, and especially once you're meeting with your team, *then* you re-read and re-re-read those fine distinctions.

What is "main" and what is "fine"? If you can restate the rule from memory—and if it makes sense—then it's main. If you need to review it, it's "fine." *Focus first on the main rules,* and expand your understanding, piece-by-piece, from there.

During class, you take no "notes." Instead, you jot down, on (or in) your outline, points that the professor makes that help you in making sense of the subject. If you're spending more than ninety seconds writing (or typing), you're writing too much. If you're writing more than the equivalent of one-half of a page—one page *at most*—you're writing too much.

Do not write down anything a student says. Ever. If it's interesting (and unrelated to law), go to them after class and ask about it. Strike up a conversation, start up a friendship. Wonderful. Otherwise, nothing uttered by a student makes its way into your outline. Period.

In fact, just to reinforce the importance of this, the only reason you're writing down anything that a *professor* says is because they're relaying what a judge has said (or what they feel is important about what a judge has said, whether they agree or not). If your professor thought about this, they wouldn't be offended, by the way. This is the essence of black letter law: it's *basic* law. These are the most basic points one can learn, and thus they're drawing upon the most basic assumptions of *thousands* of judges across the nation and over many decades of cases. The law is, to paraphrase a famous jurist, what judges say it is. And, despite the great tempests in one area or another, at one time or another, as to the basic rules especially judges are rather boring. Their reinforcement of black letter law—over and over and over—is both consistent and, once you think about it, filled with nuance and reasoned balance. *That* should be the joy of law school.

Point #2: Many if not most professors have an opinion about what they're saying. Some professors have an axe to grind. Whatever their personal take, this is important too. You should understand what that position is, why it is, and tread lightly. This includes treading carefully in the exam. Yes, they might say that they'll consider anything "well-reasoned" in opposition to their view. Don't you believe it. Especially do not believe it for an exam. While they might act carefully among their colleagues, they feel no such deference to you. At best, a well-reasoned dissent will not be marked down. More often, it will. This is human nature. If it's the tiniest bit less than well-reasoned (as it will be), it will be marked down *severely*. Do not give you professor reason to dislike the unknown writer of the exam before them.

More importantly, why get into this at all? If your professor is radical, believing that all of American law is an evil, horrid, patriarchal plot, what does that have to do with Contracts? Yes, contracts might well be an evil, horrid, patriarchal plot...but for Goodness' sake, on the exam *address the question presented*. Try like anything to avoid getting embroiled into an ideological battle. You won't win. At most, thirty second recounting that it is possible to argue that Contracts are an evil, horrid, patriarchal plot, and leave it at that. No counterpoints. Just move on.

If, conversely, your professor is a reactionary, don't go into detail as to why the Second Amendment was badly interpreted in a recent Supreme Court decision...and certainly not in Property Law. Focus on the exam. Use a clear bias of a professor against them, but *carefully*. In tiny bites at most, and by ignoring it altogether, when you can. These "tiny bites" *must* be aligned with your professor's known biases. Do not fight the valiant fight—and certainly not as a quixotic Devil's Advocate. (In Roman Catholic tradition the *advocatus diaboli,* appointed to argue against canonization, was opposed by—no kidding—God's advocate, whose job was to argue *for* canonization. In use since 1587, the post of the *advocatus diaboli* was abolished by Pope John Paul II in 1983. For either reason—choosing an unloved side or a post that lasts a mere four centuries—think carefully before accepting this responsibility.)

Are you familiar with jujitsu? This is the art of Japanese wrestling in which an opponent's strengths are used against him, often by leverage and gravity. (For example, by pulling against an opponent when he expects to land a punch.) In an exam, don't attempt even this. If your professor gets even the hint that you're being sarcastic—and they will be sensitive to this, whether or not you are—you will be penalized. And there is no appeal. Jujitsu is a terrific metaphor for law practice. In law *school,* beware. On an exam, stick to the law and facts, add a policy flourish or two, and move on.

Okay, back to your outline (which, as we're in a section on "No More Notes," should reinforce the importance of outlines over conventional notes). After the class, find a quiet spot for one-half hour to complete your task for that class. You go over your outline's section of that point of law, you re-incorporate anything that was said that made sense, you check anything that was said that did not, and you cross-check all of the above. Thirty minutes.

What next?

Next you *stop.* You're done. Do not spend more time just because you think you're supposed to. And do not spend more time chasing rabbits down tertiary legal holes. Those holes are traps. You simply do not need to know that much about the law—and, irony of ironies, if you focus on the main rules you'll begin to understand those tertiary rules intuitively, simply because they make sense. You'll find yourself simply "plugging in" section headings for what you have already intuitively learned. First, however, you must learn the primary and secondary rules. This means, among other things, staying focused on the higher levels of your outline, with only the briefest descriptions of the lower-level minutiae. Thirty *intense* minutes. Then stop.

This means that, for a 60-90 minute class, you're spending 60 minutes before and 30 minutes after. That's 5-6 hours per class per week, or 25-30 hours per week for *all* of your classes. Seem fair?

ONE MORE THING

These minutes are not spent slouched below the table, seemingly ready to fall to the floor with the slightest of turbulence. Your leg is not dangling over an armchair—or anything else. You need to *act like a lawyer*. You should be *intense*. You should intimidate the Hell out of anyone who approaches you, because—*dammit,* you're *working*. You're deep in concentration. Your mind is racing above, below, around, near, and through the topic. You are *engaged* with the legal subject. "Studying" is for wimps. You're not merely "reading" it. You're practically copulating with the law. Lady Justice, indeed.

So, would you rather spend 30 hours like this, *intensively* engaged with the law, plus 5-10 hours with your learning team (increasing to 10-20 hours the month before exams), perhaps even another 10-15 hours working a part-time job at a law office...and still have time for 5-10 hours chatting with fellow students *and* time to actually enjoy at least a part of your weekends? For second and third years, you'll probably need to spend about half as much time with each subject (because you will already know the basic legal concepts, and will be "merely" filling in the specifics of that legal discipline into the framework that is by then second nature to you, much as ABCs are to all of us)...but you'll spend more time with law review or another journal, moot court or clinics (or both), and a part-time job.

What's described above is a 60-hour workweek. This again is on the low end of law firm work...and it's also on the low end of law school "study" as it's currently done (badly) by nearly all. *Your* aim is different, higher, better. Less time. More learning. Less nonsense. More *Ah ha!* and *Well, of course!* That should be your goal, and your plan, and how you actually work.

How will you know if you're intense enough? At the end of two-and-one-half hours' work, you should be *tired.* You should need to take thirty minutes to grab a drink and chat with friends—before heading off for the next round of intense work. Clearly, if your classes prevent this exact scheduling, you'll need to be creative. The point is that it should be 2.5, not 10 hours, and it should be 2.5, not 0.5 hours. And the chatting, while important, is not as important as the work.

This type of focus is not easy. But it *is* rewarding. Among other benefits, you will not feel the flash of panic that hits others around you. And as exams approach, you will realize that you actually *understand* the law. And you and your learning team will grow increasingly able to talk through a hypothetical with insight and precision. You will, in short, be thinking like a lawyer. And you will find it enjoyable...because it is.

Pound for pound and hour for hour, this is a vastly more effective way to learn the law—and to learn what is needed in preparation for law exams. It is, however, unlike anything you've tried before, and thus the risk is that, in your nervousness, you will start falling back on old (bad) habits. One of them is note-taking. If you start to jot down more than the occasional note—say, the equivalent of more than one-half page per class—then you should do one thing: *Stop.* You're heading down the wrong path.

No notes. I mean it.

YOU CAN'T BE SERIOUS. NOTES ARE, LIKE, REQUIRED. RIGHT?

Well, yes, I *am* serious. And no, they're not required. In fact, they're downright dumb.

So why has everyone been taking notes all of these years, year in and year out, and no one has said anything? Because...the point of school (up to now) has never been to excel. Yes, you read that correctly. Even though *you* might have had that as a goal—and probably, because you're going to law school, succeeded quite admirably—that is not how the system as a whole is designed. Secondary education (and, to a large extent, now college too) are designed for the masses. They're designed to convey a reasonable amount of knowledge and information to a large number of citizens. Put simply, the object in secondary school is to ensure the "education" of the masses; the lower and higher tails are poorly served (as, indeed, is the middle in many ways). This is not pejorative; it is the essence of our educational system, and indeed was one of its greatest strengths.

Notes are, in essence, a remedial tool to help the majority of students. Notes are "required" as a way to help the average student remember what it was they heard. Law school is so far beyond that in terms of what is required, that even if notes were effective (which they are not), they would still not be sufficient.

Another major point: *you've never had competition before.* You're not part of the majority. You're at the top. Or at least you *were.* In law school, you're still not part of the "majority"—but unlike before, you might just be *below* the new average. Chances are you did well before, always or nearly always getting good grades—sometimes without even trying. How did you do this? It was possible because you were simply better than your peers. The difference, in law school—sorry to keep repeating this—is that your "peers" now includes a group of students comprised of the best handful of students from each graduating class across the nation. In essence, for the first time in your life you're not automatically "the best." With the forced curve (and an average close to a "C"), this reality can and will hit hard. *Very* hard.

A key, then, is to avoid that reality hitting you. And one of the ways to fail is to open your notebook. Don't do it. Open your mind, instead.

No, Really...No More Notes?

If you're like me, you will probably feel naked in a classroom without a writing pad and at least a few pens.

Okay, let's not fight academic genetics. Try this: take a legal pad (8.5" x 14" just to get into the legal spirit), and force yourself to write down only those elements that are truly crucial (*i.e.,* that add to your understanding of that specific legal point). Nothing from students. Only something that forwards your understanding of that subject. In other words, only something *directly related to the exam.*

At the end of each class, you should have no more than one-half of that page filled in. And, you should immediately incorporate whatever those comments are into your outlines. What is "immediate"? That day. Any later, and it will suffer the same fate of all other notes: it might as well have been a letter to the editor (rejected for poor penmanship).

At the end of each week, you should have incorporated all relevant notes into your respective outlines—and ignore the rest. If it's not relevant, it's not worth your time. This is a good reinforcement for your standard of evaluation, by the way. You will write down *only* those points that are important to your understanding of the law. Having already prepared the outline, almost nothing will meet that test—because you will already understand that point of law.

You will then file these pages in one of six legal folders, each corresponding to the appropriate subject. Why file them? First, to build good habits. And, more importantly, so that that you don't see a stack of unmanageable papers. Stacks are useless *and* demoralizing. The more disorganized you might otherwise be, the more you should force yourself into a "gross" organization at least: these folders will serve as a mental step in ensuring that whatever was discussed in class makes its way into your outline—if indeed it should be there at all—and that it is then out-of-sight, because it no longer adds to your study.

The truth? You could burn those old notes and it wouldn't make a bit of difference: what was in them is already in your head. You should thus *never look at them again*—except to laugh just before you throw them away, perhaps as you graduate and need to clean out. This is the last reason they should be filed. That makes throwing them out easier.

You should, however, keep your outlines. These you will enjoy seeing on occasion, later. You can throw out the notes and consolidate all of your outline files into one prized "file pocket" (the kind you see in law offices). As long as we're on organization and file pockets, another good habit is to have seven legal-size file pockets, into which you have files in each subject for your outline (crucial), notes (whatever), and perhaps a third for anything else that strikes you (which you won't need or use, but it will give you a place to put miscellaneous items so that they don't clutter your space). Why seven? One for each of the Six Biggies, plus one for Legal Research and Writing.

These file pockets become your automatic starting and stopping point, and reduce productivity-robbing disorganization. One colleague used a rolling cart, into which he put files pockets for each case. It was a crude but effective way to stay on top of his (mobile) projects. There are many options; find one that works for you, and stick with it.

A Second Opinion

Here's how Wentworth Miller, Yale Law grad, Rhodes scholar, and perhaps the nation's expert on law exams, phrases it:

> Here's what I say to students: I suspect you've been accumulating a mountain of notes. Most law students do. Accustomed to note-taking during years of college, law students take lots of notes: 2-3 pages per class hour longhand, more if typed into a laptop. That's 8-12 pages of notes per class per week, perhaps 30-40 pages of notes altogether each week. *Whew!* By the end of term the typical law student has amassed a literal mountain of notes, and they are a monument to busywork. If you talk to a 2L or 3L, they'll tell you that all those notes proved largely useless for exams.
>
> Your task between now and exams is simple: get rid of all your notes! I mean that. Literally, in the trash! You should come to the end of the term and have *no notes!*

This obviously gets students' attention. Given his long track record vis-à-vis law exams, Miller is perhaps an even stronger voice than mine in his advice on taking fewer notes in class, which he defines as one-half to one page of notes per class hour, not the avalanche described above.

I include this long passage here—which I hope you do read—as it's another veteran's take on where and how many law students fail. What's interesting to me is that his and my advice parallel each other—almost mirror each other—even though we'd not discussed this before. What follows are email exchanges he and I had as we delved into the topic of note-taking:

> The reason so many notes are taken, apart from habit, is because the typical law student doesn't fully grasp what is going on in class. Sure, the assigned cases have been "briefed"— procedure, facts, rule, and the rest. However, then the professor begins asking *"what ifs."* "What if the following facts were changed?" "What if this and what if that?" "Would the concurring judge have then sided with the dissent?" "Would the outcome have been altered?"

This is to hone "lawyerlike thinking," that nitpicking ability of lawyers to discern strengths, weaknesses, facts needing clarification or development, and the like as they seek to prove or disprove the objective they seek for a client. The problem is that most students don't catch on, and sit confused (and bored).

Some students, by a background in math, science, philosophy, talmudic studies, or some other discipline that encourages and inculcates close, nitpicking reasoning and thinking, pick up on the skill of analyzing as a lawyer. Not altogether, but to some extent. But most do not. The habits of critical thought that the experienced attorney is accustomed to is in the adversarial give and take of practicing law. There is no better motivation to hone the insufferably close thinking of lawyers. (Think, "…depends upon what is meant by *'is'!'*") Plus there's the thought of losing to the opposing lawyer because some small-but-significant fact or legal aspect was overlooked. Lawyers learn, often the hard way, to sweat the details.

The typical student also doesn't *really* realize he is expected and needs to know "black letter law"—legal rules, principles, statutes—cold, in order to follow the discourse in class. Moreover, neither the professor nor appellate case assigned will fully articulate such law. An outside reference such as a commercial outline is needed. Further, class discussion veers so often (and comfortingly) into larger topics surrounding the law—social and economic implications, so-called "policy"—that the precise aspects and needs of rules are obscured or ignored. Thus, the typical Harvard 1L, months into first term, cannot provide more than a fuzzy definition of battery or assault.

Confused, law students write as much down as possible with the thought, "I'll make sense of this later." Problem is…there is no "later" in law school. Every day more cases are assigned. More briefing, more notes. Because they don't understand where it is all going, what is needed, and how to get what is needed, law students cast about and waste time. A week into law school, most are playing catch up. Notes accumulate as weeks pass, and at semester's end the student realizes, upon reviewing past exams in preparation for the final exam that will determine his entire grade, that he doesn't know the law as precisely as he needs to. So the time between class and the exam that he anticipated using to review and make sense of his mountain of notes must be spent in a feverish attempt to nail down black letter rules.

No matter. Notes about things that were not fully understood when taken are now cold and of little use, even if there were time to review them. They were busywork. It simply provided comfort and a sense of industry to take them.

Contrast this student with the one who knows going into class the following three things: (1) she will need to know black letter rules precisely for the final exam, and also to follow the discussion in class; (2) neither the professor nor the assigned case will present complete and precise law, so law introduced by cases needs to researched and fleshed out via a commercial outline— and if the law remains confusing (think Parol Evidence Rule or the Rule Against Perpetuities)—then an examination of its history, evolution, and purpose in a hornbook needs to be made...prior to class!; and (3) that the facts of assigned cases will not be repeated on the exam, but at most variations thereon, and indeed assigned cases merely introduce law the student will be responsible for on the exam, often just parts thereof, and the facts of cases provide but an introduction to the law and its application. The ability to discern relevant law and apply it to *new* facts will be tested on the exam. Class discussion and *what ifs* from the professor are designed to anticipate and hone such application.

This student, also skilled in at least the rudiments of lawyer-like analysis, will take a more proactive approach to class. Her attitude going into class is not "I'll wait for the professor to explain things," but "I think I understand this—the law and how it was applied in the cases assigned." This student is not looking to take copious notes, but has the attitude, "What's new; what have I overlooked?" She also wants to get a bead on the professor: "What is he *really* interested in?" (She will thus read articles her professors have written in the past several years.) Such preparedness and perspective prompts a critical shift in attitude. The student looks ahead to the all-important final exam. Everything points to the exam. If relevant to the exam, interested! If not, it probably can be ignored. Certainly it will not be written down. Looking to the hypothetical-type exam, how to break it down into components that reveal "issues," and how to analyze those issues in roughly concise paragraphs, this student's thought is, "What do I want to take out of class and the assigned cases for use on the exam?" Class is but a means, not an end.

This student takes a critical but knowing eye and ear into class. With 2-4 line case briefs in the left-third margin of her notepad, what is relevant in class is noted in the larger margin on the right across from each brief. Her greater depth of understanding allows her to sift out the considerable chafe in a typical hour—meandering *blah blah* from a classmate, something already thought about and digested. No notes needed.

Does the professor take issue with an aspect of a rule? Believes the rule should be changed or the federal rule should trump the state version? Better note that. A *what if* introduced by the professor suggests a new way of looking at the law or a result that she hadn't considered. Better note that. The professor mentions a law review article, emphasizes a policy aspect. Write that down too.

This student is not scribbling/typing endless notes, but is more productively engaged in critical and reflective thinking about what she has already endeavored to understand. Greater comprehension and a view of how the piece—class—fits into the larger whole—preparation for the final exam—translates to far fewer notes. *No more than a page per class hour!* Often, students tell me, just a half page. At the end of each week what continues to seem relevant from these 1-3 pages is further condensed and folded into the growing course outline.

Ideally, a law student will come to the end of term, take a few notes in the final class, incorporate those notes into the largely complete course outline, and spend the time between the last class and the exam—when most are feverishly re-reading cases and collecting law—fine-tuning the completed course outline and testing it on old exams. *There are no class notes extant!*

I debated—before I mentioned the topic to Wentworth—whether I would recommend that you take no more than one-half page of notes per class, or, in the spirit of going cold turkey, no notes at all. Whichever way you decide—on a *note diet* or *cold turkey*—I hope this advice by both Wentworth and me is taken to heart, because piles of notes in law school are useless. Thus, spending time taking those copious notes is a waste of your time, and a distraction from what *is* important.

CASE BRIEFING

And now to the second major vacuum cleaner of law students' time—and the second reason so many students fall so miserably behind.

This section was added after outlining, on purpose. In book after book, and in orientation after orientation, law students are told to prepare meticulous briefs. While nice in theory, this fails in practice. And, to repackage this yet again, if you brief cases the way you're told to, you will fail. Why? Because you simply won't have time.

Case briefing is extremely labor-intensive. To prepare a good case brief takes perhaps one hour. For each case. You will have multiple cases for each class, each week. That's dozens of cases, each week. As some classes burn through multiple cases each session, that might be three or four dozen cases, week in and week out. Even if you rushed each one—which you should not do as a matter of principle—that's still twenty or more hours of your time each week. If we assume our 60-hour marker, that means that you have just a few hours left to do things like outlining and working hypotheticals and taking practice exams.

No, no, no.

Briefing fails on the expenditure side. What about the benefit side? Isn't it worth it? I mean, after all, why does everyone seem to think that's the way to learn the law?

Well, when this was first propounded as the way to learn the law, the year was sometime in the 1880s, and American law was just a wee-bit less burdened with cases. All of Torts—our case-heavy subject—might be parsed in a mere few dozen major cases and perhaps a few dozen more in the jurisdiction of choice. This, too, was in the context of the apprentice-student. Few students were full-time in the sense that we would use the term today. And so, they would be told to study a case or two—by candlelight, no doubt—and then would be shown, by their practitioner-mentor, how that case applied...in a real case. "Research" was also more primitive, and so even if a contrary case existed chances are it might not be found—especially not in other jurisdictions.

It should be needless to write, but in an age when we're in the third series of any number of *Reporters,* each with a thousand volumes and each of those volumes with 1,500 or so pages, we're talking about a *lot* of reading. A hugely difficult task, at best.

"Ah," the pro-briefing response might be, "that's not what briefing is!"

In true pre-pubescent retort, I will draw deep and respond.
"Is too!"

The idea behind case briefing is that one gleans the legal principle (rule) from the legal conclusion (holding) as that conclusion applies to the fact pattern in that case. Adding case after case after case, we begin to see a pattern, and from that pattern we begin to form general principles, exceptions to those principles, and exceptions to those exceptions. While certainly possible, this carries a number of disadvantages. First, it's a *lot* of reading. Second, these cases are not written with students in mind. Sometimes they're not well-written at all. Sometimes they're not even well-supported by the facts or the law. That aside, even a well-written, well-reasoned case will *assume* a command of the law, and will jump right into the relevant legal issue and facts.

This is why law school has been so epochally difficult for students—not to mention endlessly frustrating. Our hapless student, who sits in a stately hall and wonders what on Earth the person at the podium is talking about, thinks in despair, "Are we talking about the same case? That wasn't what *I* read! Ohmygod, did I read the right case?!" And it doesn't matter which class, or which professor, or which student. Chances are that 90 percent of every class is utterly lost 90 percent of the time. That is no way to learn the law.

This is why outlines are so crucial. They add context to the cases. Your outlines tell you those general principles, exceptions to those principles, and exceptions to those exceptions. From there, you can see how the case connects and why it's being discussed.

Outlines *must* be at the top of your priority list. If you brief cases, you must force yourself to put that below outlining in importance.

How, exactly, to brief a case?

For this I will defer. I'd written a section, and mentioned it in passing to Wentworth Miller. As it happens he has thought about this for some time, and proposes a "2-4 line brief." I liked what he wrote more than mine, and so in the interest of quality and with his permission, I include here his take on this most important topic:

2-4 Line "Case Briefing." One of the first things every student is taught to do in every law school is "brief" cases. Cases are descriptions of proceedings in an actual lawsuit, casebooks are the staple of most law classes, and the "case method" is the standard mode of instruction in all but a handful of law schools. Homework in law school consists of briefing cases assigned for the next day's class. Don't make the mistake of simply showing up for the first class assuming it will be a "hello," "goodbye." One or more cases will be assigned for that first class, and you may be called upon to recite from your brief in the unnerving ritual called the "Socratic Method."

Conventional case briefing is a culling of the procedure, facts, issue(s), rule(s), holding, and rationale from cases assigned. In the first few weeks at every law school, students are engaged every evening in the consistent, feverish process of briefing cases. Many type up these briefs. They will have them at the ready in class the next day so as to be "prepared" should their name be called. They are the foil in the professor's examination of a case for the purpose of "teaching you to be a lawyer": "Mr./Ms. _____, can you give us the facts of *x versus y?*" A few professors insist that students stand, and remain standing for perhaps ten minutes while the professor queries him or her about the case, and often turns to other students to respond to questions.

So frightening and arresting is this process, unique to law schools, that it is a staple of every law school movie, from *The Paper Chase* up to *Legally Blonde*. In the book *Law School Confidential,* the author relates how as a 1L he was so unnerved by one professor's skewering use of the Socratic Method that he chose not to go to class on the day he calculated he would be called upon. (Professors often simply move down a seating chart they have in front of them.)

Of course, law students soon realize they can't keep producing page-long briefs every night for 2-3 cases for 3-4 classes the next day. So they move to "book briefing"—notes in the margins of cases or highlighting, typically in different colors, of the brief elements: procedure, facts, etc. Should you view a law school classroom from the heavens, the opened casebooks would reveal a kaleidoscope of color.

2-4 line briefs are not book briefs. No more highlighting and notes in the margins of cases! Well, okay, maybe a few notes. Not only will this allow students to keep their books clean so they can resell them for top dollar, notes are actually incorporated into the *abbreviated* briefing process: the 2-4 line brief goes in the left margin of a sheet of paper. (Notebooks with margins one third across the page are ideal, but a simple line or mental border works just as well.)

How can procedure, facts, issue, and the rest be reflected in 2-4 lines? More than that, how can these 2-4 line briefs reflect *more* understanding than a traditional brief? The answer is in the method.

The key is approaching a case the way a lawyer would: a lawyer starts with his *own* case—a set of facts—already in mind. If the case has been cited by his opponent, he seeks to distinguish it from his own—to show that the facts are sufficiently different as to render the case meaningless or at least "distinguishable." Alternatively, the lawyer seeks a *new* case "on all fours," or close to it. This means that the facts, procedure, issue, rule, and holding are sufficiently similar to his own case to be supportive of the points he anticipates making to an opponent and before a judge. (Even if he intends to settle the case, this is how the lawyer prepares—as if it's going in front of a judge.)

The lawyer will make *very* few notes relating to the case. (Chances are he'll just photocopy the entire case.) Perhaps a ten-word synopsis of the facts. Perhaps a few notes on the rule(s). If you were to question this lawyer about the case, he could recite the salient facts, issue(s), procedure, holding, rule(s), and rationale. How? Everything about the case "fits" into a picture. The important "work" is in pulling those *case specific* facts relevant to *his* case. If called upon in a law school class, he would shine. Yet he would have only 2-4 lines of "briefing notes" in front of him.

How does this translate to a *law student* briefing a case? The law student obviously doesn't have her own case. She doesn't have an opponent. She (thankfully) doesn't anticipate arguing before a judge.

This goes to the crux of the issue: the *academic* orientation to studying that law students bring from college into law school is never redirected to the *goal-oriented focus of the practicing lawyer*. Law students come to cases with a passive, academic orientation. Memorize this, memorize that, because you may be called upon to respond. The case may or may not be of interest. The exercise bears no apparent relation to what lawyers do other than that the topic of discussion happens to be "legal."

If the law student understands what lawyers actually *do* (which they are never told, as the words "lawyer" and "attorney" are almost never heard in a law school classroom); and if law students understood that all legal roads lead potentially to a court-room—an adversarial arena—and that a lawyer's task, simply stated, is to marshal relevant law and facts to assist a client in achieving an objective (redress of an injury, ownership of a property claimed by others, staying out of jail, halting the predatory practices of a competitor business, etc.)—*then* students could put cases in a more practical context. For example, "Here's an instance of competing parties (so-and-so versus so-and-so), with competing objectives. What law and facts are marshaled by the respective lawyers to achieve the respective objectives?" The student can more actively engage as a would-be lawyer.

If, moreover, law students were versed in the nitpicking, back-and-forth, analytic process of "lawyerlike analysis," which the case method does little to instill, they would better appreciate the subtle nuances of argumentation not over entire legal rules, but instead *parts* of rules. They would understand that cases typically dwell only on those parts of legal rules that are contested. They would know to turn to other sources—commercial outlines—for more complete presentation of legal rules. They would understand that the law is not something to be grasped in the abstract—*boring!*—but they could focus on the law as a tool wielded by an attorney. They might be interested in the *how* and *why* a particular legal tool was wielded.

If, in addition, law students understood that on the final exam they would be tested on their ability to apply legal tools to new sets of facts, much as a lawyer would, they would have a proper perspective on the role of cases in their education: first, to introduce legal precepts, building in the aggregate to a body of legal understanding in torts, contracts, property, etc.; and second, to give them examples of and practice in the application of those precepts to facts, precisely the exercise in which they will be expected to exhibit skill on final exams.

Understanding all this, the student will know what she wants to glean from a case in preparation for the all-important final exams: legal tools and an understanding of how to apply those tools. If a student has in addition discovered some enthusiasm for the game of lawyerlike analysis—opposing lawyers sifting facts to make arguments on contested aspects of relevant legal rules to gain an advantage—then she will begin to take a much more active posture respecting assigned cases. She will think about, and perhaps be amused by, the arguments made in the case, and, knowing that she will never see these same facts again on an exam, but will be expected to apply the legal precepts to new facts, perhaps *take the necessary step in preparing a case that few, if any, law students do.* She must *make up new facts in her mind* (creating hypotheticals!) for the sheer pleasure of thinking about how they might alter the outcome of the case.

For example, if she changed which facts might the dissent come around to the majority view? What aspect of the facts caused judge so-and-so to feel he had to write a separate opinion? Why do we have such a rule? Is it a good rule? Should it be changed?

This is the kind of thinking that law professors want, but almost never get. A student who thinks in this way about cases (with curiosity, interest, deeper understanding) begins to anticipate what the professor will do in class the next day—posit hypothetical new facts and ask, "what if?" A student who thinks in this way about cases has the procedure, the facts, the issue(s), the rule(s), the holding, the rationale of the case *in her head!*

Much like a lawyer investigating a case, she needs but a short synopsis—a 2-4 line notation of law and facts—to remind her of all the elements of a conventional brief. Not a reminder for the next day in class. Everything is fresh in her mind the next day. But a reminder for weeks later as she prepares for the final exam. She has, of course, fleshed out the complete legal rule(s) *prior* to going to class. She doesn't *have* to go back to the assigned case ever again (as someone who does a "book brief" *will* have to do)

To be able to do a 2-4 line case brief, to be able to approach a case as a lawyer, a law student first has to learn what lawyers do and how to perform the kind of nitpicking analysis that most law graduates only learn when they get out in practice and face an opponent who is nitpicking law and facts. It is small wonder that many doubt that a case can and should be briefed in 2-4 lines. Yet that is how lawyers do it, every day.

I will let Wentworth's words speak for themselves. However you decide to brief cases, do not spend hours doing so—much less, dozens of hours. Do not fall into this trap, for a trap it is.

SECRET No. 142: HYPOTHETICALS AS THE KEY TO THINKING LIKE A LAWYER

Law professors often talk about "hypos," usually in passing reference and rarely as a direct encouragement to put hypos at the center of your law school world. In a similar way, most guidebooks do the same thing: those that mention hypos (with one exception) tend to do so in a way that utterly fails to convey how important they are.

Here it is: Working with hypotheticals is *the* key to learning how to think like a lawyer. If you work with hypos, you will be well on your way, because what is tested on law exams draws on *exactly* the same skills as playing with hypos.

Why are professors endlessly concerned with "mere" hypos? Because hypos are the same conceptually as real-world cases with real-world clients. The difference is that a hypo happens to have facts that aren't real. Often they're exaggerated—as a way to test the law (and students' understanding of that law). The legal analysis is identical. It's not possible to overemphasize this. *The legal analysis is identical.* This means that, while a law professor is reading an exam from a student, they want to know whether the student can identify the legal issues, and explore the meaning of those issues, in exactly the same way as a lawyer will need to do. *This* is "thinking like a lawyer."

If you do not work intensively with hypotheticals, you will not develop these skills as well (or at all), and you will fail. It's almost as simple as that.

The rules lawyers know as black letter law are the ABCs of thinking like a lawyer. Working hypotheticals is the process of learning how to write. ABCs are required but hardly sufficient. "Writing" is also required...but hardly sufficient (unless you want to write "See Jane run!" over and over). To build mastery to the point that *you* can think like a lawyer (which is *the* skill tested on law exams), you must first learn the ABCs and then learn how they fit together. In the process of doing both, you will move from the basic to the ever-more sophisticated. Among top law students, the discussions will sound eerily like discussions at, yes, law firms.

Okay, how about some examples? We've borrowed from Torts ('cause it's fun). How about, say, Criminal Law? Self-defense is always good for a rousing debate, yes? Being defensive, let's go with that.

The outline will list self-defense as one of the defenses to a criminal act. So, for example, here's what your outline for Criminal Law might look like:

Criminal Law

   I.   Jurisdiction: Legal situs of crime (either conduct or result)

   II.   Elements of a Crime

a. [List those here.]

III. Accomplice Liability

IV. Inchoate Offenses

V. Defenses

    a. Insanity

    b. Intoxication

    c. Infancy

    d Self-Defense

VI. Offenses Against the Person

Each of these sections will have its sub-sections and sub-sub-sections. Each should be modest (in the master outline) and a single phrase (in the summary outline). Your outline might be (and should be) a little different from every other one...but the main points will be identical. That is, after all, the whole point of the law.

Did I make this up? Not at all. This is taken directly from the summary outline I made when studying for the bar exam. Yes, I've kept them all these years, and while a bit faded they're still kinda' fun to go through, all these years later. (Now you know how much fun I am.) Here's what I have for self-defense:

    d. Self-defense

        1. Non-deadly: OK if reas believes force is about to be used on V

        2. Deadly: Maj: OK if reas ? ? ? / Min: must retreat 1st if safe, unless (1) home, (2) rape/robbery, (3) police

        3. Self-defense to Orig Aggressor: no, unless withdraw & communicate withdrawal

        4. Defense of Dwelling: Never deadly force solely to protect prop.

        5. Duress: threat from human source; Necessity: defense to all exc homicide

6. Mistake of Fact

    i. Specific intent: any mistake (even unreas); Malice/ Gen intent: reas mistake only; Strict liab: never

7. Mistake of Law: no excuse

8. Consent: only rape/kidnapping

9. Entrapment (very narrow): predisposition negates defense

So what are we to make of this? First, this seems to cover a fair amount of ground…but, when you look at it a few times, it's really not all that much. Yes, self-defense is just a small part (actually, about half) of "defenses," which is about one-fourth of Criminal Law. But think about that. All of Criminal Law fits on one and one-half pages. And, better yet, *this is all the black letter law you need to know to ace your exams*. Well, almost. Before you get excited, however, while this is just about everything you need to know, that misses the point: this is the *summary* outline. It is condensed from your master outline, which follows your digesting each of the various areas. And this *precedes* your working of hypotheticals, which is what will give you the ability to address the exam with a lawyerlike analysis. And *that* precedes your working of *dozens* of exams for each subject, each under timed conditions.

So, to get back to our example, one area Criminal Law professors like to test (because it's controversial and because there's lots of room for playing with the facts in light of the above rules) is the defense of self-defense. You might, for example, get a fact pattern on an exam that posits a series of interactions in which self-defense might or might not apply, leading to a result favorable (or not) to defendants 1 through *x*. What you'll need to do is to take the above law and weave your analysis of what happens based on the facts given to you (and those you can suppose).

There are some favorite traps, such as in defense of a dwelling. These "traps" are an attempt to get you to respond based on what you would *like* the law to say, and not what it *actually* says. Here's the fun part: you can still have strong beliefs about, say, defense of a dwelling—and get *more* credit with a genuinely lawyerlike analysis. So, let's say you're from Texas and believe that anyone caught trespassing is fair game. Indeed, you might even believe there should be legalized hunting in this regard. With, say, a limit on the gauge of shotgun allowed, and perhaps bagging limits per season. All right. Not exactly mainstream (and certainly not in Hawaii or Massachusetts), but let's go with it.

How to apply this to an exam? First, you do not start chattering about how restrictions on handguns are un-American, blah, blah, blah. Nor do you blather about how handguns are awful, yada, yada, yada. If *I* read that, that exam almost certainly gets a "D". Max. No, you start with the wording exactly as above: Deadly force is *never* a defense if used solely to protect property. There. Twelve words. That is the law of self-defense as applied to the protection of property. Note: it is not the law *as applied to defense of self,* or to *defense of others.* This is another favorite trick of professors; they're playing tricks only if you fall for them, which many students do. And students fall for them for two reasons: first, they don't know the law, and second, they argue from emotion, not the facts.

So, after dispensing with this statement and a *brief* connection with the facts, and perhaps further explication for ninety seconds (no more!) about the public policy reasons behind and criticisms of this rule (for an extra point), you move on to what the professor had *really* set up: that there are "hidden" defenses that apply to defense of self and to defense of others. So, while Defendant x will not be able to use self-defense as a defense to a criminal charge for having cheerfully blown away a trespasser in his castle, he *can* use this as a defense *if* the facts indicate that he or someone else was reasonably believed to be at risk of death or serious bodily injury. See how this works? Do not respond with generalities, and do not respond with emotion. You need to know the law, and you need to apply the law, *and* you need to apply the law *specifically,* fact by fact. No fact is left unturned. Even if irrelevant, you indicate why it is irrelevant. If relevant only if *a, b,* or *c* is true, you let the professor know that you know. In essence, you're having *fun*...and letting the professor peek in on that fun. You can (and should) throw "because x, then y" and "if z, then q." You should be able to do this for three hours or three days or three weeks—that's the meat of legal analysis, and it should become as easy as breathing.

When someone mentions defense of property, your response should be, "well, I sure hope *someone* in the picture was threatened, 'cause if not, they lose." But you get to that "easy" answer only after you know black letter law *and* how to sift through facts.

Note too that each line in the above summary outline carries with it crucial words that can and should have an extra line of explanation in the exam. This is fun! The statement is "Deadly force is *never* a defense if used solely to protect property." Within that statement, however, are *chapters* filled with nuance for each of the crucial words. What is "deadly force"? How about "defense"? That word has a specific meaning in criminal law—and slightly different meanings in other areas of the law. You need to be sure your prof knows that you know what that means. And you use a shorthand to get all of that conveyed, fast. This is another reason your study should be *intense*. It's extremely unlikely that anyone can go from lackadaisical study habits to the type of intense, and intensely-paced analysis that is needed for an "A" exam. And you're just getting warmed up. Note, for example, "solely" and "to protect property." Those were keys to the above trap.

What you boil down from commercial outlines and class discussions to a master outline (and then to a summary outline) becomes a shorthand in your mind for the tapestry of rules interwoven behind every fact pattern. When you take that tapestry and knit and re-knit it dozens of times through hypotheticals, it becomes your own. The physical outline becomes almost a distraction. I'm serious. You should be able to burn your copy before the exam and lose not one point.

So, after outlines, "working hypos" should be at the *center* of your law school world. This, in turn, leads us to a discussion of a badly misused tool: the study group.

LEARNING AS A TEAM SPORT

In the film *The Paper Chase,* the central character's study group loomed large in his success or failure. Among the storylines was the infamous 700-page "outline"—which, the implication went, would determine who got the "A" and who did not. Ironically this is true—but in exactly the opposite way. Anyone foolish enough to waste time on a 700-page outline is almost certain to do poorly on an exam. The law requires concision as well as analysis, and the black letter law required on a law exam can fit on one page. No, that's not a misprint, and no, that's not much of an exaggeration: One page.

In Scott Turow's book *One L,* study groups likewise play an important role—again with the implication (as of the time it was written, which was just after exams), that study groups made the difference.

This film and book seemed to cement a tradition of the study group, which—it was heavily implied—would determine for the grades sweepstakes who won and who lost. But instead of being a competition by individuals, would instead be a competition among groups: the "best" group wins.

The paradox is that this is right, but for reasons almost diametrically opposed to how groups are portrayed in *The Paper Chase* especially *and* how most students actually form and "use" their teams. In the film, there's a race to form teams early. There's a solemn division of who does which outline. Then there's a holing up in a hotel to cram for exams.

Wrong, wrong, and wrong.

First is a misunderstanding of what study groups are for. It is not to get an advantage over others—at least not directly. It is not to "divide" labor in outlines. It is not to cram. If you feel pressure to take any of these approaches, chances are good that your group will be a drain, not a boost, to you. Do not allow this approach to take hold in your team—and if it does, politely decline. Leave and live to study another day, with another, better team.

As part of the mad dash in the first days of law school, students tend to race in a frenzy to form study groups. This is seen, mistakenly, as a way to get an "edge" in first-year. In reality this results, often, in a mismatch of members, and in the poor performance of the group and its members—if indeed the team ever gels. What happens many times is that the group dissolves, or one or more members peel off, and the survivors are left to find new homes. Many do not, and simply continue in their own gloomy worlds. Feelings are bruised, and nearly everyone is unhappy.

Here's how to do study groups right:

First, understand the purpose and value of a study group. Its purpose is to "work" hypotheticals and exams. That's it. (Okay, to make lots and lots of food too.) If done correctly its value is enormous: a study group can make a one-letter-grade difference in the performance of its members—if not two. In fact, if one looks at the performance of the highest-performing students, chances are high that the very top students have all been in a team…together. Usually, it's quite literally a question of which member gets #1, who gets #2, and so on. Occasionally there's a loner, or someone from another team, but this is quite often how it breaks out.

To repeat: the purpose of a team is to work hypotheticals and exams, and its value is enormous: potentially the greatest in law school. Teams, well done, are crucial to success. This is because of what teams, properly run, can add to the ability to think like a lawyer (and act like one too). They can also serve as a social and emotional balance that is almost as important.

To break the bad habits that most students now have, and to emphasize how these teams should work together, I'll refer to study groups as *learning teams*. This is to reinforce that this is not "study" as in "memorize and regurgitate," "cramming," or dividing work, but *learning* as in an intense interaction that builds upon the strengths of each member: a team for learning the law. What's important is to understand why and how teams are used, to form them correctly, and to work together correctly. It so happens, as well, that I have worked in classrooms with hundreds of teams (probably close to a thousand, actually), and so can share what works, and what doesn't—and why. Again, the solution is about focused and efficient use of time. The goal is maximum reward for minimum effort. This is what teams can accomplish, if done right.

[Whining] But I Don't Want a Team!

Why are learning teams important? Four reasons I can think of immediately: (1) to restate for effect, they are crucial to the working of hypos and exams; (2) they are useful in the sharing of expenses for ancillary study materials; (3) they serve as an internal benchmark for higher-quality thinking and writing; (4) they are an important social and emotional strength. In short, for most students a strong team is the difference between an "A" and a "C"—it's almost that stark.

HOW TO BUILD A STRONG TEAM

There are three big objections about teams—and reasons most teams don't work. First is that students entering law school— panicky enough as it is—are nervous about whom to ask, and how. And so it often boils down to an awkward glance at whoever's sitting next to you with a "Wanna' start a team?" question/shrug. Second, because teams are ill-defined and often misaligned, few teams "gel," and even fewer actually accomplish what they're potentially greatest at. Third, many abandon even the possibility of a team as soon as the slightest thing goes wrong—or they reject the very idea of teams as somehow outdated and just not worth the trouble. This leads not only to disappointment, but to "proof" that teams are bunk. Mysteriously, however, the top students seem to be on teams. Good ones. Often the *same* good one.

So how should one actually go about forming a learning team? First, do not "race" at anything in law school. This means you should not rush a team. Instead, take your time, make it a point to talk with every student in your class—not a "sizing up" as much as a genuine conversation about that individual. (Note: this is exactly the same as in law practice.) It doesn't take much, just a "Hi! My name is [don't forget to insert your name here]. So, what do you think about…?"

Do not rush to offer your opinions. Instead, ask about *their* thoughts. Stop being so focused on yourself, and start focusing on where others are coming from. An amazing thing will happen: you will learn far, far more than you did when it was "all about me."

Another magical thing happens: when you engage in genuine conversation, you'll find the answers you seek—without even trying. If, however, you force yourself into conversations—sizing up each contestant as a possible match for Your Holiness—you'll likely get the incorrect impressions, and will be *less* effective in both how you go about getting what you want and in actually getting what you want. I hate to be rude, but it's not all about you. You must stop thinking about yourself. And, paradoxically, the more you re-focus on others, the better your own odds become. This is one of those intangible social skills that almost trumps an actual knowledge of the law. Almost.

In law school, this is a chance to have *fun!* And if you're doing the work you should be doing, then you'll have nothing to fear about survival. Rather, you'll be looking in a pragmatic sense about how close to #1 you get (if, indeed, it isn't #1). But...and this is key...the more you force it, the less likely it will be.

Form your learning team *carefully*. If someone asks if you'd like to join them, be polite (always) and respond that you're enjoying the process of getting to know each other, and you'd be happy to sit in...but you're not ready to commit until you see how each of the members—and the entire team—comes together. This time you should spend happily: to get acquainted with your new colleagues and perhaps to pick up a tidbit or two. Yes, this means you might "join" several teams, all the while letting each know that you're really just so gosh-darned happy to be there you'd like to share in the fun. Perhaps permanently.

In a conversation or meeting, you don't just ask about commitment...you want to *see* it. So, find out how each thinks it should be run. What you're looking for isn't the answer as much as the attitude. You'll be able to apply your own voice to the team you do choose, but reserve in your own mind the right to decide whether the fit is the right one, for you. As in any deal, it's important to be able to walk away. And, as in any setting, it's important to do so with "class."

The qualities of each member and team become apparent soon enough. Often, early teams simply fall apart: but you'll likely find one or two gems, perhaps building a new team that *will* last, and work. A team of three who work well together is vastly more valuable than a "team" of six who just go through the motions.

Ultimately, the learning team should be one that fits. If you're *Type-A-All-The-Way,* then you might seek out other Type-A souls. These tend to be huge disappointments, however, as many Type-A's mistake form for substance, and it's easy to get into a battle of egos. If you can find compatible colleagues that have different ego levels but an equal commitment to what is important (*no* to dividing outlines, *yes* to working hypos, and *yes* to working exams), then that might be your perfect team. Not everyone has to be a leader, and in fact the best teams don't have leaders (in the sense we think of the term). They do, however, have winners.

Everyone on the team *must* be on the same page. So you might share this section and see if there's resistance and, if so, whether it's reasoned—or inflexible. Every member must understand and agree: (1) outlines are individual work; (2) hypos are central to the team's purpose; and (3) exams are the team's *raison d'être* in the last third of the semester. Law exams are "merely" forms of hypos, after all. The team must also agree, collectively, about its administrative details: that members must come prepared to discuss the hypo. This is non-negotiable, and should be agreed explicitly. If a member fails to adequately prepare the outline section for that hypothetical, that member fails. And so does the team. In such a case a teammate who is unprepared is worse that unproductive: he or she is a drain. You cannot have drains. You have *work* to do.

The "punishment"? They should not attend that session.

It's funny, in a sense: Law professors have gotten the brunt of criticism as to classroom environments that are "hostile"—as indeed the fear of being called on will instill in anyone. But this isn't class. It's a *team*. And you darned well *know* what's expected of you, to the case, as well as the subject of what's being called in "class" that day. There's no "pass" in a team, and absent some serious, temporary issue, you and your teammates must be firm. If it happens once, okay. But not thereafter. You *must* hold yourselves to a high standard (as your professors certainly will), and each member must know that there is the risk of being "fired" from the team. Not out of spite, but because this is serious.

On a positive note, your learning team can and should be one of the very best parts of law school: you will have a team of like-minded colleagues with whom you can share the burdens of learning, frustrations, and occasional venting, and who will likely be continued professional allies and sounding boards. This can be an immeasurable asset to any professional. Again, this is not *the* reason you should take this seriously, but it is a solid plus.

What follows will seem odd. Yet it so happens that I have worked with academic learning teams for over a decade, and with hundreds of teams over the years have seen what has worked, and what has not. Thus, the formality I recommend, as with an outline, is more a symbol of how serious you and your team take this, rather than the essence of what's important. What *is* important is your team. Yet it won't *be* a team unless you all do agree. Here's how you can:

Your team should start with a Charter. This is the agreement that will help in formation and also the inevitable hiccups. The charter should include the following elements, in any format or wording that you agree on:

1. Contact information: land and cell numbers, email addresses, emergency contacts, and best times to call. While this might seem silly, this is one of those nagging details: when you need to contact someone, it's important to have the right information, even if it's emergency contact data, and it's important to have it when you need it.

2. An individual "skills inventory." What are you each good at, and what do you each need to focus on? This too is not a pro forma blank to be filled in: everyone has strengths, and everyone has weaknesses. Be honest, and be earnest in addressing them. If, like me, you're "big picture," say so. If you're methodical, terrific! That's a great balance. That, in the end, is what you're looking for: six big-picture types will make for one tricky team, while six methodical types will probably miss out on, yes, much of the big picture. You need both, and need to draw out the best in each. How many in a team? I recommend 3-5. Three makes for a cozy team, but with the right individuals will be far stronger given how much closer communication is. More than five and a team too easily gets unwieldy. Again, this depends as much on the members and how seriously each of them takes this (and their own responsibility) as it does on the actual number.

3. Goals of the Team. What do you expect to get out of this? Not everyone has the same goals, and that's okay. It's thus important to set this down, now. Yes, many will respond "Get an A in everything!" If so, the next parts will be a cross-check to how seriously that is really the goal. Why? Because if you don't follow these suggestions you will almost certainly not all get A's. In fact, without a solid team it's unlikely even one of you will get more than an occasional A.

4. Ground Rules. What, specifically, will the team be doing? Don't be coy. If you're going to meet once per week (the bare minimum), then you need to specify exactly when, where, for how long, and what other details apply to your group.

   a. This should not be dreary. This should be fun. Seriously. That's part of the give-and-take of hypotheticals. Thus, you should find teammates you genuinely enjoy being around, and don't feel that mixing socializing with "work" is a problem. As long as you are taking it seriously, making it an all-evening or full-day meeting with lots of food and, at the end, appropriate beverages is a marvelous way to go. For an example, skip to 5(a)(iii), below.

   b. My recommendation? Plan to meet on Sundays for a half-day. This gives you each all of Saturday to individually fine-tune your outlines for each subject. And it conveniently removes the "I didn't have time" excuse. As you get comfortable, you can fine-tune your approach, perhaps rotating leadership by subject, by week—say, two or three subjects alternated each week with a one-hour focus, each led by one member, with the remaining subjects given just twenty-minutes, or some such. As you get more comfortable, you might meet for one or two evenings mid-week to expand the focus for each subject, again on a rotating basis.

5. Ground Rules II: Expectations. This is a key. You should specify what you, as a team, agree is expected...such as preparation of individual outlines, how much time will be spent on each subject, a calendar for the semester with expected stages of hypotheticals and exams, and so on.

   a. My suggestion:
      i. Each must prepare a master outline. This must be in pace with the class. Each segment of the class (usually, just a few weeks or so) should result in no more than a half-dozen pages. The master outline should be no more than 50 pages.

      ii. Teams should meet for at least five hours per week, rising to ten hours per week (or more) before exams. Initially this is for discussion of outlines (i.e., black letter law); then for working of hypos; then for working of exams.

    iii. Food and fun are an important part. Incorporate them. One of the best teams I ever saw met for an entire day on Sundays, replete with food (and the occasional family picnic). They could just about finish each other's sentences. They had fun, and every one of them got an A.

6. Penalties. Just as you'll deal with in Contracts, there should be an up-front understanding of what happens if all does not go according to plan. Perhaps a warning, a chance to recover, a final warning (copied to all members), and, if all fails, an earnest "Sorry, this didn't work out."

The Charter is a living, not static, document. So, you should agree to revisit it at least once. What usually happens is that such a document is treated as a *pro forma* formality, which no one really cares about when written—and cares about even less thereafter—until something does go wrong. Just like in Contracts. By then, it's usually less effective than it would have been if it had been taken more seriously up-front. You needn't be ritualistic about it, but a twenty-minute, eyeball-to-eyeball meeting of the minds is important. If you want the top grades, teams are a boost to that effort. But to be a boost, the team must be the right team, working in the right ways.

    Your team will need to devote a substantial effort to, well, team work. How much is substantial? Well, that depends upon you. But it's probably not less than five hours per week, rising to ten hours per week toward the end of the semester. Even that is too low for what you'll need to accomplish, so keep that in mind. And this work *follows* the individual work that each member must have done prior to the meeting. Ideally, that should be a part of each member's daily schedule, so there's nothing extra to do. Reality does intrude, however, and it's inevitable that there's catch-up to do. Two points: you might schedule your team meetings accordingly; and if it's more than minor or occasional catch-up, that's a warning. Not a "warning" warning, but, more importantly, a warning *sign*. Law school should not and cannot be about catching up. It must be about keeping up.

As to how you might discuss this, break the objectives down. The purpose, for the first one-third of your semester, is to discuss your outlines. Note #47.5: this is *not* to *divide* your outlines. Repeat: Do not even *say* "hey, let's divvy up the outlines," and do not tolerate it. Instead, it is to engage in a serious discussion of what's in each member's outline—which each has worked on and fine-tuned *beforehand*—and to make sure each member of the team has a sufficiently detailed and meaningful understanding of those areas of the law. The outline *reflects* this understanding; it does not replace it.

It's hard to overemphasize this (although you're no doubt getting tired of the repetition): the outlines must be updated *before* your meet. If not, the team "meeting" is a waste of time. You've heard of the expression "If you want something done, give it to a busy person?" Well, having taught many hundreds (if not thousands) of students, I can spot a certain type of stellar student within the first few meetings (if not the first few minutes). This is the person for whom an "A" is actually a low standard—but not because of the grade. Rather, instead of focusing on the grade they're focused on the material. When others whine and moan about how much they have to do and how overloaded they are, these few students seem to magically produce what everyone else merely promises. Often, I learn that these star students actually have more demanding lives than nearly all of the other students in the class. One example: just such as student apologized for being ten minutes late. She was, I found out later, an immigrant who was raising *four* children—the youngest in diapers—*and* working probably 80 hours per week at her family's store. I joked about that for many classes later: "You can't complain unless you can top *her* story, yes?" Yet *these* are the students who excel. Why? Because they're efficient (they have to be) and because they spend less time moping and more time doing.

A dangerous trend happens in law school. Many students are burned out after sixteen straight years of school. Many feel that this is their last chance for freedom. And fun. Some simply don't care. So, rather than prepare, they either start and then falter, or they just go through the motions and then sputter to a stop entirely. These are the ones who are usually "scamming" for the easy way out. And they're often the ones most concerned about grades, grades, grades. In law school, there is no such way. Want to hear a secret? Law professors are actually quite happy with blind grading. It's their way of saying to these not-quite-lawyerly students: "You're not getting past *my* class!" For some professors, blind grading and the curve become a relief valve of sorts against the constant griping, whining, and general lack of preparation. They won't say this, but that's what they're thinking as the fifth person mumbles "Pass."

This is worsened by the protocol for law school: no quizzes, tests, or exams until the end. So, it's *easy* to start letting things slide—as it's nearly impossible to keep up the way most are encouraged to do it—and then, after a while, to simply let it all slide. Maybe they get called on up front, maybe they don't. Maybe they're embarrassed, maybe they're not. Either way, it's simply too much work, requiring too much faith, to stick with a regimented program. And there's an additional hurdle of a near-rejection of anything smacking of "regimentation." (How *dare* you tell me I have to…!") Your learning should not be regimented, but you *do* have to keep up.

Back to teams: A failure to have completed a section of an outline should be a violation of your charter. This is not a mere formality; anyone who has not done their work before walking in the door is *wasting your time,* and hindering your progress. One free pass, and then a long-term pass…to another team. You need to be serious about this. And you need to do *your* work, beforehand. No ifs, ands, or buts. And no excuses.

The good news? "Doing the work" means *preparing a small section of an outline, which you should be able to do in under an hour (if you're as efficient as you will be).* Two if you include scanning the cases and a bit of extra work. This gets to another paradox: efficient students get vastly more done, with vastly less fuss. If you feel yourself slipping into the "wait and whine" category, stop and re-evaluate. Don't do this for me, but for the train wreck waiting for you at the end of the line.

Teamwork should transition by the middle-third of your first term to a focus on hypotheticals. In reality this is when most teams start to gel anyway. (Note: You'll continue to work on outlines, and discuss them, but the focus will grow to include hypothetical discussions to bring these points to life.) Actually, you should begin with basic hypos almost as soon as you start. How? You start asking the "what if" questions...and then you start to answer them. These first hypos are given to you: the cases assigned to you. But don't focus on the entire case! Just the narrow point of the law that is the point of that outline sub-section. That's it.

How do you get more hypos? They're everywhere. The obvious place to start, again, is in your casebook. Those cases (and the commercial case briefs that will have condensed versions of the facts) provide ample meat: start changing the facts, and discuss what would happen. If you can't agree (after a serious discussion), then jot down a message to your professor, lay out a "what if" scenario, lay out your proposed solutions, and ask which is correct. Chances are your professor will be deeply impressed by the approach and by the lawyerlike attempt at analysis. Whether one or both "answers" are right or wrong is irrelevant; the point is that you're setting up an alternative fact pattern, and then applying the legal tests to that pattern. One reason this is so valuable, by the way, is that in the discussion you and your team will begin the process of narrowing the issues to the single legal test that applies. What will happen is that you'll end up with a series of legal tests, and a finer and better grasp of when each applies, and how. *That* is a lawyerlike analysis.

Do not write to your professor to impress.

What's the rule? *Grades are the only thing that count.* More importantly, it takes just a few occasions to impress a professor (and those occasions are better left for years two and three). More than a few occasions and "impress" turns into "annoy." Trust me on this. Some professors won't mind answering an occasional email (*i.e.,* once or twice per semester) *if* it has a clear question and shows *genuine* effort to arrive at an answer. Any less and you won't be impressing your professors in the positive. Any more than once or twice and...same conclusion. Ironically, the better the question—which almost by definition answers itself—the more you can pester without causing annoyance.

Another reason this should be infrequent: the only times that your team should be stumped is when the law itself is unsettled. In such a case, chewing through the facts and applicable test(s) is almost certain to boil down to a fairly straightforward analysis. This is less true when there is a split of authority...which again, in most cases, is answered within your team as: "if the majority rule is applied the answer is *x,* because such-and-so; if in a minority jurisdiction the answer is *y,* because so-and-such." Note that your team is doing the heavy lifting. You're asking the question, you're parsing the facts and law, and you're "answering" it with reasoning. *Answering* is in quotes because the answer is less important than the reasoning. So, it's fine to focus on how the rule applies and it's equally fine to conclude with an "It depends..." summary. What's key is the *reasoning* behind your summary: On *what* does it depend?

This reasoning is *brisk,* not pedantic. If you're spending more than 25 words, you're spending too long. This is, moreover, a *crucial* skill for exams. You must train yourself out of long-winded answers. You need to adopt an almost choppy style to address legal reasoning. You will see this as an almost brusque, but firmly to-the-point series of exchanges.

Don't forget to laugh on occasion (or, better yet, a lot), but don't mistake that for an intense focus on what you're studying. In short, your team doesn't *need* outside help. You're it. You should strive to accomplish all of the above without ever going to a professor for the answer. How? Because you will have the answers (and analyses) in front of you.

An excellent source for hypotheticals is any of the *Restatements* for the Big Six. At least one member of your team should have a copy. As with other ancillary material, this is something you can divide. Each member should buy a student-edition of the *Restatements* for one of the subjects. You should copy the fact patterns, covering the answers, and work through them together. Do not look at the analytical summaries. Instead you and your team spend 20 minutes on each scenario, recording your summary and analysis, and *then* compare how you fared with how the greatest minds in the law conceive of that rule. Seriously. Don't cheat. Force yourselves to focus on these hypotheticals, properly; they are one of the most important keys to your success. Your analysis should be detailed. Not a mere, "Oh, yeah, I got that!"—but a precise "Yes, but what about...?" It would be unusual (at least) for all members of your team to have arrived at the same conclusion, in the same way; *use* this process to make each member's thinking stronger, because each member challenges the logic of all responses—including especially one's own. If you're merely nodding your heads in agreement, you're not doing your jobs.

You should all attend LEEWS, together, as early as possible. More about this program, later. In the meantime, about six weeks before exams start, you should shift again to practicing "live"—with real exams. These can be found in your library, where there are probably dozens from your professor and others. Everyone will copy the ones from your professor, of course, and so should you. Occasionally these won't be available, but—here's the truth—it really doesn't matter. Legal reasoning is legal reasoning. Again, a law professor—any law professor—can spot legal reasoning. From our perspective, even that doesn't quite nail it: we can spot legal reasoning about as well as the golden-egg-laying duck amid the (rotten) eggs. The fact patterns are just a way to get there. And it's highly doubtful you'll get an edge with the secret old exam. The exception is when a professor actually re-uses an old exam, which is a second reason you should work *every* exam from your professors...at least once. So, look for and use it, but that's just the icing on the cake. The cake itself is comprised of the dozen exams in each subject that you and your team will take, under *timed* conditions. As with the LSAT, play a trick on yourself: give yourself 15 minutes *less*. As you near the exams, cut that to 30 minutes less. You will then debrief each exam and your answers to it, discussing not just what you got but—more importantly—what you missed, and why.

Have you ever undergone an exercise program under the tutelage of a trainer? Have you noticed the difference it makes? You can promise yourself all you want that this year will be different, that you'll lose the pounds and gain the physique that lies hidden somewhere beneath. Yet, no matter what it never seems to work. Try this: if you've not gone to a physical trainer, try it for two weeks. That's it. Two weeks. Just go to a gym (the less fancy the better) and sign up for a trainer. Just do it.

What you'll find is that your efforts are *far* more focused, and far more intense, simply because you have someone looking at you.

Yes, most trainers know a fair amount of nutrition, physiology, and kinesiology…but the real reason they're effective is simply that they're *there*. Knowing that you're observed, you do a better job. And the results are there for all to see—including you.

I once happened to see a presentation by a CEO of a major corporation to his top directors. In connecting with the company's sales efforts, he challenged them to think about why anyone would use a personal trainer at a gym.

"What do they *do!?*" he bellowed. He was not one taken to whispering.

"What is their function?!" he just about shouted.

In mock suspense and imitating someone pushing a weight with great strain above their heads, he said, again shouting, "Up!"

Then, after a second, he lowered the imaginary weight.

"Down!"

A few second more, weights back up over his head.

"Up!"

"Down!"

"Up…!"

The audience got it, and cheered. (It's hard not to be cheer-led in corporate America.)

The point? In playing with yourself, you're likely, well, not accomplishing a whole lot. You're playing games, more than preparing for exams. In playing with others—discussing outlines, hypos, and exams with a *team* of dedicated fellow students—you *have* to do better. And you will. Build a good learning team, and use it.

The section below is a test. In the classroom, the thrill is in the chase, not the capture. This is a source of frustration between professor and students: the professor wants students to learn from and even *enjoy* the dialogue; many students just want the answer.

The "answer," however, is a false trophy. Why? Because when you face a client—or partner—the facts of that case will almost certainly be different. That means that the answer will be, too.

If you find the discussion below interesting, chances are you will do well in law school...because you will be able to *use* classroom discussion, rather than simply being frustrated. You will also be more likely to enjoy your three years of law school, rather than being perpetually bored.

Finally, you will see that enjoying the discussion ties directly into the result—which happens to be the subject of the section. Or, in other words, appreciating the trail—and knowing how to follow it—will lead you to that "A" exam. In this case, the trail is an analogy that consumes six paragraphs—398 words—of your time. Your professors will follow a great many similar trails in class, in the thought and hope that those trails will help the answer at the end make better sense.

Shall we give it a go?

EXAMS: A SECRET

One of the most difficult areas of the law used to be obscenity cases, in part because of the (*ahem*) desire of local prosecutors to rid their communities of what they considered to be obscene material. Courts were then faced with the issue of how to effectively apply a legal test to what is at base a prurient (and thus inherently subjective) subject: sexual gratification. In other words, what, *exactly*, is "obscene"?

Note: if we cannot define it, is it "law"? Is it a community standard and, if so, *which* community? See how difficult this gets once you begin to apply a truly legal test—*i.e.*, one that applies across cases, with some reasonable degree of certainty and predictability? That, after all, is—or is supposed to be—the very meaning of "the law."

This is not idle chatter: the U.S. Supreme Court had to do just that. In the post-World War II era the state of Ohio (as with many states at the time) regularly banned what it considered obscene material in response to the new-fangled technologies and mass-dissemination of photography and films. Among such material was *The Lovers,* a 1958 French film—*bien sûr!*—which resulted in the conviction and $2,500 fine against Nico Jacobellis, the manager of the Heights Art Theatre in the Coventry Village neighborhood of Cleveland Heights. Hardly the place one would expect to find scandalous material—and not a small sum in those days, to be sure.

In its decision the Court floundered with a rationale: the film was constitutionally protected, but *why?*

Was it because the First Amendment permits *no* censorship? Only Justices Black and Douglas supported this view. Or that *this* film was not obscene? Justice Brennan, writing for the majority, was joined only by Justice Goldberg. No fewer than four majority opinions and two dissenting opinions testified to the jurisprudential disarray. The legal test remains muddy (and might well change), but the opinion that resonated (and one you will likely hear more than a few times in law school) was Justice Stewart's concurrence, which after juristic niceties states simply:

> I shall not today attempt further to define the kinds of material I understand to be embraced within that shorthand description; and perhaps I could never succeed in intelligibly doing so. But I know it when I see it, and the motion picture involved in this case is not that.

Your law professors will know it when they see it. They will know *within seconds* roughly what grade your exam will get.

I was challenged by a colleague on this, by the way, and thought about changing it to "a minute" or "forty-five seconds" or even a too-generous "five minutes," but the point is worth reinforcing: *in under one minute, or a few pages, your professor will know your grade,* give or take a half-letter. Despite the hugely tedious billion hours that (most) professors spend grading exams, the truth is that your professor will know your grade within seconds.

They don't know you—it's graded "blind"—or how much time you spent in the library or how many notes you took or how long your outline is—but *they will know it when they see it.*

The "it" is lawyerlike analysis. In short, your professor needs to see a *lawyer* jumping off the page. This means something quite specific: a (1) precise, accurate recitation of law relevant to the issue the professor wants discussed along with (2) a balanced, probing analysis of the relation of that law to the facts the professor took the time to make up in his "hypothetical," and (3) *only* of those aspects of the law that are problematic or determinative (*i.e.,* those that would likely be contested by lawyers arguing over the issue in a courtroom). In short, a lawyerlike analysis.

That is the "A" exam.

For anyone who has practiced law—or who has read law exams year in and year out—the quality of lawyerlike analysis (or lack thereof) jumps off the page. But here's the trick: even though the quality of the analysis is evident within seconds, it's not possible to simply write a good opening paragraph and then write gibberish. The opening paragraph will be good only if your *thinking* is good. If you have honed your ability to think like a lawyer (black letter law + working hypos), then you will have developed the skills that result in an exam that includes an opening section that shines. The rest of the exam is almost perfunctory. Almost. Your professor is hooked. And, yes, professors are amazed and delighted when they read the handful of exams each semester that are actually something that might have been written by a lawyer. The rest, to them, are varying shades of crap.

This is so important it should be stated again:

The opening paragraph will be good only if your *thinking* is good. If you have honed your ability to think like a lawyer (black letter law + working hypos), then you will have developed the skills that will result in an exam that includes an opening section that shines.

Wax on, wax off.

It is the process of practice that makes perfect. Attempting to cram for a law exam is not only foolish, it is pointless. Even a Supreme Court Justice knows that law is built on foundational steps: skip those steps (black letter law in the Big Six), and all else fails. One cannot "study" for a law exam. One studies and learns black letter law, but even that is not sufficient. Indeed, it is just the beginning. Black letter law sinks in only when one *uses* it. This requires working with hypotheticals.

*   *   *

Do you know the alphabet? No, I don't mean to insult you or your intelligence (again). It's a serious question, actually. So—if you'll bear with me—yes, this became second nature within months of first learning your ABCs. But *when you first learned them,* it was hardly second nature at the time.

Have you ever seen a child recite the alphabet before they knew it? They might, for example—*cheerfully!*—recite *"A, B, D!"* Their enthusiasm is infectious. This is *fun!* They'll soon get the rhythm of the ABC song, but not quite understanding the importance of the sequencing, they'll add or subtract letters with happy abandon. *"A-B-F-Z! Yeaaaaaay!"*

Despite the look of consternation written on parents' faces (which, come to think of it, looks more like constipation)—*My God, is my child retarded? How can they not know where "C" goes?!*—this is hardly a problem as the song itself helps to reinforce the ordering of the characters; the sequencing in turn is needed to make sure all the characters are learned (in addition to the joys of alphabetical order, but that comes later), and that none are misplaced. Soon enough, the flow of the song—and the letters—starts to make sense (or at least are memorized), and they begin to recite the letters in proper order. Still fun, but...not quite so much.

Once they know all of the ABC song, they're done, right? Well, much as we might have liked this to be true—*time for recess!*—that's not quite the end of it. Young students then learn to form short words, and then longer ones, and then basic sentences, and then longer, more-complex ones.

So how does this apply to law school? Is this some implicit insult by a stuffy know-it-all? I hope not. Even the nine justices of the U.S. Supreme Court—the wisest of them all—*regularly* cannot come to agreement on the meaning of a point of law. They do, however, know lawyerlike analysis. And they *make* black letter law.

The law, while considerably more complex than the 26 characters of the American English alphabet, is (or should be) absorbed by each person in much the same way. To the student, it takes a few times to recite the ABCs of each legal test. When entering the world of negligence in Tort Law, for example, you'll need to remind yourself more than a few times just what those legal elements were. Pretty soon, you'll remember, almost in cadence, "Duty,

Breach, Cause, Harm." If you're sufficiently enthused, then it's *Duty-Breach-Cause-Harm!* By the time you get to the exam, it should be almost the same as ABC: you don't even have to think about it. You *breathe* Duty-Breach-Cause-Harm. It's *that* basic.

The complication comes in that *Duty-Breach-Cause-Harm* is hardly enough. That's the ABC: just the first step in a lawyerlike analysis of negligence law in Torts. So you then take each of those first-level tests and break it down. Duty, for example, has its own set of rules, definitions, exceptions, and exceptions-to-exceptions. You will go through the same process with each of those sets, until each of them is DEF, GHI, and JKL to you.

So, when your professor starts to read your exam, *what they're reading is a poem.* Well, a choppy, not-very-poetic poem written in a highly condensed verse. This poem shows, from its very first stanza, that you're so far beyond mere ABC that you can actually *use* those letters. *That* is lawyerlike analysis. And that is what you must be able to do on a law exam.

So, that sounds awful purdy. But *ABC* and *wax-on-wax-off* doesn't *seem* very helpful. Dag nabit, I want the A. How do I get it?!

OKAY, THEN. HOW TO GET THE A.

It's not too often that advice is easy—especially with advice on a subject as endlessly distressing as law exams. Here, it *is* easy. (The advice, anyway.) The answer?

In a word, LEEWS.

This is the Law Essay Exam Writing System, developed by Wentworth Miller. [I will state, up front, that I receive no money from Mr. Miller or from LEEWS, or from anyone in any way connected with either, for any of my comments that follow. I have, it is true, developed (what I hope is) a friendship with him—but that too is not the reason for my endorsement here.]

Over the years I have corresponded with Miller and have been impressed with his decades-long passion to teach students how to conduct a lawyerlike analysis—and how to replicate such an analysis in a law exam. He and his associate, JoAnne Page, offer seminars around the country, and I urge you to attend one, as early as possible. They do add an expense, but—in comparison to most

CLE (continuing legal education), which costs hundreds if not thousands per seminar—it's actually quite reasonable. (It's equally reasonable, for that matter, in comparison to LSAT or bar exam prep courses.) So, while it is an added expense, it is one that will be worth it.

If that seems questionable, the two sections borrowed from Wentworth, above, might be a fair indication of what you would be getting. In particular, the 2-4 line briefing—which can save you hundreds of hours of makework—is central to his program. As always, you be the judge. This is one reason I included such long passages of his, so that you would have sufficient evidence to make a sound judgment.

Assuming you agree, you should take this as early as possible. In writing this section, by the way, I was debating whether to recommend that you take LEEWS twice. I asked Wentworth, and here's his response:

> Once is enough, *if* they do the follow-up practicing. The book suffices to refresh anything that is unclear. Sooner is better, in order to more fully implement the 2-4 line briefing and 30-50 page outlining techniques. At the end of a live program I make the point that the essay hypothetical, so confusing and formidable at the beginning of the day "is now your best friend!" Students should think, "thank goodness for the essay hypothetical." Because, yes, on paper the competition is formidable. You are probably *not* smarter or more hard-working than your classmates. They are in the library...briefing...even as you sit here! (This usually gets a laugh as students digest their advantage.) But they can brief all they want. When the smartest ones, the ones who so impressed you in class, come up against the essay hypothetical...
>
> The Blender can be mastered quickly. This plus knowing—finally—how to "analyze as a lawyer" and present concisely on paper will vault the student far beyond clueless, hapless class-mates. I was *eager* to look into the cases the professor appended [to an email] as sources of the law to be applied. Why? Because the lawyering game is *fun*. When a student gets hold of this very consistent game of legal problem-solving, law school becomes fun.

While I agree in principle, here I will disagree, gently, with Wentworth: you should plan to attend LEEWS twice. You should attend at the beginning of your first semester (or even before law school), and again at the beginning of your second semester. You should absolutely plan to attend as early as possible in your first year—even if you have to travel to take it. It's that important.

The caveat to save money: *if* you absorb LEEWS, use its primer (which means actually using it, not picking it up again a week before exams), and practice, practice, practice as he lays out, then once is enough. If, like me, you can use the additional structure, plan on attending a second time. The more important point is that LEEWS—or this book or any other study "aid" for that matter— isn't the answer. It's certainly not a secret weapon. It's a way to frame the question. The "answer" is *your work,* properly framed. So attending LEEWS twice, three times, or Hell, why not every month…isn't going to make a difference if you don't follow it. Attending once *will* make a difference, if you do. You must treat LEEWS as a framework to the solution—not as the solution itself. The solution is our old standbys: (1) learning black letter law; and (2) learning how to use it. There is no substitute for either, and LEEWS will focus your efforts as to both…in time, crucially, for exams.

IN CASE I'VE NOT BEATEN THIS SUFFICIENTLY TO THE GROUND, HERE'S HOW TO ACE YOUR LAW EXAMS, AND, AHEM, TO PROVE THAT YOU'VE GOTTEN GOOD (…AND, AHEM, AHEM, TO GET THE GOLD):

LEEWS.

WELL, I'M NOT CONVINCED. WHAT ELSE YOU GOT?

Once upon a time, a law student struggled along with the rest of his class. He learned just before impending exams of a program, LEEWS, that was being offered in a classroom far, far away. Well, far, far away in the same city. Not having money and not wishing to anger the Good Witch of the East with pleadings for additional alms, he ignored it and soldiered on.

He later learned that, with just one notable exception, every one of his classmates who'd graded on to law review had taken LEEWS. In fact, that's how he'd originally found out about LEEWS: one of these friends happened to sit next to him.

SECOND YEAR AND BEYOND

Law school splits up after the first year from a regimented, mandatory path to a nearly open field.

Many students are encouraged to take courses matching the bar exam, and the standard courses, such as Evidence for litigators or a slew of business-ish classes for those intending a transactional practice. After the exhaustion of the first year, nearly everyone is eager to avoid anything smacking of any of their first-year trauma.

The good news? Professors do take a different approach in most upper law classes: even for large classes, things tend to be in a lower key. There are a number of reasons for this, but most importantly, neither professors nor students have much appetite for more Socratic torture. This is a shame, because the Socratic Method can be a valuable tool, when done right. More often, you're in smaller classes and seminars with professors who are teaching what they're *really* interested in. After a bruising with grades, the possibility of writing papers instead of taking an exam is especially attractive for many.

My advice? Go easy. You do not need to take a course merely because it's on the bar exam. A good bar review course (which you *do* need to take) will cover everything you need, and even if you didn't take that subject before you'll find that your increased capacity and comprehension will fill in the blanks with amazing facility. That written, if you are seriously planning on litigation, or a certain practice, you should take at least most of the standard courses.

Specializations? No. Aside from litigation, and unless you have a serious, long-standing interest, don't try to force a "specialization." This is in quotes because there really aren't true specializations in law school, and most firms won't care. They seek the degree, and grades, and will put you where you're needed. Again this should tie into your interests. Choose what you genuinely *like*.

Don't make yourself miserable—with little benefit—taking what you don't.

It's important, too, not to pre-judge a subject: one colleague found herself enamored with tax law—tax law!—because it was so intricate and, to her, engaging. (This is reason #42 to work in a firm before and during law school, as you'll have a better sense of what you like—and what you don't.)

More important is who is teaching. Your four semesters remaining don't leave a huge amount of choice, particularly with sequencing and periodic offerings. You should thus think about this carefully. If the choice is between a standard course you're not terribly interested in and an off-beat course you *are* interested in, taught by someone with a good reputation, take the fun course. This is reason #87 that good grades matter: if you have good grades, your employer almost could not care less what you take. Don't go wild, but that's pretty close to the truth.

What about foreign study? If you can swing it, yes. It's a fantastical—and fantastic—adventure. *Well* worth it. (Reason #88 to do well—and reason #43 to work in a firm—is that you'll not need to worry so much about interviewing, and can enjoy your time abroad.)

What about courses outside the law school? Yes and yes. You can usually take six credits without too much fuss. There's often a request form, and it must be a graduate course with at least some reasonable bearing on what it is you're interested in. Go for it. You'll be glad you did. (Reason #89 to do well is that you'll not need to worry so much about a course in, say, musicology—which you justified by an interest in working with non-profit theater groups—and can *enjoy* your time.)

What about clinics, externships, and the like? Yes, yes, and yes. Take advantage of these, even and perhaps especially if you're not sure you'll like them. The break from conventional study will be refreshing, and you might just find yourself with something you love. In any case, it's almost always worth it. If you have nothing lined up for your first summer, you might consider a summer clinic, topped off with volunteering at an organization that interests you. Both will be worth your time.

How about seminars? Yes. Usually these require a substantial written paper, rather than an exam. For most, this is a useful trade-off: more work, but more control. You should probably take one per semester. This will free up some of your exam time, and there's almost always one (or two or five) seminars you'll find interesting.

In short, use your four open semesters to the maximum extent you can. Take a few of the "suggested" courses, sure, but don't neglect those *you* want to take, as well. In the end, you'll be glad you did.

SOCIALISM

There seem to be extremes in the social life of many law students: one crowd lets it all hang out, while the other seems preternaturally wired for social climbing. Neither is a good approach. Nor should either be yours.

You should, first, relax. Don't be so worried about what others think of you. Neither should you not care at all. You should, in all interactions, be your *better* self: courteous, generous, respectful, and, well, friendly.

This is one of those unspoken rules that is almost more important than all the others: how you behave among your future colleagues will have a *big* impact on how they will behave with you. This ranges from the practical (how many client referrals you get) to the intangible (how well-liked and respected you are). As you become a senior lawyer, you'll be amazed at how much more important the intangibles in life are.

For most, keeping this all in perspective and being concerned with how well you're treating others is, by far, the better path.

GETTING THE GOLD

Summary

There are many ways to define success: "Getting the Gold." For most law students, that means getting a good job, if not a terrific one. For us, this will be a consideration of all aspects of financial as well as personal success, from before law school on.

The rules, condensed:

1. Earnest and early preparation pays.

    a. Earnest means sincere and substantial—preparing as if your livelihood depends upon it (as indeed it does).

    b. Early means high school. Seriously. AP courses for early college credit. Honors while you can focus. Minimizing distractions and lightening your load when you can't. A laser-focus on your LSATs. A serious focus on the application process. A dedicated focus in preparing for law school before law school. And a concerted, strategic approach once in law school.

2. Prior to law school: In addition to deciding which area of the country is for you, and crafting the skeletons for your outlines, you should prepare a database of small and mid-size law firms in that area.

3. Attend LEEWS early in your first semester and again in your second semester, and re-read the primer monthly.

4. Prepare your master and summary outlines (which should be nearly complete by the middle of the semester), and use them intensively for at least one month in working hypos and old exams, under real-exam conditions. This is your primary means of "study"—Black Letter Law is assumed (and is assured with your outlines).

5   Etiquette, deportment, and integrity count—in subtle yet powerful ways. Be polite, positive, and persuasive—in interviews and elsewhere.

6. Seek a part-time job in a law firm or office. Volunteer if you have to. Work experience is a must; money is a plus. Important paradox: focus too much on just money and you're less likely

to get it. Focus on getting good, first, and the money—and options—will follow.

7. Pay attention to grants and scholarships, through your law school, the university if one is attached, and local and special-purpose organizations. This should be part of your application process, and should take about as much time.

About Success

What is *this!?*

Why are we talking about stuff we've just gone over!? I mean, really. Six of the seven summary points are primarily about Getting In and Getting Good. This can't *really* be your advice on Getting the *Gold*.

Actually, it is. If you're not too upset, and for an explanation as to why this is so, please bear with me as you read on.

*   *   *

The very model of blind grading serves—for all its imperfections— as a powerful leveler. Yes, those from families with attorneys who have inculcated the process of analytical thinking—of thinking like a lawyer—tend to produce grades at least a little better than average. Too, there are opportunities available to even those who don't get into the top law schools, or who achieve the top grades. Although both weigh heavily in the equation, in reality these are short-term considerations: a degree with honors from a top law school make it easier to make more money immediately—but they hardly make it easy. And neither is a guarantee of long-term success. After all, a successful litigator can be from any ABA-accredited law school, and with perseverance can—if you'll excuse the crudity—wipe the courtroom floor with more elevated peers who don't do their homework. It happens often enough to reinforce the rule that, in practice, one's pedigree is of concern mostly to that person. Nearly everything we're discussing fades in the background when the bailiff yells *"Oy yea, oy yea! All rise for the Honorable…!"*

A listing of the most successful litigators will show, for example, that the top defense attorneys tend to come (not surprisingly) from the top firms, and in turn from the top law schools. The top plaintiff's attorneys, however, tend to come from less-hallowed backgrounds, many from state and local schools…a lesson as to the value of the school of hard knocks. Importantly, this does not lessen the importance of Getting Good. Quite the opposite. An "up-from-nowhere" litigator had darned well *better* know the law as well as or better than a pedigreed opponent. Equally important, the lean and hungry litigator will prepare, prepare, and prepare some more (just like for law exams); it's important to assume that over-preparation is *almost* enough. That is the link. And it is true in transactional firms as well: the over-preparation is in excruciating attention to detail.

Again, these are inter-correlated variables: they're all, well, related. An intense dedication to the LSAT will almost certainly result in a higher score as compared to a half-hearted approach. This will almost certainly result in better acceptance possibilities to higher-ranked law schools, which in turn will open doors to jobs during and after law school, which in turn will greatly boost your financial picture. All depend upon a concerted effort, up front and focused on what counts.

GOLD?

Perhaps we should define what "gold" means. No, this is not an excursion into the parsing of words: We need not worry (again) about what "is" is. Rather, we should explore—or, more correctly, you should explore—what "gold" means *to you*.

This is an important question in a number of ways. If, for example, you have a family you actually like being around, or a time-consuming hobby you love, or...whatever...you should seri-ously consider whether you would *want* a high-powered, high-pay-ing job. Really. Assuming you could get such a job—which either will or will not be the case, depending upon which law school you attend and how well you do—what happens when you need to call home to tell them you'll be late for the fifth night that week?

This is *serious*. It doesn't hit most graduates until too late, but the joys of a large paycheck being to fade after the 2,500th billable hour. Actually, they'll fade long before then.

For some, such a worklife is exhilarating. Good for them. But for most, and for nearly everyone with commitments outside work, the dead-serious obligations expected of any big-firm associate all but preclude any real time spent outside the firm for at least the bet-ter part of a decade. If you're "lucky" enough to land a summer clerkship in a national firm, rather than (just) relishing in the win-ing-and-dining, spend at least a week matching the hours of the hardest-working associate there. This isn't (just) to butter up the partners in the hopes of a permanent offer; you need to know what you're getting into, and the summer clerkship is almost the antithesis of that reality.

I do not mean, by the way, to be condescending about this option. It is rewarding to practice in a powerful firm (either large or boutique), and it is clearly rewarding financially. These are important considerations. The key is whether the personal costs are worth it…to *you*. If you're in your mid-20s and relish the thought of working with high-powered people and problems, and you actually enjoy spending your time thinking about work, then that might well be the career for you. Again I'm not being sarcastic. Many individuals truly enjoy working—a lot—and I share much of that, myself. It's more than merely "enjoying" work; it's more that you can't *stop* working. The key, yet again, is whether that applies to you. While I would caution anyone against a workaholic approach, if that does apply to you and you have the energy, you might as well take advantage of both and, perhaps, ease into a more balanced life later.

It should go without saying that an approach at the opposite end of the spectrum—that of wanting simply to get by—will almost certainly result in failure. What nearly everyone should strive for is some reasonably happy middle ground: Enjoying what one does as well as what one does when not working, and balancing the many aspects of life. One saying has it as "Working to Live" rather than "Living to Work." If you find yourself either looking at the clock or ignoring it completely—either is a sign of danger.

*   *   *

The second, related part of this question is *where*. Some graduates know exactly where they want to practice, and are lucky enough to land a job exactly where they want to be. Good for them.

Others aren't so lucky. Most, in fact, will go wherever the job takes them, and as one of the realities of law practice, the larger the city, the larger the salary. Again, for those who qualify, it's awfully hard to turn down a big paycheck, particularly with massive student loans looming.

I know I've harped about this, but it *is* important. Think about this very, very carefully. There are several aspect to this issue. First, not having a preference likely means that you'll end up wherever a job happens to take you. That can be fine, or it can lead to a lifetime of missed opportunities. If you like sailing, or if you like the *idea* of sailing, then for goodness' sake figure out whether that's a real issue for you. If it is, then don't even consider moving to (or staying in) a place without water. Whatever your personal desires, define what they are, and decide where they're likely to be best used. It is these subjective elements that can make such a huge difference in our happiness. And, believe it or not, this is a large part of whether (or not) we find career success.

Consider too the practical side. A paycheck in a large city will almost certainly be worth less than a smaller paycheck in a smaller city. Before accepting an offer, if you haven't already lived in that city...go there. Visit. Spend a week. This is one of the *rare* good uses of a credit card for a vacation. But this is a *working* vacation. You want to get out in rush-hour traffic (not that you'll be in rush hour too often, as you'll be in the office, but your family will), you'll want to go to the shopping centers, cafés, stores and so on, and you'll want to get the Sunday paper and go to open houses. I'm serious. Find out what you're getting into. Chances are you simply won't believe how expensive most of the essentials are in a large city. If, for example, a decent apartment costs upwards of one-half of a million dollars, that's going to be quite a mortgage—even on a high-powered salary. Worse, it presents what are known as the "golden handcuffs"—once you're paying, say, five thousand dollars a month for a mortgage, plus a thousand per month for a status car, plus a thousand per month for student loans, plus a few thousand each month for "necessaries," as the saying goes pretty soon you're talking about real money. You can't quit...and you can't afford to fail.

There's the axiom in sales that you should buy absolutely the biggest car you *can't* afford...which will spur you to make your job a success. This derives from the "smile yourself to success" school of psycho-biz-think, and while it has some merit (I have worked with a number of individuals such as this), it is a dangerous game to play. Be sure, absolutely sure—before you roll the dice—that *you* want to play.

Yes, it's heady stuff to be suddenly on the receiving end of money that just seems to roll in. But it tends to roll out just as fast. And it can roll out even faster than it rolls in if you're not careful. It might seem unbelievable that anyone making in the six figures can ever be short of money. Think again. In fact this is just the demographic most likely to get into trouble. It doesn't take many two-thousand-dollar suits, one-thousand-dollar shoes, and twenty-dollar martinis before even a healthy monthly salary vanishes. And once it's gone, you're left with old suits, worn shoes, and…sorry to be crude…urine. We're getting a little beyond the scope of a mere law school book, but be very, very hesitant to spend money like everyone else. Live, instead, *below* your means. You needn't be a miser, but do be careful. Let that money build to a reserve that gives you both a cushion and the power to do what you want, when you want.

For the record, I have been in both positions, which is perhaps why this advice is coming on as strongly as it is. There should simply be no debate about this: save twenty percent or more of your initial income. Focus on your job, buy necessary career and personal tools, focus on your job some more…but otherwise be the quiet millionaire-in-waiting. Were I to put on my curmudgeon's hat I would write that *no one* should obligate themselves to anything close to a $500,000 + home right out of *any* school. But, as we've seen over the generations, what was once considered normal is now beneath question. How many of us would be content with a two-bedroom, one-bath, 1,200-square-foot starter home?

Financially, a modest home is without question a preferable investment than one beyond or at the limits of one's means. Among other warning signs, it's seductive but fiscally deadly to consider the mortgage interest deduction as a gain; it is, after all, a reduction of an *expense*. Be very, very careful here. Fundamentally, if you can't afford it with a 15-year loan, you can't afford it. Whatever you do, unless you've been in that market for years *and* are convinced that it's bottoming *and* has inherent strengths—such as a large university, military, or government base—it's better to rent rather than buy, at least at first. Moreover, you simply don't have time for ownership; you have a *job* to do.

WHAT ARE FIRMS LOOKING FOR?

As has been mentioned too many times I know, the law is a highly risk-averse profession. This, however, doesn't quite convey the depth of this risk aversion—or its impact on the soon-to-be law graduate. Picture this: You are a powerful law partner, in a powerful law firm. Your clients are precious, and they too are powerful. Your power relates directly to how well you serve them. When they yell "Jump!" it is you—the law *partner*—who asks "How High?"

Not exactly, but that's not too far off the mark, particularly for the biggest clients.

What is the impact of this? What, for example, would be your reaction to a mistake? What about something silly, or embarrassing? Or something major, and painful? In any case, you'd prefer not to relay bad news to your client. Even this falls short: you'd rather have a tonsillectomy without anesthesia and with the dullest instruments that have been discarded into the HazMat bin than relay bad news to your client. Your standing in the firm and legal community is riding on it. So is your livelihood. Even partners face the threat of losing their jobs if they don't bring in—and keep—sufficient business. The gold watch is long gone, and partnership is not a prize you get to keep. Partners in every firm now have to justify their existence to their firm, every year. It's the same as with associates, but with higher expectations and higher stakes.

Yet you cannot do all the work yourself. Nor would you want to. Instead, you want to be the conduit for and to the client. You want *others* to slave away over the million details—a new public offering, a major case, a merger, an acquisition—while you chat over expensive lunches with your clients. You do not want to give bad news—*ever*—and so you will do whatever you can to avoid having to give such news.

Okay. You like money and power, and you like chatting with clients over expensive meals. Check. You don't want to do all the work yourself, but you certainly don't want the work done anyone else less well that you would do it yourself, if you had to. Check. So where does that leave us? You will hire only the very best. The best of the best. Even if they screw up (and screw up they will), you'll at least have the emotional comfort of blaming it on them, or on some peculiarity, rather than on yourself.

If, for example, you decide one year to be generous and recruit from the mid-tier schools, or perhaps dip deeper into the middle of the class, what happens if something goes wrong? And it almost certainly will, at some point, in some way. Other partners will look at you—as your mistake has just cost them each a new sports car—and ask "Why did you hire *him?*" If that him (or her) is not a top student from one of the top schools, you won't have an answer.

So, lawyers and law firms go to an extreme: they go nuts over "objective" excellence. If the bar exam were graded rather than pass-fail, we would probably see a complete disregard of law school grades (and perhaps even law school rankings), and instead the same stratification would occur—only this time it would be over the score on the bar exam: the top bar exam performers would get top dollar, and each layer down would get less, in steeply descending order. The firms would *still* take only the top ten or fifteen percent.

This is a key point against which one should not rebel, as it will not change: The law is highly risk-averse. Thus, firms are highly risk-averse. Thus, they want *the best*. And *only* the best.

Do we know what "the best" is? Well, yes and no. The entire process of law professors grading students on a strict curve, while unfair on one level, does give an accurate picture of who "gets it" (at the top)—and who doesn't get it (everyone else). As firms demand only the best, they're concerned only about the viability of the top. We might not like this reality, but it *is* a reality, and the message of Getting Good is just that: if you want any hope of Getting the Gold, you must get good, first. I know I haven't been fair to things linear, and this is no exception. In this, the book is circular rather than linear: one follows the other, in a cycle. That is the way of the law, and indeed of life.

And, yes, this applies from "getting the gold" to "getting in" too. If you've gotten a bit of gold as a part-time employee at a firm during college, chances are much better that you'll have the advantage while applying to law schools. This is almost certainly true in a relative sense, as the day-to-day interactions will almost certainly help in preparations for the LSAT, references, personal statements, and the applications themselves. It will also help, by the way, in your law exams: you will have a better sense of what, exactly, a "lawyerlike analysis" is.

Further, you should not rail against what "getting good" means. That is a dead end, vocationally and emotionally. While becoming the best might not, on some cosmic scale, be represented by law exams (or the LSAT, or any other measurement), such exams *are* a fair approximation of quality—especially at the extremes. Note that this is true as well for law school rankings, or just about any other qualitative judgment. Thus, your aim should be to show that you *have* those qualities. And to show this, you must *actually* have those qualities. As much fun as can be made of certain aspects the legal industry (which most partners will, in private, be the first to agree with), when you talk with partners and senior associates at firms, you *will* be impressed. These are very, very smart individuals, and they have done their time, too.

Here's a lesson I learned in a different context that might convey some of this importance—the extreme weight placed on quality, however measured. It's a lesson I learned in a business capacity dealing with—of all people—graphics professionals. This was for ads, special announcements, and the like. That these tasks were ancillary to the real job at hand proves the point all the more, and the lesson applies equally to other professionals—including attorneys especially.

Some of these graphic designers are "professional" in name only, as they would submit work that, in my view, they should have been embarrassed to send with their name anywhere near it. As one example, I once reviewed what should have been a final copy and saw an uneven arc of blank space where two colors should have come together. It was so obviously wrong that I thought at first the wrong version had been sent. No, that was the file the designer wanted (expected, really) me to approve. It was *he* who felt put out when I pushed it back to him to fix. While I could have (and perhaps should have) made a bigger deal of it, instead I simply sent it back with corrections needed, and we went back and forth as much as we could each bear until it was passable. It should be no surprise that I never used him again. He lost many tens of thousands of dollars of future business because he was sloppy and because he didn't care.

The standard for a professional? Perfect.

Perfect means perfect. Not almost perfect. Not sort of perfect. Perfect. This is the same standard that is reqarded in practice, in law school, in the LSAT, and in applications.

Perhaps 80% of designers are technically competent (a rather shocking assertion, as it should be upwards of 98%), and perhaps only 20% or so have a good "eye" for design. In my view, both are *base* requirements for a good designer. So, it's really just the top 10-15% who are worth hiring in such a public need as design. Gee, that percentage range sounds familiar.

You might think it odd for me to go on a tangent as to something as dissimilar as law practice. In reality, these are two sides of the same coin. It is not sufficient for an attorney to be brilliant. The attorney's work product—and everything associated with that attorney—should *look* brilliant, as well. Note: I'm not referring to "flashy." If anything, understated brilliance is the mark of the true professional. But to appreciate what it is to be understated, one must know what the full-volume setting is.

Another point to be made from this tangent: Law partners do not want to hover. Well, most of them don't. They want, instead, a *professional* they can depend on to make independent judgments that carry forward the partner's direction. In other words, they want someone who can do the work. A professional. After all, if it were otherwise, why bother using an associate at all?

Thus, partners are looking for individuals who meet both requirements, within a legal context: (1) a command of the law, as well as an ability to develop a command of a particular area of the law...quickly; and (2) an ability to act like an attorney. The "game" as it is thus constructed operates to find for partners just such people. Law students do not yet have a command of the law—but the top law students have shown that they *do* have a command of the basics. Good enough. The firm can and will teach the finer points. And the firms look as well to comportment. They're not looking for James Bond-like superstars. They *are* looking for reasonably good-looking, good-acting, promotable future lawyers.

This is no easy task, and while it is easy to criticize firms, it would hardly be as easy to come up with a better strategy.

WHERE EVERYONE IS A LITTLE ABOVE AVERAGE

You will often hear, both before and after law school, about the enormous salaries that attorneys draw. This is flattering, of course, but also a dangerous misperception.

The myth of extraordinary salaries is just that: a myth. It is highly misleading to even think in terms of an "average" salary for an attorney. Why? Because the legal profession is, essentially, a giant double bell curve.

There are two fairly distinct sets of lawyers:

1. Those with "substantial" firms, which includes national, large regional, and boutique firms.

2. Everyone else.

A "boutique" firm is often a spin-off of a large firm, in which usually a handful of partners break off—taking their large-firm clients with them—to escape whatever unkindnesses are running rampant in the larger firm. A boutique firm can be a wonderful place to work. Given its relatively thin staff, however, an even greater burden on learning the law and on fitting in will be upon you.

Lawyers in certain positions, such as those in large corporations, might be viewed as being at the bottom of the first group, or at the top of the second group. This is not meant to be disparaging, as these can also be great places to work, with good pay and many lifestyle benefits unavailable to "outhouse" counsel. Likewise, attorneys working in mid- and upper-levels of government and a very limited number of nonprofit organizations—including law schools—fit in the well-paid category.

It is hard to keep writing—and reading—about this extreme focus on status, credentials, and top, top, top. It is, however, a serious reality in law practice. Firms are under the spell of the

"Cravath system," referring to the New York firm of Cravath, Swaine & Moore, which set in motion the fixation on top credentials and law-firm training as the guarantor of client service. This system has proved highly remunerative to partners at powerful firms, which of course makes it extremely difficult to even consider breaking this seductive (and ever more fragile) system. Why fragile? Because clients are increasingly unwilling to pay for associate training—and certainly not at multi-hundred-dollar-per-hour rates. The result, nonetheless, is the bimodal distribution in which we see just a small percentage earning high salaries, with a majority earning modest salaries far below the "average" for lawyers.

At the opposite end of the scale, only a *small* percentage of a solo practitioners is in group one; most get by with quite modest success. In terms of status within the profession, only a *tiny* percentage of this small percentage is treated with any respect. No, I don't think this is right, and no, it shouldn't be this way. But it is. And, after a few years in practice—and following the sections in Getting Good—you'll get a glimpse as to why this perception is too commonly justified. Importantly, all of group one is a relative minority, including no more than one-quarter of all attorneys. Our fifteen percent is a good benchmark for those earning truly significant salaries. Everyone else is either in a relatively modest-paying position, or scrambling for clients.

We should, too, define what is meant by "well paid." For some it is the miraculous million-dollar draws you might read or hear about in *The American Lawyer* or other journal. This is the fiscal equivalent of grade inflation. Very, *very* few attorneys make this much money. While doing quite well, financially, even most big-firm lawyers make salaries in the six (not seven) figures. Indeed, most attorneys in all but the largest or most specialized firms make salaries at the lower end of those six figures. This is still quite healthy—especially as compared to everyone else—but it's hardly in superstar leagues. Or in the same league as most clients, for that matter. For lack of a better ruler, let's say that to be "well paid," we're talking six figures.

For everyone else, salaries are usually in the mid-to-upper five figures. Again, not bad, but hardly extraordinary. When compared to other fields with comparable educational requirements, salaries for the bulk of the legal profession can seem downright dowdy. For those in lower-ranked law schools, the jobs are either lower-to-mid five figures, or not in the law at all. This is important to keep in mind as you're considering the assumption of your one-quarter-million-dollar investment. It is also important in predicting the options that are likely to be open to you upon graduation.

If you attend a third- or fourth-tier school, will you scramble for a decent (meaning reasonably well-paying) job? Will you be treated as a distant and disliked cousin in the family of law? In other words, are you in trouble before you even start practicing? The answer? Yes, yes, and probably.

Yes, it will be nearly impossible for you to walk into a top position, even if you're one of the top graduates. At either lower tier, a "top graduate" is measured in absolute numbers, not in percentages. So, someone who graduates in the top five—people, not percent— might have an entrée, usually into a good local firm wanting to keep good relations locally, or with partners who graduated from that school. Yes, you will have to work very, very hard both to achieve academic success and respect, and to buttress that with extracurricular value.

And now for the good news: it *is* possible to overcome almost any disadvantage. This, after all, is the American Dream. I have known (and admired deeply) "night students" who became partners in national firms; it does happen. Rarely, but it is possible. What this *will* require, however, is an extraordinary focus and self-motivation to build the relationships that will lead to that opportunity for you. Be sure, again, that that job is really the job for you. These steps might be firm and government internships and externships, judicial internships, volunteering, you name it.

This does not include pestering. This is a sure turn-off, and chances are if you badger a top-firm partner for a job, you'll be iced out just the same. You might, might have a chance with that same partner, however, if you volunteer for bar activities and build a genuine relationship in a non-interview context. To borrow again from the military, there's never a time you're not being observed.

A DIFFERENT REALITY

All this written, however, for a great majority (that is, nearly all) these steps won't happen—a family, other distractions, or simply not picking up on the rhythm of law exams quickly enough—sufficient to land that well-paying job. If not, your student debt will hang over you like the proverbial Sword of Damocles. In the fable, Damocles ["Damn-oh-cleese"] is a sycophant in the employ of Dionysius II of Syracuse, on the eastern coast of Sicily. Dionysius allowed him to switch places for one day—not terribly likely, but that's how the legend has it—and at the end of the evening meal Damocles notices a sword hanging above him, held by a single horsehair. He immediately loses his appreciation for the feast and maidens [in the original, it was boys], as he learns the lesson of the weight of responsibility.

I've a few thoughts on this. (You're shocked, yes?) As someone who's held positions of reasonably substantial authority—directly responsible for some 65 souls—and to quote from Mel Brooks, it's good to be King. Where this is an excursion worthy of the ink is in its underlying message of a cloud hanging over someone. In the law school context, the reality is that, if you don't attend a law school in the first or second tier, and if you don't perform well, *and* if you don't have some other hook or extraordinary energy and ambition, you will nonetheless end law school with student debt that will be quite cutting indeed.

I was fortunate to have attended inexpensive public schools, and worked throughout. The one private school I attended was paid for by my employer, a hugely expensive gift. I also had the benefit of free rent through homes my brothers and I renovated and one we built. Even so, after the first three degrees I entered the workforce with what felt like a heavy burden, and like most I paid for many years. I finally got sick of it and paid them off a year early; *that* was a good feeling. Had I attended private schools earlier the debt would have been far larger. Even with the luck of a job in Honolulu, far removed from the acute legal recession of the early 1990s, I doubt that I would have been able to support a much higher load, in Hawaii, on even a firm's salary. And that was more than a decade ago. The debt today with either public or private schools is higher still.

Again, this is *serious*.

If you are going to attend a law school in the third tier or below, think very, very, *very* carefully about attending a private law school if they don't also offer a sizeable scholarship. I don't like being pessimistic, but is it worth $100,000-$125,000 of debt if you're going to scramble to find *a* job? This isn't much better than a Ph.D. in English in the worst academic markets, really—and in most doctoral programs stipends usually cover at least starvation-level living. Public law schools provide a bit more leeway, as their tuition rates are lower. They're increasingly more expensive, however, and you have in addition three years' living costs. This is a financial sword that will either have a solid rope—in the form of a solid income stream—or a fraying strand of horsehair.

Part of this consideration is practical, and this is a serious, serious discussion you should have with your significant other, if you have one. In short, taking three years off and incurring tuition and book costs is an almost-insurmountable burden. Unless you absolutely, positively *have to be a lawyer,* taking such a path— unless it's a top-tier school—is almost reckless endangerment. This, by the way, is a good way to know if you're suited to law school: do you meet that "absolutely, positively" test?

There are solutions, as always. We might not always like them, but they're there.

A GOLD RUSH

Yes, much of the advice in the summary relates to first-year and even pre-law issues. This is very much the Catch-22 that is success in any field. Law school simply—well, no, not simply—is at an extreme of this vocational maxim.

Success comes in having one's academic ducks in a row. Each of these ducks will be *in* a row behind some other duck...which for our purposes extends backwards in time until even before law school starts. This is not a joke. And it's one reason law school becomes such a ghastly place for so many students: they realize, too late, that they're not even in the running for the jobs they had hoped for and even planned on. All too often, depending upon the job market they're not even in the running for *any* law job. With family expectations piled high—and student debt piling higher—a sense of desperation quickly takes hold. By then, however, it's too late. And "getting the gold" has faded to a dream. An impossible one. *This* is what causes law school to become such a bad experience for so many students.

I hate to be the one to break it to you, but this is the truth. This should not be the truth for you, but for a great many it is. This is also one reason why there are so many books about law school, and why they seem to all dance around the same subjects—some more pointedly than others. If you're reading this well before law starts, there's still time. If you're reading this during law school, there's still time. If you're reading thus just before exams, there may or may not be time, but you need to act just the same. In all cases you must re-focus in getting good especially, and in not wasting time or energy. The important point is to *focus*. It is simply not sufficient to say, "Well, I guess it's too late so I won't worry about it now." Or, "It can't really be all that bad. These are just scare tactics. I'll be fine."

If either of these approaches are yours, you will almost certainly *not* be fine. But it won't be (just) because of law exams, or because of the ever-higher competitive pressures (not least because of books like *Planet Law School* and this one). Rather, it will be because you won't *deserve* to succeed. Ouch. This might be hurtful to read, particularly if this has already happened to you, but that won't make it less true.

Law practice is filled with crises—cases or questions that arise at the last minute, or often *after* the last minute. The law partner cannot simply throw up his hands and say "Well, I guess it's too late so I won't worry about it now" or "This can't be all that important, and the opposing side must just be using scare tactics. We'll be fine." Can you *imagine* the response of a client—or other partners? (...soon to be former partners, if that were ever uttered. Even that is too vague: Imagine partners who have just received word that your cavalier attitude has just cost each of them a sports car, or vacation home, or other such trinket. This is no exaggeration, either as to value or as to effect.) Dammit, this is *serious*.

If you're going to be an attorney, and especially if you want admission to the club of high-powered (and high-paid) partners, then you'd darned well better start acting like you will need to just to *survive* in the real world of law—much less be reasonably assured of success. This means, among other things, never giving up, and never shrugging your shoulders as if you could not care less. Even if you don't care, you can be sure that your future bosses will.

Law school is about thinking like a lawyer. Getting the Gold is about *acting* like one. And part of the latter is making darned sure you're good at the former. As with the over-the-top focus on status-prestige-altitude earlier, it's useful to take a look at the model: the type of law firm that serves as the benchmark for all firms, and indeed for all law offices. This is not written lightly. Even if you decide to work at, say, a smaller firm or in a government agency or in a non-profit organization, while the specifics will differ, and while the chairs might be metal instead of leather-covered hardwood, the structure and general approach is strikingly the same. There is a model for law practice, and it is what was set in genteel partnerships from long, long ago. And even if they weren't really all that genteel, that's still the model.

A Peek Into The World Of White Shoe Law

A "white shoe" firm is the *crème de la crème,* the richest of the rich. Interestingly, these are not always the biggest law firms. One distinction, however, is that partners at such firms almost always come from money. This is not (just) because of the importance of nepotism, but also because of the importance of knowing how to act around money. Note the on-going connection: just as "thinking like a lawyer" is crucial to Getting Good, *acting* like one is crucial to Getting the Gold. In this, these firms take that to a higher level. Among other traits, they pay *special* attention to the care with which clients are treated, by everyone in the firm. To reiterate, these firms are the implicit model for all firms: there's that parallel to Harvard-Yale and...all other law schools.

Many of these firms are in New York City, for obvious reasons: that's the epicenter of wealth (or at least the flow of wealth) in the New World. One such firm, founded well over a century ago, has majestic offices overlooking the Statue of Liberty, among its other distinguished features. It hires a hundred or so new associates each year. The partners offer no apologies for a strong bias in their hiring: they recruit almost solely from just seven law schools. Although they officially recruit at a dozen, the bulk of their new hires come from just those seven—with perhaps five percent or so coming from "write-ins," or unsolicited applications from outside those dozen schools. And any such "outsider" is almost certainly in the top five—not percent, but people—in class rank.

One partner admitted that a law school is not a perfect way to evaluate candidates: "Sometimes the people with the best grades at the best schools can't make a decision." True enough. But—and here's the crucial *but* that applies across firms—"...but these facts are the only proxies we've got for intelligence and effort as people begin their careers."

Note how profoundly important that statement is: We cannot really know what we're getting (in the hiring process), but we really don't have a choice. We're under the gun, and the "quality" of a law school is just about the only way we have to predict with any accuracy who we're getting. Sound familiar? The word "proxy" is hugely important. A law school degree is no guarantee...but it's the closest that a firm can get. And it *is* correlated. It's also the only thing that a firm can reliably and easily use. Therefore, that's what the firm will use. Period.

This particular partner happened to be a third-generation aristocrat in his family, which speaks as well to the draw of elite schools. Traditionally, elite schools did not draw from the *intellectual* elite. Far from it. Many of the very smartest students went to technical or state schools—or, believe it or not, never went to college at all. The change in elite schools to a quasi-meritocracy occurred only in the past half-century, accelerating to the heights of academic elitism only in the past few decades. Nonetheless, the world of the white-shoe firm is now almost uniformly populated by the academic *and* social elite. If that is your world, good for you. If you would like for that to be your world, you have two rather steep hurdles. Among them, you will need to perform exceptionally well in law school. Even if you're in a top law school you will need to rank in the top 5-10 percent of your class. Better to simply assume that you need to rank among the top ten students; top five students if you're in a law school lower than the Top Ten. *And* you will need to act the part, which here means being not "snobbish," but in fact almost the opposite. Most who are extremely wealthy are just as turned off by such affectations as we all are. No, what they're looking for is, essentially, someone who could fill in for Cary Grant should the need have arisen. Seriously. True wealth is *under*stated. What we *think* of as wealth is a grotesque masquerade (especially among Americans): these are the *nouveau riche,* a term not generally used as a compliment. If this is your desire, you do need to spend money—but it should look natural, rather than painted. Understated elegance, not *Lifestyles of the Rich and Famous.*

Another such firm, this one with some 500 attorneys, had more than 100 from Harvard, nearly a hundred from Columbia, about 60 from NYU—and no more than 30 from any other law school. This is a pattern repeated at each white shoe and national law firm: All are interested in the tippy-top, upper crust only.

Notice what happens: if every firm is interested in the top students at the top schools, this means that those students have nearly every opportunity. Even in a poor job market they almost certainly will have at least one if not multiple job offers. What happens is a steeply cascading effect, in which each rank (whether a 5% block of the class or a literal ranking of every student) gets peremptory right over everyone below. Sorry to keep repeating myself, but it's a winner-take-all spoils process. The top student has first choice, the next student has the next choice, and so on. As the top jobs have stayed fairly constant—about 15% of the market—that means that the top 15% get what they want...and the rest scramble.

Yet there's more, as this applies both among schools as well as within them. Nearly all firms would be fine to have a pedigreed name behind an associate hire. Again, it is defensiveness at work: when the associate from Harvard/Stanford/Yale messes up, it must have been a bad day—or just a bad apple. When the same thing happens to a graduate of Podunk U—the goodwill is worn instantly thin. This results in an extraordinarily steep demand curve for new law graduates: 85% of the rewards to the top 15%; 15% of the rewards to the rest. Fair? Well, let's look at that.

It would be quite conventional to simply write, "Of course it's not fair." But, after all, this *is* the reality. And law firms, while not charged with absolute fairness, are not completely blind either. We have the statement from a partner at one of the world's top law firms, and he admits that grades and school are just a proxy. We know why firms rely on proxies. As indeed all of us do, in ways great and small. But even that doesn't quite capture it. Something must be going on. That something is *quality*.

A law firm sells two things: (1) a knowledge of the law; and (2) an ability to assist clients with that knowledge. Both of these require the ability to think like a lawyer, and the ability to act like one. The sad truth is that the bottom half of any law school class— even if they're the most lawyer-like individuals ever to grace the hallways of that school—have simply not mastered the "thinking" part. At best, they've not *shown* that they know how to think like a lawyer. Those of us in practice, and in legal education, know a great secret: the bottom eighty-five percent *don't know how to think like a lawyer*. Reading exams is torturous, and not just because it's tedious. The exams are often horribly constructed, and just as badly reasoned. They ramble, in a mad rush to get something down. This is the opposite of what legal analysis is and should be.

In a very real way, firms are simply accepting the system as it is, and dealing with it as they must. They would be happy (literally, as they would not have to waste nearly so much money) to hire law students in a way similar to medical residents. But that's not the way the system is, and it's pointless to rail against that here. It's even more pointless for you to rail against it. The answer, if the gold is what you want, is to show—through the two elements of thinking like a lawyer in Getting Good and acting like a lawyer here—that you are worth the risk.

Aren't We Ever Going to Stop with the Top-Top-Top?

I know, it is getting monotonous to read about Harvard-Yale this and top-10% that. The truth is that most of us are in neither category...and need jobs too.

The point of everything above was to give you the reality. If you doubt that this is the reality, ask a practicing attorney. Don't dance around it—they're big boys and girls. Ask them what it is they look for in a new attorney, and who they would hire...and what they would expect once they actually hire that person. Chances are you'll get more in that ten minutes than in a two-hour "here's how to impress an interviewer" workshop.

What we'll now focus on is what is helpful to everyone, including especially those who won't be the objects of vocational affection during on-campus interviews. This focus will be in several parts: first in reducing your costs in attending law school; and second in increasing your earnings. The latter is broken into a several important components: how to increase earnings before and during law school, and then after. Not much here is Earth-shattering, but the difference in financial success between those who take these seriously and those who don't is quite striking.

One last point: I do not pre-judge what it is that "success" means to you. For many during law school, this is the job with the fancy office and huge paychecks. As might not be surprising, if that's an option for you, I think you should take it—even if you don't think that's your life's goal. You can always transition to a position that is more suitable, but it will be hard to duplicate the training you will receive at a top job. A "top" job isn't merely with a big firm, by the way. For litigators, working as an Assistant District Attorney or Public Defender, or as a JAG officer, is *invaluable* practice.

Much of happiness in life is not just in getting what you want, but in being able to choose. With that in mind…

GOLD BEFORE LAW SCHOOL

A great many law students have never worked in a law office, or even had much contact with the law (on either side of it). This included me, and serves as a handicap in a number of important ways.

If you are still in college, you should seek a part-time job in a law firm. I'll use "law firm" here to include a law office. Most of what's applicable here will apply as well if you work in a government agency or non-profit. In either case, chances are the money will be lesser but the intangible rewards will be greater.

It can be almost anything, although the more professional the better. Working in the mailroom (not a figurative word but a real place), while important to the working of a firm is not likely to be as beneficial in interactions or in promotion prospects in that firm especially. (There's a hurdle even for legal secretaries—highly prized among smart attorneys—who go to law school and try to make the leap to junior associate.) Better is paralegal or a back-office function such as accounting or in the law library or, if the firm is large enough, marketing, web development, or the like. Most firms hire summer staff—including summer secretaries—to help with the sudden influx of summer associates and the overflow they create. It doesn't get much more up-close and personal than as a summer secretary.

Such a job will be a benefit not just in spending money, but in several important ways. You will gain an understanding of the basic issues that come up, and in how these are dealt with. You will gain a sense of how professionals act—both in private and with others—and in many of the nitty-gritty details of law office life. If you end up practicing in that city, you will quite likely gain an inside track with that firm when it comes time for summer and part-time employment—a *huge* advantage—and you will benefit from an on-going income that will take at least some of the sting out of LSAT, application, and other expenses.

Is there a Catch-22 with regard to grants? Yes there is. Making (and having) money will likely reduce or eliminate need-based grants. They won't however, make a difference as to merit-based scholarships, and for most the benefits far outweigh the costs. Moreover, as will be explained you should expand your scholarship horizons beyond what is often considered; the money is there.

I won't recommend manipulation—and certainly not fraud—but the criteria for grants are available just about anywhere. Take a look and decide for yourself where your energies are best spent. Chances are, for most, any income before law school will be consumed by general living expenses as well as your LSAT and LSDAS fees, LSAT prep course, and application fees. Also, chances are your salary will be modest, unless you come to a firm with experience in, say, accounting. Thus, chances are the effects on your eligibility for grants will be minimal.

*   *   *

All that comprises our collective imagination about law and law practice is made up. Whether that's Tom Cruise as a slick young buck in *A Few Good Men* or *The Firm;* Matt Damon as a hapless new lawyer in *The Rainmaker* (*much* closer to reality than *The Firm*); Reese Witherspoon in the funny and equally implausible *Legally Blonde;* Jim Carrey as the charming rapscallion in *Liar, Liar;* Richard Gere as the smooth-as-silk-tie Billy Flynn in *Chicago;* Tom Hanks as AIDS-striken Andrew Beckett in nearby *Philadelphia;* Julia Roberts as feisty non-lawyer Erin Brockovich in, ah, *Erin Brockovich;* John Travolta and Robert Duvall as dueling opponents in *A Civil Action;* Joe Pesci as the woefully (and wonderfully) Big-City-fish-out-of-Deep-South-water Vincent Gambini in the endearing *My Cousin Vinny;* Al Pacino and Keanu Reaves as the Devil and his advocate in *The Devil's Advocate;* a (much) younger Al as a fed-up litigator seeking truth *And Justice for All;* the venerable Gregory Peck as Atticus Finch in the poignant adaptation of Harper Lee's novel *To Kill a Mockingbird;* Henry Fonda as drifter Clarence Gideon who fought for and won the right to counsel in *Gideon's Trumpet;* and many, many more...these films *are* our perceptions of what the law is and what lawyers do.

That's all well and good, and entertaining. But it's not law. And it's certainly not the experience that is the bulk of one's day in the practice of law. Most of us know this, intellectually...but we don't know it, emotionally.

I always wanted to be a pilot. It wasn't until after I learned to fly that I realized the fun parts lasted seconds. Much of the rest was tedious or stressful...just like law practice. I still enjoy flying. But without an understanding of what's really involved, embarking on a career is a rather serious commitment to take. Doing so with "stars in our eyes" and without even the most basic steps to make sure that that's what we *really* want...especially when we have to *pay* for the privilege...is asking for heartache.

Consequently, you should seek employment at a law firm before law school with an eye towards what you will learn (and experiences you will be able to use)...and employment during law school for that *and* for income to defray costs.

You should maintain scrupulously good manners and ethics with that firm, and hint that you'd be happy to consider working there during your first summer, should they need the extra help. Chances are good you'll get the "of course!" response, and so you'll either have a paying job lined up—or the happy choice of that or a prestige clerkship if (and when) you ace your first-semester exams. Even if you decide that you'd rather not work at that firm, your contacts (and good manners and ethics) will pay off, as each will make it much easier to find other employment during summers and semesters.

GOLD DURING LAW SCHOOL

A part-time position during law school will provide an income (important), a deeper perspective (more important), and possibly summer and year-round jobs (very, very important). What is key— and the reason this is so important—is that the real difference is in income you earn *during* law school and in the relationships you will have established. It is not possible to overemphasize the importance of the latter especially. This is true even if you don't stay in that city: a reference from a senior partner will carry substantial weight with another firm. Possibly, if your actions are worthy and your reasons are pure, your firm's partner will make a call, all but getting you a job. *That* is the power of "networking."

There's yet another reason this is important: can you honestly answer the questions in Getting In without having worked in a law office? If you're going to spend three years plus a *lot* of money plus at least a few years if not an entire career...how will you know that that's what you want if you've never seen what it is you're deciding on?

MORE ON EMPLOYMENT

Law schools will stress that one cannot work full-time while attending first-year. This is mostly true, for understandable reasons. And it's a requirement of the ABA for all full-time programs.

The assumptions behind this rule are that it's not possible to work full-time and simultaneously study in a full-time law school program. If truth be told (and you're in the right place), while this is generally true, it's true because of the way that most law students study—which is misguidedly.

I have known a fellow law student, a new physician, who stopped attending after the first few classes. We'd thought he dropped, and he them magically reappeared for the exams. We learned that he was simultaneously going through a medical residency. (Perhaps he should have specialized in psychiatry, as what he did *did* seem rather insane.) I have deep respect for what he did, and for the astonishing self-discipline he displayed in, essentially, teaching himself the law without *any* help. Perhaps it was sanctioned by the law school (as he was in a recognized educational program); perhaps not. He did well enough not to have to worry about his standing, and had the benefit that his standing was of less importance to him than it would have been to most of us non-physicians. He embarked on a highly successful career in medical malpractice, retiring early and enjoying a much-deserved rest.

The ABA, understandably, would look askance (at least) at such an attempt nowadays. Indeed, this fellow was the exception who proves the rule. The ABA's prohibition on employment during first-year is reasonable and well-intentioned. It can also be limiting to that small percentage of students who are sufficiently focused to reasonably do both.

For another reason you might respect the ABA's commandment: even if you could undertake both (and keep your sanity), and even if it were the perfect job in a law firm (which itself is unlikely as they know the rules as well as law schools do), it is highly, highly doubtful that you could do well on your law exams. Doing well on law exams is eighty-seven times more important than having a bit of extra work experience, or money.

Such work experience would come in handy primarily if you're qualified for "regular" admission to that firm (*i.e.,* your grades put you in the top $xx\%$), or if you're hungry and they like you enough to toss you a part-time bone. The latter is more likely if it's a smaller firm. In either case, doing well is far, far, *far* more important.

Why all this fuss about a rule that few will worry about? Because, one more time, you really should look for a job in the law. Full-time before law school; part-time thereafter. Nearly all legal employers will be understanding, especially with an outstanding employee such as yourself. They will almost certainly understand that, when you enter your first year you will go on a hiatus, and chances are good that they will consider you for a summer position after your first year. This will be an important coup, it will save you time and *much* pressure, and such a position will have *enormous* benefits. You will learn by observing. Much of this will be law "in the trenches," so you'll have to be careful not to bring up too many of these points in class (as indeed you should not in any case). Second, you'll rely less on loans. You might not appreciate this until after you've graduated, but it's a *huge* benefit. Third, you'll pick up the subtle cues that mark good practice in the law. While only incidentally beneficial in law school, these are crucial in law practice—and in interviews. Fourth, you'll make contacts and even friends in the firm. Be careful how you make friends, and consider each individual within the firm as a *business* "friend," not as a buddy. Finally, this might well become a permanent home, or at least a semi-permanent job, which will be of tremendous importance in a difficult job market especially.

How much is "part-time"? Ten to twenty hours per week during second and third years. Just enough to keep you balanced away from the law school atmosphere and enough that you'll still benefit from the daily exposure to a law office (and from additional reason to focus on proper law study when not in the office), but not so much that you're siphoning too much time from study.

LAW REVIEW

Yes.

Some books go into detail about "whether or not" one should accept a position on law review, and there seems always some mythical student who turned down law review because, well, it was just too diverting of one's time.

First, let's cut the nonsense. I have never known of such a someone…and if I did, I'd be hard-pressed not to put on my lawyer hat and wonder whether that person was really cut out for life as a lawyer. That, in short, is what law review is. Endless, tedious, draining. All true. And all beside the point: law review provides an insight into life in a law firm—which is one reason firms so consistently seek it as a seal of approval—and it thus offers an unmatched boost in seeking employment.

At most schools, there's "law review"...and a handful of other journals. As with everything else in and about law school, there's a winner-take-all aspect here too. Firms will seek out law reviewers; they will yawn at nearly everything else. Keep that in mind.

You should seek membership on law review with the same vigor that you sought your place in law school. In most law schools, law review is no longer simply a "grade on" challenge; many have "write on" competitions or some mixed grade/written competition. In your write-on essay you will likely be given a stack of cases, articles, and so on, and be asked to draft a memo, essay, or some such. You're given a certain time—perhaps a week—to complete this. This should be your consuming job during that week. This is yet another reason to have spent time on outlines, hypotheticals, and exams during your first year in law school, as that saves you a week's work.

In the write-on, you absolutely do not take a partisan position. No, no, no. You must write something that is flawless and reasonably unique...but never, never, never controversial. All you need is one reader (usually there are three) who doesn't like what you write. And, as with exams, do *not* believe humans when they proclaim a fairness for all views.

I'll state now (and restate later) that I believe law review should be mandatory for *all* law students. It is a valid test, and a valuable taste. So, yes, try like the dickens to get on. And don't take no for an answer. If, for example, you miss the grade-on cutoff, and somehow your write-on essay just misses, chances are that your school's law review has a little-known (and lesser used) third option: writing a publishable-quality article. In law review parlance, a "student note." Ask. If so, do it. The article should also be flawless, reasonably unique, and non-controversial. Okay, you can rail against the Financial Accounting Standards Board, if you must.

And, by the way, if you don't want to do it because it's just too much work, think *very* seriously, now—before you're in law school—whether you want to do all *that* work. This is part-and-parcel of life in the law; from an employer's perspective, law review is proof of employability. Why? Because it is. Honestly, an article is not that big a deal to do, and you should be able to re-use parts of it. But it *is* a big deal to have *done*.

No matter what, if you don't get on, find *some* other avenue for your extracurricular (and vocational) ticket-punching. Whether that's another journal, moot court, an externship, a part-time job in a firm, you name it…this is a serious concern for your future employer. And, yes, that is why this section is in Getting the Gold, not in Getting Good.

Once upon a time I happened to see an interaction between a law student and a senior partner. It was at a recruitment event, and the student was seeking to mingle. He walked up to a group including this senior partner, who asked conversationally where he had worked the prior summer. The student tried to smile and said that he hadn't worked at a firm but had taken classes. The partner, with hardly a pause and without saying a word, simply turned away from that student.

As unbelievable as that seems, it does happen. I lost a lot of respect for that partner—as a person—and I watched the poor student slink out shortly thereafter. It should not be this way, but sometimes it is. Thus, if you're inclined to disbelieve how seriously all this should be taken, please reconsider.

SUMMERS

Full-time law school students have three summers: the one between first and second years; the one between second and third years; and the one after law school (and filled with thoughts of bar exam and actually beginning a job). Let's take these in reverse order, as the advice most important for many students will relate to the first two summers.

The Third Summer. This can be the most painful, particularly if a job is not lined up. Added to the vocational worries is the considerable stress of the bar exam itself...plus the considerable expense of the bar review course, continued costs of living, and general concerns over looming debt. Moreover, this is not merely a top/everyone else divide that seems to permeate this book (and law school), but can be very much left to the fates: I have known students with the proverbial golden pass to a top firm who have seen that pass disappear as the firm itself dissolves. Worse, firms facing internal pressures will almost certainly keep those dangers to themselves, and continue to recruit to "keep up appearances." This leads to a terrible shock to those students who had assumed their post-law school dreams were set—and all of a sudden they're back to square one. Worse than that, actually, as it's too late for them and everyone else is already scrambling. Fortunately, this doesn't happen too often, but, for everyone, it's a reminder to *always* keep good relations with *every* potential employer. Take the extra time to be courteous even *and especially* if you decide not to accept a firm's offer. This, yet again, is exactly the same standard you will employ as a professional.

Usually, you will know by the end of the fall semester in third year whether a job is set. If it's not, you'll need to spend a good portion of your energies in the ensuing six months or so to secure employment. Fortunately, the actual job of classwork is relatively less burdensome. In such a case it won't be less important, but it should take relatively less time. Even so, you'll need to raise your load back to the 60-hours-per-week level that you started with (and maintained!) in first-year. You'll need to spend half of that time re-engaging with class to boost your final grades (which might be needed), and the other half in getting a job.

Chances are a focus on larger firms will be a waste of time. This is because nearly all large firms maintain their annual recruiting cycle, and would be reluctant (at best) to disturb that by even interviewing someone outside that pattern. The only exception—sorry to keep harping on this—is the top 10/law review student who haplessly gets left in the cold by another top firm. Even that is tricky, as the best bet would be to have had an on-campus interview with that second firm already.

Thus, you should focus on smaller and mid-size firms. If you're looking to practice in the same city in which you study, clearly that makes interviewing a bit easier. If not, you'll need to orchestrate your own job fair...with you as the contestant. This is done by writing (with follow-up calls) to the effect that you'll be in X City on such-and-so date [at least a month ahead], and would they mind very much chatting with you. Chances are they might, and chances are equally good that it will be a "courtesy interview." This takes us back to the world of genteel law, in which professionals are careful to maintain good relations with any- and everyone, lest bad blood come back to haunt them.

If you are invited to a courtesy interview, you take it. Chances are it won't lead anywhere, but if you impress them it might, and if nothing else you might follow up with a request for part-time work. The key to the courtesy interview is that courtesy works both ways, and even if it leads nowhere it's entirely fine to follow up with a polite request for any references of other firms that might need assistance. That's a good approach, in any case: you're not desperate (even if you are). Rather, you're looking to help someone solve a problem. In this case, you're looking to assist a firm in whatever day-to-day needs they have. Win or lose, the smile on your face is genuine, as even if it's not an answer you want to hear that day, you're *happy* for the opportunity to chat and you'll look forward to the next time you meet—even if it's across the table.

I'm serious. This is part of what being a true professional is all about. Paradox #82.5: the more of a professional sense they get from you—that you really are an earnest, honest, hard-working soul—the more likely is an answer you *do* want to hear. Most firms don't have a "set" number of associates. They have a general sense that they have enough or that they need more—and they're almost always willing to take a second look at someone who shines.

More to the point, chances are there are *many* smaller firms with an on-going need for associates. They lack the resources that larger firms have for annual recruitment, they often don't recruit on-campus at all, and thus fall into new associates a bit more haphazardly. Often, this is by a direct reference from a judge or lawyer (who just as often have a long personal relationship with a senior partner). If you're at the front of the line in front of them, well, that bodes well for your chances.

If you have worked with a judge in an externship, or with a senior practitioner in a clinic (or part-time in a firm), now's a good time to politely ask whether they know of anyone who might have a need. Even if you think that's them, do not ask that. If they make the connection, so much the better. Your question is more polite...might they share a reference or two of folks they know? This is how business is done at all firms...happy calls among happy (even if secretly desperate) attorneys seeking guidance, a pointer or two, you name it.

If you are currently working part-time for a firm, that conversation will be a bit different, as the relationship is different. Most firms will already have raised the question internally in deciding whether to offer you a full-time job or not. Usually, this is based on what they perceive as your qualities on the job (including your social qualities among everyone in the office). Occasionally this is based on the firm's actual needs. It's difficult to overstate the subjective element: most firms operate "from the gut," not from a strategic plan. And even if they do have a plan, they'll happily violate it if they like you. Conversely, all the planning in the world won't help if they don't. So, chances are you'll have a good indication of whether that's a permanent home for you or not.

If you are offered a permanent job, think very, very carefully before turning it down. Unless you have a significantly better option, and unless you absolutely don't want to continue with that firm, it's probably a better bet to take the job, (especially if their offer includes payment for the bar review course, which it should). A lateral transfer is vastly easier for a junior associate than is landing a job in the first place.

If the question hasn't been raised, choose the right partner and the right time, and ask whether the firm has considered its full-time needs for their associates. They'll take the hint, and if nothing else that will start the ball rolling among the partners. Do not raise this if you've given hints that you will not accept (which, *ahem,* you should not have hinted). As with any relationship, the tenor is almost as important as the actual substance—and sometimes more.

As should be obvious, the probabilistic tone of all of the above lends additional credence to the importance of your earlier summers. Not least, the more of a "dead start" you face, the longer the odds. If you've been working through law school, chances are that your immediate concerns will slight. And even if they don't offer a full-time position (which would be unusual), you'll at least have income to defray your bar review and other immediate costs, *and* you'll have professional references for your job search. (Assuming, of course, that you've been a good employee and a collegial presence.)

The Second Summer. The summer between your second and third years is the one many law students use as their "real" job hunt. This, unfortunately, boils down to a two-caste system in which the top students are wined and dined by firms in on-campus interviews (OCIs) as part of a hugely expensive and misleading ritual, while the rest peer wistfully (and with growing resentment) from the outside.

If your performance on exams places you in the former group, then of course you'll have a huge advantage. Your task is to keep your proverbial nose clean, treat interviewers with respect and with an upbeat attitude, and be polite and careful at call-back interviews. As to all interviews, what they're looking for is not brilliance. They *assume* you're smart—and they don't want brilliance. They want competence. What you should focus on is in presenting the type of person who is hard-working yet pleasant to be around. Much of this can be small talk. Some of this is in knowing when to keep your mouth shut, as with anything remotely political, off-key, or otherwise controversial. Don't do it. It's a no-win scene. Be your most pleasant self.

If your exams are not much to write home about, then instead of staring through the gates wistfully, it's time to get to work. The same process that is recounted above should be employed: you must find your own job. In addition you should add the possibility of a judicial or governmental summer job. Many agencies have just such positions—and some don't use what they have budgeted because it's just too much trouble to orchestrate. If so, they want someone so as to preserve the next year's budget. So, you'll need to do their work for them. Find the possible offices, and see what you can see. An orchestrated effort can elicit dozens of possibilities even in smaller cities, and chances are you'll find some with at least a willingness to consider you.

If you cannot find a paid summer position, consider an unpaid clerkship and ask your dean for law school credit. You can almost certainly get it (often in conjunction with a professor's approval, which should also be fairly easy to get), and in this way, although you're not getting paid (and you are paying tuition), you're at least getting law school mileage out of it. And, chances are, a fairly easy "A"...if you take your job seriously and have good relations with the supervising professor. When speaking with the dean or professors, by the way, you must be unfailingly polite—same standard, yes?—and also ready with back-up information as to the position, legal research responsibilities, and so on.

More importantly, you will almost certainly get something more valuable: based on the quality of your work, you will likely get a serious vocational boost from the judge you work for. One colleague landed his job with the firm based on a phone call from a local judge for whom he clerked. The clerkship was full-time and paid, but was not a "prestige" one. The judicial nod was enough. And it wasn't about the firm "getting an inside track" as to that judge, as we rarely appeared there; the fact that this judge thought highly of his clerk—and our future associate—was sufficient. And, sure enough, as he started work with the firm his qualities were in fact what the judge had assured. That's the way the legal world (and the rest of the world, for that matter) works.

In either event, the value of a part-time job in a firm is reinforced. Whether you intend to continue working at that firm, what you're gaining is invaluable: references, a knowledge of law practice and of professionalism, and, last, money. If you're not working yet, part of your task should be to find part-time employment. This should ideally start during your first summer, but should not be delayed through the first part of your fall semester in second year: many of these part-time positions are advertised with your school's career services office, but many more are available (whether advertised or not) in just about every firm there is. If you're interested in non-profit work, excellent! Search what's available, and make your inquiries. If you're lucky you might secure a part-time position funded through an agency or grant. If not, as with the externship see if you can get law school credit for the work you do. Though it might seem a throwaway phrase—and while money *is* important—it's the least important of what you're gaining. In a real sense, it's merely a short-term benefit in light of the long-term value of building your professional knowledge, deportment, and contacts.

There might be more to write about this, but there's not. In either category this is the time during law school when you need to focus on full-time employment for your second summer, and part-time employment for your second year.

The First Summer. The summer between your first and second years is often one in which paid employment is difficult or improbable. The exceptions are usually at top law schools, for top students, and for students who have worked at a firm previously or who arrange their own employment. As a result, many students decide to take summer classes, or perhaps a clinic or externship, or (more fun!) take the summer off.

It should not be surprising that, while enjoyable, the last option—basking in the summer breezes—is not the better path in terms of your long-term financial goals. Many firms will look askance at this, as indeed they'll not look favorably, in general, on summer classes. Why? Because the assumption is that the best students will be employed...even in first year. While some firms will look deeper to where the person was employed, the truth is that employment in any law office is a category higher than any other option.

One challenge for the first summer is that...you're busy! You're working on all that you need to work on to do well on exams, and the last thing you need is for someone like me to chatter on about devoting more time to interviews. Tell you what. These usually are the secondary interviews in the spring, and again are usually for those who did well in first-semester exams. (Which, of course, is a somewhat misleading indicator.) If you are in the running, of course you should take advantage of OCIs.

If not, here's a task to add to your list of things to do *prior* to law school. Before you get to the law school's doors, create a database of firms in the area in which you want to practice. (Thus, it's a good idea to already know the location as part of Getting In.) You will generally have a list that can be filtered in a number of ways. The biggest firms will usually not hire part-time employees for legal work, but instead might hire for ancillary positions (such as in office administration or accounting). Consequently, these are actually not the best places to look. Instead, look to smaller and mid-sized firms.

Why waste your time if you're then invited to OCIs? Because it won't be a waste of time. If you're assembling a list of smallish firms and are able to land a first-year clerkship at a huge firm... what's the problem? At worst, you send a polite note to the small firm you've contacted in the spring, perhaps with a recommendation that you refer your most able friends there. You must be impolite never (never!)—but firms know the score, and few will begrudge you your better opportunity. How you handle this will be almost if not more important than what you actually do.

How much time? Perhaps a half-dozen hours to find the firms, and a bit more to play with them in the database. How to find them? The NALP, or Association for Legal Career Professionals (don't ask) has a number of useful links, including information on recruitment (at www.nalp.org) and a hugely valuable directory of law firm recruiters (at www.nalpdirectory.com). The directory tends towards larger firms, but they do have quite a number of smaller ones as well. For database compilation you'll need a login, which is available only to students of a member law school. Thus, unless you can get access via a local law school's placement office, you get to manually input data. Chances are you can get access if you explain your request at your nearest law school. As always, be super-courteous. Another benefit is that these offices will have at least general information of interest, and most career counselors will be glad to show you the ropes. For most, merely seeing what's available and taking an hour or so to familiarize yourself with the resources is time very well spent. You should, as well, begin building your own database, whether with the access above or during your winter break. Don't spend too much time—it really is quite fast—and do get familiar with what's there.

Another resource to check is Martindale-Hubbell, the directory of lawyers and firms (at www.martindale.com). This is the authoritative reference as to firms especially, and as above you'll find a wealth of information just seconds away. There are a number of useful filters, such as searching for firms by location, size, and specialty. Unless you have a clear preference *and* expertise (say, a degree in engineering or medicine), chances are you should focus on a broad search of firms in the cities you're interested in of medium and smaller sizes. These are, in essence, your "ace in the hole," or, perhaps, your ace in law school.

Again, this research should be done before law school or during your winter break...and before the smallish spring recruiting season during your first year. If done earlier, such as in college, this is two aces: you will build a relationship with a firm and its attorneys and staff, and you will build an awareness that will almost certainly improve your application.

AFTER LAW SCHOOL

This is the section that nearly everyone focuses on—landing the perfect job—but as should be apparent, this is almost pointless without going over (again!) everything before.

There are a few wrinkles that we might still discuss.

First are the "Other" law jobs—the ones that few put at the top of their list. Often this is for a fair reason, as these jobs tend not to pay as much as the OCI jobs do. But just as often, these jobs have advantages that are not as well considered, and for at least some students are a better fit.

HIDDEN IN PLAIN SITE

Let's start with smaller firm jobs. In any city and town there will be numerous smaller firms. Many have just a handful of lawyers, some with just one or two (or no) associates. Many of these are "quaint" practices; some struggle; many do well, but often not spectacularly so. These can be wonderful places in which to work, but clearly, there's not a lot to connect you with them. And, if you do connect, chances are you will be paid modestly. On the upside, if there is a good fit, you might well inherit the practice, adding to what would then be a healthy partner's draw. Often, these are quite literally family firms.

Why are they "wonderful" places in which to work? Because they are. The stress level is usually a fraction of that in a larger firm, and the assumptions are typically far more family-friendly.

As you move up the scale, you'll find many mid-sized firms, often populated with a dozen or so attorneys, and, as with smaller firms, often tilted towards full partners—as there isn't the "sweatshop" track as exists in large firms. Because these firms don't focus on summer recruitment, if you have a legitimate reason for wanting to work there (you need something more than "I need a job!"), and if they happen to need help (they often do), chances are you can almost literally write your own ticket.

Why a focus on firms, firms, firm—even smaller ones? Well, for starters that's where the law is practiced. And, from a practical standpoint, that's where the money is. Not just in terms of salary, but also in terms of part-time work, connections, referrals, and such not-so-minor details as bar review course fees (which most firms will pay without a second thought on your behalf).

There is a world of clerkship that is also hidden in plain sight. These are the clerkships for "lesser" judges, some of which are unpaid and nearly all of which are modestly paid. The upside to these is that the connections of that judge are almost certainly sufficient to help you in your career—and job search. Clearly, the boost is strongest in the jurisdiction in which the judge sits. Most judges are mindful of their power—informal as well as formal— but even so, not many firms would resist hiring a clerk from a judge they could conceivably come before. This assumes, of course, that you do a solid job (at least) for your judge-boss.

Not least, with any court you will learn many, many aspects of law practice. You will, in addition, learn what makes for *bad* practice...and bad legal research and writing. You will be astounded at how much bad practice there is—and how much of a difference a good practitioner makes—and you will learn the differences between the two. This is yet another reason firms are so willing to take a chance on a judicial clerk. It might seem like stepping off a cliff, but clerking for a judge—any judge—is a vocational coup. To reinforce a point I've already overdone, you *must* think seriously about where you want to practice. With that, and with the right judge, your career is all but set.

ALL THAT YOU CAN BE

A category of gold deserving of its own special mention is the military. We don't often think of military service as a golden opportunity, but for professionals in medicine and law Uncle Sam offers unique benefits. In law, the JAG or Judge Advocate General corps is the military's law firm. In fact, given the military's needs, it's dozens of firms, each with dozens of branches and many, many tasks. These range from contract evaluation to dealing with rowdy sailors and soldiers (airmen tend to be a bit more sedate) to handling the many personal tasks for the million-plus men and women in uniform to working near and sometimes in combat zones. Given the size of the military, however, nearly all JAG officers deal with the more mundane aspects of life—but in an environment more reminiscent of a large DA's office than a walnut-paneled law firm.

For those willing to commit (there's not much room for commitment-phobics here), one *big* benefit is that a military gig is, well, a *job*. Once the papers are signed, physicals passed, and arm raised, Uncle Sam offers you a commission as an officer (and, often, a fair amount of scholarship money), and you offer a few years of your life. On the upside, this means that you will spend just about zero time worrying about finding a job; yours is waiting. This is a benefit that is hard to overstate. So much so that you'll have to be careful as many of your friends will be envious and even resentful of your "easy" path.

On the downside, of course, the commitment on your end is not insignificant. Aside from push-ups, there's the matter of the actual differences between civilian and military worlds. Law students rarely study the UCMJ, or Uniform Code of Military Justice, but if you do serve, this code in turn serves as a legal overlay, obscuring more than a few elements of law—constitutional and otherwise—that apply in the civilian world. Honestly, this is rarely a problem, absent an inclination to go AWOL or protest your favorite hundred causes. For most, the comforts of a military life become quite, well, comfortable. Beware, however, that it's often a "love it or hate it" reaction.

A little-known relief valve is that officers who drop from a program will—generally—be dismissed administratively. This means a "separation" that severs the relationship. Thus, if you find that you really, truly don't like it, chances are you do have the option to drop and never set foot on a military installation again in your life. This is, however, at the discretion of the service. Confirm the current policy if it's a concern for you—and ask to see it in writing. Whom to ask? Be *very* careful with military recruiters. It's fine to give them the "body"—their own yield—but don't rely on them for professional advice. They often deal with enlisted recruits, and will probably have little knowledge of special programs such as for JAG officers. Work through a national office, and don't be coy. Ask for the name of a JAG commander, and track down the office responsible in that branch for JAG officers and recruitment. Chances are, by the way, that a local JAG officer would be happy to show you their office and routine. Go. Whether you raise your right hand or not, it will be a valuable look-see at the world you're about to enter. And, yes, they can get you on base (post, whichever); just be darned sure you have all your personal and automotive documentation.

That aside, the military life offers unique professional advantages. You'll deal with issues that most of your colleagues will have just about zero chance of encountering. You'll have responsibility and authority earlier—sometimes far earlier. You'll have more authority—sometimes far more—than even partners would be comfortable with. You'll likely travel, perhaps a lot. You'll quite possibly be involved in issues that will be staggeringly important, such as dealing with war crimes or rules of engagement or refugee crises or the like. For the right person, military service is about the best there is.

You should not think that a military obligation—typically a half-dozen years or so for an officer who receives a scholarship—precludes work in a firm. In fact, the experiences you receive will quite likely open doors that might otherwise be firmly shut. If, for example, you find yourself with a "B" average, jet off to the JAG corps, and serve your several years, chances are high that you can secure a job with a top firm dealing with, say, defense contracts or aerospace clients. In this, your military service "trades up" based on your work, which if you select and are granted the right specialty ties directly into work that is done at a partner-level in a firm. Yet another benefit is that your professional bearing will be light years ahead of most civilian associates: there's not much that duplicates the professional training offered in the military. You likely won't get "extra" credit for "time served," but you almost certainly would join "in rank," or in the year that you would have been in as an associate.

Even if you don't find or choose work in a firm, you will be at an advantage in most government positions—which tend to be favored because they mirror the good-but-not-great-pay/interesting-to-fantastic-work/great-lifestyle-including-evenings-and-weekends-free that JAG officers grow accustomed to. Not least, veterans receive a sizeable preference in hiring for most government jobs, and a fair number of administrative judges served as JAG officers. Nothing to sneeze at, that.

What if you find out, after you commit, that your grades enable you to work for a high-powered (and super-high paying) firm? If so, you'll have the best of both worlds. Chances are strong that such a firm—in fact, all firms—would still look at you favorably after a minimum hitch with the military. The experience you'll receive, as well as the professional bearing you'll learn, will almost certainly be appreciated, so that as above you'll be able to enter a firm with salary and perks commensurate with the firm's track. Chances are, in such a case you'll find a great many doors open to you besides the big firms, and odds are good that you'll find many of those quite attractive as well. Not least, quite a number of JAG officers find the qualitative elements of their jobs intoxicating, and thus either stay in or find themselves in defense-related positions outside of law-firm practice. Most importantly, *you'll* be doing the choosing.

The second part of "most importantly" is a practical one: in most cases, you should be able to qualify for a scholarship that will significantly help with law school expenses. There are even programs for a lucky few in which the military pays your full tuition *and* a salary. These are highly competitive, of course, and are usually only available to a small number of active-duty military. I have heard of some Reserve and National Guard members qualifying—

depending up on the "needs of the service" at the time—so do ask. If granted this is an amazing opportunity: zero tuition and full pay...plus a job.

The pay is good but not great. The benefits are good, and the overall experience is likely to be *much* better than for the typical junior associate. The issue of pay might be a serious psychological barrier, but for most an officer's pay compares roughly to a non-prestige junior associate (and, adjusted for hours, to top associates)—and with Uncle Sam you're working for the biggest firm of them all.

And as the saying goes, it's not just a job...

GOOD ENOUGH FOR GOVERNMENT WORK

If you're not interested in military service you might still find another variety quite high on your list: this is the realm of government law.

Just about every aspect of government is filled with lawyers. The whole purpose of much of government life is, after all, the creation, regulation, enforcement, and interpretation of law.

The truth? Many in law school (and practice) hold their noses in distain or even contempt of government lawyers. Usually, this is a misplaced emphasis on money, and often, yes, grades. I once heard a partner nearly sneer, "He's a *government* lawyer." Knowing that particular partner, I'd be willing to bet that that mere government lawyer was far, far happier.

The nitty-gritty? The reality is that much government work is far more interesting than most private work. Moreover, there's usually a far wider array of potential government work than there is in a firm. This depends on which agency and where you happen to be, of course. Most government offices are quite similar to private firms in their approach to office matters: papers in, procedures followed, papers out.

There is a crucial difference, and it's one not measured in money. This is the life of a government lawyer. All jokes aside, chances are good that a government attorney works 40 hours a week...or close to it. There are hardly any lawyers in *any* private practice—large, medium, or small—who work only 40 hours per week. The government lawyer has evenings and weekends free, and usually a full four weeks' vacation...plus all those official holidays. It's a darned nice lifestyle, when you think about it.

What are you giving up? Well, money for one thing. If you're in the running for a big-firm job, chances are a government position will offer one-half or less what you would make. The choice, then, is the value you place on your time. If, for example, you have children and really don't intend to spend 60-80 hours a week at the office, you've some serious thinking ahead of you. One alternative is to work for the big firm for a few years, with the thought to transition to a more-relaxed position. Chances are you'll be able to do this, and a government job will be one possibility. Odds are that this approach will land you at least as good a job at a comparable pay grade than if you worked your way up. In the end, the real test is that you ask and answer the question for yourself, rather than floating on the currents that take you somewhere you won't want to be.

On the other side of the money equation, here's something to consider: one reason we even have this discussion is that we have developed such a bizarre set of values. It's only when a new lawyer can make $100,000 or $150,000 or $200,000 that we start asking, gee, that buys a lot of goodies, yes? This begins to warp our sense of what a job is. It certainly starts to warp our sense of what is "normal"—and what is needed.

A relative minority earn as much as an attorney in government practice, who might earn perhaps one-half of the amounts above. Is that "enough"? Well, it depends upon perspective. If you want the high life, fast cars, faster women, and so on...then no, it won't be. Actually, even the $200,000 won't be, believe it or not.

If, however, you're content with a decent home in a decent neighborhood with a lot more time to putter around the house, that $60,000 or so will be just fine. There's a whole block of neighbors earning less than that, and they're puttering just the same.

A friend from law school surprised me with his lack of concern about things law school-ish. I found out that he intended to parlay his prior experience in the state legislature and a new law degree for a job on the staff of...some office in the state legislature. His goal was comfortable, and achievable. It also made more sense the more I thought about it. It's easy to think that life in a some non-descript government office will be somehow less likely to fulfill one's inner potential, but in reality there's a lot less separating that from a fancy law firm than we might think. One the one hand you have metal desks, good-but-not-great pay, often big-picture work, and a lifestyle that is simply unattainable otherwise—and on the other hand, a fancy office, great-to-stellar pay, challenging but sometimes thankless work, and a lifestyle that is usually highly stressful and constraining. Any job can be intoxicating...if you want it to be. As always, the choice is yours.

*   *   *

All of the above is just part of the law school cost-benefit equation. One way to improve the financial picture, aside from increasing revenues, is to decrease your costs.

GRANTS AND SCHOLARSHIPS

This might seem like yet another throwaway subject, but it's amazing how few students explore even a substantial fraction of the money that is available.

Mostly, this is understandable. Before law school, you generally don't have the access to pre-packaged grant and scholarship information, such as is maintained in law school offices. Consequently, most students rely on whatever the law school tells them is available—and whatever they're lucky enough to qualify for. In most cases, grants and scholarships (which need not be repaid) are a fraction of tuition.

There's an open secret: there's a *lot* of money out there. But you have to find it. And, no, this is not something you should look for via some quasi-scam book or "service." The money is out there, and *you* need to find it.

How? Generally, this money is available to worthy candidates from an array of organizations. Often, it's fairly modest for each grant—$500 here and $1,000 there. But, when bills must be paid—especially for impoverished students—that's hardly worth sneezing at.

You first challenge is to check with every organization you conceivably belong to. If a parent works at a company, chances are it has some scholarships. Often these don't come with too many strings, such as an intent to practice in a certain field, an essay requirement, or the like. If you or any of your family (or even distant relatives) are members of *any* organization, take a look. Union, fraternity, sorority, glee club, you name it. Chances are there's some scholarship money in there somewhere. If you are interested in any field—any field!—check out the organizations in that field. Chances are there's some scholarship money in there somewhere. Sure, you might have to write an essay...which, come to think of it, is great practice.

In short, if you want "free" money, you must spend at least a few dozen hours scouring for it.

There's more. Even if the scholarship comes with limitations or strings—as is often the case—that's not the end of the story. Chances are, even if the "fit" between you and the scholarship isn't perfect, the person or committee deciding who gets the money has a great deal of leeway. I know of one case in which a grant (for $2,500) was expressly limited to a nursing program. A student—who was a nurse in an MBA program—asked whether she could apply anyway. The answer? Yes. And she got the scholarship. She was the only one who applied, believe it or not. A $2,500 question, asked and answered.

In another case, I was asked to be on a committee to distribute scholarships for a women's organization. We interviewed dozens of young women who faced all manner of hardship. The process was both heartbreaking and uplifting, as we heard story after story of how these young women had overcome enormous burdens. One, for example, had been sold into quasi-slavery as a "mail order bride," had had a son, had escaped, and was attempting to complete an associate's program. Might some have exaggerated? Sure. But the storytelling began to tell its own story: it was fascinating to see how each of these candidates approached fairly deep questions of their lives, all in how they approached education. In short, we were "okay" to be fooled, as long as the ulterior motive was education.

What happened? The members of the committee and I—not much liking the task of deciding upon just a few "winners"—reset the competition. We kicked in more money, thus funding scholarships for nearly half of the women.

Such opportunities *are* there. You must find them, and you must make the effort.

Public Interest?

If firms and governments provide much of legal employment, there is a vast need in public-interest organizations. These are often poorly paid...and highly rewarding. So, I'll state up front that if this is you, you have my genuine respect: what you will do in such an organization will be hugely important to your clients. I have known a number of public-interest attorneys, and without exception they are truly decent...and far happier.

We still face, however, a rather difficult hurdle: while many students going in to law school profess a desire to work in the public interest, almost no one still has this imperative toward graduation. One book states that fewer than five percent of law students want to take a public-interest job. While true on its face (at the end of law school, anyway), this misses a deeper and more intractable issue: the real problem is money. But it's not just what everyone focuses one; it's about choices one makes before and in law school. That's what we should discuss. So let's.

The first question is how much debt you end up with. This might seem like yet another throwaway phrase, but a $125,000 student loan (on top of undergraduate loans) will, even if consolidated, total a *lot* of money out the door each month, beginning sooner after graduation than seems possible. Enough that a public-interest job will be insufficient to cover rent, a car payment, and the loan repayments—much less food and the occasional movie. Consequently, if you are considering—seriously—public interest work, you must factor in your "carrying capacity" for debt. In yet one more paradox, it is the very top private law schools that are implementing debt-forgiveness programs, although these are likely to extend to others and from government sources. Again, if you're serious, these are serious avenues to explore, and the earlier the better. Part of how you can know is to take a job, or volunteer, in a non-profit before and during law school.

The second question relates to your expected lifestyle. If you have (or develop) a taste for $20 martinis, and unless your trust funds have ample reserve, you almost certainly cannot maintain such a lifestyle on public-interest employ. (Note: while I *am* critical of $20 martinis—at least in the context of a world with $20 monthly incomes—the deeper question is whether that is your preference, and whether you're willing to take one path or another for that preference. As always, the choice is yours.) More to the point, ask whether you would be content with a modest lifestyle, in a modest home…likely something along the lines of what you grew up in. If so, an amazing world of possibilities opens up. Seriously. If you're hoping and attempting to close on a half-million dollar apartment, you'll find yourself stretched even on a firm's salary. If, however, you're content in a smallish, oldish (and surprisingly comfortable) home, your income needs fall substantially, which in turn open any number of opportunities.

Public-interest work can be immensely satisfying, and can make your save-the-world aspirations and self-image before law school come true. The psychic rewards are there. The challenge is to balance those against the vocational chips you'll trade in exchange. For most, it's worth it. For you, that's the question.

WHAT IF IT'S NOT FOR YOU?

Get out.

If you realize that you truly, honestly don't want to be a lawyer, get out. This will be hard, not least in the emotional hurdle of disappointing others…and yourself. But, more importantly, do not let others "force" you into something you will hate—even (and perhaps especially) if that force is implied. Do not let *yourself* force you into something you will hate. As painful as the break is, if it's truly a break you need to make, then make it.

Much as it's easy to see this as a "failure," in truth it can be a hugely beneficial decision. Again, this assumes that this is not something done on a lark, or a result of embarrassment in class (no one but you will ever remember!), but rather is a distillation of a semester-long, nagging feeling that you're in the wrong place. If so, then take yourself out. Live to fight another day.

All of the student loans and time and energy spent won't be wasted. It will instead be a valuable lesson...if you do something else worthwhile. Dropping out should not be a rejection of law school, but rather a decision *toward* something else. Something better. For you.

AND FOR EVERYONE ELSE...

The advice in this book will, by virtue of your merely raising the issue and paying attention to it, almost certainly help you as you move from pre-law to law student and on to law graduate and new lawyer and eventually to senior partner, general counsel, or just General.

If any point is unclear, unanswered, or unwise, please let me know. My email address is thane@fineprintpress.com, and I welcome all comments—the good, the bad, and the vitriolic. I would especially welcome comments as you're in and after you've graduated from law school—in between bar exams and late-night research—as to what worked well and what might work better.

In all of this, and whichever path you decide to take, I wish you the very best.

Aloha.

OBITER DICTA

I know only too well my predilection for detours, frolics, and other diversions, often at the expense of a more direct, more easily digested prose. This, in my perhaps deluded mind, is part of what makes the law fun.

If you've found these detours, frolics, and other diversions half as annoying as I sometimes do, I hope you have skipped them without hesitation and in good health. For those interested (or morbidly curious)—and for those who will someday sit on the ABA's Board of Governors—I invite you to read on:

*   *   *

Our system of legal education, while it has many strengths, is deeply flawed in ways that harm the very fabric of our legal system—and, consequently, in ways that put our society at risk.

Notably, this is not a good-versus-bad, rich-versus-poor harangue. Indeed, it is possible to argue that the haves should *insist* upon rules aimed to limit their excesses—and not because the poor deserve it, as often they do not. Rather, the rich have much to gain by a poor who do not suffer. Thus, in essence, the concept of *noblesse oblige* has as much to do with long-term self-interest as with noble altruism.

Our legal system is stratified to an extent that results in greater, not lesser, social inequality. But this is not merely because the poor, huddled masses are left in the cold. Rather it is because *most* Americans are in the deep-freeze when it comes to matters legal. In essence, only the very wealthiest of clients—most corporate, a few individuals—can afford legal representation at what should be considered an acceptable level of legal competence. An entire class of solo practitioners, scrambling for work and too busy to focus on filling in the details that were left out in the three years of law school and in the bar exam…make mistakes costing their clients dearly. Even highly paid attorneys neglect their clients' genuine concerns more often than they should. This is a critique shared among many in legal education, resulting in, among other soul-searching, the MacCrate Report in 1992.

Arguably, the concerns in that report are too lightly stated, and too lightly taken. Much of the resulting inequality affects far more than a "mere" disenfranchised fraction. Rather, the practical limitations of the law as it exists in the United States excludes the *majority* from reasonable representation. Most Americans either never use counsel when they should, or are ill-served by the counsel they do have.

Rather than encompassing some small percentage—say, the bottom 15%, a socioeconomic class of genuine concern to few— the percentage of those ill-served by our profession is the obverse: the *vast majority*—perhaps the top 85%—receive no effective benefit from our educational and legal systems when they need it. And the indirect benefits that do exist are borrowed from past legal innovations (such as mortgages and employee ownership), since at risk of being overtaken with usurious derivations ungoverned by basic legal doctrine or systemic controls (such as predatory lending abuses and executive theft). That these abuses might be answered by first-year legal principles—such as long-neglected Agency Law—only heightens the betrayal our system visits upon our and future generations. That only a relatively thin upper-crust benefits from all that our legal system is set up to provide ultimately costs the wealthy (almost) as much as it costs the poor. And the great middle, which until now survived most encounters in a calmer legal sea, is set adrift. This should not be.

It is so, at least in part, because law students graduate and have not the faintest idea how to actually practice law. Not tertiary questions of the best provision to use in such-and-so a document, but a complete lack of awareness of what document must be used, what other documents might work, and what each should look like. Were this written of medical education, there would be congressional hearings on the matter. And so, practitioners are left to teach what law school did not. The bigger the firm, the better the teaching—which further exacerbates an already great divide. This is an economic as well as moral deadweight, resulting in personal as well as societal costs, disproportionately borne by the lower *and* middle classes.

Our fixation on academic status, which seems to have reached unparalleled heights, is misguided—both morally and societally. While competition has its place and its value, we now use it as a proxy for rewards far out of proportion or any reasonable limits. In this brave new world, clients are no longer subjects of genuine concern, but rather are objects of greed and contempt. This can't help but infect the very nature of the legal world—our legal world—and, by excess, legal education.

Moreover, our system of competition...isn't. We neglect such large parts of our secondary school populations there is no reasonable chance for them to compete. And so, they fail; they were never real contenders. In this, much of legal education is a rigged game, fixed long before the admissions process begins by mutual, self-satisfied consent among a variety of players...all of whom agree with great voiced concern and none of whose children are ever seriously at risk. Worse, the occasional disadvantaged student actually makes it in...giving lie through rarity to what no one wants to admit. And we wish not to admit this because fixing it would be hard work. Harder than rearranging our deck chairs. In this, we are all, eventually, at risk.

So, in our role, what *should* legal education look like?

*　　*　　*

LAW SCHOOLS: THE FACULTY

The idea of a professional school that excludes genuine professional knowledge is dangerous as well as illegitimate.

Legal Apartheid. The ABA should reject the model of legal education that places the teaching of the law as distinct from and superior to the practice of the law. There is no such thing as a "theory" of law that does not have practical implications. And, if it did, it should be disqualified for discussion in law school as *ultra vires*. And, yes, I say this as someone who *loves* theory.

This is not to argue the converse, that practitioners should take over the teaching of law. Again, this goes to a dangerously false dichotomy: that one either learns "big picture" law (theory and lofty Shibboleths) or pedestrian, real-world law (what is taught, presumably, by lesser teachers who have dirtied their hands in practice). This pseudo-intellectual snobbery is treacherous and limiting.

Practice Makes Perfect. New law faculty should have, as a requirement not capable of easy waiver, a minimum of ten years' work experience in law practice or in a legal capacity—roughly the equivalent of earning partnership in a firm. In reality, even this captures just the beginning of a practitioner's exposure to and knowledge of real-world implications of the law.

The current practice of hiring assistant professors with just a few years (or no) practical experience is shockingly inappropriate in a professional school. Among practitioners, experience under a partner level (or even at a senior associate level with a half-dozen years' experience) is insufficient to impart a true understanding of law practice or its many demands and qualities.

Law schools should rebalance their academic with practitioner faculty. The benefits of legal research are significant, but they're hardly sufficient to occupy the time of *all* the nation's law faculty—and do a disservice to the aspirations and potential contributions of talented senior and retired practitioners and judges (many of whom, if truth be told, are every bit as credentialed and smart—and vastly more knowledgeable—than their brethern at the podium).

The current tenured/adjunct divide should also be rebalanced so as not to continue an academic caste system that has an impact very much harmful to students. Among other needs are more senior practitioners, including especially judges, senior partners, and general counsel, to complement in an integrated way the curricular offerings. These should not be merely as adjuncts, but rather full members of the faculty (even if teaching part-time). If not academically suitable, why are they there?

Back to the Future. Pre-law requirements should be reinstated for admission to law school, equal to a 30-credit "super-minor" in undergraduate studies. This should not be a degree in itself, and while requiring significant coursework could fit in the lower-division requirements for most undergraduate programs.

Required courses should include: business law (3 credits); Latin (3 credits); legal history and jurisprudence (3 credits); logic

(3 credits); textual interpretation (3 credits); and some combination of advanced mathematics (calculus and above), statistics, and computer or other hard science (15 credits).

Business law provides a useful backdrop for much of real-world law, condensed in a straightforward format. Latin is as useful for linguistic and logical fluency as much as for insights into the common law. Legal history and jurisprudence might provide some of the big-picture missing for most law students. Logic especially should be approached not from the perspective of philosophy as it is currently taught, but rather from the perspective of the *use* of logic; in essence, identifying the ways in which logical arguments are defective and in which logic is *mis*used. Textual interpretation might focus on Talmudic, ecclesiastical, and other religious as well as jurisprudential modes of evaluating and synthesizing texts; the former components would not be "religious," but would focus instead on method and effect. The mathematics and science requirement would probably constitute the single most important boost to students' ability to think critically. And, despite the unfortunately well-deserved reputation that law school has as a sanctuary for those who "don't like math," this is precisely the population most in need of this foundational analytical toolbox. Survey courses would not count.

This should first be a "plus" in admissions, and, when appropriate, a requirement.

Perfect Before Practice

Curricula. The legal curricula should be redesigned so that the core of legal education is the use of the hypothetical as the pedagogical model. The focus on black letter law should rightly be pushed onto the law student, but in an open and honest way: starting with vocabulary, structure, and themes, the student would build (and be capable of reproducing) an outline as the fundamental requirement for each subject. This would be structured at a pace in keeping with classroom discussion.

The Socratic Method. Socratic Dialogue should be employed, but not one-on-one. Instead, teams of students would prepare a single case (or, as appropriate, a set of related cases) for discussion, and would be expected to engage with the law professor in an extended and integrated dialogue as to the rule(s) at hand. A student failing to contribute would be given one additional chance, and upon a second failure would receive a grade for the course one letter grade lower.

Integration. The legal curricula should be integrated such that major topics are taught together, with interrelated lessons and assignments. These should follow the combinations described in Getting Good—such other combinations as faculty deem appropriate.

Agency Law and Remedies should be re-incorporated in, within, or among the first year courses.

Open Minds. Classroom rules should be radically changed: (1) no electronic devices of any kind; (2) no writing instruments.

Collegiality. Learning teams should be incorporated as a mandatory, structured part of law school. Team formation should occur at the end of the first two weeks of law school, preceded by rounds of leaderless activities focused on legal terminology and concepts. Students would choose their own teams, by weighted voting. Each would get 500 votes to choose up to five partners. Teams would then be assigned, and would be responsible immediately for case preparation for classroom discussion.

A Review of the Law. Law review should be mandatory. Law reviews would be published online.

Students seeking the prestige that is associated with law review as it currently exists would, in addition to their duties, be required to produce and have accepted a student note for publication in a journal at another law school.

Grading. Grades should be based on three factors: (1) web-based MBE-styled tests of black letter law; (2) the reproduction of an outline; and (3) the final exam.

Thirty percent of the course grade would be determined by web-based quizzes, which would be conducted in five-minute sessions at the beginning of each class. Class periods would last at least 90 minutes. Students who were late would receive no credit for that day's quiz. A biometric identifier would be used to verify the test-taker.

The content of the quizzes—ten multiple-choice questions—would correspond to the subject of that day's class, as modeled by the professor via an electronic randomizer tailored to a descriptive assessment of black letter law, curved nationally.

Twenty percent of the course grade would be determined by the outline exam, which would be taken via a timed, web-access test available up to two weeks prior to the final exam. Students could re-take the outline exam as often as they wished, and the highest score would be recorded. A biometric identifier would be used to verify the test-taker. The outline exam would not be curved, but would be based on computer-generated analysis of the number, sequencing, and co-location of each component (but not requiring a single "true" outline). For example, an outline for Tort Law would start with "Intentional, Negligent, Strict," and then within Negligence to "Duty, Breach, Cause, Harm," and then filling in the aspects of each of those subsections. Pasting into the test program would be disabled; students would be required, closed book, to complete the outline from memory.

Fifty percent of the grade would be the final exam, which would be a combination of three components: (1) a section crafted nationally and modeled upon (or by) the National Conference of Bar Examiners (responsible for the multistate bar exam); (2) a short-answer section; and (3) one essay. The first component would be 60 minutes; no exam could exceed 3.5 hours. Professors could collapse parts two and three into a single essay. All exams would be open-book. Exams would be curved nationally as to the first component, which would count for 40% of the exam, and not curved as to the second and third components. The distributions of the latter components could not exceed 15% "A" grades or 30% "B" grades.

Legal Research and Writing. These should be the focus of second year, supervised in and integral to clinics and externships involving real clients and cases. These should be year-long programs, incorporating all aspects of law practice: client counseling, drafting, negotiation, litigation, fees, law-office management, and the like. Such a program should be supervised by senior practitioners, who would hold the rank (even if part-time) of full professor.

The Bar Exam. Legal education should be restructured such that the bar review and bar exam are incorporated into and as the final semester of study. In essence, the multistate bar exam and the core legal doctrines are taught and tested as part of law school. The final semester would be a mandatory 15-credit sequence, culminating with the MBE and 18 (of 22 possible) one-hour essays given over a four-day period during final exams.

Nine essays would be from the core legal doctrines: Agency Law; Civil Procedure; Constitutional Law; Contracts; Criminal Law and Procedure; Evidence; Professional Responsibility; Remedies and Restitution; and Torts.

The remaining nine essays would be chosen randomly from the following areas: Administrative Law; Bankruptcy; Business Associations and Securities Regulation; Commercial Paper; Conflict of Laws; Consumer Protection; Employment Law; Family Law; International Law (Public and Private); Property Law: Personal and Intellectual Property; Property Law: Real Property; UCC Article 2 (Sale of Goods); UCC Article 9 (Secured Transactions); and Wills, Estates, and Trusts.

States could require their own jurisdiction-specific topics— which could be offered and administered in any other state upon proper application—but would be encouraged to accept and administer the in-school exams.

All bar exams would be administered in law schools, whether or not taken by current graduates.

Law schools could (and should) incorporate proprietary bar review courses as this sequence, which would be pass/fail, based on passing the bar exam itself. The nine core legal doctrines could be graded A-F, with the grade based on performance in that respective section of the bar exam.

Three Plus Two Plus One. The professional requirements for admission to the bar should be tailored to more closely resemble that of the medical profession.

A legal internship should be required, consisting of one year at a judicial, legislative, or government office. Judges at all levels and jurisdictions as well as legislators and other government officers would benefit from research assistants who would, optimally, be paid a nominal salary.

A legal residency should also be required, consisting of one year (for general practice) or two years (for specialized practice) at a law firm or other law office. Graduates would be paid a modest salary. Assignment to law offices would be made in a manner similar to that of medical residents.

Debt repayment would be deferred during the internships and residencies. Law schools would receive no tuition, and could charge only a modest fee for transcript recordation.

Upon completing three years of study and a minimum of two years of post-graduate work, the student would retake the one-day multistate bar examination, and upon passing (at a higher standard equivalent to an 80% comprehension) would then be admitted to the bar. If not meeting that threshold, the student would retake the entire bar exam.

How Many? The number of law school positions should be appraised by a joint commission of the ABA and Congress, the latter for funding of externship positions.

Seeing the world. No student should be admitted to law school within two years of graduation from college.

Comparative Law. Study for one semester at a foreign law school should be required. This should be during the first semester of the third year.

Pro Bono Publico. Students who continue post-externship work with a public-interest focus should receive a remission of one-third of their law school debt for each year of service.

Pro Bono Discipulus. As part of practitioners' pro bono responsibilities, each law and pre-law student should be assigned to a practitioner-mentor.

About the Author

Thane Messinger is a graduate of California University of Pennsylvania, tucked away in southwestern Pennsylvania; Texas State University–San Marcos, south of Austin; the University of Texas School of Law, deep in the heart of Texas, where he made mischief as an associate editor for the *Texas Law Review;* and Harvard University, somewhere in the Northeast. He also studied at Tunghai University, in Taiwan, and at Mansfield College, Oxford University, England. With two decades in business, law, and education, he divides his time between Austin, Texas and Honolulu, Hawaii. Admittedly dreary locales, but, as the saying goes, someone has to do it.

Messinger is the author of, among other works, *The Young Lawyer's Jungle Book: A Survival Guide,* now in its second edition and twelfth year. He is an editor of *Jagged Rocks of Wisdom: Professional Advice for the New Attorney; Later-in-Life Lawyers: Tips for the Non-Traditional Law Student;* and *The Slacker's Guide to Law School: Success Without Stress.*

Perhaps most importantly, he's not nearly as curmudgeonly as he seems. Well, okay, he is too. But he *does* have redeeming qualities.

Hang on. I'm thinking.

INDEX

A

Admissions
  objective criteria   59-60
  overview   60-61
  "Three Stacks"   85-88
  yield   58, 104
Advice   22-25
Alcohol   158
Applications
  fees   99, 126
  gambling   59
  impact of cycles   52-53
  number of   52-54
Arguer-as-lawyer   34-35
Atlantic Monthly, The   78
Ann Arbor, Michigan; city of   97, 133
Athens, Georgia; city of   133
Attention, a lack of   162
Austin, Texas; city of   97, 133
Ave Maria School of Law   110

B

BAR/BRI (bar review)   172
Best Law Schools' Admissions
Secrets (book)   60
Bimodal distribution   54-56
Black letter law
  definition of   199
  examples   193-97, 220-23, 278-80
  generally   23, 142, 160-61, 186-87
Boulder, Colorado; city of   133
Brown-nosing   18, 199, 248-49
Burnout   170-71
Business law   39-40
"Business of studying law"   183-87
Business school (MBA)   50-51, 55

C

"Canned briefs"   241-42
Cases
  briefing   170, 272-78
  casebooks   240

color-coding   23, 188-89, 223, 275
Case Western Reserve Univ.   94, 116
Casinos   58-59
"Catch-22" (film)   191-92
Chicago, city of   97, 103-04, 131
Civil Procedure   105, 234-36
Classroom participation
  see Participation
College courses   140
Collegiality   130
Columbia University   39, 90
Commercial outlines   241
Constitutional law   227-34
Contract law   141-43, 209-17
Cornell University   108
Criminal law and procedure   224-27
Curll, Joyce Putnam   60

D

De Soto, Hernando   204
Dictionaries   242
Diversity   54, 76
Document reviews   41
Dorks   19
Double bell curve
  see Bimodal distribution
Doubts   51-52
Dropping out   357
Drugs   158
Duke University   108

E

Economist, The   78
Efficiency versus laziness   168-71
Engineering (degree in)   50, 76
English (American)   79
Entrepreneurship   51
Environmental law   127-28
Examples & Explanations (series)   241
Exams
  doing well   246-48, 297-304
  poor quality of   175-76